Introduction to
Accounting Information Systems

Visit the *Introduction to Accounting Information Systems* Companion Website at **www.pearsoned.co.uk/boczko** to find valuable **student** learning material including:

- Multiple choice questions to test your understanding
- Links to relevant sites on the web
- Assignment questions that help develop your analytical skills
- Flashcards to test your understanding of key terms
- Chapter summaries that provide a succinct guide to each chapter's contents.

Introduction to
Accounting Information Systems

Tony Boczko
Hull University Business School

PEARSON

Harlow, England • London • New York • Boston • San Francisco • Toronto • Sydney
Auckland • Singapore • Hong Kong • Tokyo • Seoul • Taipei • New Delhi
Cape Town • São Paulo • Mexico City • Madrid • Amsterdam • Munich • Paris • Milan

Pearson Education Limited
Edinburgh Gate
Harlow
Essex CM20 2JE
England

and Associated Companies throughout the world

Visit us on the World Wide Web at:
www.pearson.com/uk

First published 2012

© Pearson Education Limited 2012

ISBN: 978-0-273-73938-8

British Library Cataloguing-in-Publication Data
A catalogue record for this book is available from the British Library

Library of Congress Cataloguing-in-Publication Data
A catalog record for this book is available from the Library of Congress

10 9 8 7 6 5 4 3 2 1
15 14 13 12

Typeset in 9/12pt Stone Serif by 35
Printed and bound in Great Britain by Ashford Colour Press Ltd, Gosport, Hampshire

For Janine, Christopher and Jessica . . . and of course Max

Contents in brief

Contents in detail

Supporting resources

Visit **www.pearsoned.co.uk/Boczko** to find valuable online resources

For students, the companion website provides:
- Multiple choice questions to test your understanding
- Links to relevant sites on the web
- Assignment questions that help develop your analytical skills
- Flashcards to test your understanding of key terms
- Chapter summaries that provide a succinct guide to each chapter's contents.

For instructors:
- Complete Instructor's Manual
- PowerPoint slides that can be downloaded and used for presentations.

For more information please contact your local Pearson Education sales representative or visit **www.pearsoned.co.uk/Boczko**

List of articles

List of figures and tables

Figures

Tables

Guided tour

CHAPTER 1

Information systems in accounting and finance – an overview

Introduction

This chapter provides an introductory overview of accounting information systems. It considers issues related to the role of accounting information systems in the supporting of corporate operations and decision-making processes, and in the fulfilment of stewardship obligations and responsibilities.

Learning outcomes

By the end of this chapter, the reader should be able to:

- Describe the nature and context of accounting information systems
- Describe the major characteristics of contemporary accounting information systems
- Critically comment on the social, economic and political roles of accounting information systems
- Illustrate an awareness of the role of accountants and accounting and finance-related specialists in contemporary accounting information systems
- Demonstrate an understanding of the structure of accounting information systems

Introduction – This section gives you a brief overview of the coverage and purpose of each chapter.

CHAPTER 1

Information systems in accounting and finance – an overview

Introduction

This chapter provides an introductory overview of accounting information systems. It considers issues related to the role of accounting information systems in the supporting of corporate operations and decision-making processes, and in the fulfilment of stewardship obligations and responsibilities.

Learning outcomes

By the end of this chapter, the reader should be able to:

- Describe the nature and context of accounting information systems
- Describe the major characteristics of contemporary accounting information systems
- Critically comment on the social, economic and political roles of accounting information systems
- Illustrate an awareness of the role of accountants and accounting and finance-related specialists in contemporary accounting information systems
- Demonstrate an understanding of the structure of accounting information systems

Learning outcomes – Listed at the start of each chapter, these bullet points identify the core learning outcomes you should have acquired after completing the chapter.

Articles – These topical extracts feature real-world examples, and include commentary that highlights the practical application of accounting in the business environment.

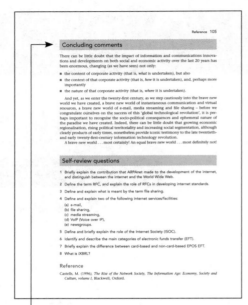

Concluding comments – Following the final section of each chapter there is a brief summary that provides an overview of the main issues.

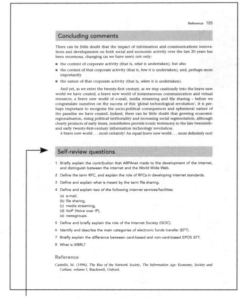

Self-review questions – These short questions encourage you to review and/or critically discuss your understanding of the main topics covered in each chapter.

References – References at the end of each chapter directs you to the most up-to-date and relevant information.

Introduction

Aims of the book

This book offers an insight into the nature, role and context of accounting-related information within the competitive business environment, and explores how companies use a range of theories and technologies to assist not only in the maximisation of shareholder wealth but also in the management and control of corporate resources. It is concerned primarily with accounting information systems – as an organisational arrangement of processes and procedures that employ both tangible and intangible resources to transform data, more specifically economic data, into accounting information. In doing so, such systems play an important role in four related areas of corporate activity:

1 Transaction processing management and the supporting of business operations.
2 Resource management and the fulfilment of stewardship obligations.
3 Information management and the supporting of decision-making processes.
4 Financial management and the fulfilment of legal, political and social obligations.

It is an understanding of each of these roles that informs the issues addressed by this book, a book which considers the following areas:

- systems thinking;
- control theories;
- accounting information systems and information and communication technology;
- architectures, topologies, and networks;
- contemporary transaction processing cycles and systems;
- systems analysis, development and design;
- e-commerce and the virtual economy;
- risk, fraud and computer crime;
- internal control and systems security; and
- accounting information systems audit.

The aims of this book are:

- to promote an understanding of the role of accounting information systems in the maintenance, regulation and control of business-related resources;
- to develop an appreciation and understanding of the practical issues and organisational problems involved in managing accounting information systems;
- to deploy systems thinking, control theories and information theories as an integrated conceptual framework for understanding the contemporary nature of accounting information systems;
- to develop a recognition of the importance of information and communication technology in corporate accounting information systems management, development and design;

- to promote an understanding of the importance of effective information management and transaction processing controls;
- to provide a framework for the evaluation of corporate transaction processing cycles, systems and processes;
- to identify the objectives and nature of internal control/security, and promote an understanding of the strategies a company could adopt to minimise exposure to corporate risk;
- to promote an understanding of the internal control issues associated with alternative transaction processing architectures and system topologies; and
- to provide an understanding of basic systems audit strategies.

Student learning features

Each chapter contains:

- an introduction presenting a brief discussion on the relevance and importance of the issues discussed in the chapter;
- a set of learning objectives presenting a summary of expected competencies to be gained by the reader; and
- a selection of self-review questions designed to encourage the reader to review key issues presented in the chapter.

On-line support for students

A website supporting this book is available containing:

- a selection of assignment questions;
- multiple choice questions for each chapter;
- a glossary of key points.

On-line support for lecturers

A website supporting this book is available containing:

- PowerPoint slides related to each chapter;
- solutions to web-based assignment questions;
- a (single semester) teaching guide.

Acknowledgements

Author's acknowledgements

My thanks to the following people for their assistance in the preparation of this book:

- Christopher James Boczko for his assistance and expertise on numerous technical aspects of this book,
- Katie Rowland at Pearson Education for her patience and professionalism, and
- the various anonymous reviewers for their constructive and helpful comments.

Publisher's acknowledgements

We are grateful to the following for permission to reproduce copyright material:

Figures

Figure 2.1 from *Sociological Paradigms and Organizational Analysis: Elements of the Sociology of Corporate Life*, London: Heinemann (Burrell, G. and Morgan, G. 1979), © Sociological Paradigms and Organizational Analysis: Elements of the Sociology of Corporate Life, by Gibson Burrell and Gareth Morgan, 1985, Ashgate.

Tables

Table 9.1 from Security Breaches Survey 2010 Technical Report (April 2010), PriceWaterhouseCoopers and InfoSecurity Europe www.infosec.co.uk/.../isbs_2010_technical_report_single_pages.pdf, INFOSEC; Table 9.2 from: Information Security Breaches Survey 2010 Technical Report (April 2010), PriceWaterhouseCoopers and InfoSecurity Europe www.infosec.co.uk/.../isbs_2010_technical_report_single_pages.pdf, INFOSEC.

Text

Article 4.2 from www.telegraph.co.uk/technology/news/8586235/ICANNS-dot-com-shake-up-paves-way-for-hundreds-of-new-addresses-and-domain-names.html, *The Telegraph*, 20 June 2011, © Telegraph Media Group Limited 2011; Article 4.3 from www.planetbiometrics.com/article-details/i/413/, Science Media Partners Ltd, Article provided by Planetbiometrics.com; Article 8.1 from www.nfcworld.com/2011/01/27/35762/orange-and-barclaycard-set-date-for-uks-first-commercial-nfc-service, SJB Research, Reproduced from NFC World (www.nfcworld.com) by permission of SJB Research; Article 8.2 from Mobile phones bring the cashless society closer, *The Guardian*, 28/05/2011 (Miles Brignall), Copyright Guardian News and Media Ltd 2011; Article 10.1 from ICO fines T-Mobile workers for data theft *The Inquirer*, 13/06/2011 (David Neal), The Inquirer; Article 10.2 from Self-destruct laptops foil thieves A 'self-destruct' technology kicks in when a laptop is moved from its designated space www.v3co.uk, Incisive Financial Publishing Ltd, Guy Dixon 19 Feb 2008; Article 11.1 from OFT to act on 'Big Four' audit firms, *The Telegraph*, 18/05/2011 (Helia Ebrahimi), © Telegraph Media Group Limited 2011.

In some instances we have been unable to trace the owners of copyright material, and we would appreciate any information that would enable us to do so.

Part 1

A CONTEXTUAL FRAMEWORK

Part 1 of this book presents an introductory overview to the theoretical and practical contexts of accounting information systems.

Chapter 1 explores the social, political and economic context of accounting information systems. It considers the practical role of accounting information systems in supporting corporate decision-making processes and the fulfilment of stewardship obligations and governance responsibilities.

Chapter 2 looks at the key features of systems thinking and considers why such thinking has become fundamental not only to the contemporary priorities of capital, but, more importantly, to business organisations and accounting information systems.

Chapter 3 examines the issue of control as a political construct, dominated by the priorities of capital, and considers the application of control theory in the development and management of accounting information systems.

CHAPTER 1

Information systems in accounting and finance – an overview

Introduction

This chapter provides an introductory overview of accounting information systems. It considers issues related to the role of accounting information systems in the supporting of corporate operations and decision-making processes, and in the fulfilment of stewardship obligations and responsibilities.

Learning outcomes

By the end of this chapter, the reader should be able to:

- Describe the nature and context of accounting information systems

- Describe the major characteristics of contemporary accounting information systems

- Critically comment on the social, economic and political roles of accounting information systems

- Illustrate an awareness of the role of accountants and accounting and finance-related specialists in contemporary accounting information systems

- Demonstrate an understanding of the structure of accounting information systems

Business management and the need for information

In a business world increasingly dominated by, and indeed reliant upon, information, accounting information has become central to enabling social, political and economic activities to be rendered knowable, measurable, accountable and manageable. More importantly, such information has become pivotal in the adjudication of rival claims between competing social constituencies both inside and outside the company.

Accounting information is implicated not only in conditioning the flows of capital investment and business resources, but also in assisting in determining/measuring the effectiveness of business institutions and organisations, through which differing levels of social, political and economic power are expressed. Indeed, there is an intimate relationship between a company's search for comparative advantage, the elimination of competitive threats and the maximisation of shareholder wealth, and its need for and dependency on accounting information.

This dependency is of course not a creation of the globalising nature of twentieth-century capitalism. It is merely a redefining of needs and priorities that have existed since the dawn of commercial market activity. Indeed, every company needs information to survive, information that can be used not only to:

- justify expansion and contraction,
- rationalise closure,
- defend closure and relocation, and
- justify increases in product/service prices,

but can also be used to:

- control activity,
- compare performance,
- ensure accountability,
- facilitate surveillance, and (perhaps most important of all)
- enforce regulations.

Such information can of course take many forms: from marketing information on customer relations and product pricing strategies, to human resources management information on organisational employment levels/policies and staff profiling/recruitment strategies; from operations management information on production timetable/schedules to financial accounting/management information on corporate profitability, on investment/financing strategies and dividend policies.

This book is concerned primarily with accounting information and with the systems, processes and procedures involved in its production and dissemination. Information such as:

- external financial reporting statements – for example, the income statement, the balance sheet and the cash flow statement;
- internal management accounting statements – for example, performance budgets, costing reports and activity reports;
- financial management information – for example, short-term working capital management, long-term investment strategies, and dividend/debt policies.

While the provision of such accounting information can, and indeed does, provide many benefits, benefits such as:

- the reduction of transaction uncertainty and business risk,
- the promotion of business confidence,
- the reduction of risk of financial loss, and
- the facilitation of organisational planning and controlling,

the central role of such information is one of governance, whether internal governance in terms of operational management processes and strategy development, or external governance in terms of corporate financial statements and corporate accountability.

But what do we mean by the term information?

Information – toward a political context

There are many definitions of what 'information' is. For example Stafford Beer (1979) suggested that information is that which changes us. Davis and Olson (1984: 200) extended this notion of change by suggesting that information is '. . . data that has been processed into a form that is meaningful to the recipient and is of real perceived value in current or prospective actions or decisions'.

This theme was also continued by Murdick and Munson (1986) who suggested that information is a sign or set of signs that predispose a person into action and is distinguished from data because data are not stimuli to action but merely strings of characters or uninterrupted patterns.

Blokdijk and Blokdijk (1987), however, suggested that information is not merely concerned with action–process–reaction. They put forward a more value-orientated definition, suggesting that information was what connects with man's consciousness or conscious being, and contributes to his knowledge and ultimately his well-being.

A common theme in all the above is the notion that information is data that have been processed in such a way as to be useful to the recipient. Such a theme suggests three separate but clearly interrelated contexts.

First, 'data that have been processed' suggests a processing context. This implies that the value of information is associated with a notion of change – of transformation.

Second, 'in such a way as to be useful' suggests a structural context. This suggests the value of information resides not only in its component parts and their relationship but also in the underlying structure – the logical arrangement – the nature/context of the language/sets of symbols used.

Third, 'to the recipient' suggests a communication context. This implies that the value of information is associated with the notion of assembly – of recording – of transmission, and of communication using a shared symbol set designed to promote understanding. In other words information is not information until it has been communicated and understood.

Implied in all the above definitions is the idea that information can in some way 'reflect' reality. That is, information possesses objective characteristics independent of the user and can therefore be processed like any other business resource. Such a perspective assumes that reality can be mirrored, more or less 'truly' or 'fairly', and that accounting information can not only provide a faithful picture of that economic reality, but also, as the nature of business transactions and economic activity evolves, that refinements to accounting information and accounting systems and practices can be introduced to ensure their continuing faithfulness.

Clearly, this is not the case. Information as a body of knowledge, or as a set of rules and procedures, is collected, created and/or designed for a purpose – to satisfy an 'assigned' role imposed by human agency.

Interrelated notions of process, of structure, and of communication are clearly dependent upon human agency and can therefore be neither politically nor socially neutral. They are embedded within social arrangements – within cultural and organisational contexts. The generation, management and application of information have social, political and economic consequences, consequences usually designed to sustain existing socio-political relationships and arrangements. In other words, information, or more specifically the use of information, is not only intentional, it is, perhaps more importantly, politically constructive.

Indeed, while the significance of information, especially accounting information, cannot be understated, it is also important to recognise that the generation and communication of information is anything but a neutral and unbiased technical activity (see Gray *et al.* 1996), and that notions of relevance, of reliability, of understandability, of validity, of usefulness, and of timeliness are 'politically imposed' characteristics, or (more appropriately) 'politically constructed' characteristics.

Accounting information systems – nature, context and purpose

Previously we considered the issue of 'information'. Before considering the broad nature, context and purpose of accounting information systems, perhaps it would be useful to consider first a broad introductory definition of the notion/idea of 'system'.

There is no universally accepted definition of the term/notion of system. Where a biologist/medical scientist may use the term system to define for example bodily parts or structures anatomically or physiologically related, a chemist may use the term system to describe matter in which there exists more than one substance in a number of different phases. A geologist may use the term system to describe a formation of rock strata created during a period of geological time, while a mineralogist may for example use the term to define categories and/or divisions into which crystals may be placed on the basis of unique, identifiable characteristics. Whereas an astronomer may use the term system to describe a group of associated extraterrestrial bodies, an engineer may use the term system to define any independent assembly of electronic, electrical, or mechanical components forming a self-contained unit. A sociologist may use the term system to describe any scheme of economic classification, social arrangement and/or political stratification, while a psychologist may use the term system to describe an individual's physiological or psychological makeup. And, finally, perhaps an economist may use the term system to describe a group or combination of interrelated, interdependent, or interacting elements forming a collective entity, whereas a political scientist may use the term system to define opinions of thought, points of view or established doctrine(s) used to interpret a branch of knowledge.

Clearly, the notion or context of 'what a system is' in each of the above definitions varies, depending on the nature of the knowledge/characteristics/components being considered. Nevertheless, they all contain a number of similar themes – if sometimes by implication only.

First, they all contain a common root meaning – that is, there is a notion of methodical or coordinated assemblage; a collection or grouping of similar items, objects, elements, and/or components.

Second, they all suggest that in general, stronger correlations (relationships) exist between one part of the system and another, than between one part of the system and parts outside the system. In other words, a system can broadly be regarded as a set of related objects/components whose relationship to each other is stronger than their relationship to their environment, a relationship to each other resulting in the constitution of an identifiable whole, separate from the environment.

Third, as a complex of directly and/or indirectly related significant objects or elements, they all suggest that such objects or elements operate together to attain a prescribed goal, aim or objective. More importantly, as a bounded set of objects/components, a system is capable of responding to external stimuli to undertake whatever functions are required to achieve/maintain the system's objective.

For example the discovery of a new virus strain may cause biologists to review their understanding of medical physiology. The emergence/development of a new global economic cycle may cause economists to review their understanding of how social and political interrelationships impact on economic institutions, or the discovery of a new star cluster may cause astronomers to review their understanding of the universe as a developing system.

It should, however, be noted that such responses to new data/new conditions/new relationships are neither automatic nor apolitical. Such responses/interpretations are imposed by human agency – they are not only socially created, they are politically constructed.

What is a system?

These core attributes of collection and commonality, of relationship and of purpose, aim, and response to change, have perhaps best been summarised by Beishon and Peters (1972), who suggested that a system is an assembly of parts, where the parts or components are connected together in an organised way, are affected by being in the system, and are changed by leaving it.

. . . and, an accounting information system?

Gelinas *et al.* (2005: 15) maintain that an accounting information system is merely '. . . a specialised subsystem of the management information system, whose purpose is to collect, process and report information related to financial transaction'. Such a definition is related to what are often described as the organisational/relational contexts of accounting information systems.

Wilkinson *et al.* (2001: 7), however, suggest that an accounting information system is '. . . a unified structure within a business entity such as a business firm that employs physical resources . . . to transform economic data into accounting information'. Such a definition is related to what are often described as the procedural and/or functional contexts of accounting information systems.

While the above definitions do differ in some minor aspects, a common identifiable theme in each is the notion that an accounting information system is a cohesive organisational structure: a set of directly and indirectly interrelated processes and procedures, objects and elements, events and activities – a collection of resources and other components designed for a purpose. But what purpose?

Romney and Steinbart (2008) maintain that the purpose of an accounting information system is to process transaction data to provide users with information, that it is a system which collects, records, stores and processes data to produce information for decision makers. Vaassen *et al.* (2009) suggest that the purpose of an accounting information system is to provide information for decision making and accountability to internal and external stakeholders.

Again a common theme in each of the above definitions is the notion that accounting information systems possess two common interrelated purposes:

1 to provide users with information – or a *decision-facilitating function*: that is, a function concerned with assisting decision making/decision makers by providing 'useful' information; and

2 to support decision making and facilitate control – or a *decision-mediating function*: that is, a function concerned with controlling and inducing alternative forms of behaviour in transacting parties where conflict exists and/or mediation is required.

To provide users with information

There are of course many aspects of accounting/financial management information – all with their own unique definition of role, purpose and nature – but in general terms, three categories can be identified.

First, financial accounting information – that is, information generally concerned with external performance reporting. Such information is often retrospective, historical in nature, very structured, and often externally controlled. It is transaction orientated, and concerned with the recording, classification and presentation of financial transactions in accordance with established concepts and principles, accounting standards and extant national/international legal requirements.

Secondly, management accounting information – that is, information generally concerned with assisting in the formulation of corporate strategies and policies, with the planning and control of business activities, with decision making and corporate governance. Such information is often predictive, unstructured and internally controlled.

And, thirdly, financial management information – that is, information generally concerned with processes associated with the acquisition of finance, and the efficient management and development of both long-term and short-term resources. It is concerned primarily with financing and investment decisions made in pursuit of maximising the wealth of corporate shareholders, and minimising risk associated with longer-term decision making.

To support decision making and facilitate control

Here it is possible to identify four integrated purposes/objectives of an accounting information system:

1 To sustain and reinforce organisational operations – that is, transaction processing management.

2 To support decision making by internal decision makers and ensure the objective transformation of economic/financial data into accounting information – that is, information management.

3 To discharge obligations relating to stewardship and control the acquisition, management and disposal of organisational resources – that is, internal systemic control.

4 To fulfil legal, social, and political responsibilities and encourage alignment with extant regulatory requirements – that is, external systemic control.

Again, all of the above four purposes are closely interrelated.

First, to support organisational operations suggests that accounting information systems should facilitate the collection, recording, and processing of business transactions. This is clearly related to supporting decision making by internal decision makers and ensuring the objective transformation of economic/financial data into accounting information, which implies that a corporate accounting information system should facilitate the generation of information not only for decision-making purposes, but also for purposes of accountability – to both internal and external stakeholders.

Second, to fulfil obligations relating to stewardship and control the acquisition, management and disposal of organisational resources suggests accounting information systems should provide information/assurances to ensure assets do not enter or exit the company/organisation without appropriate authority. Again this is clearly related to fulfilling legal, social, and political responsibilities and encouraging alignment with extant regulatory requirements, which implies that accounting information systems should not only seek to ensure and maintain the integrity of information generated, but should also seek to maintain/ensure where possible the objectivity and validity of that information.

More importantly, from a functional business context, while information management activities are closely related to transaction processing management activities (as suggested earlier), such activities nevertheless have a clear defining impact on internal and/or external systemic control activities.

Contemporary contexts of accounting information systems

The heart of contemporary market-based capitalism is the notion of resource or commodity exchange – a temporal and spatial displacement of resources which is the foundation of conventional economic activity and therefore the determinant of corporate profitability, wealth maximisation and continued corporate survival. Indeed, in today's highly competitive (some would say chaotic) global marketplace companies must not only be flexible and adaptive, they must also be responsive to social, political and economic change. One consequence of this need for continued flexibility and adaptability is that accounting information systems, as an essential part of a company's arsenal of competitive technologies, have become increasingly complex; a complexity not only related to notions of security, of control, and risk reduction but increasingly influenced by:

- ever increasing volumes of accounting/financial management data and business data processing,
- ever increasing demands of internal and external users to reduce data processing times,
- an ever more critical emphasis placed on correct processing,
- an increasing importance of detail management,
- ever increasing computerisation of accounting/financial management transactions, and
- the ever increasing requirement/demand of market participants to minimise management/regulatory intervention in competitive business activities.

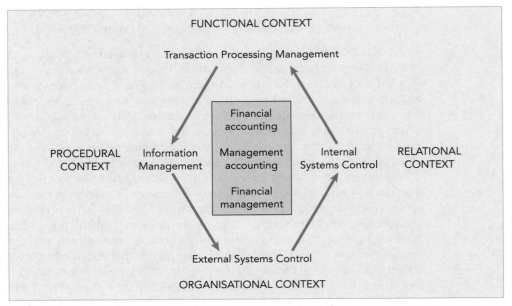

Figure 1.1 **Alternative contexts of corporate accounting information systems**

Accounting information systems are by their very nature created resource structures – that is, they emerge from a need/desire to protect, control and manage resource activities and wealth creation processes. They are created by human agency, the purpose of such systems being to provide a decision-facilitating function and a decision-mediating function.

This duality of function or purpose can be, and indeed often is, interpreted in a number of alternative contexts (see Figure 1.1). Such contexts include:

- a procedural/processing context,
- an organisational and relational context, and
- a functional context.

Procedural/processing context

From a procedural/processing context, accounting information systems are essentially data transformation management systems – that is, the purpose of such a system in this context is to facilitate five key procedures (see Figure 1.2):

1 Data collection.
2 Data maintenance.
3 Data management.
4 Data control.
5 Information generation.

The procedural context is of course closely related to notions of input (data collection), process (data maintenance/data management) and output (data control and information generation), and is concerned primarily with ensuring the proper execution of a certain procedure, and/or series of procedures to guarantee appropriate processing – to

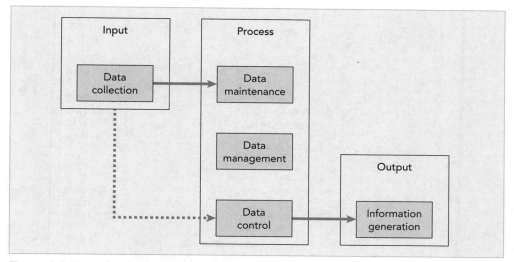

Figure 1.2 Procedural context of corporate accounting information systems

ensure correct data storage, data maintenance and data/information retrieval and removal/ disposal. Key issues within this procedural/processing context are often related to:

- limiting data redundancy – (reliability),
- ensuring data consistency and standardisation – (efficiency),
- promoting where possible data integration – (spatial constraints),
- ensuring data accessibility – (user control), and providing data flexibility – (modification), and
- ensuring data security – (integrity) – by providing appropriate data capture and entry facilities – (accuracy).

They generally involve ensuring:

- the provision of appropriate data capture and data input procedures – for example, hard copy (physical) input or pre-formatted data-entry (virtual) input;
- the adoption of appropriate processing methodology – for example, periodic (batch) processing, immediate processing, on-line processing, real-time processing and/or distributed processing;
- the development of appropriate maintenance procedures – for example, data correctness, data accuracy, data relevancy, master file security, and media access restriction; and
- the development and implementation of appropriate output procedures.

Clearly such a procedural contextualisation of accounting information systems is closely related to decisions concerning the use of information and communications technology (software and hardware) and the development of physical and virtual (non-physical) information networks.

Organisational and relational context

From an organisational context, accounting information systems are essentially hierarchical information systems – that is, they are designed to assist in:

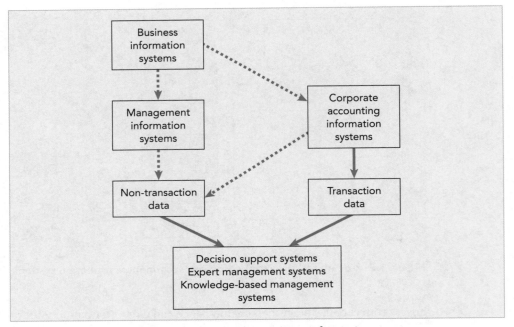

Figure 1.3 Relational context of corporate accounting information systems

- defining business strategies/policies,
- embedding information into tactical decision-making processes, and
- providing useful information for operational control purposes.

From a relational context, accounting information systems are essentially a component part of an integrated corporate information system (see Figure 1.3). That is, they exist as an essential part/component of a company's overall management information system.

Such a context is, of course, related to a range of internal/external factors such as:

- the size of the company and the complexity of corporate structures/lines of accountability;
- the organisation of the company and the intricacy of data/information flows;
- company maturity and the current stage of corporate evolution/development;
- internal psychological factors and the underlying nature/philosophy of management behaviour/activity, and the related attitudes of information users;
- external environmental factors (including social/political/geographical factors) and the levels of risk and competition the company faces; and
- company resources and the availability of financial resources for investment in systems development.

Key issues within this organisation and relational context are often related to:

- ensuring information standardisation,
- promoting where possible information consistency,
- ensuring appropriate levels of accessibility,

- ensuring appropriate levels of integration, and
- providing sufficient levels of information flexibility,

and generally involves ensuring:

- the provision of appropriate communication structures/procedures,
- the adoption of appropriate procedures of accountability, and
- the development of appropriate information models.

Clearly the organisational and relational context of accounting information systems is closely related not only to the development and maintenance of appropriate management decision support systems and strategic information systems, but also, and more importantly, to the development and maintenance of flexible knowledge-based information systems.

Functional context

From a functional context, accounting information systems are essentially transaction processing systems; that is, they are designed to mirror a company's cycles of operation and/or business activity – the temporal and spatial displacement of resources founded on the following:

- tangible/intangible products and services absorb resource expenses,
- resources are bought and sold,
- resources are converted,
- equity is increased and/or diminished,
- debts are incurred and/or liquidated.

Such activities can be analysed within the context of four functional subsystems (see Figure 1.4):

1 A *revenue* cycle – generally consisting of a marketing system, a transportation system, and a sales and debtor system.

2 An *expenditure* cycle – generally consisting of an acquisition control system, a receiving and inspection system, and a purchasing and creditor system.

3 A *conversion* cycle – generally consisting of a stock control system, a production control system and a payroll system.

4 A *management* cycle – generally consisting of a cash receipts and payments system, a fixed assets and property system, and a general ledger system.

In general two categories of functional contexts can be identified:

- ***Category 1 Companies with a dominant flow of commodities***
    - *Type 1(a) Retail and distribution companies*
        - (i) Consumer-based retail
        - (ii) Non-consumer-based retail
    - *Type 1(b) Manufacturing and production companies*
        - (i) Continuous production
        - (ii) Non-continuous production

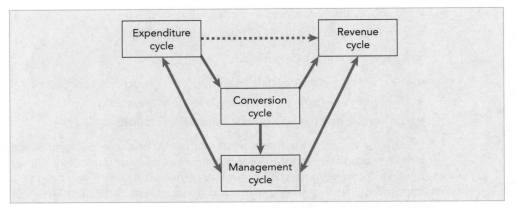

Figure 1.4 Functional context of corporate accounting systems

- *Category 2 Companies with no dominant flow of commodities*
    - *Type 2(a) Companies with a limited flow of commodities*
        - (i) Limited owned commodities
        - (ii) Limited non-owned commodities
    - *Type 2(b) Time/space-based companies*
        - (i) Specific time/space
        - (ii) Non-specific time/space
    - *Type 2(c) Knowledge/skills-based companies*
        - (i) Time-based specific knowledge/skills
        - (ii) Supply-based non-specific knowledge/skills

Each of the above will of course place different emphasis on different aspects of their transaction processing systems. (We will discuss these categories and sub-categories in more detail in Chapter 7.)

Key issues within this functional context are often related to the need to control, authorise and record the impact of resource movements; that is, they are issues related to internal control and:

- the separation of administrative procedures, and
- the separation of functional duties,

and generally involve ensuring:

- the provision of relevant control procedures,
- the adoption of appropriate custody procedures, and
- the development of accurate recording procedures.

Clearly such a functional context of accounting information systems is closely related to the development and maintenance of appropriate internal control procedures and the development and maintenance of flexible audit, risk reduction and fraud management strategies.

Accounting information systems – social and political context

As suggested earlier, accounting information systems are created resource structures – political structures that possess a range of general characteristics:

- they are goal orientated – that is, they are purposeful;
- they are generally comprised of a range of interacting components (subsystems);
- they exist/function within a hierarchical context;
- as systems they have a defined boundary; and
- as systems they possess synergistic qualities.

Accounting information systems have many users and involve many different groups of stakeholders. More importantly, such systems are subject to a range of social, political and economic influences and controls – both internal and external to the company.

Internal influences on accounting information systems

Such influences include issues related to:

- the size of the company;
- the knowledge base and intellectual capacity of the company (and its employees);
- the structure/organisation of the company, and the complexity of information demands and requirements;
- internal management factors/features; and, of course,
- the availability of company resources.

External influences on accounting information systems

External factors would include issues related to:

- political influences such as company law requirements, and other legal/political requirements imposed by quasi-governmental organisations;
- social influences such as professional reporting standards requirements, like UK GAAP (General Accepted Accounting Principles), IFRS (International Financial Reporting Standards) and other professional pronouncements;
- economic influences such as market regulatory requirements (London Stock Exchange requirements), and other industry standards/regulations;
- technological influences such as hardware/software technology constraints.

Organisational users

Because of the vast the range of influences affecting the functional nature/capacity of accounting information systems, the continued survival and growth of a company increasingly depends on the supply of effective accounting information to a wide range of diverse stakeholder groups – both internal and external to the company (see Figure 1.5).

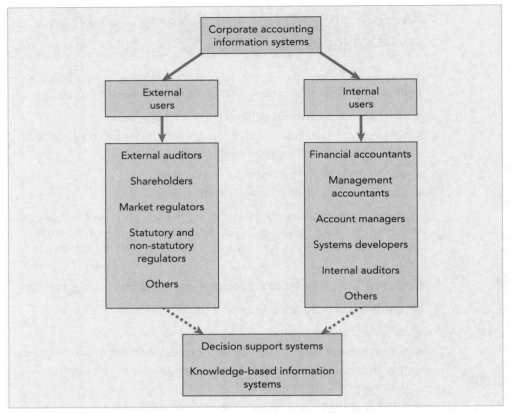

Figure 1.5 Organisational users of corporate accounting information systems

Clearly the nature, size, location, and complexity of the company will have a direct impact not only on the range of accounting information systems users, but also on the types of information various stakeholder groups may require. For example, a large diversified UK-based multinational company would have a greater range of accounting information systems users and information demand requirements than, say, a small, regional, single-purpose, private limited company.

Internal users of accounting information systems

The primary internal users of any accounting information systems would be:

■ financial accountants,

■ account managers,

■ management accountants,

■ systems developers,

■ internal auditors, and

■ other departmental managers.

Many of these users would be generally concerned with outputs from the corporate accounting information system. For example, outputs such as:

- income statements,
- financial statements of affairs and balance sheets,
- cash flow statements,
- performance budgets/reports,
- costing and activity reports, and
- financing summaries.

Others would of course also be interested in:

- accounting information systems inputs, for example the collection/recording of relevant business transactions;
- accounting information systems processes, for example the processing and maintenance of proper accounting records; and
- accounting information systems controls, for example the application of appropriate regulatory requirements and standards.

Those using these would in particular include, for example, the financial accountant, the internal auditor and, perhaps, the systems developer.

External users of accounting information systems

The primary external users of any accounting information systems would be:

- shareholders,
- external auditors,
- shareholders and potential lenders,
- market regulators,
- government regulators,
- taxation authorities,
- suppliers and creditors, and
- other interest groups such as trade unions, employee groups and other social/political agencies.

As with internal users, many of these external users would be generally concerned with outputs from the corporate accounting information system; for example, outputs such as published income statements, balance sheets and cash flow statements.

Again, as with internal users, some external users would also be interested in inputs, process, and relevant controls. These would, for example, include the external auditor, government regulators, market regulators and, of course, taxation authorities, and their interest would generally derive from some legal and/or institutional requirement.

Accounting information systems – problems/fallacies

Like many created resource structures – often very bureaucratic resource structures – there are many problems and fallacies surrounding the effective use of accounting information systems. Some of these emerge from the narrow roles assigned to such systems. Others emerge from misunderstandings over the nature, purpose, and use of information.

Problems with accounting information systems

Accounting information systems only represent a subset of a company's information system – a subset concerned primarily with data collection, data maintenance, data management and data control. Consequently, accounting information systems are only able to produce information in a limited context – mainly quantitative information. More importantly, such information is invariably historical in nature.

Secondly, such systems, because of the underlying political nature of information and information systems, only generate information consistent with a particular perspective or 'world view' – a functional liberal economic/market-based view. The reason for this is purely historical.

Traditionally, accounting information systems were, and to some extent still are, grounded in what has often been called a 'value-driven approach' – that is, an approach in which the management of financial outcomes such as profitability, levels of shareholder dividend, gearing and other financing issues often take priority over other issues. Such an approach, while clearly supporting conventional liberal economic wisdom – the maximisation of shareholder wealth – unfortunately leads to:

■ a rigid conceptual understanding/definition/model of the company,

■ an overemphasis of the 'procedural/process' context of accounting information systems,

■ an implicit faithfulness in outputs that is consistent with the 'reflectivist' contextualisation of information, and

■ a 'single stakeholder' perspective of accounting information systems that rejects any alternative perspective other than those consistent with wealth maximisation.

An alternative approach is one that has often been called an 'events-based approach', an approach which advocates that a company should focus on managing relevant business events or sequences of events as opposed to managing values in financial statements. Such an approach not only supports a business 'multi-stakeholder' view rather than the 'single-stakeholder' view, but also acknowledges the shortcomings of conventional notions of accounting and accounting information systems.

Accounting information systems – a contemporary framework

A key theme throughout the book is an acknowledgement that accounting is a creative process – a social construct designed to portray (in a particular way) the outcome of the temporal and spatial displacement of resources. It is an active 'political' technology of capital accumulation – wealth creation – directed toward preserving already dominant social structures and hierarchies, and is as such purposive, rather than inherently purposeful.

More importantly, accounting information systems as created resource structures are the 'practical embodiment' of this 'socially constructed' art form. Such systems are designed to maintain a particular set of processes consistent with the implied 'socio-political' purpose of accounting.

So, given the 'socio-political' nature of accounting/accounting information, and the constructed political nature of accounting information systems, is it possible to have a theory of accounting information systems?

Not really! The search for an underlying theory of accounting information systems is rather like the 'search for the holy grail'. An underlying theory of accounting/accounting information does not and will never exist.

While some academics and some accountants may refer to the Statement of Principles issued by the Accounting Standards Board (1999) as a broad conceptual framework – a possible theoretical framework – such a view is mistaken and founded on misconceived notions of accounting/accounting information's neutrality and objectivity.

Similarly, an underlying theory of accounting information systems does not and will never exist.

However, that is not to say that a broad theoretical framework – or more appropriately a broad thematic context – cannot exist. It is this thematic context that forms the basis of discussion in Part 2 of this book – a thematic context founded on three interrelated notions/ideas/theories:

1 Systems thinking.

2 Control theory.

3 Information theories.

Concluding comments

As we have seen, accounting information systems are socially, politically and economically important. Not only do they affect all levels of management decision making and various internal and external groups of stakeholders, they are, more importantly, an enabling 'political' resource that plays a leading role in obtaining and sustaining competitive advantage and maximising the wealth of shareholders, and are without doubt an increasingly critical success factor in the search for corporate survival.

Self-review questions

1 Define the term comparative advantage and explain its relationship to wealth maximisation.

2 Define 'information'.

3 'Information is the most valuable resource a company can possess.' Discuss.

4 'The purpose of a corporate accounting information system is to provide information, and support decision making.' Discuss.

5 What role does accounting information play in the regulation of corporate activity?

6 Explain what is meant by the functional context of accounting information systems, and why the understanding of such context is important for accounting information systems managers.

7 What are the main influences (internal and external) on accounting information systems?

8 Who are the main users of accounting information systems?

References

Accounting Standards Board (1999), *Statement of Principles for Financial Reporting* available at *http://www.frc.org.uk/asb/technical/principles.cfm*.

Beishon, J. and Peters, G. (1972), *Systems Behaviour*, Harper Row, London.

Blokdijk, A. and Blokdijk, P. (1987), *Planning and Design of Information Systems*, Academic Press, London.

Davis, G.B. and Olson, M.H. (1984), *Management Information Systems: Conceptual Foundations, Structure and Development*, McGraw-Hill, London.

Gelinas, U.J., Sutton, S.G. and Hutton, J.E. (2005), *Accounting Information Systems*, South-Western College Publishing, Cincinnati.

Gray, R., Owen, D. and Adams, C. (1996), *Accounting and Accountability*, Prentice Hall, London.

Murdick, R.G. and Munson, J.C. (1986), *Management Information Systems: Concepts and Design*, Prentice Hall, London.

Romney, M. and Steinbart, P. (2008), (11th edition) *Accounting Information Systems*, Prentice Hall, New Jersey.

Stafford Beer, A. (1979), *The Heart of Enterprise*, Wiley, London.

Vaassen, E., Meuwissen, R. and Schellman, C. (2009), (2nd edition) *Accounting Information Systems and Internal Control*, Wiley, Chichester.

Wilkinson, J.W., Cerullo, M.L., Raval, V. and Wong-On-Wing, B. (2001), *Accounting Information Systems*, Wiley, New York.

CHAPTER 2

Systems thinking

Introduction

This chapter explores a wide range of issues related to contemporary systems thinking and provides an introduction to how systems thinking has been, and indeed continues to be, an extremely important framework in understanding the increasingly dynamic and chaotic business world.

Learning outcomes

By the end of this chapter, the reader should be able to:

- Define a system and describe the main features of systems thinking
- Distinguish between soft systems and hard systems
- Critically comment on the importance of systems thinking to contemporary capitalism and to wealth-maximising organisations
- Illustrate an awareness and understanding of systems terminology
- Describe and critically evaluate from a systems perspective the key socio-political factors that constrain wealth-maximising organisations

Systems thinking

Systems thinking* is a contemporary interdisciplinary study. It is a study of organisation and relationship, independent of any substance, type, spatial or temporal scale of existence. Such thinking seeks to investigate the principles common to all complex entities, and the models (often mathematical in origin) which can be used to describe them.

With its origins in biology, systems thinking was first proposed by the biologist Ludwig von Bertalanffy (1936) as a reaction to what he viewed as the reductionism of contemporary science. Von Bertalanffy sought to emphasise the holistic nature of real systems: to emphasise that real systems are open to, and interact with, their environments, and so can acquire qualitative properties through processes of acquisition, adaptation and change – processes of emergent evolution.

Rather than reducing an entity, or organisation, or process to the properties of its constituent parts or elements, systems thinking focuses on the arrangement of and relationships between the parts which connect them into a whole. This idea of looking at the whole is a concept commonly referred to as holism – a concept that has enormous consequence in contemporary financial reporting issues.

Since it is the particular set of relationships and/or organisation that determines a system, independent of the concrete substance of the systems elements, the same concepts and principles of organisation can be, and indeed have been, used to analyse and explore issues from an eclectic range of disciplines – for example sociology, economics, physics, biology, information technology, and many more. Indeed, nearly 70 years after von Bertalanffy's proposition, systems thinking has evolved to a situation where its terminology has become integrated not only into common business language, but into everyday language – for example, the health-care system, family system, social system, human systems, information systems, banking systems, political systems, and many more.

Hard system/soft system

Clearly while all of the above types of systems do possess a range of common relational elements, they do nonetheless represent an enormous diversity – a diversity founded on, for example, varying degrees of humanism (objectivity/subjectivity) and/or varying degrees of predictability and stability – a diversity which can be categorised as 'hard systems' thinking and 'soft systems' thinking.

For our purposes we will use the framework (see Figure 2.1) developed by Burrell and Morgan (1979), a framework/understanding constructed on two simple dimensions/ criteria:

1 An ontological dimension, that is, a subjective/objective criterion.

2 An ethical/contextual dimension, that is, a change criterion or a scale ranging from radical and chaotic change to regulation and stability.

Within the ontological dimension, a subjective view/assumption would perceive social reality/system to be the product of an individual and/or a shared consciousness, whereas

---

* The term 'systems thinking' is used in preference to 'systems theory' and/or 'general systems theory'.

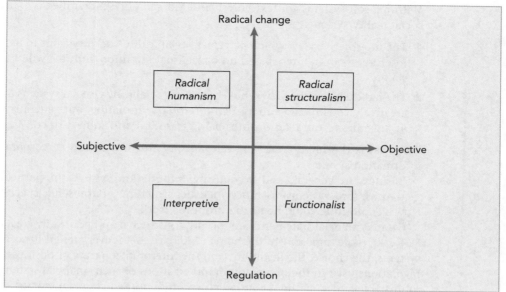

Figure 2.1 Burrell and Morgan – four paradigms of analysis

an objective view/assumption would perceive social reality as having a hard, objective, externally determined existence, separate from the individual.

Within the ethical/contextual dimension, a sociology of regulation would perceive social reality/system to be based on consensual agreement, with stability achieved through discussion and cooperation, whereas a sociology of radical change would perceive social reality as containing widespread contradictions and conflict, with cohesion existing as a consequence of one group's domination over another.

While such a framework neither implies nor distinguishes between:

■ a social reality/system whose purpose/meaning is provided by society or an individual (or group of individuals) – that is, a perpetuity/mechanistic explanation, or

■ a social reality/system whose progress and purpose are externally imposed as a doctrine of final causes – that is, a teleological explanation,

it does provide a structure within which two broad categories of systems (or views of social reality) can be identified:

■ a hard systems view, or hard systems thinking, and

■ a soft systems view, or soft systems thinking.

Within a hard systems context Burrell and Morgan (1979) identified two views:

1 The functionalist view which perceives social reality/systems to be real, external to the individual, structured, purposeful and stable. Individuals are regarded as no more than a component part, with understanding based on identifying relationships and regularities.

2 The radical structuralist view which perceives social reality/social systems to be real, structured, but generally unstable. Again human intention is secondary; however, understanding is based on identifying contradictions, irregularities, and conflict.

Within a soft systems context Burrell and Morgan (1979) identified two further views of social reality/systems:

1 The interpretive view which perceives social reality/social systems to be humanist and interpretive in nature – based on consensual intention and free will, but nonetheless stable.

2 The radical humanist view which perceives social reality/social systems to be humanist, creatively constructed and as such interpretive in nature, but generally unstable with arrangements and relationships being transient and subject to continuing change.

But what is the importance and relevance of this distinction to corporate accounting information systems?

Business in general, and accounting information systems in particular, are often viewed as hard systems, as functionalistic, structured, purposeful, specific, and stable. However, nothing could be further from the truth!

Clearly financial statements are socially constructed and politically created statements. However, more importantly, the human interface that is ever present in corporate business systems, the choice, the flexibility, and the interpretive nature of business standards and regulations used in the preparation (and creation) of such financial statements all result in unstable and sometimes contradictory, often unpredictable outcomes.

What is a system?

As suggested in Chapter 1, there are a number of alternative definitions of a system. For example, a system can be defined as an entity which can maintain some organisation in the face of change from within or without, or, more simply, as a set of objects or elements in interaction to achieve a specific goal.

For our purposes we will define a system as a complex of directly and indirectly related elements which operate to attain a goal or objective, in which the goal or objective is often used as the key controlling element, the function of the system being to convert or process energy, information, or materials into a product or outcome for use inside the system, or outside of the system (the environment), or both.

Furthermore, we will assume three key groups of ideas. First, all systems, whether hard or soft, have a number of common elements (see Figure 2.2):

■ input,

■ throughput or transformation process,

■ output,

■ an external environment and boundary,

■ control,

■ feedback and, where appropriate, feedforward, and

■ a goal and/or objective.

Second, all systems possess the following fundamental, if somewhat generic, characteristics:

■ all systems consists of a set of objectives and their relationships;

■ all systems tend toward equilibrium (or balance);

■ the constant interaction between systems results in a constant state of flux/change;

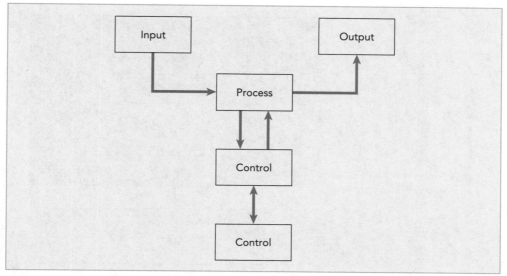

Figure 2.2 **A diagrammatic representation of a system**

- all systems are composed of interrelated parts – that is, a hierarchical system/subsystem relationship;
- where such subsystems are arranged in a series, the output of one is the input for another – therefore, process alteration in one requires alterations in other subsystems;
- the parts of the system (subsystems) constitute an indissoluble whole;
- although each subsystem may be a self-contained system, it is nonetheless part of a wider and higher order;
- each subsystem works together towards the goal of the higher system;
- the system (and subsystems) must exhibit some predictability; however, some systems are very complex and are impacted by an infinite number of other systems, and as such can never attain total predictability of effects;
- the value of the system is greater than the sum of its parts (or individual subsystems); and, finally,
- to be viable, all systems must be strongly goal-directed, governed by feedback, and have the ability to adapt to changing circumstances – that is, exhibit properties of emergent evolution; and
- no systems exists in isolation. A system interfaces with other systems that may be of a similar or different nature.

Third, we will assume that systems exist within a range of differing levels of complexity. As suggested by Wren (1994), nine alternative levels of complexity can be identified within systems thinking (see Figure 2.3):

Level 1 A structural framework, a static, predictable and descriptive system.

Level 2 A clockwork system – a semi-dynamic, moving, and predictable system, that must be controlled externally.

Level 3 A cybernetic system – a semi-dynamic and predictable system, capable of self-regulation within certain limits.

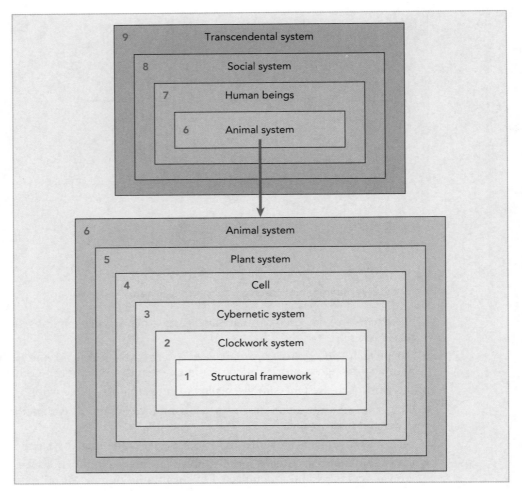

Figure 2.3 Levels of complexity

Level 4   A cell – an open and dynamic system, programmed for self-maintenance under changing external conditions.

Level 5   A plant system – an open, dynamic, and genetically determined system, capable of self-regulation through a wide range of changing external and internal conditions.

Level 6   An animal system – an open, dynamic, and genetically determined system that adjusts to its environment by making internal adjustments and by forming simple social groups.

Level 7   A human being – an open, dynamic, and self-regulating system that is adaptive through wide circumstances because of the ability to think abstractly and communicate symbolically.

Level 8   A social system – a system more complex than an individual, more open to environmental influence, and more adaptive to circumstance because of collective experience and a wider reservoir of skills.

Level 9   A transcendental system – a system that is freely adaptable to circumstance and change because it rises above and extends beyond the boundaries of both individuals and social systems. This may infer a teleological underpinning.

Clearly in each of the above there are a number of distinguishing characteristics.

First, there is a distinction between a static system and a dynamic system. A static system is a system in which neither the system elements nor the system itself changes much over time in relation to the environment (for example Level 1). A dynamic system is a system which is not only constantly changed by the environment, but also changes the environment in which it exists (for example Levels 4 to 9). Levels 2 and 3 could perhaps best be described as semi-dynamic (or semi-static), since control and influence is generally externally imposed/moderated.

Second, there is a distinction between an open system and a closed system. An open system is a system which is interactive with the environment, exchanging information, energy and/or raw materials for information, goods and/or services produced by the system. Such systems are generally self-regulating and capable of growth, development and, more importantly, adaptation. Examples of such systems would range from nature-based systems such as the human body and other plants and animals, to created organisational systems such as banks and financial institutions, manufacturing plants, governmental bodies, associations, businesses, and many more.

A closed system is a system which is not interactive with its environment. Fixed and often automatic relationships exist between system components, with no exchange with the environment. Such systems are generally incapable of growth, or any form of development/adaptation, and as such possess limited life. Examples of such systems would range from nature-based systems such as a rock as an example of the most closed type of system, to a mechanistic process such as an autonomous piece of manufacturing machinery, to detached social systems such as families and/or communities that are isolated from society and resistant to any outside influence.

This distinction between an open system and a closed system also encapsulates what is called the 'principle of equifinality'. We will discuss this principle later in the chapter; however, for the time being we can define the principle of equifinality as the capacity of an open system, because of its interactive nature, to reach its final state or achieve its goal(s)/objective(s) in a number of different ways, unlike a closed system, which can only achieve its final goal(s)/objective(s) or state based on its initial conditions.

Understanding the context of systems thinking

Although some social systems (and institutions) may, in the short term, appear to be isolated and detached from their environment, such isolation is, in a systems sense at least, limited. Prolonged detachment often results in systems failure, that is, the system becomes disorganised or entropic, or external influences intercede and the system becomes interactive with its environment, whether by choice or by imposition.

Clearly, then, the sustainability of a social system is dependent on its interactivity, that is:

■ monitoring change in the environment,

■ understanding the relationship between parts of the environment, and

■ understanding the effects of change in the environment.

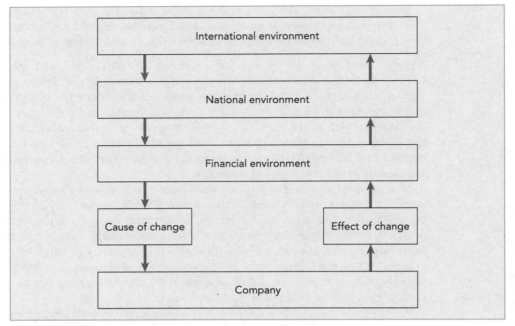

Figure 2.4 The systems view of the financial environment

However, because all social systems are created, constructed and artificial, their inter-activity is often moderated and generally controlled, that is, they exhibit characteristics of both open and closed systems – they are semi-open (or semi-closed) systems.

A semi-open system is a system which exchanges known or prescribed inputs and outputs with the environment – that is, such systems are generally constructed and/or artificial processes and generally regulate interaction with the environment. As a con-sequence such systems are capable of sustainable growth and emergent development, where competition for limited resources may exist. Examples of such systems would of course be the business and financial environment and created social/organisational systems such as companies (see Figure 2.4).

For example, for the company, prescribed inputs and outputs of resources and information are regulated not only by legal requirements and codes of practice but, more importantly, by market pressures of supply and demand, and internal resource constraints.

Systems change because of an event, or a series/sequence of events over time between or within systems. Such events can and often do cause multiple events (or change) in other systems. Where an event is a repetitive sequence such a sequence is known as a cycle. From a systems perspective, cycle(s), or cycling, may be used to either retain and/or enforce balance within a system – that is, to maintain equilibrium – or to stimulate growth – that is, to attain a higher level of integration.

The attainment of a different level of integration through a series/sequence of events is often known as spiralling – that is, where there is a sequential effect as a result of a series of events that magnifies the initial effect. Spiralling that has an increasing integrative effect is known as positive spiralling. Spiralling that has an increasingly disintegrative effect is known as negative spiralling.

Before we move on to a consideration of the key elements of a system and systems thinking, perhaps it would be useful to provide some context to this notion of system, and the notions of events, cycles and spiralling.

Applying systems thinking

Modern society (modernity)

Modern society, or modernity, is merely a complex (and often chaotic) arrangement of social, political and economic institutions, an arrangement that is ever changing and ever evolving – an arrangement composed of four interrelated environments (see Figure 2.5):

1 The political environment – the nation state.
2 The economic environment – market-based capitalism.
3 The social environment – processes of surveillance.
4 The technological environment – industrialism.

While such an unsophisticated definition of modernity has many limitations, it does nonetheless provide a framework of modern society by which we can locate and contextualise the main focus of our discussion – the corporate entity.

As a system, modern society, although open to continuous change and enormous environmental influence, the outcomes of which are often random and unpredictable, is nonetheless a controlled system – at least within the context of a regulatory and hopefully representative democratic political framework. It is in essence a semi-open system.

Financial environment

As an intrinsic component of modern society, the financial environment (see Figure 2.6) is a complex, but nonetheless constructed institutional system that can be analysed on many different/distinct levels – perhaps two of which are particularly important for our discussion.

First, we could analyse the financial environment as an institutional system historically founded on commodity production and exchange; that is, in a contemporary context, a socially constructed network through which processes of wealth accumulation are

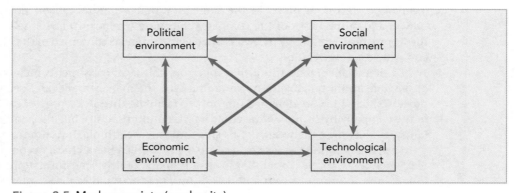

Figure 2.5 Modern society (modernity)

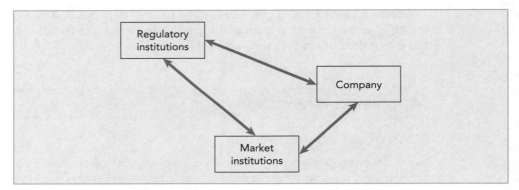

Figure 2.6 Financial environment (capitalism)

legitimated – through which the search for profit and gain take place. It is an inter-connected network/web of individuals, companies, commercial banks, government central banks, and various quasi-regulatory agencies who buy and sell not only tangible but, increasingly, intangible assets and resources.

Clearly, while the activities of each group can and indeed do affect the overall functioning of the market, by far the most influential group are the corporate entities – the wealth-creating entities: the companies.

Second, we could analyse the financial environment as an integrated virtual network/web – a virtual information system whose physical reality is represented by a collection of geographically dispersed trading centres located around the world – for example, in London, New York, Hong Kong, Singapore, Frankfurt, Brussels and Amsterdam. In essence, it is a global marketplace, trading in financial instruments and corporate ownership, which has grown considerably over the last 20–30 years; a virtual network independent of, but closely related to, commodity production and exchange.

Company (cycles of operation)

At the core of modern society, and indeed of the contemporary financial environment described above, is the company – a constructed social entity. But what do we mean by a company?

In a legal context a company is an artificial person created by law that not only has legal rights and obligations in the same way that a natural person does, but whose powers and duties (both of the company and those who run it) are closely regulated by the Companies Acts and by its own created constitution as contained in the Memorandum and Articles of Association.

In a financial context, this artificial person, this legal construct is merely a collection of tangible and intangible resources and assets, the management (and decision-making processes) of which are designed not only to facilitate the safekeeping of capital invested in the company by corporate stakeholders (risk minimisation), but also, and more importantly, to maximise the wealth of its shareholders (wealth maximisation).

In a systems context, however, a company is (using a hierarchical decomposition context) merely a complex black box whose primary goal is 'transformation process' – of inputs into outputs, of needs and desires into products and services, of market demand into market supply – and, of course, ultimately wealth creation. It is a collection of

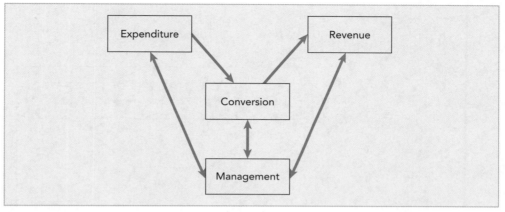

Figure 2.7 Company (cycles of operation)

systems, procedures and processes whose *Weltanschauung* or 'world view' is clearly located within the above financial contextualisation, but nonetheless limited by the above legal contextualisation.

As with modern society, and with the financial environment, we will take a fairly simplistic systems view of the company (whatever the nature of the business undertaken), and contextualise the company's activities/procedures/processes or, more appropriately, cycles of operation, as follows (see Figure 2.7):

- a revenue system,
- an expenditure system,
- a conversion system, and
- a management system.

More importantly we will consider the company to be a semi-open system seeking greater integration within its systemic environment – that is, the financial environment, and ultimately modern society.

Systems thinking – the full picture

Systems thinking – key elements of a system

In the earlier discussion, a system was deemed to have a number of common elements (see Figure 2.8):

- *Input*: the data, energy and/or raw materials transformed by the system.
- *Transformation process*: the function or purpose of the system that is the process or processes used by the system to convert data, raw materials or energy from the environment into information, products and/or services that are usable either by the system itself or by the environment.
- *Output*: the information, product and/or service which results from the system's transformation process.

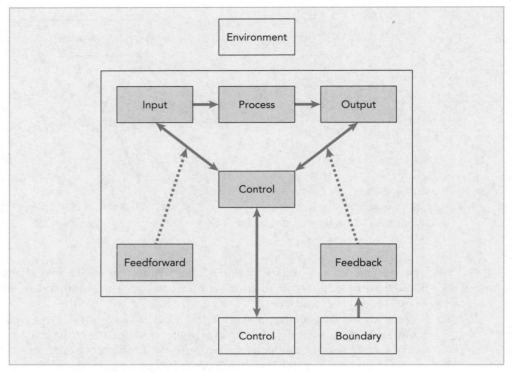

Figure 2.8 Key aspects of systems thinking

- *Systems boundary*: the functional barrier between systems (or subsystems), that is, the line or point where a system or subsystem can be differentiated from its environment or from other subsystems. Such a boundary can be rigid or permeable, tangible or intangible, physical or virtual.
- *Systems environment*: the part of the environment external to the system.
- *Control*: the mechanism for regulating performance to expectations, that is, the activities, processes and procedures used to evaluate input, throughput and output in order to make corrections.
- *Feedback*: information about some aspect of output that can be used to evaluate and monitor the system and to guide it to more effective performance.
- *Feedforward*: information about some aspect of input that can be used to modify the system's processing procedures, and to guide it to more effective performance.
- *Goal/objective*: the overall purpose for existence of the system, or the desired outcome of the system, that is, its reason for being.

Input

Input can be defined as the data, energy and/or raw materials transformed by the system. Input may be externalised, that is, obtained directly from the system's external environment, or it may be internalised, that is, the product of or output from another subsystem within the system's environment.

Transformation process

The transformation process is the function or purpose of the system – that is, the process or processes used by the system to convert data, raw materials or energy from the environment into information, products and/or services that are usable either by the system itself or by the environment.

Output

Output can be defined as the information, product and/or service which results from the system(s) transformation process. Output may be externalised, that is, generated for and delivered directly to the system's environment, or it may internalised, that is, it is the product/input of another subsystem within the system's environment.

Systems boundaries

The systems boundary is a functional barrier that exists between systems (or subsystems), a line or a point where a system or subsystem can be differentiated from its environment, or from another subsystem, or set of subsystems. A systems boundary can of course take many forms – it may be rigid or permeable, tangible or intangible, physical or virtual – but whatever its form, it is essentially a specified demarcation that enforces a limit within which the element/components/attributes of a system and their interrelationships can be explained. That is, the system's boundary is that which defines the systems.

For example, in many biological, geological and created mechanical/physical systems, such systems boundaries are often tangible and readily identifiable – a membrane surrounding a biological organism, or a physical border between two countries, or the body/shell of a motor vehicle. In many sociological and socio-political systems, however, such boundaries tend to be intangible and often virtual in nature, and as such are often difficult to identify. More importantly, such systems may possess many alternative boundaries that may be in a constant state of flux as a result of changing environmental conditions. For example, what is the boundary of a company – that is, at what point does an employee enter the company in a systems context? Is it when the employee crosses the physical boundary that separates the company premises from the outside environment? Or is it when the employee becomes an employee of the company?

Systems environment

The systems environment is that which is external to the system.

A systems environment could be described as not only all those objects, elements, components and attributes not in the system, but, more importantly, all objects, elements, components and attributes within specified limits, that may have influence on, or be influenced by, the operation of the system(s). That is, a systems environment does not only comprise those external elements whose change may affect the nature, context, properties and functioning of the system, but includes all those elements that are themselves affected by the system's behaviour.

Systems control

We will explore the issue of control in more detail in Chapter 3, but for the time being we will define control as that which guides, directs, regulates and/or constrains the behaviour of a set of variables. It is a mechanism designed to regulate, monitor, and/or compare performance to expectations – that is, the activities, processes and procedures used to evaluate input, throughput and output – and where necessary make appropriate corrections.

Such control can be either by means of feedback – where information about some aspect of output is used to evaluate and monitor the system and to guide it to more effective performance – or of feedforward – where information about some aspect of input can be used to modify the system's processing procedures, and to guide it to more effective performance.

Systems objectives/goals

The ultimate objective/goal of a system, or its raison d'être, is dependent not only on the nature and context of the system, but, more importantly, on its hierarchical location. For example:

- For modern society it could be the reproduction and/or maintenance of existing social relationships and power structures.
- For the financial environment it could be the reproduction of existing modes of regulation and regimes of wealth accumulation.
- For the company it could be the accumulation of wealth by means of the temporal and spatial displacement of assets and resources.

Equifinalty

Systems thinking recognises that semi-open systems and open systems can achieve their objective(s)/aim(s) in a variety of ways – using varying inputs, processes, methods and procedures. As suggested by von Bertalanffy (1968: 40): '. . . the same final state may be reached from differential conditions and in different ways'.

Systems adaptability

For closed systems the achievement of any objective/goal often requires little external invention because such systems, by definition, require little environmental interaction to function. However, for semi-open and open systems the achievement of any objective/goal almost certainly requires some ongoing monitoring of the systems environment and systems adaptation where appropriate.

Why? Because for such systems both input and output are affected by changes in the systems environment, and certainly in a business context where a systems environment is rarely constant, stable and predictable, the successful achievement of any objective/goal or set of objectives/goals requires carefully planned change. A lack of monitoring, and where necessary adaptation, may lead not only to increased disorganisation, or *entropy*, but more importantly, to a failure to meet ongoing objective(s)/aim(s).

Shared and overlapping systems

One common feature of all systems, not only socially constructed open and semi-open systems, is that a system and/or subsystems can belong to more than one systems or subsystems – that is, it is possible, and often common for a system not only to possess

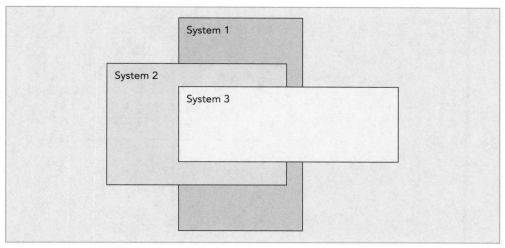

Figure 2.9 Shared/overlapping systems

multiple ownership/membership of other systems and subsystems, but also to interact at different levels with different systems/subsystems (see Figure 2.9).

Such multiple ownership/membership is particularly important where changes are made to systems.

Interconnections

All systems are interconnected either by way of input and/or output, or by processing relationship. Often systems/subsystems will be connected to a number of systems/subsystems simultaneously – interacting and exchanging data and information at various levels of activity. The number of interconnections can be calculated as:

$$(n \, (n - 1))/2$$

For example, a system with 4 interrelated subsystems would have $(4 \, (4 - 1))/2 = 6$ potential interconnections (see Figure 2.10).

As a system increases in complexity (number of subsystems), the potential number of inter connections also increases. For example:

- A system with 10 interrelated subsystems would have $(10 \, (10 - 1))/2 = 45$ potential interconnections.
- A system with 50 interrelated subsystems would have $(50 \, (50 - 1))/2 = 1,225$ potential interconnections.
- A system with 100 interrelated subsystems would have $(100 \, (100 - 1))/2 = 4,950$ potential interconnections.

Decoupling

If subsystems are interconnected, such interconnectivity implies not only spatial and temporal coordination but, more importantly, functional integration. Decoupling occurs where (see Figure 2.11):

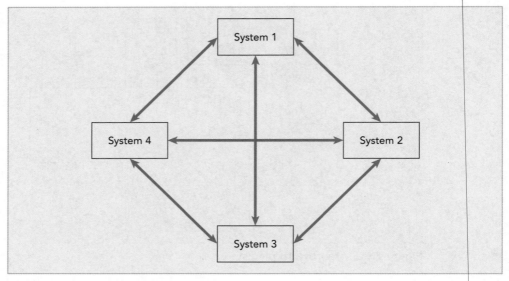

Figure 2.10 Systems interconnections

- a number of systems (or subsystems within a system) operate with a degree of independence, and/or
- an interconnection between two systems and/or subsystems is suspended either temporarily or in some instances permanently.

While many reasons can exist to justify/rationalise such decoupling, such decoupling can nevertheless be difficult and problematic in terms of:

- the costs involved,
- the time period involved,
- the consequences of a loss of subsystems connectivity and control, and
- the possibility that such decoupling could result in long-term sub-optimisation.

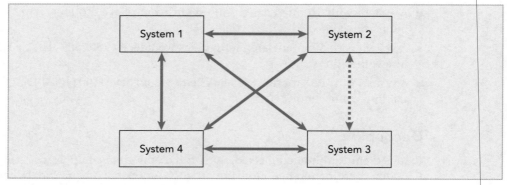

Figure 2.11 Systems decoupling

Multiple and conflicting objectives

Large systems may possess a number of objectives or a hierarchy of objectives (see Figure 2.12). Although subsystems objectives should contribute to achieving the objective of the systems as a whole, in some instances such objectives may conflict.

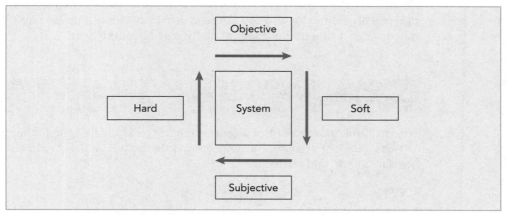

Figure 2.12 Multiple/conflicting outcomes

Systems constraints

Many systems, especially socially created systems, have constraints imposed upon them, for example operational limitations, resources shortages, and/or structural difficulties (see Figure 2.13).

Such constraints may well be temporary but can nonetheless severely restrict the system's ability to achieve its aim(s)/objective(s).

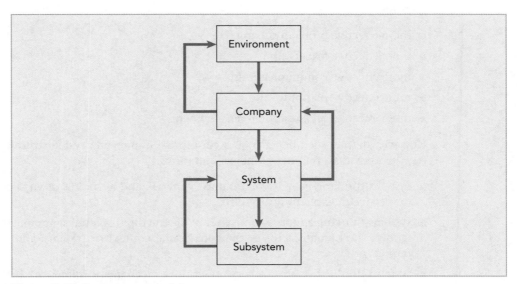

Figure 2.13 Systems constraints

Sub-optimality

Subsystems should work towards the goal of their higher systems and not pursue their own objectives independently.

Where a subsystem seeks to pursue its own objectives/agenda to the detriment of higher objectives, or the decoupling of a number of systems has reduced the overall efficiency of the systems as a whole, or changes in a systems environment have not been correctly accounted for and as a consequence have reduced the overall efficiency of the system, then a situation of sub-optimality may be said to exist.

Concluding comments

Systems thinking arose out of a generic interest in finding a general theory of similarity between different systems – a fundamental methodology that could address problems associated with, and related to:

- order,
- structure, and
- organisation,

the aim being to provide a set of unifying principles of organisation that could be applied to all organisations at all levels of complexity (von Bertalanffy 1968).

In essence, systems thinking addresses a number of structural and relational issues that are common to a vast range of interdisciplinary studies (including business and finance). Perhaps more importantly, systems thinking provides a framework – a conceptual model that can be applied to a diverse range of scientific and business areas. Indeed, business practitioners and management scientists have learned a great deal about organisations and how they work by utilising a systems perspective, the benefits of which have been identified as:

- more effective problem solving,
- more effective leadership,
- more effective communications,
- more effective planning, and
- more effective organisational development.

However, despite such benefits, as a conceptual framework, systems thinking neverthe-less does possess a number of major limitations:

- systems thinking is by its very nature 'general', and as such is often accused of being ineffective in explaining anything,
- systems thinking adopts a somewhat hard-structured analytical approach, and rejects/ignores the human factor or the behavioural context of systems; and perhaps more importantly,
- systems thinking imposes a very prescriptive mechanistic framework that necessitates the use of an overly functional analytical context.

If systems thinking possess so many limitations – why is it used?

A simple yet incisive question! Perhaps three main reasons exist.

First, in the context of contemporary capitalism, systems thinking provides an assessable (if somewhat limited) framework that can be used not only to monitor but, more importantly, to control business activity.

Second, as a broad conceptual model systems thinking provides an acceptable (?) conceptual version of how the physical aspects of capital appear/move within the business environment.

Third, systems thinking provides a rational (if again somewhat limited) basis on which conceptual models of organisational structures (including those of a company) can be constructed.

Self-review questions

1 Briefly explain the term 'systems thinking'.

2 Distinguish between a soft system and a hard system.

3 What is sub-optimality?

4 What is the transformation process, and why is knowledge of organisational boundaries important?

5 Why are systems boundaries so important?

6 What are the key features of a closed system and an open system?

7 If a sales system has 14 subsystems, how many possible connections could there be?

8 Distinguish between a closed system and an open system.

References

Burrell, G. and Morgan, G. (1979), *Sociological Paradigms and Organisational Analysis: Elements of the Sociology of Corporate Life*, Heinemann, London.

von Bertalanffy, L. (1936), 'A quantitative theory of organic growth', in *Human Biology*, vol. 10, pp. 181–213.

von Bertalanffy, L. (1968), *General System Theory: Foundations, Development, and Application*, George Braziller, New York.

Wren, D.A. (1994), *The Evolution of Management Thought*, Wiley, New York.

CHAPTER 3

Control – management by design

Introduction

The aim of this chapter is to ascertain the key features of control theory and explore how and why control (and control theory) has become fundamental to:

- ensuring the efficient and effective use of corporate resources,
- facilitating cooperation in the achievement of corporate objectives/goals,
- minimising the impact of unpredictable disturbances on corporate activities, and
- ensuring the reliability and relevance of information – in particular accounting information.

Learning outcomes

This chapter explores a wide range of issues related to control theory and its application in the development and management of accounting information systems, and provides an introduction to how control theory has been, and indeed continues to be, a highly relevant context for understanding the increasingly complex nature of twenty-first-century corporate activity.

By the end of this chapter, the reader should be able to:

- Explain the contextual nature of control
- Understand the importance of control in complex systems
- Describe the basic elements of control
- Critically evaluate the relevance of environmental factors on control
- Distinguish between feedback and feedforward and explain their importance in control

Control and a trust in systems

Historically, in a corporate context at least, trust was in the majority of cases placed in, or assigned to, people – as representatives of the corporate entity. Physicality, it appeared, ruled! Today however, trust is no longer merely assigned to people or individuals. It is assigned to systems – the networks, the procedures and the interconnections that exist within and between companies and other organisations.

Consider the following:
Imagine you are an elderly customer entering a bank – to deposit money into your current account. At the bank counter you are greeted by a counter clerk – who will deal with your transaction. An elderly customer may well believe that as the transaction takes place, there is a trust relationship (however limited) between them as the customer and the counter clerk – a trust that is founded on the assumption that the correct procedures will be followed, that the transaction will be properly processed, that the money will be paid into the correct current account – your account.

In reality, however, this is not the case. As a customer you have (in the majority of cases at least) often no knowledge of the bank clerk – who he/she is – apart from, say, a name badge and evidence that the bank clerk actually works for the bank (we will discount here any possibility that the bank clerk may be an impostor or villain waiting to defraud the bank!).

The customer's trust is placed not only in the individual bank clerk, but also in the system that the bank clerk represents – more importantly, in the systems that actually facilitated the bank clerk's presence at the counter to deal with customers in the first place!

Okay, so trust is an important characteristic of contemporary corporate activity – both customer-based activity and corporate-based activity – but exactly what do we mean by trust?

Trust is essentially a belief – a firm belief – in the reliability, honesty, veracity, justice, strength, etc., of a person or thing. Trust is historically a product of human nature – a human construct designed to protect; a construct designed to minimise uncertainty and risk. In an anthropological context trust was, and indeed continues to be, associated with notions of cultural kinship and community – with notions of hierarchy and deference, with respect and responsibility, with locality. However, contemporary society – or modernity – has, with all its complex processes and interconnections, detached social relations from their local contexts – from their community, from their local hierarchy – and restructured them often across infinite spans of time and space.

Such complex processes are often referred to as 'disembedding mechanisms' (see Giddens 1990). Disembedding mechanisms are those aspects of contemporary society that allow individuals and/or organisations such as companies to create and develop distance relations (see Figure 3.1).

While there are various such mechanisms in operation in a market capital context, there are perhaps two key and important disembedding mechanisms:

1 a trust in the use of symbolic tokens (for example, money), and

2 a trust in expert systems (for example, a body of reflexive knowledge).

In contemporary society, as individuals we cannot produce or manufacture everything we need, or want, or desire. We live in an exchange environment in which we trade our services for a 'variable' financial reward depending on our skill/knowledge/abilities – a financial reward which we then use to acquire the things we need, or want, or desire.

More importantly, we cannot know everything we need to know.

The world is too complex, and because of this we depend on others to help us navigate through the complexity – to demystify the complexity, to make that complexity less complex – although this process of demystification is far from straightforward, and rarely apolitical!

Obviously there is again a price attached to such knowledge, such information – to such demystification – and so again we are intrinsically associated with and/or connected to the exchange environment – the market process. And, as we enter the second decade of the twenty-first century, our trust in the use of these symbolic tokens – of these expert systems – has been given further urgency by the impact of technology. Just think of a modern society without credit cards and debit cards and e-commerce and e-banking and everything else 'e'-based!

So, in a contemporary context at least, trust is no longer 'just' a confidence in the reliability of a person or persons. It is, more importantly, a confidence in the reliability of a system or a set of procedures and/or process(es) – on a particular outcome or an event. Indeed, contrary to popular belief, the requirement for trust – for the existence of a trust-based interrelationship – is not a lack of power. It is a lack of knowledge or understanding, a lack of ability – a lack of information.

And, here it seems that market-based capitalism is not without a sense of irony.

Why? Because as the changing dynamic of the global market becomes ever more complex, and individuals become more and more dependent on symbolic tokens and expert systems; as companies become ever more integrated, interconnected and inter-dependent, ever more technology orientated – ever more virtual – they have become ever more disembedded and spatially remote, ever more dependent on the active creation and development of distance relations.

It is perhaps important to note that this trust in systems can be either explicit – that is, through formally agreed contractual agreements – or implied – that is, through the development of informal indirect dependencies/relationships.

More importantly, as a system or set of systems evolves and expands (or, more appropriately, as 'political' participants within or responsible for the system or systems facilitate

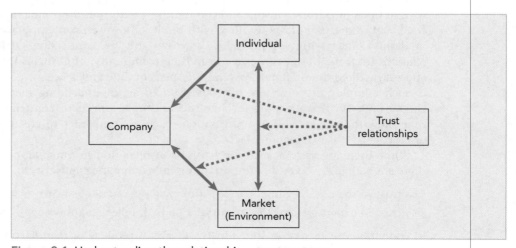

Figure 3.1 Understanding the relationship – trust systems

such an evolution) they do so not only by creating more and more interconnections but also by eliminating redundant systems and inert connections. For example, a company can enter a new market by:

- the development of a new range of products and/or services, and/or
- the acquisition of an existing company.

Whichever strategy is adopted, the expanding company will create and seek to sustain new interconnections and new interdependencies while at the same time possibly destroying and/or relinquishing others.

And so? Well, as these changing interconnections become ever more complex – as the level of interconnectedness and interdependency rises – so boundaries become ever more difficult to monitor and to control. Such boundaries become increasingly more porous, and their effectiveness becomes increasingly more unpredictable. As a consequence, the level of risk and inherent uncertainty within the system or systems rises – that is, the potential for entropy or chaos or failure increases.

(Remember we are talking here about semi-open 'created' systems, whose environment is at best volatile and at worst extremely erratic, and where interconnections and interdependencies are created and destroyed in an often chaotic and random manner.)

As the potential for risk and inherent uncertainty rises – as the risk of possible failure and the level of insecurity rises – so the level of trust in the system or systems rises up to a point, a point at which the cost of such trust in systems outweighs the possible benefits to be gained.

Consider the following:
DFL plc is a large, established, international company seeking to expand its business activities into a developing country. Clearly, risks will exist – certainly in terms of country risk. For example, country risk could arise out of a country's government's actions/policies that seek to either expropriate corporate assets and/or profits, impose discriminatory pricing intervention policies, enforce restrictive foreign exchange currency controls, and/or impose discriminatory tax laws.

On a more socio-political level, such country risk can also arise out of a country's government's actions/policies that seek to impose social/work-related regulations that offer preferential treatment of domestic companies, restrict the movement of corporate assets and resources, and/or impose regulations that restrict access to local resources.

Clearly, then, the influence of such government actions/policies on a company's commercial activities can be substantial, with the impact of any one of the above producing considerable fluctuations in a company's short-term ability to generate profits and therefore maintain/maximise shareholder value. Moreover, in the long term, the impact of such policies can dramatically affect a company's ability to repatriate and/or reinvest such profits for future growth.

To minimise such risk and uncertainty, the company would most likely hope to develop, create and foster a range of risk-minimising strategies that could, for example, include:

- obtaining insurance against the possibility of any potential expropriation of the company's assets;
- negotiating with host governments potential concessions and/or guarantees;
- structuring the company's financial and operating policies to ensure they are acceptable to, and consistent with, regulatory requirements;

- maintaining high levels of local borrowing to safeguard against the possibility of government action adversely affecting exchange rates;

- encouraging the movement of surplus assets from host country companies to the home country companies;

- developing close social/political relationships with host country institutions;

- internationally integrating production to include host country and home country companies to ensure host country companies are dependent on home country companies;

- locating research and development activities, and proprietary technology, in the home country to reduce the possibility of expropriation;

- establishing global trademarks for company products and services to ensure such rights are legally protected domestically and internationally; and

- encouraging local participation in company activities, and inviting local shareholders to invest in these activities.

Each of the above would invariably involve developing interconnections and interdependencies with a range of organisations – the greater the perceived risk the more intense the interconnections and interdependencies – essentially to minimise any possible boundary incursion and protect the company from any possible risk of loss and/or other adversity.

There is, however, a second important issue to consider. That is, as the level of interconnectedness and interdependency rises – as the level of trust in the system or systems rises – so does the 'imposed' level of monitoring and control. In fact, as complexity and uncertainty within a system or interconnected systems rise, so the systems themselves become less concerned with the underlying context/rationale for such trust and a means of efficient operation, and more and more concerned with governance and control – an adaptation process that since the twentieth century we have come to call bureaucracy.

But why does this so-called adaptation occur?

Put simply, in a corporate context at least, this silent conversion – this quiet almost 'velvet revolution' – occurs as systems within a hierarchy attempt to minimise at best any possible loss or at worst complete failure, not only of the company but of the market as a whole!

In essence, as lower-level systems become increasingly more interconnected and more integrated into higher-level systems, so the higher-level systems can and do exert greater and greater influence and control on the lower-level systems. This can be good because, in a corporate/market sense at least, it can lead to the creation of a so-called 'level playing field' – a fair, albeit competitive, marketplace. However, it can, on the other hand, lead to excessive surveillance and regulation, and thus lead to unfair competition and potential abuse. Indeed, an endemic attribute of the ever-expanding influence of the marketplace – of market capitalism – is that features and system characteristics that often start out as 'facilitators' of commercial activity can (and very often do) eventually end up as conduits of 'economic politicisation' and 'bureaucratisation'.

Why? Because such endemic risk and uncertainty – as emergent features from the ever-changing interconnections and interdependencies – result in:

- an increasing need for environmental surveillance to monitor how these ever-changing interconnections and interdependencies may cause potential failure and possible loss, and

■ an increasing use of regulation and control to minimise the impact of such ever-changing interconnections and interdependencies.

Why? Because such thinking not only lies at the foundation of liberal economic thought, it is (in a contemporary context at least) now the dominant ideology within the contemporary global marketplace!

Okay, so now that we have a general context for control let's have a look at how control is a key component of the so-called corporate governance triad:

■ the framework of governance – regulation,

■ the process of governance – surveillance, and

■ the context of governance – control.

Regulation, surveillance and control

As suggested earlier, in a superficial context (albeit an often overly emphasised context), the hierarchical nature of the marketplace provides a contextual mechanism through which companies not only exchange goods and services, but generate income and profit, and thus provide a context for their future survival. It is, however, also a highly integrated and dynamic systemic framework – a socio-political framework through which companies seek to:

■ interpret and understand the context of environmental change, and

■ manage, and where appropriate minimise/maximise the consequences of, such environmental change.

More importantly, it is a framework through which contemporary notions of corporate governance – of accountability and of responsibility – are both articulated and operationalised.

Corporate governance is, as suggested by Cadbury (2000), concerned with holding a balance between the economic, social (and political) goals of the individual and of the community. A (pro) active corporate governance framework is essential to:

■ encouraging (and ensuring) the efficient and effective use of resources, and

■ requiring accountability for the stewardship of those resources.

Thus, the aim of corporate governance is to align as closely as possible the interests of individuals, of companies and of society, and involves a control framework founded on regulation, on surveillance, and on control.

Regulation

Regulation relates to the provision of prescribed rules of operation and codes of practice that are designed to provide a framework not only for uniformity of action but also for accountability/responsibility for such action. Consequently, such prescribed rules of operation/codes of practice are normally process and/or procedure related – that is, they define, they facilitate, and they constrain not only what can be done but, more importantly, how it can be done, where it can be done, and when it can be done.

Although, in a corporate context, modes of regulation/rules of operation/codes of practice may be seen as 'democratically negotiated' they are in fact:

■ often imposed – whether internally and/or externally,

■ often hierarchical in content – that is, they operate at different socio-political levels, and

■ generally pluralistic in context – that is, they may not only have multiple origins, they may also impact on different levels within an organisation in different ways.

Indeed, in a 'free' market context, regulations generally evolve from a combination of pressures from the state, the market, and the community – although invariably the levels of pressure exerted in the struggle to manage/enforce regulatory pronouncements is not necessarily reflective of that order.

Surveillance

Surveillance is synonymous with notions of supervision – of close observation – and relates to any process or mechanism through which information on, or knowledge of, the efficiency and effectiveness of extant modes of regulation/codes of practice/rules of operation can be obtained. Whereas, in a societal context, surveillance is often associated with contemporary notions of a 'Big Brother' type imposed control and overly invasive bureaucratic monitoring of social and economic activities and processes, it is essentially (in a corporate context at least) an economically driven political process – a process concerned primarily with appropriating information and knowledge as both a current and future basis of power, of control, of gain. Thus, in a corporate context, surveillance processes exist to assist companies in:

■ seeking out opportunities and managing competition,

■ understanding and controlling change (political and technological),

■ mediating disputes,

■ making decisions, and (ultimately)

■ enforcing regulations.

Control

There are many definitions of control. For our purposes, we will define control as two distinct but interrelated activities. First, we will define control as the processes/mechanisms through which compliance with extant modes of regulation/codes of practice/rules of operation are monitored and enforced. Second, we will define control as the power/ability to influence either directly or indirectly another's (either individual and/or corporate entity's) activities.

In a broad sense, notions of control encapsulate an ability to determine, facilitate, and/or constrain such activities by enforcing adherence to and compliance with approved systems, policies and procedures – to ensure the maintenance of hierarchical responsibilities and accountabilities.

Although control may be:

■ internal/external,

■ direct/indirect,

■ formal/informal,

- voluntary/statutory,
- facilitating/constraining,
- mechanistic/organic,

the socio-political context of control as an organisational mechanism is neither socially neutral nor economically impartial. Control is a political process at the centre of which is the need for access to, and use of, information and knowledge.

But what is the purpose of control?

In a corporate context, at least, as a 'constructed artificial process', the purpose of control is designed to assist a company in:

- promoting environmental fit,
- minimising the impact of environmental (socio-economic) disturbances,
- providing a framework of conformity (organisational isomorphism),
- promoting the coordination of action and resource utilisation, and
- promoting the socialisation of people and procedures.

In essence, control operates on three economically determined but nevertheless socio-political levels.

First, a symbolic level in which controls are designed to further corporate/organisational value beliefs. The focus of such controls is the corporate community, with the primary purpose of such controls concerned with the values embedded in a company's/organisation's action(s).

Second, a behavioural level in which controls are designed to monitor and evaluate process/procedure outcomes. The focus of such control is the company/organisation member, with the primary purpose of such control concerned with directing and coordinating behaviour towards specific outcomes.

Third, a resource allocation level in which controls are designed to measure and evaluate the conduct of exchange-based mechanisms. The primary focus of such controls is the transacting party or parties, with the primary purpose of such controls concerned with providing an efficient mechanism for conducting exchanges.

In a broad sense, the symbolic and behavioural levels of control are perhaps closely associated with market-based notions of effectiveness, whereas the resource allocation levels of control are closely associated with the notion of efficiency.

And perhaps herein lies the interesting political divide that continues to dominate contemporary UK political and economic thought!

Why? Because in a traditionalist context:

- a more right-wing notion of economic activity would tend to favour a more 'market-place' driven rationalisation of control and thus prioritise the notion of efficiency over effectiveness – for example, control based on determining value for money measures and/or resource usage and wealth creation; whereas
- a more left-wing orientated notion of economic activity would tend to favour a more socially inclusive rationalisation of control and an agenda emphasising the notion of effectiveness over efficiency.

However, while UK political and economic thought has (certainly during the latter part of the twentieth century and the early part of the twenty-first century) become less differentiated politically, with:

- the Labour party moving their political axis towards a more centre 'left' or, as some would say, a more centre 'right' agenda, and
- the Conservative party floundering their political axis around the centre 'right', and,
- the Liberal Democrats attempting to determine their political axis in the centre 'somewhere',

the alternative perceptions/notions of control still persist. Just look at the 2010 UK elections!

Corporate context of control

As we saw earlier in this chapter, in a corporate context control is fundamentally an artificial construct – a construct whose increasing importance is directly correlated with the endemic risk and uncertainty associated with:

- the increasing complexity of the global marketplace, and
- the ever more eristic nature of market capitalism.

Whereas its very existence – as an imposed socio-political function – is founded on the need to:

- monitor and regulate the influence of environmental disturbances (macro influences), and
- minimise the impact of incorrect/inefficient internal systems (micro influences),

its effectiveness is essentially determined first by the existence of:

- adequate information,
- effective channels of communication, and
- efficient organisational structures,

and second – and perhaps more importantly – by the socio-political context through which such controls are politicised and operationalised, that is, whether controls are:

- coercive,
- mimetic, and/or
- normative.

For the moment, however, it would perhaps be useful to recap on a number of key control contexts identified in the discussion so far:

1 Control is a primary management task – as part of the wide corporate governance ethic.

2 Control processes and procedures exist/function as a facilitator of organisational action.

3 Control mechanisms are socially constructed political processes designed to ensure that operations/activities proceed and/or comply with extant modes of regulation/codes of practice/rules of operation.

4 Control is necessary because unpredictable environmental disturbances occur that can result in:
   (i) actual performance deviating from expectations, and/or
   (ii) a failure (whether passive or active) to comply with extant modes of regulation/codes of practice/rules of operation.

To illustrate the basic elements of control, for the remainder of Chapter 3 we will consider control as a mechanism for the identification and management of deviations from expectations, as described in 4(i) above. The description in point 4(ii) above will form the basis of our discussion in Chapter 4.

Basic elements of the control cycle

In a broad context, a systemic control cycle (see Figure 3.2) will consist of the following:

- *An expectation*: a standard and/or requirement specifying expected/anticipated performance – that is, a performance plan and/or a resources budget.
- *A measurement process*: actual results are quantitatively determined – usually by the use of an organisational sensor.
- *A comparison*: actual results are compared to requirements/expectations to determine a quantitative estimate of performance – usually by the use of an organisational comparator.
- *Feedback*: deviations and variations between expectations and actual performance are reported to a higher level control unit.
- *Action*: outcome and/or instruction activities resulting from the control process – usually by the use of an organisational effector.

The control cycle may also include feedforward – in which action is taken in anticipation of possible deviations and/or variations.

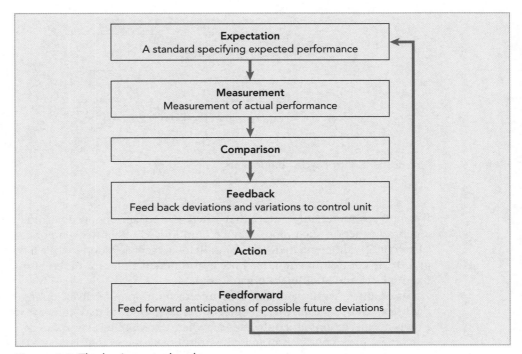

Figure 3.2 The basic control cycle

Understanding systemic control

Feedback and feedback loops

In cybernetics and control theory, feedback is a process whereby some proportion of the output signal of a system is passed (fed back) to the input. Often this is done intentionally, in order to control the dynamic behaviour of the system. In corporate systems, control is generally exercised by the use of feedback loops. The term feedback loop refers to a 'systemic connection' and can comprise any mechanism, process, procedure and/or action either physical (that is, manually orientated) or virtual (that is, essentially computer orientated) which gathers data on past performance from the output side of a system or set of interconnected systems.

These data are used to direct future performance by adjusting the input side of a system or set of interconnected systems. The component parts of a feedback loop would be (see Figure 3.3):

- *A sensor*: an organisational system(s) for measuring actual outcomes.
- *A comparator*: an organisational system(s) for comparing actual outcomes with expectation.
- *An effector*: an organisational system(s) used to issue instructions based on comparisons.

A feedback loop can have many levels, for example single feedback loop (one level) (see Figure 3.4), double feedback loop (two levels) in which a higher order control facility is introduced (see Figure 3.5), or multi-loop feedback in which a number of higher order control facilities exist.

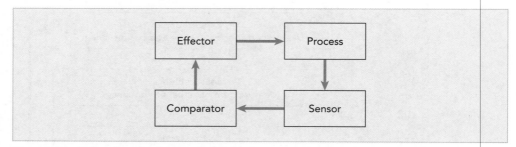

Figure 3.3 **Control cycle components**

It is perhaps important to note that where more than one feedback loop exists within a control function such loops may be (and indeed often are) temporally, spatially and hierarchically differentiated. That is, individual feedback loops, while a component part of a single control function, may occur at different times (or different intervals), at different places and at different organisational levels.

For example, within a double loop and/or multi-loop feedback arrangement, the initial loop (at say, for example, an operational/tactical level) may consider small variations between expectations and outcomes so, where appropriate, action can be taken to adjust outcomes. Since control is exercised within the system – that is, there is no interaction with the external environment – such a control function would normally be regarded

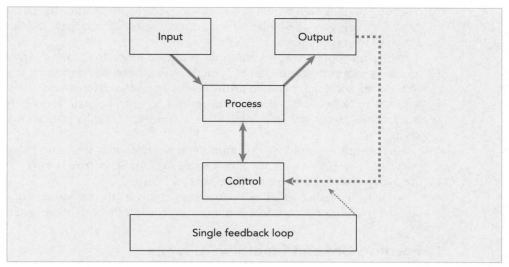

Figure 3.4 A single feedback loop

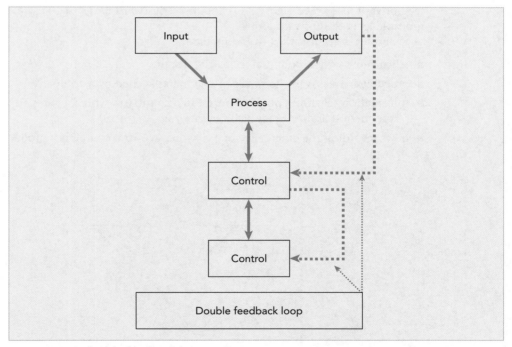

Figure 3.5 A double feedback loop

as a closed system, would be fairly mechanistic, more than likely automated and, in contemporary accounting information systems, probably computer based. A higher-level loop (or loops) may consider large or excessive variations between expectations and out-comes and/or consistency of expectations over a range of company locations and/or reporting periods, and would therefore be concerned with the strategic or 'big picture' view. Such a higher-level loop (or loops) may, where appropriate, take action to revise/ review plans/expectations.

While interconnecting (or nesting) feedback loops to create multi-level loops has become commonplace in contemporary corporate control systems, it is perhaps worth considering something known as the law of requisite variety (Ashby 1956). The law of requisite variety provides that for full control, a control system should contain controls at least equal to the system it is intended to control. This fairly abstract rule provides two key points.

First, simple control systems cannot effectively control large complex systems – that is, closed feedback systems are only suitable for simple systems; complex systems require open loop feedback and feedforward control systems.

Second, increasing levels of control may result in the imposition of excessive time delays and additional costs which may render the system both redundant and inefficient.

Feedforward and feedforward loops

A feedforward loop is designed to react to immediate or forthcoming deviations and/or variations by making adjustments to a system or set of interconnected systems. As with feedback loops, feedforward loops can and often do exists on many levels – as single feedforward loops (see Figure 3.6), double feedforward loops (see Figure 3.7), or indeed multiple-level feedforward loops.

Examples of feedforward would include:

- advance news of a potential industrial dispute,
- probable increases in the prices of raw material used by a company,
- information regarding political unrest in a country in which a company has a number of production and/or retail facilities, and/or
- news regarding the emergence of a new market for a company's products.

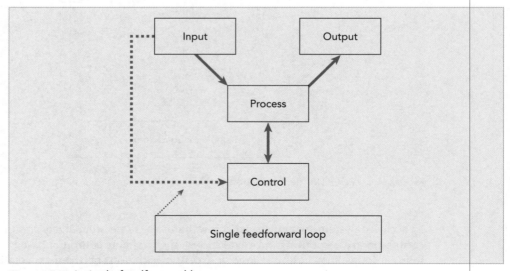

Figure 3.6 A single feedforward loop

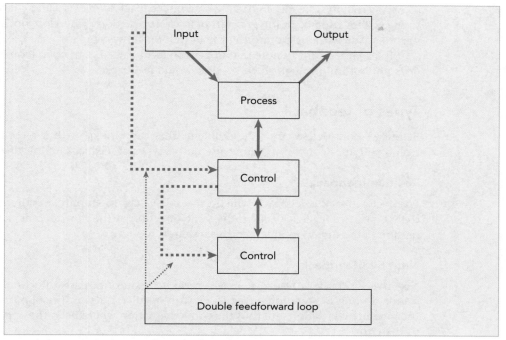

Figure 3.7 **A double feedforward loop**

In many instances such events are beyond the control of the company, and as such all that the management of the company can do is to attempt to minimise/maximise the possible adverse/favourable consequences of such environmental disturbances by the active maintenance of feedforward procedures, processes and mechanisms.

It is important to note that the two types of control explored above – namely, 'feedback' and 'feedforward' – are not mutually exclusive. Feedforward control systems are often combined with the feedback control systems. Why?

First, feedforward control systems facilitate a rapid response to any environmental disturbance, and, as such, feedback control systems merely act to correct any error in the predetermined adjustment made by the feedforward control system.

Second, feedforward control systems do not have the stability problems that feedback control systems can and often do have – especially in feedback control systems that require some human intervention. Feedforward needs to be pre-calibrated whereas feedback does not – that is, feedforward control applies to disturbances with known effects: the management of a company can only react to forthcoming disturbances if it is able to assess the potential effect of such disturbances.

Closed and open loop systems

A closed loop system is a system of feedback loops where control is an integrated part of the system – that is, feedback, based on output measurement, is 'returned' back into the system to facilitate appropriate modification to the systems input. An internal quality control cycle within a company's production process would be a good example of such a system.

An open loop system is a system where no feedback loop exists and control is external to the system and not an integral part of it. Control action is therefore not automatic and may be made without monitoring the output of the system.

It is also important to note that in general feedforward is an open loop inasmuch as it does not 'return' through the process as would feedback.

Types of feedback

Before we consider some of the problems that can emerge within a control system, it would perhaps be useful to define alternative types of feedback and feedforward.

Positive feedback

Positive feedback is feedback which causes a system to amplify an adjustment result – that is, positive feedback acts in the same direction as the measured deviation and thus reinforces the direction in which the system is moving.

Negative feedback

Negative feedback is feedback which seeks to reduce/minimise fluctuations around a standard or an expectation – that is, negative feedback acts in the opposite direction to the measured deviation and thus the corrective action would be in the opposite direction to the error.

Types of feedforward

While it is not customary to distinguish between positive and negative feedforward, it is possible for each variant to exist.

Control systems – a reality check

In the real world of complex business, organisations will invariably possess integrated control systems that consist of both feedback and feedforward – possibly at a double, if not greater multiple, nested level (see Figure 3.8).

Such integrated control systems are necessary because:

- companies are invariably hierarchical and comprise many interconnecting systems and subsystems;
- relying on a single loop feedback may result in action being taken too late, which may increase the possible risk of failure;
- relying on a single loop feedback may result in incorrect action being taken which may also increase the possible risk of failure;
- relying only on feedback may not alert the company to environmental changes that may have a significant impact on future activity; and
- feedforward, while important, would not on its own be able to instigate the appropriate corrective action where inefficiencies exist.

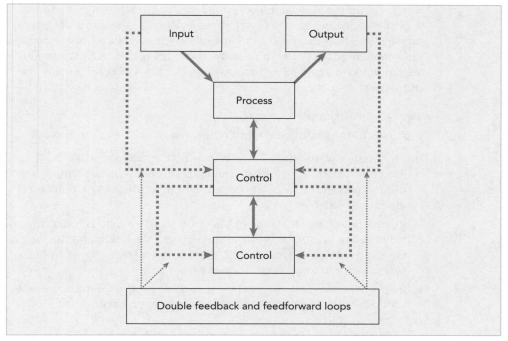

Figure 3.8 Feedback and feedforward control loops – the full picture

Problems in control action

There are many issues that have an impact on the effectiveness and efficiency of a control system. Such factors include:

- timing of the control action,
- delays in the control action/system,
- internal contradiction,
- the political nature of management control systems,
- behavioural aspects of control systems, and
- organisational uncertainty.

Clearly this is not an exhaustive list, but merely illustrative of the possible problems a company could face. However, the first three issues warrant further discussion.

Timing of control action

There can be little doubt that control action is most effective when the control time lag is short – that is, when the time difference between the determination/measurement of a deviation from expectations and the implementation of action to redress the divergence is short.

For example, monitoring budgetary performance is commonplace in many large companies. If a large deviation between expected performance (budget) and actual performance was to occur in a large manufacturing facility of a national company, in say month 2 or 3 of the financial year – let's say the overspend is the result of excessive raw material wastage due to poor quality raw materials – then waiting until month 5 or 6 or even later could result not only in excessive losses being carried by the production facility, but also in possible losses being incurred in other areas of the company due to possible loss of trade etc.

Why might such delays occur?

Problems in the timing of control action can happen as a result of:

■ Inefficient organisational structure – that is, excessive levels of management. For example, where the company requires information concerning possible deviations from expectations to be processed and monitored by a number of managers at a number of different levels.

■ Inappropriate reporting period/lack of speed – that is, excessive waiting periods between the identification/measurement of a deviation and the making of that information available so that control action can be taken. For example, where budgetary performance in May is not made available until June.

■ Ineffective information content – that is, where the information available for control action is either inaccurate and/or lacking in appropriate detail.

. . . and a possible solution to any of these problems?

Difficult to say – but as a general rule control decisions/action should where at all possible be made at the lowest possible hierarchical level; that is, as close to the event (the source of the deviation) as possible.

Delays in the control cycle

Whereas eliminating

■ inefficient and out-of-date organisation structures,

■ inappropriate reporting periods, and

■ ineffective and redundant information content

may improve the effectiveness of the control action, it is also important that corporate control systems should seek to ensure that:

■ control action is taken as soon as possible after any deviation has been identified/ measured,

■ environmental disturbances are recognised and acted upon as soon as possible, and

■ the concentration of control action is correctly focused on those areas of greatest potential risk.

Nevertheless, and often despite the best actions of corporate managers, delays in control action can and indeed do arise – at various stages of a control cycle. Such delays would, for example, include:

■ collection delays,

■ assessment delays,

■ decision-making delays,

- implementation delays,
- impact delays,
- control delays.

Internal contradiction

Internal contradiction or 'push/pull' problem arises from conflict resulting from the existence of multiple control factors within a system and/or group of interconnected systems. In a corporate context, such internal contradiction can arise where a system and/or subsystems boundaries are ill defined, and a system and/or subsystem objectives/ goals are contradictory. For example, a company while seeking to maximise shareholder wealth may nevertheless possess a range of secondary objectives that may, at least in the short term, result in contradictory pressures existing within the company: for instance, seeking to maximise high-quality product specifications, or attempting to maintain high levels of employee development, while seeking to minimise/reduce overall costs.

The existence of such multiple objectives is clearly not uncommon, and the role of corporate strategic managers is to ensure that such conflicting objectives are prioritised and accommodated as painlessly as possible – that is, with as little financial loss as possible – since such conflicting objectives can, if not appropriately managed, result in the inefficient use of resources and, in a systems context at least, possible entropy and ultimately systems failure.

Concluding comments

Control, trust in systems, feedback, feedforward, control loops are now an endemic part of corporate activity. They are a product of:

- the ever more virulent spread of 'market-based' competitive capitalism, and
- the increasing 'public/media' demands for greater corporate responsibility and accountability – for more effective corporate governance.

The need to

- undertake surveillance of corporate systems and activities,
- regulate and monitor corporate activities,
- control and monitor corporate procedures and processes

is now a paramount preoccupation of many corporate managers – a preoccupation conditioned only by a single overarching objective: maximising shareholder wealth, again and again and again, year after year after year! Indeed, such notions of control, of trust (in systems not people), of feedback, and of feedforward have become commonplace not only in financial accounting but also in management accounting and in financial management.

In a corporate context, if the possession of information and knowledge is the fundamental component for the exercise of management power, then the 'corporate system and/or interconnected subsystems' is/are the conduit(s) through which that management power is exercised, and control is the mechanism through which that management power is maintained. Management not only *through* design but, more importantly, *by* design!

Self-review questions

1 Why is control necessary?

2 What is meant by the term 'trust in systems'?

3 What are the basic elements of a control cycle?

4 What is a feedback loop and what are the key components of a feedback loop?

5 What is a feedforward loop?

6 What are the key components of a feedforward loop?

7 Distinguish between negative feedback and positive feedback.

8 Why is the law of requisite variety important in control systems?

References

Ashby, W.R. (1956), *An Introduction to Cybernetics*, Chapman & Hall, London.

Cadbury, A. (2000), *Global Corporate Governance Forum*, World Bank, New York.

Giddens, A. (1990), *The Consequences of Modernity*, Polity Press, Stanford, CA.

Part 2

INFORMATION SYSTEMS IN ACCOUNTING AND FINANCE

Part 2 of this book provides a contemporary perspective on accounting information systems.

Chapter 4 explores a range of innovations enabled by information and communication technology and considers the impact of such technology on the operations and management of accounting information systems.

Chapter 5 examines the increasing role of networking and networks in accounting information systems. It explores alternative topologies and architectures and the increasing impact of developing information technologies.

Chapter 6 looks at issues related to information management, data processing and databases, and considers the importance of effective information management and accurate data processing.

Chapter 7 examines the cyclical nature of the four major transaction processing systems within accounting information systems: the revenue cycle, the expenditure cycle, the conversion cycle and the management cycle.

Chapter 8 explores the practical aspects of e-commerce, in particular the uses of e-commerce innovations and technologies in transaction-related activities. It also considers the problems and opportunities presented by the integration of e-commerce facilities into corporate accounting information systems, and the regulatory issues related to the use of e-commerce.

CHAPTER 4

Accounting information systems and the information age

Introduction

This chapter considers the social, political and economic impact of information and communication technology enabled innovations on corporate activities, services and facilities – in particular accounting information systems. It also examines the increasing dependency of accounting information systems on these innovations, and explores how and why the selected adoption of innovations enabled by information and communication technology has become fundamental to the future of contemporary capitalism.

Learning outcomes

This chapter explores a wide range of issues related to innovations enabled by developments in information and communication technology and their implications in regard to the functioning and management of accounting information systems. By the end of this chapter, the reader should be able to:

■ Consider and explain the impact on accounting information systems of innovations enabled by information and communication technology

■ Demonstrate a critical understanding of the social, political and economic aspects/consequences of developments in information and communication technology

A brief history of information and communications technology

'Technology is society' (Castells 1996: 5)

There can be little doubt that the late twentieth and early twenty-first century has seen what some would describe as an unrestrained explosion of technological innovation – innovation that has revolutionised the nature and context of social relations and transformed the very fabric of social life. This self-accelerating process of technological innovation and development with a pervasive and integrative capacity to facilitate operations and communications in *real time* has clearly contributed to a reconfiguration of:

- the socio-economic relationships of production,
- the political notions of power and control, and
- the social contexts of knowledge and experience.

Some regard such technological innovation and development as having enabled the creation of new global interdependencies and interrelationships – new global interconnections characterised by the emergence of:

- the new global informational economy,
- a new integrated global network, and, of course,
- the new network corporate, increasingly dependent on information and communication technology to contribute to, and participate in, the increasingly volatile flows of information now at the heart of contemporary capitalism.

For others, however, such technological innovation and development has merely fragmented the very foundations of social life,[1] and has not only become intertwined with rising inequality and social exclusion throughout the world, but has, more importantly, contributed to the resulting increase in economic regionalisation, political territoriality and social segmentation.

Why? Clearly the technological innovation and development over the last 20 or so years has opened up many new possibilities – many new opportunities. It has also presented many challenges: it has not only challenged the political landscape of social interrelationships, it has also changed the economic context of those interrelationships. That is, it has not only changed the focus of power within the so-called new global network, it has also reinforced the concentration and flow of wealth within that network – especially between the corporate entities that contribute to and participate in the new integrated global network.

The internet[2] . . . the world is out there!

A brief history of the future

There can be little doubt that the idea for, and indeed the development of, an international computer network intended to facilitate communication between geographically dispersed computer users was not the brainchild of a single individual nor a single group of individuals. Its cultivation, its sponsorship, and its promotion was the product of applied research and development undertaken by a vast number of unrelated yet inventive and forward-thinking individuals and organisations, located not only throughout the USA but, importantly, throughout the world. Indeed, while the very existence of this so-called internet is perhaps made more remarkable by the episodic and fragmented context of its history, and the contentious and conflict-ridden controversies associated with its early development, there can be little doubt that in a contemporary context, as an information and communication facility, the internet has revolutionised the very fabric of polity, society and, indeed, economy.

But what exactly is the internet?

In a technical context, the term internet (as an abbreviation of the term internetwork – see below) refers to a publicly accessible worldwide system of interconnected computer networks that are connected by internetworking[3] and transmit data by packet switching[4] using a standardised internet protocol,[5] and/or other agreed protocols/procedures. The internet is a created structure. It is a composed architecture – an interconnected configuration comprising thousands and thousands of smaller networks.

What types of networks?

Some of the networks are academic and some commercial, some domestic and some government-based – all of them carry a vast array of information and communication services, including, for example, e-mail messages, electronic data, on-line chat, and the interlinked web pages and other documents that comprise the World Wide Web.

. . . and the foundations of the internet?

Surprisingly enough, the general foundations of the internet can be traced back to the late 1950s and early 1960s. Indeed, it came about because of:

■ increasing frustration and dissatisfaction with contemporary communication facilities, and

■ the growing realisation of the need for more efficient and effective communication between the increasing numbers of users of computers networks and information and communications systems,

which resulted (according to many academics) in the creation and development of the ARPAnet,[6] in the USA – a quasi military/academic network which, for many, is inextricably associated with the birth of the contemporary internet.[7]

Why? For many, the ARPAnet was not only the core network in the early collection/ group of networks that formed the original internetwork, it was and indeed remains the intellectual predecessor of the internet – as the first packet switching network. More importantly the ARPAnet or, more specifically, its developers and researchers, were fundamental in the development of a number of innovative networking technologies – including open architecture networking[8] – technologies responsible for facilitating internetworking not only across limited regional networks, but across vast geographically dispersed computer networks, irrespective of their underlying characteristics and location.

As suggested above, the early internet, based around the ARPAnet, was:

■ restricted to non-commercial uses such as military/academic research,

■ government-funded, and

■ limited (initially) to network connections to military sites and universities.

It was, however, the transition of ARPAnet from NCP to TCP/IP[9] as a network standard that enabled the sharing of the ARPAnet internet technology base and resulted in initially the partitioning of its use – between military and non-military – and eventually the complete removal of the military portion of the ARPAnet to form a separate network, the MILnet. Indeed, by 1983, network connections to the ARPAnet had expanded to include a wide range of educational institutions/organisations and a growing number of research-related companies.

In 1986, the US National Science Foundation (NSF) initiated the development of the NSFnet, a university network backbone which coincided with the gradual decommissioning of the ARPAnet during the 1980s. Continued research and development during the late 1980s (for example, the development of a domain naming system in 1984), and early 1990s (for example the arrival of the first commercial provider of internet dial-up access – world std.com) promoted an increasing public awareness and a growing public interest in the internet – an interest that resulted in the emergence and development of a number of commercial networks both in the USA and in Europe.

And so the commercial use of the internet was born – although not, it should be said, without heated and often confrontational debate!

By 1994 NSFnet had lost its status as the backbone of the internet, with the other emerging competing commercial providers in the USA, in Europe, and indeed further afield creating their own backbones and network interconnections. Indeed, by 1995 the main backbone of the internet was routed through interconnected network providers, commercial restrictions to access and use of the internet were removed, NSF privatised access to the network they had created and developed . . . and the internet took off! Within a year or so, the word internet had become common public currency and it is now an essential aspect of everyday social, political and economic activity.

It is difficult to estimate precisely how big the internet is because:

■ The internet is neither owned nor controlled by any one person, company, group, government and/or organisation. Consequently accurate empirical data regarding the internet – its size and its usage – are not only difficult to obtain, but, more importantly, difficult to substantiate and difficult to validate.

■ The internet is an organic ever-changing structure, an ever-evolving entity, an ever-developing network whose exponential rates of growth (certainly in the last 10 years) continues to belie even the most optimistic of approximations.

It should also be noted that the internet is not a global network – irrespective of much of the commercial and political hyperbole surrounding its emergence into the global economic psyche. There still remain many parts of the world (for example, some countries within the African continent, some parts of Asia and some parts of South America) where access to the internet continues to be severely restricted, not only for social and techno-logical reasons but, increasingly, for political and economic reasons.

Controlling the internet – names, standards and regulations

Due perhaps to the fragmented nature of its development, perhaps to the very nature of its underpinning technology, the internet as a social phenomenon has developed a significant cultural ethos – an ethos predicated on the notion of non-ownership: the idea that the internet as a virtual social network is not owned or controlled by any one person, any one company, any one group, or indeed any one organisation.

Nevertheless, the need for some standardisation, for some harmonisation, for some control, is necessary for any social network – especially a communication/information exchange network established on the ever-shifting foundations of technological innovation, development and change.

Names

Because a global unified namespace is essential for the internet to function properly, in September 1998 the Internet Corporation for Assigned Names and Numbers (ICANN) – a non-profit-making organisation – was created as the sole authority to coordinate the assignment of unique identifiers on the internet, including domain names (historically in English), internet protocol addresses and protocol port numbers.

ICANN's headquarters are in California, USA, and although its operations are overseen by a board of directors representing both commercial and non-commercial communities, there continues to be little doubt that the US government continues to play a pivotal role in approving changes to the domain name system. Although recent years have seen a number of attempts to reduce not only the influence of the US government on the activities of ICANN, but also the influence of ICANN itself, ICANN continues to retain a firm grip on its role as the key internet naming authority, with many critics fearing that the possible privatisation of ICANN will lead to the ultimate commercialisation of the internet.

For ICANN, recent years have seen three key developments that will have a major impact on the functionality of the internet.

1 In October 2009, ICANN approved the use of international domain names – that is, domain names in a language other the English (see Article 4.1). The first non-English domain names were issued in May 2010 to the United Arab Emirates, Saudi Arabia, the Russian Federation, and Egypt.

Article 4.1

IDN ccTLD Fast Track Process Launch

ICANN is pleased to announce the launch of the IDN ccTLD Fast Track Process.

Non-English speakers across the globe will soon have access to the Internet addresses completely in their own language. The Internet Corporation for Assigned Names and Numbers (ICANN), the organization charged with overseeing the Internet's naming and numbering systems, is today launching a process for delegating a number of internationalized top-level domains.

IDNs are domain names that include characters other than the currently available set of the English alphabet (the 26 letters 'a–z', numbers 0 to 9, and hyphens). ICANN Chairman Peter Dengate Thrush noted, 'The IDN program will encompass close to one hundred thousand characters, opening up the Internet to billions of potential users around the globe.'

ICANN President Rod Beckstrom described the importance of this change to the global Internet community, 'Over half the Internet users around the world don't use a Latin-based script as their native language. IDNs are about making the Internet more global and accessible for everyone.'

Starting November 16, 2009 ICANN will accept requests from representatives of countries and territories around the world for new Internet extensions that represent their country name and are made up of non-Roman characters.

Once the requests are evaluated and approved, Internet extensions are expected to come online in many countries during 2010.

'This is the biggest technical change to the Internet's addressing system – the Domain Name

→

System – in many years,' said Tina Dam, ICANN's Senior Director of Internationalized Domain Names. 'Right now, it's not possible to get a domain name entirely in for example Chinese characters or Arabic characters. This is about to change.'

It's important to note that ICANN will not accept direct registration applications for second-level domain names – the part before the Internet extension or suffix – from individuals, companies, or organizations. The ability for people to get a domain name in their language will come later – through a process determined by the entity that successfully applies for an IDN country-code top-level.

The IDN ccTLD Fast Track Process is available online now, including an online request form, a manual describing how to apply, a list of Frequently Asked Questions, ICANN's final implementation plan, and brief history of the Fast Track process.

Source: ICANN website, 16 November 2009. Available at *www.icann.org.*

2   In February 2011, ICANN announced that the IANA (Internet Assigned Numbers Authority)[10] had distributed the last batch of its remaining IPv4 addresses to the world's five Regional Internet Registries.[11] The Registries began assigning the final IPv4 addresses immediately within their regions and it is expected that the allocation will be completed by early 2012. That means the long awaited transition to and allocation of IPv6 addresses may well begin in early 2013.

3   In June 2011, ICANN approved final guidelines on a new host of web addresses which will now allow companies to purchase URLs ending in their brand name (see Article 4.2), and has perhaps opened the door to a possible revolution in domain names.

Article 4.2

Dot com shake-up paves way for 'hundreds of new addresses'

Emma Barnett

A new host of web addresses have been approved by the internet domain regulatory body, which will see domain names end in almost any word, as opposed to the standard .com suffix.

The Internet Corporation of Assigned Names and Numbers (ICANN), the non-profit group which controls the internet domain name system, has approved the changes today at a conference in Singapore, which will see hundreds of new domain endings, such as .google or .NYC (for website pertaining to New York City).

ICANN has today announced its final guidelines on a new host of web addresses which will allow companies to purchase URLs ending in their brand name. For example the clothing company Gap could buy the ending '.gap' instead of 'www.gap.com'.

The issue of buying a relevant web address has become one of frustration for both individuals and companies alike, which, coming later to the web party than the early adopters, have found that they cannot buy the web URL of choice. It has often already been taken by someone else – who they then have to pay high sums of money to in order to reclaim themselves online. Such 'cyber squatters' will regularly not give up their internet spot and cannot be easily contacted.

Web experts have said that ICANN's proposals, to essentially open up a new online market-place, where new addresses are available for those brands and individuals who have lost their identity online in the first and second wave of the web, could be significant.

For instance, the fact that even Apple does not own iPad.com but could now potentially own all websites ending in .Apple, should its submission be successful, is something the technology titan is expected to at least consider.

→

There are currently 22 generic top-level domain names (gTLDs), as well as about 250 country-level domain names such as .uk.

However under the new proposals, there will be several hundred new gTLDs.

'ICANN has opened the internet's addressing system to the limitless possibilities of the human imagination,' said Rod Beckstrom, president and chief executive officer for Icann.

'No one can predict where this historic decision will take us.'

Theo Hnarakis, chief executive of Melbourne IT DBS, a digital branding consultancy which advises companies on such matters, argues that brands need to take this opportunity seriously.

'The application process will only be open for 60 days. After that, the process will be closed for another three years so companies need to think about this hard and fast.'

Hnarakis told The Telegraph that companies who were serious about their brand being digitally represented needed to consider the option as it is important for businesses to be trusted and easily findable online.

'These new domain names represent an amazing opportunity for companies to really stamp their brand online, instead of having to take on URLs which don't have their exact brand title in. It's an issue of trust online and this could be a good way for some companies to reclaim their brand.'

20 June 2011

Source: Available at www.telegraph.co.uk.

Standards and regulations

In a contemporary context, broad control of internet development and innovation is now exercised through a series of documents referred to as RFCs (Requests For Comments). These are a series of numbered internet informational documents and standards widely followed by all those involved in developing internet-related/internet-based technologies.

As a series of documents, the RFC series began in 1969 as part of the original ARPAnet project; the first RFC (surprisingly called RFC 1[12]) was written and published in April 1969. Today, such RFCs are the official publication channel for the Internet Engineering Task Force (IETF),[13] the Internet Architecture Board (IAB),[14] and the wider internet community. RFCs are published by an RFC Editor,[15] who is supported by the Internet Society (ISOC),[16] but accountable to the IAB.

It is perhaps important to note that once published and issued, an RFC is never de-published,[17] but is rather superseded by the publication of a new RFC. An official list of RFCs which are currently active, or have become adopted internet standards (see below) and/or have been superseded is regularly published by the RFC editor.[18]

How are RFCs produced and how does an RFC become an internet standard?

While RFCs can be promoted through a variety of processes and procedures, the majority of RFCs are now produced by working parties of technical experts. Such working parties/ groups would publish what the IETF refers to as an internet draft[19] to:

■ facilitate comment and review, and

■ promote discussion and critique

prior to submission to the RFC editor for publication.

. . . and such an information procedure works?

Surprisingly, it does! In managing to avoid both the ambiguities sometimes found in informal regulatory pronouncements, and the bureaucracy always found in formal regulatory pronouncements, the widespread adoption and acceptance of RFCs continues to define the workings of the internet. (For more details about RFCs and the RFC process, see RFC 2026 'The Internet Standards Process', Revision 3 (1996).[20])

. . . and internet standards?

The acceptance of an RFC by the RFC Editor for publication does not automatically make the RFC a standard. Promotion to, and recognition of, an extant RFC as an internet standard (with the prefix STD) by the IETF occurs only after many years of experimentation, many years of use, and widespread acceptance have proven an extant RFC to be worthy of the designation internet standard.

And yet even after being designated an internet standard, many are still commonly referred to by their original RFC number. For example: STD 1 Internet Official Protocol Standards[21] is still frequently referred to as RFC 3700, its original designation prior to becoming an internet standard.

Clearly, the internet regulatory process and the issue and promotion of internet drafts, the adoption and publication of RFCs and the development of internet standards is an evolving standardisation process, a control procedure whose informality has perhaps been its greatest success.

Will such (regulatory) informality remain? We will have to see . . . but let's hope so!

The internet today

In a contemporary context, the internet is more than just a complex arrangement of hard wired physical connections. It is more than just a growing collection of wireless interconnections. It is more than just the sum of its infrastructure. The internet – as a communication and information exchange network – is an interconnected series of:

- multi-lateral agreements/commercial contracts (for example, peering agreements which are legal contracts that specify exactly how internet traffic is to be exchanged), and
- technical specifications or communication protocols that describe how data/information is to be exchanged over the network/the internet.

Indeed, the internet protocol suite[22] was consciously and deliberately designed to be autonomous of any underlying physical medium. As a consequence, any communications systems/network – whether hard wired or wireless – that can carry two-way digital data can be used for the transmission of internet traffic.

Some of the most popular services on/uses of the internet are:

- electronic mail (e-mail),
- file sharing,
- media streaming,
- VoIP (Voice over IP),
- internet relay chat,
- newsgroups,
- the World Wide Web,
- blogs and bloggging.

E-mail

Electronic mail (or e-mail) is a method of composing, sending and receiving messages, together with any associated attached files of text data, numeric data, and/or images, via an electronic communication system/network – usually the internet. We will discuss e-mail later in this chapter.

File sharing

File sharing is the activity of making a file of data/information, or files of data and/or information, available to others, a sharing that can be accomplished in many ways, for example:

- data/information file(s) can be e-mailed to (an)other user(s) as an e-mail attachment,
- data/information file(s) can be uploaded to a website and/or an FTP[23] server for download by (an)other user(s), and
- data/information file(s) can be placed into a shared location or onto a file server using a peer-to-peer (P2P) network[24] for instant access/use by (an)other user(s).

Clearly one of the key benefits of any network (especially the internet) is the ability to share files stored on a server with many other users. While all of the above represent adequate mechanisms for this task, where a vast amount of file sharing occurs, especially between many users, such traffic – such file sharing – may best be served by the use of a website and/or an FTP server, or a peer-to-peer (P2P) network.

For example, many companies operate websites/FTP server facilities from which product catalogues, service information and/or corporate literature can be downloaded. Many professional associations use secure FTP facilities to provide information to members only, and many educational institutions – schools, colleges and universities – now use secure FTP facilities to provide student access to data/information files, with many also using blackboard[25] to facilitate and control/restrict student access.

Although file sharing is a legal technology with many valid and legal uses (as indicated earlier), there nevertheless remain two major problems/concerns surrounding this – especially around file sharing[26] using peer-to-peer (P2P) networks:

- the anonymity of such file sharing, and
- the questionable legality of such file sharing, especially where copyright concerns exist.

Although some successful prosecutions have been brought before the courts in an attempt to close down and/or force those responsible for the development and management of P2P file sharing networks to legitimise their facilities/activities, it would nonetheless appear that such companies may well be fighting a losing battle.

Why? First, because the ongoing development of a generation of decentralised peer-to-peer protocols is severely restricting the potential effectiveness of court action for file sharing and copyright infringement. Second, because of the growth of groups supporting the use of file sharing technology and questioning the legitimacy of the so-called 'corporate witch hunt' for illegal file sharers – for whatever socio-political reason. See, for example, the Electronic Frontier Foundation (EFF),[27] and perhaps also the openDemocracy website at *www.openDemocracy.net*.

Media streaming

The delivery of media can be classified into two categories:

1 Delivery systems through which media can be delivered for concurrent consumption[28] – for example, television and radio.

2 Delivery systems through which media can be delivered for deferred consumption – for example, DVDs, books, video cassettes and audio CDs.

The term media streaming is often used to describe category 1 above – that is, delivery systems and/or facilities through which the simultaneous delivery and consumption of on-line and real-time media occurs, and is invariably applied to media that is distributed over computer-based networks. However, as we shall see, category 2 above (delivery systems for deferred consumption) are now increasingly dependent on on-line media streaming – although some would categorise it as file sharing!

Although the basic concepts of media streaming had been well established as early as the 1970s, and the technical questions and problems regarding the feasibility of computer-based media streaming delivery systems[29] had been resolved as early as the 1980s, it was not until the mid/late 1990s that dependable computer-based media streaming became a reality, as a result of:

- the establishment of standard data/information protocols and formats;
- the development of reliable networking technologies;
- the growth in network capacity and usage, especially the internet; and, of course,
- the increased processing capacity of the modern PC.

Today, not only do many of the existing radio and television broadcasters provide live internet media streams of programme broadcasts but a new breed of 'internet only' broadcasters have emerged that provide a range of audio and video programming, from technical 'live' web casts to specialised video and audio programming much of which is often unlicensed and very often uncensored!

There can be little doubt that media streaming has, and indeed will continue to, revolutionise corporate activity – not only those aspects associated with product delivery, but, perhaps more importantly, those aspects associated with service/process management – for example, media streaming (in particular web-cam-based media streaming technologies) for intra-company video conferencing. Media streaming technology brings with it many social, economic, and legal issues – many of which remain unresolved.

VoIP (Voice over IP)

Voice over Internet Protocol (also known as VoIP, IP telephony, internet telephony, and digital telephony) is the routing of audio – in particular voice conversations – over the internet and/or any other IP-based network (for example, a local area network and/or a corporate intranet). Essentially it is the use of internet protocol networks to carry voice phone calls, inasmuch as voice data flows over a general-purpose packet switched network, instead of traditional dedicated, circuit switched voice transmission lines.

What are the main advantages and disadvantages of VoIP?

The main advantages of VoIP are:

- *faster innovation* – that is, product innovation and development is dictated by the market, resulting in faster adoption of new or advanced features;
- *lower cost* – that is, telephony service using VoIP costs less than an equivalent service from traditional sources; and
- *increased functionality/portability* – that is, calls are always routed to a recipient's VoIP phone. Calls can be made and received anywhere without additional cost.

The main disadvantages of VoIP are:

- *lack of reliability* – that is, power supply disruption/failure could significantly affect performance;
- *geographical anonymity* – some VoIP systems do not yet provide e999 facilities for emergency calls and as a consequence it can be difficult to route callers to appropriate emergency centres/facilities;
- *security* – like any internet-connected device, VoIP telephone systems are susceptible to attacks, as are any internet-connected devices, in that vulnerabilities (for example, insecure passwords) can result in:
  - denial of service attacks,
  - the theft and use of customer data,
  - the illegal recording of confidential conversations, and
  - the interception of voice mailbox content;
- integration into global telephone number system – although in the UK telephone numbers are regulated by OFCOM,[30] in some countries there is no widely adopted number standard for the allocation of numbers for VoIP.

So will VoIP replace traditional telephony?

Probably not . . . well, not in the immediate future. Why not?

First, because problems still remains with regards to VoIP system's ability/capability to adequately service the requirements of a vast range of devices that depend wholly or in part on access to a quality voice-grade telephony for some or all of their functionality. Such devices would include, for example:

- fax machines,
- conventional modems,
- fax modems,
- digital satellite television receivers that require a permanent telephone connection (for example, SkyHD (see *www.sky.com*)), and
- burglar alarm systems which are connected to the regional call centre through which a link (sometimes automated) is provided to the emergency services.

Second, the regulatory framework for VoIP is still in its infancy – and while both EU and UK telecommunications regulators have proposed, issued, and subsequently revised, regulatory pronouncements and codes of practice for providers, much still needs to be done.

Although some companies have migrated from traditional copper-wire telephone systems to VoIP systems primarily to reduce their telephony costs, it remains unlikely that either the corporate office environment of the near future or the consumer home of the near future will use anything remotely like pure VoIP telephony.

Currently, the most popular VoIP providers are: Vonage (*www.vonage.co.uk*), Skype (*www.skype.com*), BroadVoice (*www.broadvoice.com*) and SunRocket (*www.sunrocket.com*).

It should, however, be noted that unlike other VoIP services, Skype is a peer-to-peer system rather than a client-server system.[31] It makes use of background processing on computers running Skype software and as a result is often banned by company network administrators on security grounds. On 10 May 2011, Microsoft acquired Luxembourg-based Skype Communications for £5.2 billion – the ultimate aim being to integrate Skype communication technologies into Microsoft's phenomenally successful Xbox.[32]

Internet relay chat (IRC)

Internet relay chat is a form of instant communication over the internet. Originating in Finland,[33] internet relay chat is essentially a huge multi-user live chat facility designed primarily for group (many-to-many) communication in discussion forums called channels, although it can be and sometimes is used for non-group (one-to-one) communication.

With a number of interconnecting internet relay chat servers located around the world, internet relay chat allows people from all different countries to participate in real-time conversations. It is, therefore, not surprising that, for many users, internet relay chat is where the internet becomes a living thing!

So how does internet relay chat work?

To use internet relay chat, users need access to a web browser and an IRC client programme. Once an IRC client programme has been installed, users can log onto an available IRC server, select an appropriate channel,[34] log into a chat session and, after learning a few basic commands and text protocols, converse by typing messages that are instantly sent to other chat session participants.

. . . and for companies?

Surprisingly, many companies (especially IT companies) now hold regularly scheduled, secured chat sessions – between company representatives, customers and clients – not only to provide technical information and advice on products and services offered by the company, but also to gain feedback on product/service developments and enhancements, and opinions on possible future developments/innovations. So, far from being merely a chat facility for the lost and the lonely hearted, internet relay chat can be a valuable and important business/marketing tool.

As of April 2011, the top 100 IRC networks served more than half a million users with hundreds of thousands of channels operating on a total of roughly 1,500 servers out of roughly 3,200 servers worldwide.

Newsgroups

Newsgroups are often referred to as repositories[35] although those which exist within the Usenet[36] system are perhaps more appropriately referred to as discussion groups since they are used primarily for the distribution of messages posted from many users at many different locations.

Within Usenet, newsgroups are arranged into a number of hierarchies, as follows:

- **comp.*** – for discussion related to computer-related issues/subjects,
- **humanities.*** – for discussion related to humanities (for example, literature, culture, philosophy),
- **misc.*** – for the discussion of miscellaneous issues/subjects not appropriate to any other hierarchy,
- **news.*** – for discussion on or about Usenet,
- **rec.*** – for discussion related to recreational activities/undertakings,
- **sci.*** – for discussion related to scientific issues/subjects,
- **soc.*** – for discussion related to social issues/subjects, and
- **talk.*** – for the discussion of contentious issues (for example, religion/politics).

There are also a number of alternative newsgroup hierarchies:

- **alt.*** – for discussion of 'alternative' issues/subjects,[37]

- **gnu.*** – for discussion of issues related to the GNU project of the Free Software Foundation (see *http://www.gnu.org.*), and

- **biz.*** – for discussion on business related issues/subjects.

(Note: in all the above * is referred to as a wildcard extension.)

A number of newsgroups exist within each of the above hierarchies. For example:

- within the comp.* hierarchy – *comp.ai* for general discussions on artificial intelligence;

- within the news.* hierarchy – *news.admin.net-abuse.email* for discussion of abuse of e-mail by spammers and other parties, *news.groups* for discussion on the creation and deletion of newsgroups;

- within the rec.* hierarchy – *rec.sport.soccer* for general discussion of world football; and

- within the sci.* hierarchy – *sci.geo.earthquakes* for general discussion on earthquakes, volcanoes, tsunamis and other geological and seismic events.

. . . and many, many more.

Briefly, for a new newsgroup to be created, it must be introduced and discussed within *news.groups* (see above) and a resolution for adoption be voted upon. If two thirds of those voting are in favour (and there are 100 more votes in favour than against), the resolution is passed and the new newsgroup can/will be created.[38]

So how do newsgroups work?

Newsgroup servers are hosted by various companies, organisations and academic institutions, with many ISPs (internet service providers) hosting their own, or at least renting a news server for the use of their subscribers. See, for example, Google news groups available at *http://groups.google.com.*

How are newsgroups accessed?

There are two ways to access the Usenet newsgroups:

1 With the use of newsreader programme (most of the popular web browsers, like Internet Explorer, Netscape and Mozilla, provide integrated free newsreader facilities), or

2 With the use of a web-based Usenet service – for example:
   - Google – see *http://groups.google.com*
   - Interbulletin – see *http://news.interbulletin.com*
   - Mailgate – see *http://www.mailgate.org*
   - News2Web – see *http://services.mail2web.com/FreeServices/Usenet*
   - WebNews-Exchange – see *http://www.webnews-exchange.com.*

The World Wide Web

There can be little doubt that the one internet application most people are familiar with is the World Wide Web.

What is the World Wide Web?

The World Wide Web is a portion of the internet. It is a facility that operates over the internet. It is essentially a multi-media information space into which information and resources are placed and made available to other users. The World Wide Web facilitates access to information and other resources over the medium of the internet using the HTTP protocol (see below) to transmit data and allow World Wide Web based applications and services to communicate with each other. In essence, the World Wide Web is an eclectic collection of interlinked[39] multi-media web documents (usually referred to as web pages) that are accessible using a web browser.[40]

While the underlying idea of the Web can be traced back to 1980 and to ideas initially proposed by Tim Berners-Lee[41] and Robert Cailliau, it was not until November 1990 that Tim Berners-Lee published a formal proposal for the World Wide Web.[42] In August 1991 Tim Berners-Lee posted a summary of the World Wide Web project on the alt.hypertext newsgroup[43] and this effectively marked the debut of the World Wide Web as a publicly available service on the internet.

How does the World Wide Web work?

The World Wide Web is essentially comprised of three basic standards:

1 The Uniform Resource Identifier (URI),[44] which is a universal system for referencing resources on the Web, such as web pages.
2 The HyperText Transfer Protocol (HTTP), which specifies how a web browser and a network server communicate with each other.
3 The HyperText Markup Language (HTML), used to define the structure and content of hypertext documents.

A web page or other resource on the World Wide Web can be accessed (using a web browser) in two different ways: by using the URL (Uniform Resource Locator) or web address of the web page required, or by following a hypertext link on an existing web page.

And then what happens?

The server name aspect of the URL is converted into an IP address using the domain name system (DNS) – a global, distributed internet database. An HTTP request is then sent to the web server working at that IP address for the web page that has been requested. The HTML text, graphics and any associated files that comprise the requested web page are then returned to the user making the request. The user's web browser renders the web page as instructed incorporating where required any images, links and/or other resources as necessary. It is this rendering that produces the web page the user will see.

What are the social implications of the World Wide Web?

In a contemporary context there can be little doubt that the World Wide Web has revolutionised the global interpersonal exchange of information on a scale that was unimaginable even a few years ago. It has allowed/enabled a sudden and extreme decentralisation of information and data unprecedented in human history. Unfettered by the demands of the physical world, the virtual nature of the World Wide Web and the digital nature of its content have presented an unparalleled opportunity for people, separated by geography and time, to mutually develop – to share/exchange – social/cultural experiences, political ideologies, cultural ideas and customs, advice, and literature and art. A sharing that appears to know no boundaries!

Blogs and blogging

A blog (a blend of the term web log) is a type or a part of a website. Blogs are usually maintained by an individual (or company) with regular entries of commentary, descriptions of events, or other material such as graphics or video. Entries are commonly displayed in reverse-chronological order.

Most blogs are interactive, allowing visitors to leave comments and even to message each other, an interactivity that distinguishes them from other static websites. A typical blog combines text and images, and links to other blogs, to other web pages, and/or to other media related to its topic. The ability of readers to leave comments in an interactive format is an important part of many blogs.

Blogs can be differentiated by type and content. While most blogs are primarily text-based, visual and audio blogs have become increasingly popular – for example, art blogs, photo blogs, video blogs, MP3 blogs and audio blogs (or podcasting). Twitter is an example of text-based micro blogging where limitations are imposed on the length of the text blog.

In terms of content, the most popular content blogs are:

- *Personal blogs*: an ongoing diary or commentary by an individual. These are the traditional, most common blogs.

- *Corporate blogs*: used internally to enhance the communication and culture within the company, or, externally, for marketing, branding or public relations purposes.

- *Genre blogs*: these focus on a particular subject, so, for example, political blogs, news commentary blogs, travel blogs (also known as travelogs), fashion blogs, and music blogs.

The internet . . . the good, the bad and the great divide!

As an emergent phenomenon of the late twentieth and early twenty-first centuries, the internet is an elaborate and intricate socio-technical system, a large-scale, highly engineered, highly complex system, whose growth and expansion has continued to astound and amaze even the most optimistic of users, developers and commentators.

And yet, while there can be little doubt that in a technical context the internet (and its component services) has provided facilities/services that were once deemed to be the stuff of science fiction, the socio-political impact of the internet technology (or indeed lack of internet technology) has often reinforced traditional socio-cultural differences and related socio-economic disadvantages. There still exist great disparities in opportunity to access between developed and developing countries, disparities which continue to reinforce the global digital divide, in which the technologically rich get richer, and the technologically poor get poorer – perhaps not in absolute terms but certainly in relative terms.

Indeed, while the internet has undoubtedly revolutionised contemporary processes of communication, and dismantled once traditional (almost sacred) spatial and temporal boundaries, it has, more importantly, enabled a greater socio-cultural sharing of ideas, knowledge and skills, and facilitated greater economic trade and the global movement of goods and service – anytime, anyplace, anywhere. Yet, the rewards and benefits from these changes, from these opportunities, have been, and indeed continue to be, shared by the very few.

Far from facilitating greater knowledge/information access, encouraging greater social mobility, stimulating greater political democracy and promoting sustained economic growth, the contemporary internet (with its Western-influenced internet culture) has, for some, merely:

- exacerbated historical politico-economic differences,
- re-entrenched socio-cultural prejudices and inequalities, and
- reinforced the so-called 'north–south divide'.[45]

. . . and the future?

While many problems remain, for example, ADSL[46] and broadband access remaining rare or even non-existent in some less developed countries, it is hoped that the increasing use of, for example, wireless internet access and satellite-based internet access will help to equalise the distribution and availability of internet technologies and (hopefully) help to reduce the ever-growing digital divide.

E-business – tomorrow's world . . . today!

E-business,[47] or electronic business, is any business process that is empowered by an information system – which, in a contemporary context, invariably means the utilisation of information and communication technology enabled innovations, including of course web-based technologies. It enables companies to:

- connect both internal and external processes with greater efficiency and flexibly, and
- operate more closely with suppliers and/or related companies to better satisfy the needs and expectations of customers and clients.

Effective e-business involves:

- the development and introduction of new revenue streams through the use of e-commerce (see below);
- the enhancement of information and communication relationships with customers, clients and related companies; and
- the development of efficient, effective and secure knowledge management systems.

Whether conducted over the public internet or through the use of internal intranets (internal internet-based networks) or through the use of secure private extranets, e-business is clearly more than just e-commerce.

Why? Because, in facilitating the integration of both intra and inter company/organisation business processes and procedures, e-business now encapsulates the whole range of business functions, activities and services, from the functions central to a company's value chain, to the activities central to a company funding cycle, to the services that support both the commercial and non-commercial operations of a company/organisation.

For our purposes, we will explore e-business in the context of the following categories, where innovations have been enabled by developments in information and communication technology:

- E-commerce, including:
  - electronic data interchange (EDI),
  - electronic funds transfer (EFT), and
  - electronic mail (e-mail).
- Accounting and finance.
- Resource planning and management systems.
- Other innovations enabled by new information/communications technology.

Developments and innovations in e-commerce

E-commerce or electronic commerce is often defined as the buying and selling of goods and services, and the transfer of funds, through digital communications – via the internet, especially the World Wide Web – but is perhaps more appropriately defined as a paperless inter-company/organisation and/or intra-company/organisation exchange of business information using a range of related information and communication-related technologies. This can involve:

- electronic data interchange,
- electronic funds transfer,
- value chain activities,
- on-line transaction processing,
- supply chain activities,
- automated inventory management systems,
- automated data-collection systems, and
- electronic communication systems (for example e-mail).

In a historical context the term e-commerce originally meant the undertaking of commercial transactions electronically, using information and communication related technologies, for example, electronic data interchange – to send and receive commercial documents electronically, and electronic funds transfer – to send and receive funds electronically.

In a contemporary context however, the term e-commerce has become synonymous with a wide range of interrelated activities associated with the sale/purchase of goods and services via the internet-based World Wide Web.[48]

During the early/mid 1990s, many business and economic analysts forecast that internet-based e-commerce facilities would soon become the major retail vehicle, but it was not until the late 1990s/early twenty-first century that a number of US and European companies began to fully develop their web-based services, including the integration of e-commerce facilities. And, despite the 'dot com' collapse in 2000 and 2001, which saw the spectacular demise of a large number of so-called pure e-commerce companies,[49] many established companies and organisations have continued to recognise the enormous added value (wealth-creating opportunities) of increasingly sophisticated but user-friendly e-commerce capabilities/facilities.

Is e-commerce a global phenomenon?

No, not really! As at the end of 2010, while e-commerce has become well established across much of the world, for a number of African, East Asian and South American countries it remains an emerging facility/capability. Indeed, in some third world countries, including some African countries, it remains almost non-existent.

The key requirements for effective e-commerce are: a website, electronic data interchange (EDI) facilities, electronic funds transfer (EFT) facilities, and electronic mail (e-mail) facilities.

Websites

A website or WWW site is merely a collection of related web pages or, to be more precise, a collection of related HTML[50]/XHTML[51] documents – accessible via HTTP,[52] on the internet, using a web browser. Remember the World Wide Web is merely a term used to describe all the publicly accessible websites in existence on the internet.

The related pages of a website are accessed from its home page located at its web address or, more appropriately, its URL.[53] While it is the URLs of the related web pages that arrange and organise them into a related hierarchy, it is the hyperlinks[54] between the pages that:

■ control how the website reader/visitor understands and comprehends the overall structure, and

■ determine how the web traffic[55] (amount of web users) flows between the different aspects of the website.

No longer restricted to the PC domain, website pages are increasingly accessible and indeed viewable through the use of a range of portable media devices (for example, PDAs, mobile phones, etc.) that possess internet browsing capabilities, internet functionality and, of course, internet connectivity.

What types of websites exist?

There are many different types of websites, some of which allow free access, some of which require a subscription to access part of their content, and others which require a subscription to access all of their content.

Some examples of website types would include:

■ *A company/business website*: a website used for the promotion of a company, business and/or service – for example *www.tesco.com* and *www.lloydstsb.com*.

■ *A commerce site (or e-commerce site)*: a website used for purchasing goods and services.

■ *A community site*: a website where persons with similar interests communicate with each other.

■ *An archive website*: used to preserve valuable electronic content threatened with extinction.

■ *A database website*: a website whose main use is the search and display of a specific database's content.

■ *A directory website*: a website that contains varied contents which are divided into categories and sub-categories – for example *www.google.co.uk* and *www.yahoo.com*.

■ *A download website*: a website used for downloading electronic content, such as software, games, etc.

■ *A professional website*: a website designed specifically for members of a professional association – for example *www.accaglobal.com* and *www.icaew.co.uk*.

■ *A game website*: a website that is itself a game or 'playground' where many people come to play.

■ *An adult website*: a website dedicated to the provision of pornographic literature, images and movies.

■ *An information website*: a website that contains content that is intended merely to inform visitors, but not necessarily for commercial purposes – for example *www.dti.gov.uk*.

■ *A news website*: a website dedicated to dispensing news and commentary – for example *www.ft.com* and *www.timesonline.co.uk*.

■ *A search engine*: a website that provides general information and is intended as a gateway to other websites – for example *www.google.co.uk* and *www.yahoo.com*.

- *A web portal*: a website that provides a starting point, a gateway, or portal, to other resources on the internet or an intranet.

. . . and of course many websites would invariably fall into more than one of the above categories/types!

Note: Many addresses or domain names used for the World Wide Web begin with 'www' because of the long-standing practice of naming internet hosts (servers) according to the services they provide. The use of 'www' is not required by any technical or policy standard, indeed many websites exist without it. Many established websites still use 'www', or they create other subdomain names such as 'www2' or 'www3' etc. Such websites are mirrors used for managing user traffic and server load balancing. Indeed, in some cases the specific host name may be obscured, creating the appearance that the user is viewing the 'www' subdomain, even if they are actually viewing a mirror site.

Electronic data interchange (EDI)

Electronic Data Interchange (EDI) is the exchange of structured and pre-defined information using agreed message standards and transmission protocols from one computer application to another by electronic means and with a minimum of human intervention. Perhaps more accurately, EDI is the specific interchange methods agreed upon by national or international standards[56] for the transfer of business transaction data. These standards prescribe which pieces of information are mandatory for a particular document and which pieces are optional.

What type of business transaction data is EDI used for?

EDI can be/is used to:

- transmit documents such as invoices, purchase orders, receipts, shipping documents and other standard business correspondence electronically between companies, organisations and/or business partners,
- transmit financial information in electronic form, and
- transfer financial payments and/or funds (a process usually referred to as electronic funds transfer (EFT)).

EDI is now widely employed in a variety of business-related industries, including:

- banking and financial services,
- manufacturing, and
- retailing.

Why is EDI used as opposed to traditional paper-based systems?

First, traditional paper-based systems:

- are invariably slow and often extremely bureaucratic,
- are often labour intensive and costly,
- increasingly suffer from low levels of accuracy and high levels of human error, and
- are often subject to processing delay resulting in often excessive uncertainty.

On the other hand, EDI-based systems are:

- less bureaucratic and less paper-based – and are therefore environmentally friendly (use less trees!!),
- flexible and simpler to use – usually allowing one-time data entry,
- time efficient – promoting the speedier more efficient flow of information, and
- very accurate – reducing possible handling errors because there is less human interface.

How does EDI work?

Within a typical EDI transaction between two trading partners (a source company and destination company), the following steps would normally take place:

Step 1 Preparation of EDI documents by source company – the collection and storage of data/information onto an electronic file or database.

Step 2 Outbound translation by the source company – translation of electronic files/database into a standard pre-determined structured and formatted document according to an agreed specification.

Step 3 Communication by the source company – transmission and routing of each file to the appropriate client destination e-mail box (via the internet) according to the destination set in the file.

Step 4 Inbound translation by the destination company – retrieval of data file from their e-mail box and translation of the data file from the pre-determined structured and formatted document into the specific format required by the company's application software.

Step 5 Processing of EDI documents by the destination company – processing of the received data file by the client company's internal application system.

Historically, the transmission/communication of EDI involved using a value added network (or VAN) – a third-party network performing services beyond the transmission of data (See Figure 4.1).

In recent years however, there has been (as we have all witnessed) a dramatic growth in the use of e-commerce via the internet and consequently the use of such networks has become increasingly rare – although some high security VANs are still in operation. It was the development of Multipurpose Internet Mail Extensions (MIME) as an enhancement to internet e-mail that enabled e-mail to carry a wide variety of alternative types of traffic – colloquially known as MIME types – including, of course, the sending of EDI transactions[57] using the internet.

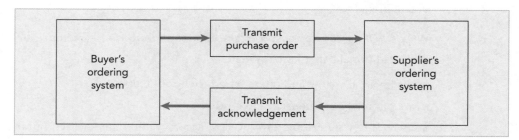

Figure 4.1 Traditional information interchange using EDI

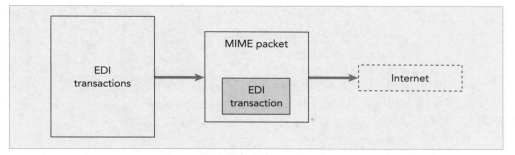

Figure 4.2 Information interchange using EDI over the internet

In a broad sense, the sending of EDI transactions – using the internet[58] – is fairly straightforward and merely involves translating the transaction document into MIME format and transmitting the message using e-mail from the source company to the destination company (see Figure 4.2).

What are the main advantages and disadvantages?

The main advantages are:

- the low transaction cost,
- low cost of transmission,
- the ease of use – no need for a dedicated private system/network, and
- reduction in the need for/use of physical documentation.

The disadvantages are:

- bandwidth may not be guaranteed and therefore transmission speeds may be affected, and
- security may be compromised by using the internet (as a public network) for the transmission of EDI information.

In general the benefits of EDI can be categorised as:

- (internal) value chain benefits, and/or
- (external) supply chain benefits,

with the potential value chain benefits including:

- a more efficient flow of resources,
- an increased overall competitiveness,
- a reduction in net operating cycle times/procedures,
- a lower overall operational costs, and as a consequence
- an improved cash flow,

and the potential supply chain benefits including:

- an increase in potential suppliers and/or customers, and
- an expansion of the corporate trading activities and the possibility of greater market access.

There are of course many risks arising out of the use of the EDI systems, in particular:

- risks associated with transmission – for example:
  - data completeness,
  - data accuracy, and
  - data authenticity, and
- risks associated with verification – for example
  - data authorisation,
  - data access, and
  - error detection and correction.

Electronic Funds Transfer (EFT)

Electronic funds transfer (EFT) is a generic term describing the transfer of funds between accounts by electronic means rather than conventional paper-based payment methods, or more specifically, the transfer of money initiated through an electronic terminal, an automated teller machine (ATM), a computer, and/or telephone. The term also applies to credit card payments, debit card payments and all automated payments including direct debits, standing orders, direct credits, and/or other inter-bank transfers using BACS.[59]

There are three broad types of EFT:

- CHAPS-based EFT,
- BACS-based EFT, and
- point-of-service-based EFT,[60] or EPOS EFT.

Both CHAPS-based EFT and BACS-based EFT would generally be used for business-to-business electronic funds transfer (known as B2B-EFT), whereas BACS-based EFT may in addition be used for business-to-consumer electronic funds transfer (known as B2C-EFT) and consumer-to-business electronic funds transfer (known as C2B-EFT).

Within EPOS EFT there are two (possible) categories:

1 card-based systems,

2 non-card-based systems.

Card-based point of service EFT, or card-based EPOS EFT can be further divided into two categories: cardholder 'present' transaction (known as pPoS EFT) and cardholder 'not present' transaction (known as nPoS EFT) (see Figure 4.3).

CHAPS-based EFT

The Clearing House Automatic Payments System (CHAPS) is an electronic bank-to-bank UK-only payment system. It is used by both banks and building societies, where money is required to be transferred from one bank/building society to another on the same day – that is, where a customer/client requires a secure, urgent, same-day payment. Under the auspices of APACS,[61] CHAPS Clearing Company Ltd:

- administers and manages the payment scheme(s), and
- provides the central infrastructure for same-day payment services.

Primarily for high value transactions, the company processes RTGS (real time gross settlement) payments in both sterling and euros.[62]

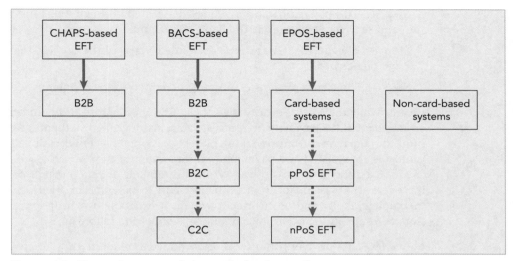

Figure 4.3 Alternative types of electronic funds transfer

The main users of CHAPS are:

- banks and building societies – for inter-bank transfers and the movement of funds within the financial system, and

- companies and businesses – for the transfer of funds from one company's/business's bank account to another company's/business's bank account.

It is very rare for private individuals to make personal CHAPS payments.

How are CHAPS payments/transfers made?

Most of the UK banks and a majority of the larger UK building societies are *direct members* of CHAPS, with the smaller UK banks and building societies being *indirect members* with access to the CHAPS payment system through a direct member.

Payments/transfers are made electronically and should start and finish on the same day. CHAPS payments/transfers can commence at 6.00 am each day and payments/transfers usually have to commence before 4.00 pm for same-day settlement – although there is a facility to make late payments up to 5.00 pm. Payment/transfer instructions can be made electronically, usually using internet or other secure/private electronic banking facilities – often the case for regular users, although a substantial number of instructions for CHAPS payments/transfers are still, somewhat unbelievably, made by customers filling in forms . . . manually![63]

Within a CHAPS payment/transfer, the various stages would be as follows:

Step 1 A company requests (probably electronically) and authorises its bank to make a CHAPS payment/transfer out of its account.

Step 2 The paying bank (the bank of the company making the CHAPS payment/transfer request) validates, verifies, and authenticates the request.

Step 3 The payment/transfer request is submitted/forwarded to a central processing centre.

Step 4   The payment/transfer request is cleared through the inter-bank payment and settlement system via the Bank of England.

Step 5   The payment/transfer is forwarded via a central processing centre to the recipient's bank.

Step 6   The payment/transfer amount is credited to the recipient's account.

Clearly, while there exists a vast range of CHAPS procedural/security protocols designed to ensure that CHAPS payments/transfers are authorised, verified, authenticated and validated prior to the payment/transfer taking place, occasionally – very occasionally – procedural protocols are violated and payments/transfers can, put simply . . . go wrong! How?

That's a difficult one to answer. While it is difficult to obtain details of specific issues, in general the vast majority of problems tend to be associated with the provision of incomplete, faulty and/or incorrect payment instructions which in exceptional circumstances results in the occurrence of one or more of the following:

■ *timing delay* – payment/transfer is not actioned as requested and the payment/transfer is not completed on the same day,

■ *payment errors* – funds are transferred to an incorrect account, and/or

■ *value errors* – an incorrect value of funds is transferred.

Clearly, given the often high value of the payment/transfer, the consequences of such a failure can be extensive, wide-ranging and extremely damaging, both legally and financially.

BACS-based EFT

Bankers Automated Clearing System (BACS) was formed in 1971 (having previously been known as the Inter-Bank Computer Bureau), its main task being to provide a central clearing function for bulk automated payments. In 1985, BACS changed its name to BACS Ltd and expanded its membership to include building societies. Following a corporate governance review during 2003, BACS Ltd was separated into two companies:

■ BACS Payment Schemes Limited (BPSL) – to govern and administer the scheme,

■ BACS Ltd – to process payments and develop/enhance processing technologies.

In October 2004, BACS Ltd was re-branded as Voca Ltd.[64] In 2007, Voca Ltd merged with the UK national switch provider LINK Interchange Network Ltd, and is now called VocaLink Ltd.

BACS Payment Schemes Limited (BPSL) is responsible for:

■ administering the scheme's payment rules and standard,

■ providing advice on best practice,

■ enhancing the quality of clearing, settlement and payment services,

■ ensuring compliance with the Bank of England regulatory requirements, and

■ developing new payment services to meet the needs of corporate customers and consumers.

VocaLink Ltd is responsible for:

■ ensuring secure transaction processing facilities are provided,

■ providing flexible and reliable payment engines,

- developing and enhancing clearing, settlement and payment services, and
- developing new payment services to meet the needs of both corporate customers and personal customers.

BACS Payment Schemes Ltd has two main products:

- direct credit, and
- direct debit.

While many of the above payments are submitted directly to BACS, currently over 50 per cent of organisations/companies make their direct credit and direct debit payment submissions through an Approved Bureau[65] rather than submitting directly to BACS. Why?

For a number of reasons, for example:

- the organisation/company may only make a small number of direct credit and/or direct debit payments transactions per month, or
- the organisation/company may be unable to fulfil all of the criteria to be able to make direct submissions to BACS – for example a newly established SME with a low turnover.

Okay, so what about direct credit and direct debit payments?

Direct credit

Direct credit is a secure transfer service which enables organisations to make EFT directly into bank and/or building society accounts.[66] Direct credits are mainly used for paying wages and salaries, although they are also used for a wide variety of other applications, such as supplier payments, payments of pensions, payments of employee expenses, insurance settlements, payments of dividends and/or interest, and payment refunds.[67]

For the paying organisation/company, the main benefits of direct credits are:

- payments are prompt and cleared on arrival into the customer/recipient account,
- payment transfer process is safe and secure, and
- payment process is time efficient and inexpensive.

Although the processing cycle for direct credit transactions is described as a three-day cycle, the actual minimum period between the transaction submission and the cleared payment into the recipient's account is actually only 36 hours.

Direct debit

A direct debit is an instruction from a customer to their bank or building society to authorise a third-party organisation/company to collect varying amounts from their account.[68] In the UK, approximately 60,000 organisations/companies, and approximately 55 per cent of the UK paying population, use direct debit services to collect a variety of regular and/or occasional payments including utility payments, insurance premiums, council tax payments, mortgages and/or loan repayments, and subscription payments.

For the paying customer/client, the main benefits of direct debits are:

- payment is automatic,
- direct debit payment is often cheaper than cheque payment (although not always),[69]

- the payment process is convenient,
- the payment process is safeguarded/guaranteed.[70]

Faster Payments Service

The Faster Payments Service (FPS) is designed to reduce payment times between customer accounts in different banks – from three working days using the long-established BACS system to near real time. (For transfers between customer accounts at the same bank it is instantaneous – that is, real time. For transfers between customer accounts at different banks it can take up to three hours.)

Although CHAPS already provides a limited faster-than-BACS service for low-volume, high-value transactions, the FPS is focused primarily on the large-volume, low-value transactions.

APACS was responsible for the development and delivery of the Faster Payments Service, which was officially launched on 27 May 2008 when the day-to-day operations and management of the service was transferred to the CHAPS Clearing Company Ltd.

The original founding members of the Faster Payments service were: Abbey (now Santander UK), Alliance and Leicester (now Santander UK), Barclays, Citi, Clydesdale and Yorkshire Banks (National Australia Group), Co-operative Bank, HBOS, HSBC, Lloyds TSB, Nationwide Building Society, Northern Bank (Danske Bank), Northern Rock, and Royal Bank of Scotland Group (including NatWest and Ulster Bank), which represented approximately 95 per cent of the payments made in the UK.

Because the FPS is intended for low-value transfers, banks continue to use BACS for outgoing transfers of amounts which exceed the individual bank's specified value. In September 2010, the value limit for all payment types was raised to £100,000; however, individual banks and building societies can and indeed do continue to impose their own value limits for both corporate and consumer customers.

SEPA

The Single Euro Payments Area (SEPA) is an EU and EPC (European Payments Council) initiative designed to:

- remove inter-country payments barriers and create a single set of standards for euro payments across the EU, and
- align the cost of cross-border transfers with that of domestic electronic transfers, resulting in overall cost reductions.

SEPA is underpinned by the Payment Services Directive (PSD),[71] which provides the legal foundation for the creation of an EU-wide single market for payments. The Payments Service Directive has now been implemented in national law in all the member states of the EU.

The SEPA-compliant cross-border schemes were introduced in early 2008 and the SEPA Credit Transfer (SCT) scheme was launched as a euro payment scheme which allows transfer payments to be made between any pair of SEPA countries, as well as enabling euro payments within the UK.

In late 2009, SEPA Direct Debits (SDD) was launched. This allows Direct Debit originators to collect pan-European Direct Debits from any of the SEPA countries using a single Direct Debit service instead of the existing country-specific services.

It is expected that the SCT and SDD schemes will replace existing national payment schemes, and, although specific dates have not been agreed, it is likely that the SEPA schemes will become fully operative in 2013 for SEPA Credit Transfers and in 2014 for SEPA Direct Debits for cross-border and local payments across all EU member states.

For payments using the SEPA scheme it will be mandatory for cross-border euro payments to make use of International Bank Account Numbers (IBANs) and Bank Identification Codes (BICs). It is expected that their use will be mandatory for domestic euro payments from 2013.

EPOS-based EFT

Card-based EPOS systems

For most individuals, point of service or EPOS-based EFT is perhaps the most common of all EFT types, one which the vast majority of individuals will use on a regular basis – monthly, weekly, even perhaps daily. There is an enormous (and ever increasing) range of cards/card schemes available which can be divided into two categories:

1 *Payment cards*:[72] for example, debit cards, credit cards, store cards (affinity cards and/ or own brand cards), charge cards, and stored-value cards (for example an e-money smart card or an e-purse).

2 *Non-payment cards*: for example, loyalty cards, ATM cards, cheque guarantee cards, and e-money smart cards.[73]

Our discussion will be restricted to payment cards.

First, however, some definitions:

- *The cardholder*: the customer with a payment card and an agreed amount of purchasing power.[74]

- *The merchant*: the business that accepts a payment card as a method of paying for goods or services.

- *The acquirer* (or acquiring bank):[75] the bank and/or other financial institution acting as a payment processing company and a link between the merchant[76] and the card issuer.

- *The card issuer*: the bank, building society or financial institution that issues a card to a cardholder and maintains the cardholder's account.

There are two types of EPOS processing:

1 On-line processing using an EFT system – cardholder present.

2 On-line processing using an EFT system – cardholder not present.

On-line processing using an EFT system – cardholder present (pPoS EFT) normally involves four stages:

1 a validation stage,

2 an authorisation stage,

3 a settlement stage, and

4 a reconciliation stage,

with the key systems requirements being:

- an active on-line PoS terminal and secure communication link,

- appropriate card validation software and card authorisation software,

- approved settlement software (acquirer and card issuer).

At the validation stage the merchant enters the customer's card data into their system by requesting the customer insert their card into a smart card reader (chip and PIN). The authorisation software validates the card.[77]

At the authorisation stage the merchant needs to authorise the transaction to ensure that the customer/cardholder has sufficient funds to finance the purchase. If the transaction value is less than the agreed MSA[78] limit, the EFT system will/can authorise the transaction off-line. If the transaction amount is equal to, or above, the MSA limit, the transaction details will be forwarded on-line to the acquirer for authorisation. The merchant will receive either a transaction authorised[79] or transaction declined[80] or transaction referred[81] response.

If the transaction is authorised the customer/cardholder will be requested to input their PIN into the smart card holder key pad. If the PIN entered is incorrect following a number of attempts, the merchant **must** decline the transaction.

At the settlement stage details of all transactions marked for payment are sorted and forwarded to the appropriate acquirer for settlement (payment). The acquirer will acknowledge receipt and confirm the validity of the transactions and the accuracy of the data. Once all data checks have been satisfied the merchant will be reimbursed accordingly.

At the reconciliation stage the merchant receives transaction reports including point of service source files, settlement files and acquirer acknowledgement files, to ensure that no settlements remain unpaid.

On-line processing using an EFT system – cardholder not present (nPoS EFT) are normally associated with:

■ mail-order-based transactions,

■ call-centre-based transactions, and of course

■ web-based (e-commerce) transactions.

Such on-line processing is normally associated with so-called distance contracts,[82] that is, contracts where there has been no face-to-face contact between the consumer and a representative of the company/organisation selling the goods and/or services or someone acting indirectly on the business's behalf – such as someone in a showroom, or a door-to-door sales person – up to and including the moment at which the contract is concluded.

The validation stage and the authorisation stage are more or less the same whether the customer/cardholder is present or the customer/cardholder is not present, the key difference being that the customer/cardholder will be requested to provide details of the card's security code (or CSC) which is a three- or four-digit value printed on the card or signature strip but not encoded on the magnetic stripe. MasterCard, Visa and Diners Club have a three-digit card security code – the code is not embossed and is always the final group of numbers printed on the back signature panel of the card. American Express cards have a four-digit code printed on the front side of the card above the number. It is printed flat and not embossed like the card number.

To accept point of service EFT (both off-line and on-line payments), a company must have a Merchant account (and ID[83]) issued by an acquiring bank. In addition, to process on-line payments a company/organisation must also have:

■ an Internet Merchant account (an ID), and

■ an approved Payment Service Provider (PSP).[84]

Non-card-based EPOS systems

A non-card-based system is any point of service EFT system that operates without the need for a debit card/credit card *and* external authentication such as a signature match or PIN. While a wide range of biometric[85] technologies using behavioural and/or physiological characteristics – for example, voice recognition, signature recognition, fingerprint recognition, iris recognition, face recognition and hand geometry recognition – are now widely used in a range of security systems, for point of service EFT systems at the present time, there is no widely used biometric system in operation.

Biometric identification technologies are essentially pattern recognition systems, and generally involve four stages:

1 *Enrolment* – that is, creation of a record associating a specific identifying biometric feature with a specific individual.

2 *Accumulation* – that is, storing a record of the biometric feature, either in a permanent non-movable facility (for example a centralised database) or on a decentralised portable storage module (for example on a smart card).

3 *Acquisition* – that is, when identification is required, a new sample of the biometric feature is acquired (for example new iris scan and/or a new fingerprint scan).

4 *Matching* – that is, the newly acquired sample is compared to the stored sample. If the newly acquired sample matches with the stored sample, there is a positive identification.

Where a single biometric measurement is used for identification purposes the system is referred to as unimodal[86] (that is, a biometric system which relies on a single source of biometric data, information or evidence for identity authentication). Where two or more biometric measurements are used concurrently for identification purposes, such a system is referred to as a multimodal biometric system (that is, a biometric system which relies on multiple sources of biometric data, information and/or evidence for identity authentication). Where a single biometric measurement is used for identification purposes but is used concurrently with another form of variable input – for example a number, or word, or phrase – such a system is referred to as a unimodal + (or a mono-modal +) biometric system (that is, a biometric system which relies on a single source of biometric data, information or evidence *and* an additional input variable for identity authentication).

Many of the biometric identification technologies that have been tested in point of service EFT systems, including the recently failed 'pay-by-touch' system,[87] have been unimodel + (or monomodal +) systems, that is:

■ the initial biometric measurement establishes/determines the identity of the individual, and

■ the additional input variable confirms the identity of the individual.

Clearly, while the use of biometric identification technologies in point of service EFT systems remains in its infancy, there can be little doubt that the development of such systems continues to remain a high priority with many card providers. (See Article 4.3.)

Article 4.3

MasterCard develops Indian biometric payment solution

MasterCard Worldwide has developed a payment solution for India's Aadhaar ID number project.

The solution will enable citizens with Aadhaar numbers to perform payment transactions using UID numbers with biometric authentication.

According to MasterCard, the solution is based on the Unique Identification Authority of India (UIDAI) platform and MasterCard's payment network and family of brands. The solution will promote financial inclusion by enabling Aadhaar account holders to move away from cash and towards electronic transactions.

The technology supports prepaid, debit and credit payment products. It will enable participating banks to issue a 16-digit Primary Account Number (PAN) to individuals enrolled into Aadhaar. 'MasterCard has developed a direct interface with Aadhaar to perform UID biometric authentication of such payment transactions,' says the company.

'With this solution, payment transactions will be performed using the Aadhaar authentication infrastructure and MasterCard's authorization, clearing and settlement infrastructure.'

For the proof-of-concept, MasterCard has integrated and collaborated with ElectraCard Services (ECS) and Integra Micro Systems (Integra) for front-end processing and terminal deployment respectively. Today's demonstration will showcase a working model of this integration that brings advantages of scale, flexibility and innovation.

13 December 2010

Source: Available at *www.planetbiometrics.com*.

What are the advantages and disadvantages of EPOS EFT systems?

The advantages of using EPOS EFT systems are:

- the increased speed and accuracy of such funds transfers,
- the reduced costs of such transactions, and
- the improved efficiency of such transaction processing.

The disadvantages of using EPOS EFT systems are:

- the increased lack of transaction transparency,
- the investment cost required to enable such a system, and
- the substantial in-house management required to ensure such systems continue to operate efficiently and effectively.

Electronic mail (e-mail)

As suggested earlier, e-mail is a method of composing, sending and receiving messages, together with any associated attached files of text data, numeric data, and/or images, via an electronic communication system. In a contemporary context, the majority of e-mail systems today are interconnected via the internet using the simple mail transfer protocol (SMTP),[88] facilitating the flow of e-mail to anywhere in the world almost instantaneously.

A brief history of e-mail

As suggested earlier, e-mail systems not only predate the internet, e-mail systems were both essential to and instrumental in the creation and development of the internet as we know it today.

The exact history of e-mail is at best vague, at worst ambiguous, and frequently the source of heated academic debate. However, what is generally acknowledged is that the use of e-mail emerged in the mid/late 1960s as a simple communication resource for users of single 'stand-alone' mainframe computer systems to allow them to send and receive messages – a facility that was rapidly developed and extended to users of networked computer systems, allowing users to transmit messages to, and receive messages from, different computers within a network.

Again, the history of precisely how the migration of e-mail from stand-alone mainframe computers to networked computer systems occurred is unclear. However, it is recognised by many academics and practitioners that the ARPAnet was one of the main contributors not only to the development and evolution of contemporary e-mail, but also to its exponential growth in popularity – from geek technology to killer application![89] Indeed, it was the widespread recognition (especially by those without access to the ARPAnet) of the benefits and advantages of e-mail as a means of communication that stimulated the development of a number of alternative protocols for the delivery/routing of e-mail among users on groups of time-sharing computers on different of networks – including ARPAnet, BITnet[90] and NSFnet.[91] Of course, the rest is history!

Contemporary internet-based e-mail

What is an e-mail message?

An internet-based e-mail message would normally comprise two major components:

1 *A header* which contains the message summary, sender details, receiver details and other information about the e-mail.

2 *A body* which contains the message itself (with a signature block[92] at the end of the message).

A header would usually contain at least four defined fields:

1 *From*: the e-mail address of the sender of the message.

2 *To*: the e-mail address of the receiver of the message.

3 *Subject*: a brief summary of the contents of the message.

4 *Date*: the local time and date when the message was originally sent.

Other common header fields would include:

- *Cc*: sometimes referred to as carbon copy (old typewriting terminology) but is more appropriately defined as copy correspondence,
- *Bcc*: blind carbon copy, or more appropriately blind copy correspondence,[93]
- *Received*: tracking information generated by mail servers that have previously handled a message,
- *Content-Type*: information about how the message has to be displayed, usually a MIME[94] type.

How do you send/receive e-mail messages?

To send and/or receive e-mails a user must have an active internet connection and access to an active e-mail system, either:

- a stand-alone e-mail client, like Outlook Express, or
- a web-based e-mail client (webmail), for example Hotmail or Yahoo, that use an e-mail service appearing on a web page and allow users to read and write e-mails using a web browser.

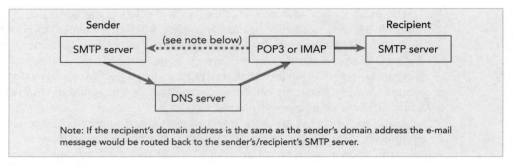

Figure 4.4 Contemporary e-mail

The e-mail system itself merely consists of a number of different interconnected servers, for example:

■ an SMTP server – to deal with outgoing mail,
■ a DNS[95] server – to locate domain names, and
■ a POP3 server or an IMAP server – to deal with incoming mail.[96]

See Figure 4.4.

Many people (and companies) are, however, choosing to use web-based e-mail, mainly because:

■ e-mail messages can be accessed and/or used anywhere – providing the user has access to a web browser and an active internet connection, and
■ webmail service providers offer a range of add-on features/facilities, for example:
  ■ e-mail filtering,
  ■ address book facilities,
  ■ e-mail spam detection,
  ■ mail retrieval,
  ■ anti-virus checking of mail attachments,
  ■ dictionary, thesaurus and, spelling checking facilities . . . and many more!

However there are some disadvantages, for example:

■ users must stay on-line to access e-mail messages,
■ some commercial webmail services providers limit individual user e-mail storage capacity, and
■ access to webmail services can be affected by slow network/internet connections.

In addition, some recent problems have questioned the usefulness and security of e-mail, for example:

■ the increasing occurrences of e-mail spam or spamming – that is, the unsolicited mass distribution of e-mail messages,
■ the growing threat from malicious intruders, and
■ the increasing incidences of e-mail-transmitted computer viruses or, more specifically, e-mail worms,

Recent years have, nonetheless, seen not only an enormous increase in the volume of e-mail traffic, but, perhaps more importantly, have witnessed a widening dependency, especially of companies, on e-mail messaging and e-mail-related services.

Innovations in accounting and finance

There can be little doubt that business management and financial reporting have been revolutionised by developments in information and communications technology, such as the availability and increasing sophistication of computer hardware, the growth of ever more advanced communication facilities, the adoption of increasingly complex networking technologies, and the widespread introduction of application specific computer software.

Computer-based accounting systems

Computer-based accounting is a term used to describe application systems that assist in:

- the recording and processing of accounting transactions data, and/or
- the production and provision of financial information for:
  - internal management reporting – for the coordination and management of business activities, and/or
  - external stakeholder reporting – in accordance with regulatory requirements (for example, the Companies Act 2006).

Because such computer-based accounting systems can have many diverse origins, for example, they can be:

- developed in-house by a company/organisation,
- purchased 'off-the-shelf' from an external third-party supplier by a company/organisation, or
- purchased 'off-the-shelf' from an external third-party supplier by a company/organisation and modified for local settings applicable to the company/organisation,

they can vary enormously in complexity, adaptability, flexibility, functionality, and of course cost.

In a contemporary context, a computer-based accounting system is typically composed of various (sometimes integrated) software modules, servicing a range of accounting-related functions, and would include the following:

- sales ledger management,
- sales order processing system,
- purchases ledger management,
- purchase order processing system,
- general ledger management,
- fixed asset management,
- cash book management,
- inventory management control,
- payroll and human resources management,
- product/process costing, and
- budgetary control.

Most contemporary, computer-based financial accounting systems provide:

- fully integrated general ledger, sales ledger, and purchase ledger systems,
- integrated transaction audit services,
- performance evaluation facilities,
- report writing solutions (for example, VAT reporting),
- financial statement preparation facilities,
- real-time on-line transaction processing facilities,
- customisation and connectivity facilities (for integration with other software applications),
- multi-currency consolidation software (for multi-company groups),
- fully integrated e-business solutions (for web-based transaction processing), and
- XBRL (eXtensible Business Report Language) tagging (see later).

Sales ledger management

The aim of sales ledger management software, and sales order processing system software, is to ensure:

- the acceptance of authorised orders only,
- adherence to sales processing procedures and company/organisation credit policies,
- adherence to company/organisation invoicing procedure,
- adherence to company/organisation pricing and discounting policies, and
- the proper management of customer (debtor) accounts.

Sales ledger management software is therefore designed to:

- manage sales transactions, and
- maintain customer accounts (debtor accounts).

The main features would include:

- on-line maintenance of individual customer (debtor) accounts,
- on-line transaction history,
- multi-currency processing facilities,
- on-line customer account analysis (using a range of categories[97]),
- on-line credit management facilities,[98]
- on-line customer (debtor) payment history analysis,
- on-line invoicing procedures,
- flexible discount facilities, and
- multi-presentational/flexible communication facilities.

Sales order processing system

Sales order processing system software is used to process customer orders.

Such a system is normally integrated with a company's/organisation's stock management system, and would control the processing of sales orders from the initial recording of an order, to the despatch of goods, and the update of stock control and accounting modules.

The main features would include facilities for:

- multi-pricing options,
- on-line management of repeat orders for the same customers,
- on-line goods return/credit note management,
- multi-currency processing,
- flexible customer account details,[99]
- on-line order acknowledgement,
- customer prioritising,
- order consolidation (that is, consolidating a number of orders into a single invoice),
- inventory tracing (from inventory to order to despatch to invoice), and
- flexible invoicing procedures.

Purchases ledger management

The aim of purchase ledger management software and purchase order processing system software is to ensure:

- adherence to purchase processing procedures and company/organisation payment policies,
- all goods and services are ordered as needed,
- all goods and services are verified and safeguarded until needed,
- all invoices are verified and validated before payment,
- all transaction records are accurately maintained,
- the proper management of supplier (creditor) accounts, and
- the acceptance of authorised orders only.

Purchase ledger management software is therefore designed:

- to process purchase transactions, and
- maintain supplier accounts (creditor accounts).

The main features would include:

- on-line maintenance of individual supplier (creditor) accounts,
- on-line transaction history,
- multi-currency processing facilities,
- on-line supplier account analysis (using a range of categories[100]),
- payment list creation and editing facilities,
- automated payment processing,
- on-line debtor payment history analysis, and
- multi presentational/flexible communication facilities.

Purchase order processing system

Purchase order processing systems software is used to process orders for goods and services from suppliers.

Such a system is normally integrated with a company's/organisation's stock management system, and would control the processing of purchase orders, including:

- the production of supplier documentation, and
- the update of stock control and accounting modules

The main features would include:

- on-line matching of purchase invoice to delivery notes and purchase orders (including multiple delivery notes and purchase orders),
- on-line management of goods returned to suppliers for credit or replacement,
- multi-currency processing facilities,
- on-line authorisation of orders,
- on-line order prioritising facilities, and
- inventory tracing facilities (from inventory to order to despatch to invoice).

General ledger management

General ledger management software is designed to record and summarise all nominal account transactions accurately so that timely and useful financial reports may be generated.

The main features would include:

- on-line maintenance of individual nominal accounts,
- on-line creation of memorandum accounts in the nominal ledger,
- on-line nominal account analysis using a range of categories,
- batch journal entry facilities,
- pre-payment and accrual facilities, and
- multi-presentational facilities.

Fixed asset management

Fixed asset management software is used to record details of company/organisation fixed assets – both tangible and intangible.

The main features would include:

- on-line maintenance of individual asset records, including acquisition and disposal, and
- on-line maintenance of depreciation/amortisation records.

Cash book management

Cash book management software is designed to provide control of all bank-related activities (receipts and payments), including cash, cheques, credit cards, standing orders and direct debits.

The main features would include:

- on-line maintenance of individual bank account records,
- multi-currency processing facilities,
- batch data entry facilities,
- on-line creation of automatic direct debits and standing orders,
- on-line bank reconciliation facilities, and
- multi-presentational facilities.

Inventory management control

Inventory management control software is designed to record and control inventory movement in relation to:

■ raw materials and components,

■ work in progress, and

■ completed products.

The main features would be:

■ on-line maintenance of individual inventory records,

■ active inventory level management facilities (using specified minimum and maximum inventory level controls),

■ multiple location inventory management facilities,

■ alternative inventory valuation facilities,

■ on-line inventory tracking facilities,

■ inventory source information (for example, suppliers),

■ automated stocktaking procedures, and

■ multi-presentational facilities.

Inventory management control software may also integrate purchasing and production/manufacturing systems activities, and may involve for example, the use of stock management and materials/manufacturing resource planning software.

Payroll and human resources management

The aim of payroll and human resources management software is to ensure:

■ all legal and statutory requirements are complied with,

■ employees are appropriately qualified,

■ employees are remunerated at appropriate levels,

■ all statutory deductions are correctly made.

Payroll and human resources management software is therefore designed to:

■ record and control employee movements/changes, and

■ calculate and manage payroll payments to employees.

The main features would be:

■ on-line maintenance of statutory personnel files,

■ on-line maintenance of employee status changes,

■ periodic verification of employee records and status,

■ calculation and payment of statutory deductions, and

■ on-line preparation of payroll and pay advices.

Product costing/process costing

Whereas product costing systems are designed to accumulate cost data related to the production/manufacture of individual product units/service units, process costing systems are designed to accumulate costs for an entire production/manufacturing process.

Product costing/process costing software is used to maintain both financial and non-financial data related not only to complete but also to part-completed customer products and/or client services.

Such software may be integrated with/connected to:

- the sales order processing system, and/or
- the purchase order processing systems, and/or
- the inventory management systems.

Budgetary control

In a broad context:

- Budgeting as a planning process/procedure can be defined as the activity of translating corporate decisions into specific financial plans, usually short-term plans (within the context of longer term financial plans of course).

- Budgetary control as a controlling process/procedure can be defined as a reactive (after the event) financial control process in which actual performance and/or results for a defined period of time are compared with expected performance/(flexed) budgeted results.

The aim of the former is to provide 'a financial framework within which corporate/organisational activities may occur', whereas the aim of the latter is to identify deviations (or variances) from the agreed financial framework and, where appropriate, recommend suitable remedial action (where required).

. . . and budgeting and budgetary control software?

For many companies, such systems are merely integrated software modules within existing financial accounting software – usually linked to (part of) the general ledger management systems, assisting in:

- the development of annual budgeted financial statements (profit and loss account, balance sheet, and cash flow statement), and
- the periodic monitoring of actual income and expenditure in comparison with budgeted expectations.

What are the advantages of such integrated budgeting/budgetary control systems?

Such integration provides:

- the ability to transfer financial transaction data directly from the general ledger management system to the budgeting/budgetary control system thereby reducing the timescale of budgeting/budgetary control activities,
- the ability to transfer financial transaction data to other integrated data manipulation/data analysis software packages and thereby facilitate scenario modelling/simulation,
- the ability to secure and control the transfer of financial transaction data thereby minimising the possibility of potential errors, and
- the ability (with the more sophisticated budgeting/budgetary control systems software) to integrate not only quantitative financial data, but also qualitative non-financial data.

Resource planning and management systems

Resource planning and management systems would include the following:

- corporate resource planning systems, and
- customer/client relationship management systems.

Corporate resource planning systems

Corporate resource planning systems (also known as corporate resource planning software) are essentially management information systems that seek to integrate and automate operations-related and production-related business practices/activities. Such practices/ activities can include manufacturing, logistics, stock management and inventory, selling and distribution, and finance and accounting. Indeed, because corporate resource planning software can be and often is used to manage and control a diverse range of business activities – from production and inventory management, to sales and delivery management, to invoicing and credit management, to human resource management – it is often intimately connected to supply chain management systems.

What is the aim of a corporate resource planning system?

The main aim of a corporate resource planning system as an information system/process seeking to integrate all related processes, procedures, and protocols is to maximise the use of all the resources within an organisation, and thereby improve resource efficiency and operational effectiveness . . . and of course profitability. Such resources would include:

- all infrastructure processes and procedures (including organisation relationships),
- all resource-based activities (including business support systems – for example, information technology and related communication systems), and
- all human resource capabilities, skills and competencies.

Essentially, corporate resource planning systems are multidisciplinary/multifunctional workflow management systems, the key to which is:

- the migration of control procedures from the execution phase to the implementation stage,
- the integration of measurement points into the corporate resource planning system, and
- the concentration of responsibility within systems procedures.

Although the corporate resource planning vision is a single coordinated company/ organisation wide integrated database and user interface, in reality – mainly for pragmatic organisational reasons – many corporate resource planning systems and applications are only loosely integrated, with the possibility of the existence of a number of interrelated databases and user interfaces, each sharing data/information within pre-defined security protocols/parameters.

There are, of course, many problems and risks associated with the implementation of a corporate resource planning system. For example, employees may view the development and implementation of a company/organisation-wide corporate resource planning system as a downsizing exercise leading inevitably to a reduction in employee numbers, and may therefore resist its implementation. In addition, culture clashes/management problems may result from inconsistencies between corporate resource planning system requirements, corporate/organisational capabilities and management expectations.

What are the advantages and disadvantages of implementing a corporate resource planning system?

For many companies the benefits from such a system include:

■ lower inventory management costs – for example, reduced ordering costs and lower carrying costs,

■ reduced selling, distribution and transport costs,

■ more flexible production processes and reduced production costs,

■ reduced financial accounting and record-keeping costs,

■ greater operational efficiency resulting in lower investment in assets, and

■ more efficient production coordination and scheduling resulting in reduced production down-times and reduced stock-outs,

all of which increase operational transparency and production efficiency, allowing for greater product/service customisation (where required) which, together with lower overall costs, may increase market share and, of course, profitability.

The main disadvantages are:

■ systems may not only be expensive to acquire/develop, to install and to maintain but difficult to use/implement;

■ systems may distort/fragment systems boundaries, accountabilities and lines of responsibility, and as a result adversely affect employee morale;

■ internal management politics may resist the sharing of internal data/information; and

■ centralising system procedures and processes may result in high organisational risks (for example a potential failure could have widespread implications).

In addition, because of the integrated nature of such systems, once the systems are established, switching costs may be very high thus reducing future flexibility and strategic control.

. . . and the next generation?

Fully integrated, fully interactive browser-based, platform-independent, IP technology-enabled corporate resource planning system software.

Customer/client relationship management systems

Customer/client relationship management can be defined as the implementation and coordination of the processes and procedures designed to improve company/organisation interaction with customers/clients, the aim being to better serve the needs and demands of customers/clients and increase satisfaction and loyalty.

Emerging during the 1990s as part of a strategic movement to reflect the central role of customers/clients in determining the strategic positioning of a company, in a contemporary context such software systems are essentially integrated databases which seek to provide a coordinated analysis of information/knowledge related to customer/client activity/

behaviour, which can be used/exploited in determining the focus of market-based retail activity, and ultimately the maximisation of company/organisation revenue income . . . and as usual, of course, profit.

What information would such a customer/client relationship management system be concerned with?

Such information – sometimes referred to as market cycle information – would include, for example:

- customer profiling information,

- transaction activity information,

- market segmentation information, and

- customer response/behaviour prediction.

While many critics of the trend for customer relationship management systems have suggested that the storage and use of such customer/client related information is by no means a contemporary phenomenon, it is, of course, the use of information and communication technologies that has revolutionised the capabilities of such systems – especially in terms of the collection, processing and management of such information.

What are the main problems of such systems?

The main operational problems stem from five issues:

1 *The technological issue* – that is, what information and communication technologies will be used for the collection, processing, and analysis of customer/client information.

2 *The administration issue* – that is, what methodologies will be used for the integration of heterogeneous collections of customer/client information.

3 *The information issue* – that is, what internal data/information structure will be used and how detailed will the data/information be (that is, what levels of abstraction will be used).

4 *The acquisition issue* – that is, what knowledge discovery procedures and/or data/information acquisition processes will be used.

5 *The security issue* – that is, who will be allowed access to the data/information, and on what basis will such access be determined and approved.

Although there can be little doubt that such integrated customer/client relationship management systems have a number of company/organisation benefits, generally related to the 3 Es (economy, effectiveness, and efficiency), the commercialisation of customer/client information that occurs in the use of such systems has resulted in many questions being raised concerning the socio-political legitimacy of such systems – in particular the data protection issues associated with the collection and storage of confidential customer/client information.

However, despite such questions, the astronomical growth in popularity that such customer/client relationship management systems have enjoyed over the last few years is perhaps an indication that they are now a necessary feature of a company's/organisation's portfolio of business-related management systems and, given the ever more competitive nature of the business environment, are perhaps here to stay.

Other innovations enabled by new information/communications technology

There are a number of generic innovations widely used in accounting information systems, perhaps the two most important being spreadsheets and databases.

Spreadsheets

A spreadsheet is a computer program that displays – in rows and columns – a group of interrelated cells in a two-dimensional arrangement, a program that allows for the entering, editing and manipulating of alphabetic and numeric data, and the undertaking of complex mathematical operations.

There are of course many versions/types of spreadsheet available, perhaps the most widely known being Microsoft's Excel (part of the Microsoft Office suite – available at *www.microsoft.com*). While it is generally recognised that the inventors of the spreadsheet are Dan Brinklin and Bob Frankson – who created/developed the VisiCalc spreadsheet using, as suggested by Brinklin, a blackboard/spreadsheet paradigm to view the results of underlying formulas – it was Mitchell David Kapor (the founder of Lotus Development Corporation in 1982) and Jonathan Sachs who designed the Lotus 1-2-3, a spreadsheet, released in January 1983, that became the 'killer application'[101] of the 1980s and

- revolutionised the use of PCs, and
- contributed significantly to the success of IBM PCs in the corporate environment.

However, market domination by Lotus 1-2-3 was short-lived!

Originally marketed as a spreadsheet program called Multiplan,[102] in 1982, the first version of Microsoft Excel was released for the Apple Mac in 1985, with the first Windows version being available in November 1987. By mid 1988, Microsoft Excel had begun to outsell Lotus 1-2-3, elevating Microsoft Inc. to the position of leading PC software developer – a position the company has maintained (although not without a number of legal, commercial, and technical battles) ever since. It also, perhaps more importantly, augmented the profile of spreadsheets – from merely interesting add-on software technology to an indispensable business tool – so much so that in a contemporary business context the term spreadsheet has now become synonymous with accounting and finance. Indeed, in providing:

- user-defined data input facilities – increasingly integrated into either other spreadsheets and/or other software applications, to facilitate direct input;
- user-defined data editing and data manipulation facilities – including facilities to perform complex iterative calculations using user-defined processes (macros) and input variables, link-related spreadsheets and multi-dimensional spreadsheets; and
- user-defined data output using a range of textual and graphical features;

spreadsheets have become an indispensable 'everyday' tool in accounting and finance, and are now widely used in many diverse areas, for example:

- in financial accounting:
  - performance analysis, and
  - accounting adjustment calculations (for example, depreciation and doubtful debt provisions)

- in management accounting:
  - break-even analysis,
  - cost apportionment,
  - sensitivity analysis,
  - scenario analysis (including limiting factor analysis),
  - pricing,
  - budgeting, and
  - variance analysis
- in financial management:
  - capital investment appraisal,
  - risk assessments, and
  - finance scenario analysis.

Databases

A database can be defined as an organised body of related data or, perhaps more appropriately, a logical and systematic collection of interrelated data, managed and stored as a unit, a key feature of a database being the structural relationship between the objects represented in the database (called data elements) – a description of which is often referred to as a database schema. There are, of course, a number of alternative ways of organising a database schema – that is, alternative ways of organising the relationships between data elements stored in a database. Such alternative ways are termed database models (or data models), the most common being:

- the flat data model,
- the hierarchical data model,
- the network data model,
- the relational data model, and
- the object-oriented data model.

(Databases are discussed in further detail in Chapter 6.)

. . . and finally

XBRL

In the UK, the filing on-line of iXBRL (in-line eXtensible Business Reporting Language) corporation tax information became mandatory for all companies filing corporation tax returns (CT600) with HMRC (Her Majesty's Revenue and Customs) after 31 March 2011 for year endings after 31 March 2010.

But what is XBRL?

XBRL (eXtensible Business Reporting Language) is an established standards-based way to communicate business and financial information. It belongs to a family of languages known as XML (eXtensible Markup Language). Essentially XBRL is a way of tagging data within financial statements – similar to the use of bar codes on retail products. Such tags allow computer software to extract and analyse the data not only within a single financial statement but, more importantly, comparatively across many different sets of financial statements.

To tag data, XBRL requires a dictionary or taxonomy to define what the tags are, how they are to be used and what they mean. The HMRC taxonomy for the corporation tax computations currently uses 1,360 tags but will be extended to 4,561 tags by 2013. Separate taxonomies exist for:

- UK IFRS financial statements (3,725 tags),
- UK GAAP financial statements (5,292 tags), and
- UK Common Data (for example company name, financial reporting period).

Because the data within financial statements cannot be easily converted into an XBRL format, HMRC has developed iXBRL (in-line XBRL), in which a financial statement can be presented not only as a human readable document with its original formatting, but can also be read by computer software.

What must be produced in iXBRL format?

In the UK the following statutory information *must* be submitted through the on-line Government Gateway using the following formats:

Information/form	Required format
Corporation Tax Return (CT600)	XML
Corporation Tax computation	iXBRL
Statutory financial statements	iXBRL
Other supporting schedules	PDF

How can a company produce financial information in an iXBRL format?

For corporation tax computations there are two options for submitting iXBRL-format financial information:

1 Use the HMRC's free product which also includes a link to Companies House for the filing of small, non-audited company financial statements.[103] This option is only practical if the number of computations (the data content) submitted to the HMRC is very low.

2 Use purchased corporation tax software – most corporation tax software packages now produce corporation tax computations in iXBRL format.[104]

. . . and statutory financial statements?

For the production of the statutory financial information in iXBRL format, a company can:

1 Use the HMRC's free on-line product (only appropriate for small, audit-exempt financial statements).

2 Use new fully-integrated financial accounting software or existing financial accounting software updated to produce iXBRL financial statements.

3 Use Word/Excel to produce financial statements and outsource to a third party to generate iXBRL financial statements.

To manage the transition to iXBRL filing, HMRC has produced on-line guidance for companies, which is available at: *www.hmrc.gov.uk/ct/mandatory-online-filing.pdf*.

Concluding comments

There can be little doubt that the impact of information and communications innovations and developments on both social and economic activity over the last 20 years has been enormous, changing (as we have seen) not only:

- the content of corporate activity (that is, *what* is undertaken), but also
- the context of that corporate activity (that is, *how* it is undertaken), and, perhaps more importantly
- the nature of that corporate activity (that is, *where* it is undertaken).

And yet, as we enter the twenty-first century, as we step cautiously into the brave new world we have created, a brave new world of instantaneous communication and virtual resources, a brave new world of e-mail, media streaming and file sharing – before we congratulate ourselves on the success of this 'global technological revolution', it is perhaps important to recognise the socio-political consequences and ephemeral nature of the paradise we have created. Indeed, there can be little doubt that growing economic regionalisation, rising political territoriality and increasing social segmentation, although clearly products of early times, nonetheless provide iconic testimony to the late twentieth- and early twenty-first-century information technology revolution.

A brave new world . . . most certainly! An equal brave new world . . . most definitely not!

Self-review questions

1 Briefly explain the contribution that ARPAnet made to the development of the internet, and distinguish between the internet and the World Wide Web.

2 Define the term RFC, and explain the role of RFCs in developing internet standards.

3 Define and explain what is meant by the term file sharing.

4 Define and explain two of the following internet services/facilities:
   (a) e-mail,
   (b) file sharing,
   (c) media streaming,
   (d) VoIP (Voice over IP),
   (e) newsgroups.

5 Define and briefly explain the role of the Internet Society (ISOC).

6 Identify and describe the main categories of electronic funds transfer (EFT).

7 Briefly explain the difference between card-based and non-card-based EPOS EFT.

8 What is iXBRL?

Reference

Castells, M. (1996), *The Rise of the Network Society, The Information Age: Economy, Society and Culture, volume I*, Blackwell, Oxford.

Notes

1 For Castells, such fragmentation is the result of: 'societies . . . [being] increasingly structured around the bipolar opposition of the the Net and the Self' (Castells 1996: 3). For Castells, the Net metaphor relates to/symbolises the new emergent organisational formations and structures based on the pervasive use of networked communication media – formations and structures that are now characteristic of many companies, communities and social movements. The Self metaphor relates to/symbolises the activities through which individuals attempt to reaffirm their identities under the conditions of structural change and instability – structural change and instability that is symptomatic of the organisation and (re)organisation of social, political and economic activities into dynamic networks.

2 In formal usage, the word Internet was traditionally written with a capital first letter, while in less formal usage the capital letter was often dropped (internet). Up to the beginning of this century, the former dominated the media and the published press. However, since 2000 a significant number of publications have adopted the latter, less formal, usage. It is this latter version that is used in this text.

3 Internetworking involves connecting two or more distinct computer networks together into an internetwork, using a device called a router (a computer network device that forwards data packets across an internetwork through a process known as routing) to connect them together and allow traffic to flow between them.

4 In computer networking, packet switching is the dominant communications procedure in which packets (units of information carriage) are individually routed between computer network nodes (devices).

5 The Internet Protocol (IP) is a data-oriented protocol that is used by source and destination hosts for communicating data across a packet-switched internetwork.

6 The Advanced Research Projects Agency Network (ARPAnet) developed by ARPA (Advanced Research Projects Agency) of the US Department of Defense.

7 For some, the urgency afforded to the development of the ARPAnet by the US government authorities was a direct consequence of the scientific success illustrated by the Russian Sputnik programme, especially Yuri Gagarin's successful spaceflight on 12 April 1961.

8 In an open-architecture network, the individual networks may be environment specific – that is, separately designed and developed with their own unique interface which it may offer to users and/or other providers, including other internet providers.

9 The Internet Protocol Suite is the set of communications protocols used for the internet and other similar networks. It is commonly also known as TCP/IP named from two of the most important protocols in it: the Transmission Control Protocol (TCP) and the Internet Protocol (IP).

10 Operated by ICANN, IANA (Internet Assigned Numbers Authority) is the organisation that oversees global IP address allocation and other Internet Protocol-related symbols and numbers. IANA delegates the allocation of IP address blocks to Regional Internet Registries (RIRs).

11 The five Regional Internet Registries (RIRs) are:

   1 African Network Information Centre (AfriNIC) for Africa.
   2 American Registry for Internet Numbers (ARIN) for the United States, Canada, and several parts of the Caribbean region.
   3 Asia-Pacific Network Information Centre (APNIC) for Asia, Australia, New Zealand and neighbouring countries.
   4 Latin America and Caribbean Network Information Centre (LACNIC) for Latin America and parts of the Caribbean region.
   5 Réseaux IP Européens Network Coordination Centre (RIPE) for Europe, the Middle East and Central Asia.

12 RFC 1 was written by S. Crocker, University of California, Los Angeles. It was published on 7 April 1969, and was entitled 'Host Software'.

13 The Internet Engineering Task Force (IETF) is responsible for the development and promotion of internet standards. It is an open, all-volunteer organisation. It possesses no formal membership, nor any formal membership requirements. For further information see *www.ietf.org*.

14 The Internet Architecture Board (IAB) (for further information see *www.iab.org*) is responsible for overseeing the technical and engineering development of the internet by the Internet Society (ISOC) (see below). The board oversees a number of task forces, of which perhaps the most important are:

- the Internet Engineering Task Force (IETF), and
- the Internet Research Task Force (IRTF) (for further information see *www.irtf.org*.

15 The RFC Editor is:

- the publisher of RFC documents,
- responsible for producing the final editorial review of the RFC documents, and
- responsible for maintaining a master file of RFC documents, called the RFC Index.

The RFC index is available at *www.rfc-editor.org/rfcsearch.html*. Currently, the RFC Editor is a small group funded by ISOC. For further information on the RFC editor see *www.rfc-editor.org*.

16 The Internet Society (ISOC) is an international organisation responsible for promoting internet access and use, and 'to assure the open development, evolution and use of the Internet for the benefit of all people throughout the world'. ISOC membership is comprised of individuals, companies, non-profit-making organisations, government agencies and educational institutions such as colleges and universities. For further information see *www.isoc.org*.

17 For some the major advantage of the tradition of never de-publishing obsolete RFCs is that as a series of documents they form a continuous historical record of the development and evolution of internet standards.

18 Current RFCs are available as an RFC index at *www.rfc-editor.org/rfc-index.html*.

19 A list of extant internet drafts is available at *www.rfc-editor.org/idsearch.html*.

20 The full text of RFC 2026 is available at *ftp.rfc-editor.org/in-notes/rfc2026.txt*.

21 The full text of STD 1 is available at *ftp.rfc-editor.org/in-notes/std/std1.txt*.

22 The Internet protocol suite (sometimes called the TCP/IP protocol suite) is the set of communications protocols that implements the protocol stack on which the internet is established and on which it effectively operates. A protocol stack is a hierarchical arrangement of layers in which each layer solves a set of problems involving the transmission of data. Higher layers within the protocol stack are logically closer to the user, and deal with more abstract data. Lower layers within the protocol stack are more distant from the user, and deal with the translation of data into forms that can eventually be physically manipulated.

23 File Transfer Protocol (FTP) is a software standard for transferring computer files between computers and/or networks of computers which possess widely different operating systems. FTP belongs to the application layer of the internet protocol suite.

24 A peer-to-peer (or P2P) network is typically comprised of 'large informal connections', and is useful for many purposes, including:

- sharing data/information files especially where such files contain audio and/or audio data, and
- real-time data transmision, such as telephony traffic.

We will discuss P2P networks in greater detail in Chapter 5.

25 Further information on blackboard is available at *www.blackboard.com*.

26 File sharing is distinct from file trading inasmuch as downloading files from a peer-to-peer (P2P) network does not require uploading files.

27 Founded in 1990, the Electronic Frontier Foundation (EFF) is a US-based non-profit-making organisation whose main aim is to 'educate the press, policymakers and the general public about civil issues related to technology', in the context of today's digital age. More information on the Electronic Frontier Foundation is available at *http://www.eff.org*.

28 The term consumption is used here to mean any, or a combination of, the following:
   - reading – if the media is text based,
   - hearing – if the media is audio based,
   - viewing – if the media is video based.

29 For example, protocol issues/requirements, data corruption issues, data recovery procedures and transmission guarantees.

30 UK Office of Communication.

31 Chapter 5 provides an explanation of the differences between a peer-to-peer network and a client-server network.

32 See 'Microsoft to Acquire Skype', at *http://www.microsoft.com/presspass/press/2011/may11/05-10corpnewspr.mspx*.

33 Internet relay chat was created by Jarkko Oikarinen (nickname 'WiZ') in August 1988 to replace a program called MUT (Multi User Talk) on a bulletin board system called OuluBox in Finland. The prominence and profile of internet relay chat grew enormously during 1990–91 when it was used by many Kuwaitis to report on the Iraqi invasion of Kuwait in August 1990 and on the gulf war in 1991, and by many Russians to report on attempted coup, the *August Putsch,* in August 1991. Internet relay chat was also used in a similar way during the coup against Boris Yeltsin in September 1993.

34 It is not uncommon for an IRC server to have dozens, hundreds or even thousands of chat channels open simultaneously – some channels are more or less permanent, others less so.

35 A central location where data/information is stored and maintained.

36 Usenet is a distributed internet discussion system through which users (or more apporpriately usenetters) can access and distribute messages (often called articles) to a number of distributed newsgroups. The functionality of the system is maintained through a large number of inter-connected servers, which store and forward messages from each other. And the difference between Usenet and the internet is?

   The internet is the worldwide network of computers communicating to each other with the use of a specific communications protocol (TCP/IP) which is used by a vast range of applications. Usenet is essentially an application – a multi-user BBS (bulletin board system) – that allows people to talk to each other on various subjects/issues.

37 The alt.* hierarchy contains a vast number of sub-hierarchies/newsgroups for the discussion of a wide range of topics – some geographically orientated, some culturally determined, many in a language other than English.

38 The procedure/criteria for the creation of a new group within the alt.* hierarchy should be discussed in alt.config., and their adoption is not subject to the strict rules/voting procedures required for other hierarchies.

39 That is, interlinked using a hyperlink, which is essentially a reference in a hypertext document to another document or other resource.

40 A web browser is a software application that enables a user to access, display and interact with HTML documents (web pages) either:
   - hosted by a web server, or
   - held in a file system.

   The most popular web browsers for personal computers (PC and Mac) include:
   - Microsoft Internet Explorer (see *www.microsoft.com/windows/ie/default.mspx*),
   - Mozilla Firefox (see *www.mozila.org*),
   - Opera (see *www.opera.com*) and
   - Safari (see *www.aple.com/safari*).

41 Tim Berners-Lee now heads the World Wide Web Consortium (W3C) (see *www.w3.org*), which develops and maintains standards that enable computers on the Web to effectively store and communicate different forms of information.

42 This document – Berners-Lee, T. and Cailliau, R. (1990), 'World Wide Web: Proposal for a hypertext project' – is available at *http://www.w3.org/Proposal*.

43 See *http://groups.google.com/group/alt.hypertext/msg/395f282a67a1916c*.

44 A URI (Uniform Resource Identifier) identifies a particular resource; a URL (Uniform Resource Locator) not only identifies a resource, but indicates how to locate the resource – that is, the URL functions as a document/web page address.

45 A disparity in technological progress and development, between those nations/countries able to develop and invest in information and communication technologies and those unable to develop and invest in information and communication technologies, continues to reinforce and indeed widen existing economic differences and inequalities between:

 • the most developed nations/countries of the world – for example, Canada, the United States, Japan, and those countries that comprise the EU, and
 • the less developed and/or developing nations/countries of the world – for example, many African and Latin American nations/countries, and some Southeast Asian nations/countries.

 Broadly speaking, this global divide is often characterised as the north–south divide – between the northern wealthier nations/countries and southern poorer nations/countries.

46 Asymmetric Digital Subscriber Line (ADSL) is a data communications technology that enables faster data transmission over conventional telephone lines than a conventional modem can provide.

47 The term e-business is often attributed to Louis V. Gerstner, Jr., Chairman of the Board and Chief Executive Officer of IBM Inc. from April 1993 to December 2002.

48 Some commentators refer to such activities as web commerce.

49 Dot-com companies were the collection of mainly start-up companies selling a range of products and/or services using a range of information and communication related vehicles – in particular the internet. Their exponential proliferation during the late 1990s dot-com boom was matched only by their spectacular decline in 2000–01.

50 HyperText Markup Language (HTML) is a markup language designed for the creation of web pages and other information viewable with a web browser. HTML is used to structure information-identifying text such as for headings, paragraphs, lists, etc.

51 Extensible HyperText Markup Language, or XHTML, is a markup language with the same semantics possibilities as HTML but a much stricter syntax.

52 HyperText Transfer Protocol (HTTP) is the primary method used to convey information on the World Wide Web.

53 Uniform Resource Locator, or web address, is a standardised address name layout for resources (such as documents or images) on the internet.

54 A hyperlink is merely a link or a reference in a hypertext document to another hypertext document and/or other resource.

55 Web traffic can be analysed by viewing the traffic statistics found in the web server log file, an automatically generated list of all the pages served, or 'hits'.

56 There are in fact three major sets of EDI standards:

 1 UN/EDIFACT(United Nations/Electronic Data Interchange For Administration, Commerce, and Transport).
 2 ANSI ASC(X12) (American National Standards Institute Accredited Standards Committee X1256).
 3 UCS (Uniform Communications Standard).

 UN/EDIFACT is an international standard, recommended by the United Nations, and predominant in all areas outside of North America, while ANSI ASC (X12) and UCS are popular in North America.

57 The sending of EDI transactions – using the internet – involves translating the transaction document into MIME format, and then using e-mail to transmit the message from the source company to the destination company.

58 EDI on the Internet is also called 'open EDI' because the internet is an open architecture network.

59 BACS (Bankers Automated Clearing System) is operated by BACS Payment Schemes Limited. The organisation is a membership-based industry body, established and owned by the major UK banks to provide the facility for transferring funds (via direct debit, direct credit and/or standing order), with their role being to:

- develop, enhance and promote the use and integrity of automated payment and payment-related services, and
- promote best practice among those companies who offer payment services.

For further details see *www.bacs.co.uk*.

60 Also known as point of sale.

61 The Association for Payment Clearing Services (APACS) is a non-statutory association of those involved in providing payment services. The principal aim/task of APACS is to administer, coordinate, supervise and manage the major UK payment clearing schemes through three operational clearing companies:

1 BACS Ltd (now Voca Link Ltd).
2 CHAPS Clearing Company Ltd.
3 Cheque and Credit Clearing Company Ltd.

62 CHAPS Clearing Company Ltd currently has 22 direct members of which 14 are members of CHAPS Sterling and 20 are members of CHAPS Euro.

63 Although the payment/transfer will be made electronically, the sending bank will need to undertake a range of authorisation, verification, authentication and validation checks prior to the payment/transfer.

64 For further information on Voca Ltd see *www.voca.co.uk*.

65 Approximately 600 BACS Approved Bureaux exist throughout the UK. They each carry the BACS seal of approval and are inspected at least once every three years to assess their technical competence and operational integrity in accordance with the requirements of the BACS Approved Bureaux Scheme. The following areas are normally assessed:

- physical security,
- computer operations,
- applications and systems support.

66 The control of a direct credit payment normally resides with a payer's bank.

67 During 2005, nearly 200,000 organisations used BACS for supplier payments, payments of pensions, payments of employee expenses, insurance settlements, payments of dividends and/or interest, and payment refunds.

68 The bank and/or building society holding the payer's account is both responsible for and answerable for all payments (including direct debit payments) made for that account.

69 Some organisations/companies sometimes levy an additional (interest) charge on customers for paying by direct debit.

70 All direct debit payments are protected by three safeguards:

(i) an immediate money back guarantee from the bank or building society if an error is made,
(ii) advance notice from the recipient company/organisation if the date and/or the amount of the direct debit changes,
(iii) the right to cancel.

71 The Payment Services Directive (PSD, 2007/64/EC) is a regulatory initiative from the European Commission (Directorate General Internal Market) designed to regulate payment services and payment service providers (as defined in the Directive) throughout the European Union (EU) and European Economic Area (EEA).

72 The main card schemes are MasterCard and Visa, which together account for nearly 90 per cent of all the payment cards in circulation.

73 See Chapter 8 for further details on e-money.

74 For debit cards, this will be the amount of money in the cardholder's account (together with any overdraft facility). For credit cards, this will be the amount of money that the card issuer is prepared to lend the cardholder (the credit limit).

75 The acquirer (or acquiring bank) will be responsible for:

- forwarding transaction requests from the merchant to the card issuer so that the cardholder's identity can be verified and to ensure that the cardholder has sufficient funds available to support the transaction;
- acting on behalf of the card issuer and authorising transactions where a referred transaction requires further information from the card holder;
- collecting the settlement files from the merchant;
- forwarding settlement files to the appropriate card issuer;
- reimbursing the merchant with the funds payable on the transactions (less the merchant service charge); and
- maintaining a Hot Card File – a record of all cards reported as being either lost or stolen.

Examples of UK acquirers:

- Royal Bank of Scotland.
- Barclays Merchant Services.
- NatWest Streamline.
- Lloydstsb Cardnet.
- HSBC Merchant Services.

76 It is possible, and indeed often the case, that a merchant has more than one acquirer.

77 If the system has Hot Card checking facility the customer's card number will be checked against a list of lost or stolen cards provided by the banks or other financial institutions/organisations. If the customer's card number matches a card number on the list, the merchant *must* decline the transaction and *retain* the customer's card.

78 Merchant Service Agreement.

79 The acquirer has agreed the transaction and has confirmed that the customer/cardholder has the funds available and that the merchant will receive payment for the transaction.

80 The acquirer has refused the transaction. No explanation will be offered by the acquirer; that is, the merchant will not be informed why the transaction was declined.

81 The acquirer has requested further information before deciding whether to authorise the transaction. For example, the acquirer may request the merchant to obtain further confirmation of the identity of the customer/cardholder before a decision on whether to authorise or decline the transaction is made.

82 The Consumer Protection (Distance Selling) Regulations (2000) define a distance contract as:

any contract concerning goods and services concluded between a supplier and a customer under an organised distance sales or service provision scheme run by the supplier who for the purposes of the contract makes exclusive use of one or more means of distance communication up to and including the moment that the contact is concluded.   (2000: s3)

83 A merchant ID is a unique electronic ID assigned to a merchant by an acquiring bank.

84 A Payment Service Provider provides payment gateway services to enable a merchant to process, authorise, settle and manage credit/debit card transactions.

85 The word biometric is derived from the Greek words *bios*, meaning life, and *metrikos*, meaning to measure.

86 Sometimes referred to as monomodal.

87 Pay-By-Touch was a US-based privately held company which enabled consumers to pay for goods and services with a swipe of their finger on a biometric sensor. It allowed secure access

to credit card, loyalty, health-care, and other personal information, through the unique character-istics of an individual's biometric features, thereby creating a highly secure anti-identity-theft platform. Due possibly to mismanagement, and to financial problems, Pay-By-Touch ceased trading in March 2008.

88 Simple Mail Transfer Protocol (SMTP) is the standard for e-mail transmission across the internet. It is a simple, text-based protocol, where one or more recipients of a message are specified (and in most cases verified to exist) and then the message text is transferred.

89 A killer application is the term used to describe a computer (software) program that is so useful that people will buy a computer hardware and/or operating systems simply to run the program.

90 BITnet was a cooperative US university network founded in 1981 at the City University of New York.

91 US-based National Science Foundation network (NSFNet) which formed a major part of the central network/core of the internet.

92 A signature block is a block of text automatically appended at the bottom of an e-mail message that essentially signs off the message. Information usually contained in a signature block may, for example, include:

- the sender's name,
- the sender's e-mail address, and
- other contact details where appropriate – for example, website addresses and/or links.

93 Here the recipient of this copy will know who was in the *To:* field, but the recipients cannot see who is on the *Bcc:* list.

94 Multipurpose Internet Mail Extensions (MIME).

95 The Domain Name System (or DNS) is a system that stores information about host names and domain names in a type of distributed database on networks, such as the internet. Of the many types of information that can be stored, most importantly it provides a physical location IP address for each domain name, and lists the mail server accepting e-mail for each domain.

96 POP is an abbreviation of Post Office Protocol, and IMAP is an abbreviation of Internet Mail Access Protocol.

97 For example, customer analysis by:

- geographical location,
- volume of trade, and/or
- payment history.

98 For example:

- sending out debtors letters, payment reminders, and statements of account;
- making provisions for doubtful and bad debts;
- holding/closing accounts.

99 For example, multiple delivery addresses for each customer.

100 For example, supplier analysis by:

- geographical location,
- account type, and/or
- credit terms.

101 The term killer application is often used to describe a computer software program that users find so useful they will buy the required computer hardware simply to run the software application.

102 Multiplan was an early spreadsheet program developed by Microsoft in 1982. It was initially developed for computers running operating systems such as CP/M, MS-DOS and Apple II (with the Apple Mac version being Microsoft's first GUI (graphical user interface) spreadsheet).

103 See: *http:/www.hmrc.gov.uk/ct/ct-online/file-return/joint-filing.htm.*

104 HMRC have a website which lists suppliers of such software and whether it currently produces the CT600 and will generate and submit the iXBRL tax computations.

CHAPTER 5

Networking – creating connections

Introduction

This chapter considers a range of issues related to soft-type networks, hard-type networks and semi-soft-type networks, and explores the implications of such networks for accounting information systems. It examines issues related to the development and control of alternative network architectures and topologies, and considers how information and communication technology, and the adoption of alternative network architectures and topologies, have affected the computer-based processing of transaction data.

Learning outcomes

By the end of this chapter, the reader should be able to:

- Describe the major characteristics of, and interrelationship between, soft-type networks, hard-type networks and semi-soft-type networks

- Consider and explain the socio-political context of networking

- Demonstrate a critical understanding of the implications of alternative network architectures and topologies on accounting information systems

Understanding differences

There can be little doubt that within contemporary Western society, certainly during the latter part of the twentieth century and the early part of the twenty-first century, much of the growing demand for greater interconnectivity and greater organisational/institutional networking has resulted from the increasing dominance of an almost singular economic philosophy.[1] This is a philosophy whose foundation lies within the social politics of economic liberalism and the free pursuit of wealth accumulation, and whose organisation and continued success is dependent upon a structure of defined economic networks and social interconnectivity, an interconnectivity necessitated by:

- the ever-increasing numbers of market-based participants,
- the ever-increasing complexity of market-based interrelationships, and
- the ever-increasing geographical diversity of market-based activity.

Indeed, from the earliest social networks to the emergence of complex interrelated institutional networks and the development of virtual networks, the purpose of such networks – their raison d'être – has remained unchanged: to provide an 'interconnectivity of trust' through which the use of data, information, assets and resources can be managed, coordinated, organised, structured and, perhaps most importantly, controlled.[2]

All networks, whether they are physical, social, or indeed virtual, possess three important characteristics:

1 **An architecture** – a specific design for the inter-operation of the components that comprise the network.
2 **A topology** – a specific shape or relational map that describes the network.
3 **A protocol** – a set of rules that prescribe and govern access to, engagement with, and communication within the network and/or between a network and other interrelated networks.

We will classify networks into three different types (see Figure 5.1):

1 soft-type networks – or social networks,
2 hard-type networks – or physical networks, and
3 semi-soft-type networks[3] – or logical (virtual) networks.

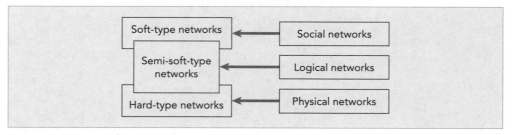

Figure 5.1 Types of network

Soft-type networks

In a social context, a network can be described as a set of relationships and/or interconnections between individuals and/or groups of people, and refers to the inter-association between individuals and/or groups of individuals, designed to:

- share commonalities,

- form communities (or expand existing communities), and

- exchange information, knowledge and/or resources.

We will refer to these networks as soft-type networks – networks in which the dominant feature is mutual communication, social interaction and exchange within a politically constructed framework/arrangement.

Such soft-type networks can be divided into two categories:

1 a social network which is created, developed and sustained for the benefit of the self, and

2 a business network which is created, developed and sustained for the benefit of the entity (for example the company or mutual association).

Hard-type networks

In a structural context, a network can be described as a physical construct and defined by the components that comprise its underlying physical structure. For example, using an information and communication technology context, a network can be defined as:

- a group of devices connected by a communications facility, the primary use of which is the exchange of data and/or information, or

- a configuration of data processing devices and software programes connected for data and/or information interchange, or

- a group of computers and/or computer related devices (for example, a server) connected by a communications facility and/or telecommunications link, that share data and/or information, and/or resources/facilities.

We will refer to these as hard-type networks – networks in which the dominant feature is a structured interconnectivity. Such hard-type networks (in particular, information and communication technology-based networks) may be either:

1 permanent – for example, a structure defined by physical interconnections and communications links, such as Ethernet cabling and/or fibre optic cabling, or

2 temporary (or intermittent) – for example, using a non-physical wireless interconnection and communication links, such as digital links, and/or satellite facilities.

Furthermore, given the highly structured (some would say mechanistic) nature of such networks, outcomes and performance are generally seen as certain and predictable, with performance often measured in quantifiable terms.

Semi-soft-type networks

From a process context, a network may also be defined as an abstract organisational construct, a construct that is superimposed on all or part of one or more interrelated physical networks and through which data/information is made available, and/or resources and activities are coordinated and managed.

Such networks are sometimes referred to as logical networks,[4] a good example of which is, of course, the internet and associated derivatives, intranet and extranet.

We will refer to these networks as semi-soft-type networks – networks in which the dominant feature is representational interconnectivity or, more appropriately, a conceptual description/constructed representation concerned only with the interconnections and pathways that comprise the network.

We will now look at each type of network in more detail.

Soft-type networks

As suggested earlier, an entity-focused soft-type network is in essence a social network that exists within a political framework – an interconnected assembly of network actors[5] who are linked by mutual interrelationships and interdependencies[6] which, while social in nature, are often political in context, and invariably economic in origin. It is the interaction (directly or indirectly) of these network actors that influences the ongoing social, political and economic activities of the network and, as a consequence, determines:

■ how effectively data/information flows within the network,

■ how efficiently data/information is used within the network, and

■ how patterns of trust and mechanisms of control are developed, established and fostered within the network.

Such interactions are determined by the interaction/interface of a range of characteristics, the most important being:

■ architecture-related structural characteristics – normally influenced by, for example:
  ▪ the nature and purpose of the network, and
  ▪ the nature of the social connectedness within the network,
■ topology-related functional characteristics – normally influenced by, for example:
  ▪ the type of relationships/links possible within the network, and
  ▪ the frequency of social contact within the network,
■ protocol-related control/management characteristics – normally influenced by, for example:
  ▪ the proximity of individuals within the network, and
  ▪ the risk profile/nature of network activities.

Soft-type networks – architectures

In a soft-type network context, the architecture provides the structure/framework through which the aims and objectives of the network are realised. While such architectures can vary enormously between networks, they can nonetheless be located, on a (somewhat subjective) scale, between:

■ a formal and highly structured architecture, and

■ an informal/casual architecture.

Formal

A network with a formal-type architecture can be loosely defined as a regulated social arrangement/network of people and/or groups of people designed to facilitate interaction, communication and the exchange of both knowledge and resources.

Informal

A network with an informal-type architecture can be loosely defined as a social arrangement/network of people and/or groups of people designed to facilitate casual interaction – without a formal regulated framework.

In reality, of course, most soft-type networks are rarely ever completely formal, that is rule-bound, or rarely ever completely informal, that is rule-less. Instead, such networks tend to be a combination of both formal and informal types – a complex layering or blending of both formal and informal architectures,[7] a blending that historically has, in a corporate context at least, been associated with/dominated by the ever-changing demands of the marketplace and the priorities of capital accumulation.

Soft-type networks – topologies

In a soft-type network context, a topology provides the specific shape or the relational map of the organisation/network. Again, while such topologies can vary enormously between networks, they can (again) be located on a somewhat subjective scale between

- a bureaucracy, or bureaucratic topology, and
- an adhocracy, or adhocratic topology.

Bureaucracy

A bureaucracy can be defined as a form of social network/organisation exemplified by a hierarchical division of labour, a formal chain of command, and a prescriptive (and often imposed) framework of anonymity, and is a (socio-political) network structure often associated with (and championed by) the German sociologist Max Weber, but highly criticised by Karl Marx.

As artificial/created social networks, typified by the existence of highly structured and highly standardised processes and procedures, in a contemporary context bureaucracies are (within varying degrees) the most common type of topology employed within the UK corporate sector. And while many alternative types of bureaucracy exist, they are (despite their inherent problems) designed primarily to promote stability and equality and provide for the allocation of:

- jurisdiction and responsibility,
- processes, procedures and resources, and
- hierarchical authority/control.

Adhocracy

An adhocracy can be defined as a non-bureaucratic networked organisation or, in other words, an organisation/social network in which there is an absence of hierarchy and/or formal constitution. These were developed (or emerged) in the mid 1940s and early 1950s for soft-type networks in which autonomy, flexibility and creativity were considered to be the core requirements for sustained survival and continued success.

Providing for greater flexibility, greater adaptability, and greater responsiveness to change – especially in periods of uncertainty and continuous change – adhocracies are characterised by:

- the absence of formal rules and regulations,
- the absence of hierarchical structures of authority, and
- the absence of procedural standardisation and/or formal organisation,

and typified by a core desire to maintain – at all costs – the autonomy and sovereignty of network actors/participants.

Soft-type networks – protocols

In a soft-type network context, the protocols provide the regulatory context of the organisation/network, that is, the management framework within which the network functions and undertakes its activities. Designed primarily to:

- reduce network variability,
- minimise possible instability,
- moderate the impact of future uncertainty and unpredictability, and
- secure future sustainability,

such protocols – such rules and regulations – are invariably the product of an often complex and highly politicised process, the outcome of which is invariably determined by the type of architecture and the type of topology adopted by/imposed upon the network.

Locating soft-type networks

We can locate a soft-type network on two distinct scales, based on:

1 The type of network architecture – ranging from formal to informal.
2 The type of network topology – ranging from bureaucratic to adhocratic.

Using the former (network architecture) as vertical scale, and the latter (network topology) as a horizontal scale, we can create an intuitive representation – albeit a somewhat simplistic representation – on which to locate alternative soft-type networks. This representation provides a range of four categories (see Figure 5.2):

1 Formal bureaucracy.
2 Formal adhocracy.
3 Informal bureaucracy.
4 Informal adhocracy.

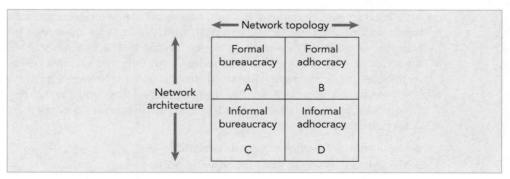

Figure 5.2 Soft-type networks

An established retail/distribution company, or a manufacturing/production company, or indeed a time/space-based company, because of:

■ the nature and interconnectivity of their activities,

■ the hierarchical complexity of their activities, and

■ the dependency on routine formalised processes and procedures,

would, for example, tend to adopt a more formalised, more bureaucratic structure, and would perhaps be located within the formal bureaucracy region of the model (see area A in Figure 5.2).

An established knowledge/skills-based company, or profession-based company, dependent not on routine formalised activities but on:

■ individual (or group) skill,

■ individual professional knowledge and competence, and/or

■ individual (or group) creativity and inventiveness,

would, for example, tend to adopt a less formalised, more adhocratic structure, and would perhaps be located within an area that overlaps a number of regions (see area B in Figure 5.2).

On the other hand, a non-established company, or indeed a newly developed/emerging company, may well adopt a less formalised, albeit nonetheless bureaucratic structure, to accommodate:

■ the need for entrepreneurial flexibility, and

■ the need for accountability,

and would perhaps be located within an area that overlaps both the formal bureaucracy and informal bureaucracy regions of the model (see area C in Figure 5.2), although eventually, as the company becomes more established, the priorities of accumulation and the pressure of the marketplace may well force such a company into either area A or area B (or out of business!).

Finally, non-corporate-based soft-type networks, for example, a charity or mutual association, would – depending of course on their size and the range of their activities – adopt a less formalised/more adhocratic structure, and perhaps, especially if small, would be located within an area that overlaps a number of regions (see area D). Larger, more established networks, on the other hand, may well adopt a more corporate-orientated bureaucratic structure, and perhaps move into the formal bureaucracy region of the model (see area A in Figure 5.2).

Hard-type networks

For our purposes we will define a hard network as an information and communications system that interconnects computer systems at different locations and:

■ facilitates the transfer and exchange of data and/or information, and

■ allows the sharing of software, hardware (for example, other peripheral information and communications devices), and/or processing power.

Such a network may be fixed, cabled and permanent, and/or variable (flexible), wireless and temporary.

There are essentially two categories of hard network:

1 A hard network whose primary purpose is to facilitate interpersonal (person-to-person) communication.

2 A hard network whose primary purpose is service provision – for example, of a bank ATM network.

Hard-type network – architectures

The term network architecture refers to the design of a network, that is, the basic layout or configuration of an information and communication system/computer system, and includes:

- the relationship of a network with/to any associated system,
- the physical configuration of the network,
- the functional organisation of the network,
- the operational procedures employed in the network, and
- the data formats utilised in the network.

There are many alternative types of network architectures, the most common being:

- wide area network (WAN),
- metropolitan area network (MAN),
- local area network (LAN),
- personal area network (PAN),
- client–server network, and
- peer-to-peer network.

Note: Computers and/or other information and communication devices within a network are called nodes,[8] and computers and/or other information and communication devices which allocate resources are called servers.[9]

Before we look at each of these alternative types of networks in a little more detail, it would perhaps be useful to consider/explain some of the components that would comprise a hard network.

Hard-type network – connecting components

A hard-type network is the physical reality of the network and comprises a range of connected components and equipment necessary to perform data processing activities and provide communication management within a network.

Computer workstation

All user computers connected to a network are called workstations or computer workstations, and are referred to as network nodes. The phrase connected to a network usually means computer workstation that is configured with:

- a network interface card,
- appropriate networking software, and
- the appropriate physical cables – if the network is hard wired, or
- the appropriate transmission/receiving devices – if it is a virtual/wireless network.

While a computer workstation does not necessarily need/require independent storage capacity – because data files can be saved on the network file server – most computer workstations do possess storage capacity, if only for use as a backup facility in the event of network problems.

File server

A file server stands at the centre of most networks and is, in essence, a computer that:

- stores and manages data files and software (for example, end users' files),
- manages the use and availability of shared resources,
- provides network users with data, information and access to other network resources, and
- regulates communications between network nodes.

A file server may be dedicated – that is, the computer workstation used as a file server is used *only* as a file server, or non-dedicated – the computer used as a file server is also used for other network related tasks, for example it may also be used, simultaneously, as a network workstation. Any computer workstation can function as a file server, and whereas the characteristics and specifications of a file server would depend on the size and nature of the network the file server will serve, the functionality of a computer workstation as a file server is dictated by the network operating system (NOS) – whether it is a Windows Server System or a UNIX Server System.

Network interface card

The network interface card (often abbreviated to NIC) is a piece of computer hardware that is designed to provide for computer communication within a network. It is the physical connection between the computer workstation and the network. The vast majority of network interface cards are internal – within the computer workstation – built into the computer workstation motherboard. The network interface cards used in a network are a major factor in determining the speed of the network and the performance of a network.

Most NICs are designed for a particular type of network, protocol and media, although some can serve multiple networks.

Repeater

A repeater merely amplifies the signal (the data/information message) it receives and rebroadcasts it across the network. It can be separate device, or it can be (and often is) incorporated into a hub or a switch.

Hub

A (standard) hub acts as a convergence point of a network allowing the transfer of data/information.

There are three types of hub:

1 *A passive hub* – which allows the data/information to flow.
2 *An intellegent hub* – which allows data/information transfers to be monitored.
3 *An active hub* – which allows the data/information to flow but regenerates/amplifies received signals before transmitting them along the network.

Bridge

A bridge facilitates the connecting of a new network (or network segment) to an existing network (or network segment) and/or the connecting of different types of hard-type topologies. The purpose of a network bridge is to ensure that only necessary data/information flows across both sides of the network. It can be a separate device, or can be (and often is) incorporated into a switch. To achieve its purpose, a bridge can be used to:

■ monitor the flow of data/information traffic across both sides of the network, and

■ manage network traffic to maintain optimum performance across the network.

Switch

A switch (or switching hub) is a device which filters and forwards data/information across a network. Most switches are active, that is, they amplify the signal (the data/information message) as it moves from one network node to another network node.

Switches are often used in a star topology, and/or a star ring topology (see later).

Router

A router is a networking component which transfers data/information from one network to another and in a simple context is very similar to an intelligent bridge, inasmuch as a router can/will:

■ select the best network path to route a message – using the destination address and origin address,

■ direct network traffic to prevent head-on collisions – using the topology of the network where necessary, and

■ prioritise network paths and links when particular network segments are busy.

Network connections – wired connections

Physical cabling is the medium from which the majority of network connections are created, and through which data/information is transmitted across a network from one network node to another. There are, of course, several types of cabling currently in use – the choice of cable depends on the size of the network, the topology of the network and the network protocol.

Network connections – wireless connections

The term wireless networking refers to technology that enables two or more computers/computer networks to communicate using standard network protocols but without wired connections – for example a wireless local area network (LAN).

For connectivity a wireless network may, for example, use high frequency radio signal connections, or infrared connections, or laser connections to communicate between network devices – and may be:

■ line of sight broadcast based – in which a direct unblocked line of sight must exist between source and destination, or

■ scattered broadcast based – in which transmission signals are transmitted in multiple directions (which can then bounce off physical objects to reach their destination).

There are two kinds of wireless networks within which each computer/terminal can communicate directly with all of the other wireless-enabled computers to share data/information files and network resources:

(i) *An ad hoc wireless network* – that is, an improvised and/or temporary impromptu network.

(ii) *A peer-to-peer wireless network* – that is, a defined network of computers/terminals each equipped with a wireless networking interface card.

Wide area network

A wide area network (WAN) is a network which covers a wide geographical area, often involving an array of computer and/or information and communication devices.

Typically, a wide area network would consist of two or more interconnected local area networks (LANs), connected using either:

- public communication facilities – for example, the telephone system, and/or
- private communication facilities – for example, leased lines and/or satellite-based communication facilities.

The best example of a wide area network would be the physical network underpinning the internet.

We can distinguish between two types of wide area network:

1 A centralised wide area network.

2 A decentralised (or distributed) wide area network – which is essentially a wide area network comprising two of more interconnected local area networks.

Centralised wide area network

The main distinguishing feature of a centralised wide area network is that there is no (or very little) remote data/transaction processing. All processing is controlled and managed centrally. Such an arrangement is useful where data transactions are homogeneous, for example:

- a bank ATM system,
- a hotel central booking facility,
- an airline booking facility.

The advantages of a centralised wide area network are:

- it provides for a concentration of computing power,
- it provides economies of scale,
- it facilitates a database approach (or a standardisation approach) to data/transaction processing and data management, and
- it promotes greater security and control.

However, the disadvantages of a centralised wide area network are:

- it can be inflexible, and change can be difficult to implement,
- it can be/may be unresponsive to user needs,
- network software can be costly, and
- centralisation may increase vulnerability to disaster.

Decentralised (distributed) wide area network

The main distinguishing feature of a decentralised wide area network is that there is intelligent remote data/transaction processing, that is, processing is decentralised within the network. Such an arrangement is useful where data transactions are heterogeneous, that is, individual data transactions may possess unique characteristics that require local processing.

The advantages of a decentralised wide area network are:

■ it is an efficient and effective means of sharing information, services and resources, and

■ it is flexible, responsive, and adaptive to user demands/requirements.

The disadvantages of a decentralised wide area network are:

■ it can be difficult to maintain operationally – especially when a large number of local area networks (each with a large number of users) comprise the decentralised wide area networks;

■ it can be difficult to manage and control data transactions and processing activities – especially peer-to-peer type local area networks; and

■ security can be difficult to implement effectively.

Metropolitan area network

A metropolitan area network (MAN) is in terms of geography an intermediate form of network – a network covering a geographical area (for example, a city/metropolitan area) larger than the area covered by a large local area network (LAN) but smaller than the area covered by a wide area network (WAN). It is a term used to describe the interconnection of local area networks (LANs) into a single larger network, usually to offer a more efficient connection to a larger WAN.

A MAN typically uses a wireless infrastructure or an optical fibre connection for inter-site connection and, like a wide area network, is usually owned by a consortium of proprietors.

The advantages of a metropolitan area network are:

■ it can provide an efficient connection to a wide area network,

■ it can facilitate the sharing of regional resources, and

■ it can be used to provide a shared connection to other networks.

The disadvantages of a metropolitan area network are:

■ it can be inflexible, and

■ it may be unresponsive to user needs.

Local area network

A local area network (LAN) is a network of computers and/or information and communication devices, usually privately owned and within a limited area – often at the same physical location, for example within a company or organisation that share:

■ a common communications link, and/or

■ a common group of interrelated resources, and/or

■ a common processing facility/network operating system,

the purpose being to facilitate the exchange and sharing of information and resources.

In a wider, less restricting context, a local area network may comprise a number of smaller interconnected local area networks within a geographically compact area – for example, within a large corporate office and/or university campus – usually connected using a high-speed local network communications backbone.

In smaller local area networks, workstations may act as both client (user of services/resources) and server (provider of services/resources). Such a network is sometimes called a peer-to-peer network, because each node (workstation) within the network possesses equivalent responsibilities.

In larger local area networks, workstations may act as client only and may be linked to a central network server. Such a network is sometimes called a server network, because clients (individual workstations) rely on the servers for resources, data, information, and processing power.

The advantages of a local area network are:

- it is an efficient and effective means of sharing information, services, and resources, and
- it is flexible, responsive, and adaptive to user demands/requirements.

The disadvantages of a local area network are:

- it can be difficult to maintain operationally – especially when a local area network has many users,
- it can be difficult to control – especially peer-to-peer type local area networks, and
- security can be costly.

A local area network is distinguished from other kinds of network by three characteristics:

1 Size.
2 Transmission technology.
3 Topology.

Personal area network

A personal area network (PAN) is a computer/information and communication network used for communication between a computer and information and communication technology devices close to one person. Typically, the coverage area of a personal area network will usually be only a few square metres, with such a network used for:

- intra-personal communication – that is, communication with/between different technologies/devices, and/or
- up-linking – that is higher level technology networking, for example connecting to the internet.

A personal area network may be either physical, using a wired connection, or virtual, using a wireless connection.

Client[10]–server network

A client–server network is a computer architecture which provides a convenient way to interconnect and distribute software programs and hardware resources and facilities efficiently and effectively across different locations – a computer architecture in which each computer on a network is either a client[11] or a server, inasmuch as:

- clients are PCs or workstations on which users run applications,
- servers are computers and/or processes dedicated to managing and allocating network resources, and
- clients rely on servers for access to network resources and/or processing facilities.[12]

Such client–server architecture is sometimes referred to as a two-tier architecture – that is, client–server architecture in which the user interface runs on the client and the resource is held by/stored on a server. The application logic can run on the client and/or the server. Alternative, newer, and increasingly popular client–server architecture is called a three-tier architecture – that is, client–server architecture in which:

- the client's computer/workstation runs the user interface – the first tier,
- the functional modules for the processing of data run on an application server – the second tier, and
- the database management systems that store the data required by the second tier run the database server – the third tier.

The advantages of the three-tier client–server architecture (and the reasons for its increasing popularity) are:

- the separation between application server and database server facilitates easier modification and/or updating,
- the separation between application server and database server facilitates the easier replacement of one tier without affecting the other tiers within the network, and
- the separation of application functions from database management functions/systems facilitates more effective load balancing.[13]

Client–server networks can be both WAN-based and/or LAN-based, and tend to be the norm for most corporate-based systems. Indeed, the client–server network architecture has become one of the central ideas of computing and information systems, with most computer-based business-related applications using the client–server model.

In a client–server environment, files are stored on a centralised, high-speed file server, with appropriate access made available to clients, usually with the use of a user name and password, because nearly all network services – like printing services, e-mail and FTP services – are routed through a file server. A file server is designed to:

- allow clients/users access to their own directory,
- allow clients/users access to a range of public or shared directories in which applications and data are stored, and
- allow clients/users to communicate with each other (via the file server).

File servers can be used to:

- supervise network traffic,
- identify and detect inefficient network segments/facilities, and
- monitor client/user activities.

The main advantages of client–server architecture are:

- It is a cost-effective way to share data, information and resources between a large number of clients.
- It provides improved scalability[14] – that is, it allows the number of network connections (and the number of clients/users) to be increased/decreased as needed.
- It supports modular applications inasmuch as software applications can be separated into identifiable modular portions on specific identifiable servers.
- Network/application upgrades can be stored on the file server, rather than having to upgrade each client/user's PC.

The main disadvantages of client–server architecture are:

- It can be difficult to ensure configuration information is up to date, current and consistent among all of the network devices.

- It can be difficult to synchronise upgrades – especially on very large client–server networks.

- Redundancy and network failure procedures/protocols can be expensive and difficult to implement.

Peer-to-peer network

A peer-to-peer network (often abbreviated to P2P) is a network in which each workstation (or PC) within the network has equivalent responsibilities and capabilities.

In essence, a peer-to-peer network facilitates the connection of a number of workstations (or PCs), so that network resources may be pooled together. For example, individual resources connected to a workstation (or PC), such as various disk drives, a scanner, perhaps even a printer, become shared resources of the network and available to, or accessible from, any other workstation (or PC) within the network.

Unlike within a client–server network, in which network information is stored centrally on a centralised file server and made available (subject to security protocols of course) to client workstations (or PCs), within a peer-to-peer network data and information are stored locally – on each individual workstation (or PC) within the network. In essence, each workstation (or PC) within a peer-to-peer network acts as:

- client or user node, and
- server or data/information store.

Structurally, there are three categories of peer-to-peer network:

1 A pure peer-to-peer network.
2 A hybrid peer-to-peer network.
3 A mixed peer-to-peer network.

In a pure peer-to-peer network, a peer acts as both client and server. Such a network would possess neither a central server nor a central router.[15]

In a hybrid peer-to-peer network, a central server maintains information on individual peers, and responds to requests for information about peers. The central server would not normally store process/transaction files. Individual peers would normally be responsible for:

- hosting the information,
- informing the central network server which files they require, and
- downloading and/or transferring any shareable resources to other peers within the network as requested.

A mixed peer-to-peer network would of course possess characteristics of each of the above.

An example of peer-to-peer networking is collaborative computing – also referred to as distributed computing – in which idle, unused, or spare CPU processing power and/or disk space on a workstation (or PC) in the network is or can be utilised by another workstation

(PC) within the network. Collaborative computing is most popular with science-based research organisations where research projects may require vast amounts of computer processing power.

The advantages of a peer-to-peer network are that it is:

■ simple to create,

■ easy to build, and

■ inexpensive to maintain.

In addition:

■ Increased network users create increased network capacity – that is, since one of the underlying concepts of peer-to-peer networks is that all clients provide resources (resources including bandwidth (communication capacity), storage capacity and computing power), as the number of nodes (clients/users logging-on) increases, and demand on the system increases, so the total capacity of the system increases.

■ Increased operational resilience – that is, the distributed nature of peer-to-peer networks and the replication of data over multiple peers – increases the robustness of the network, thereby reducing the possibility of failure.

■ There is no single point of failure – especially in non-index-based pure peer-to-peer networks – which enables peers to locate data and/or media files without reliance on a centralised index server.

The disadvantages of a peer-to-peer network are:

■ There is no central store for files and applications, and as a result such networks can become fairly insecure.

■ Maintaining software on individual computers within a peer-to-peer network can be time-consuming.

■ Speed and performance can be poor – especially within large peer-to-peer networks.

There are, of course, several major problems/concerns surrounding file sharing – in particular file sharing using peer-to-peer (P2P) networks – especially for companies. The most important of these problems/concerns is network protection and security, a problem which emerges from the very architecture of the network itself.

Why? First, because anonymous peer-to-peer networks allow for distribution of material with little or no legal accountability across (potentially) a wide variety of jurisdictions and, second, peer-to-peer networks are (increasingly) the subject of malicious attack, examples of such attacks being:

■ poisoning/insertion of viruses – providing corrupt and/or infected data files,

■ denial of service/filtering attacks – inserting malware[16] (or spyware[17]) to reduce network efficiency,

■ defection attacks – using network resources without contributing to the network capacity,

■ identity attacks – harassing network users,

■ spamming attacks – sending vast amounts of unsolicited data/information across the network.

The most appropriate defence – to minimise possible security threats – is to introduce:

■ access policies to monitor network access – a protocol-based approach to monitor and prevent intrusive network traffic being received through the P2P clients, and

■ content policies to monitor/control the files – a surveillance-based software solution approach to actively search for files based on their type, their name, their signature or even their content.

Hard-type networks – topologies

The term network topology refers to the shape/map of a network, and relates to:

■ how different network devices are connected to each other, and

■ how each of these network devices communicates with each other.

Topologies can be:

■ *physical* – that is, relating to hard-type networks, and/or

■ *logical* – that is, relating to semi-soft-type networks.

Whereas a physical topology would describe the physical connectivity of a network – that is, how network devices are physically connected – a logical topology would describe how data and information flow within a network.

For the moment we will consider physical (hard-type network) topologies.

What types of physical (hard-type network) topologies are there?

The most common types of physical (hard-type network) topologies are:

■ bus topology,

■ ring topology,

■ star topology,

■ mesh topology, and

■ hybrid topology.

Note: The star topology (and the tree topology – see later) is often referred to as centralised topology, whereas the mesh topology is often referred to as a decentralised topology.

Before we look at each of these topologies in a little more detail it would perhaps be useful to consider the key factors that would dictate the designing/selecting of a network topology.

These main factors would include:

■ the financial cost of installing the network topology,

■ the technical viability of the network topology – for example, maintenance and faultfinding/troubleshooting,

■ the potential scalability of the network topology and the potential for future expansion,

■ the required capacity of the network topology, and

■ the physical nature/constraints of the network topology – for example, the geographical distances involved.

Okay . . . so let's look at these alternative types of network topology.

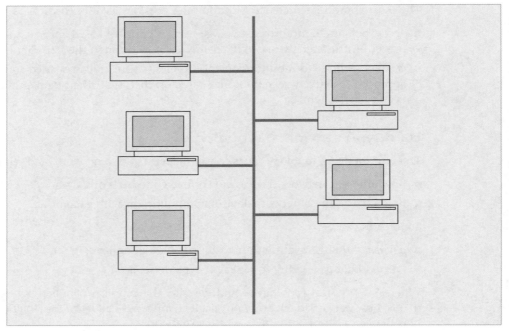

Figure 5.3 Bus topology

Bus topology

A bus topology (also known as a linear bus topology) is a topology in which a set of clients are connected through a shared communications line or a central cable, often called the bus, or the network backbone.[18]

There are two alternative types of bus (or connection lines):

1 *A regular bus* – in which each network node is directly attached to the network backbone by means of a shorter cable connection (see Figure 5.3).

2 *A local bus* – in which each network node is attached directly to the network backbone in a daisy-chain configuration (see below).[19]

Within a bus topology, communication signals are broadcast to all nodes on the network. Each node on the network inspects the destination address of the signal as it travels along the bus – or the communication link. Remember, every node in a network will have a unique network address – either a data link control address (DLC), or a media access control address (MAC). If the signal's destination address matches that of the node, the node processes the signal. If the address does not match that of the node, the node will take no action and the signal travels along the bus.[20]

In general, a bus topology is regarded as passive[21] inasmuch as the nodes situated on the bus simply listen for a signal – they are not responsible for moving the signal along the bus or communication link.

However, whilst such a topology is perhaps the simplest and easiest method to use to connect multiple clients, at multiple nodes, operationally, such a network topology can nonetheless be problematic. Why?

Consider the situation where two or more clients using two or more different network nodes want to communicate at the same time, using the same bus/network connection. To minimise the consequences of such a situation, a bus topology would employ:

- a scheduling protocol – to queue network traffic and prioritise communication, and

- a collision avoidance protocol – to monitor and control access to the communication link or, more appropriately, to the shared bus – often using a media access control protocol, technically referred to as a carrier sense multiple access.[22]

The advantages of a bus topology are:

- they are easy to build and implement,

- they are simple to extend, and

- on a small scale, they are relatively cheap to set up.

More importantly, a network employing such a topology is generally more resilient to failure inasmuch as failure at one node does not affect the operational capacity of other nodes on the network.

The disadvantages of a bus topology are:

- they can be difficult to administer – especially larger networks,

- operationally they can be slow, inasmuch as network performance may reduce as additional nodes are added, and

- maintenance costs can be higher, certainly in the longer term.

In addition:

- The size of such networks may be limited – that is, limited cable length means limited number of nodes.

- Such networks are generally regarded as fairly insecure and easy to hack into, in addition to which a single virus infection at a node within the network will often affect all nodes within the network.

As indicated earlier, using a local bus to connect/attach each network node directly to a network backbone creates a daisy-chain configuration – a topology in which each network node is connected in a series to the next network node.

Within a daisy-chain configuration, communication signals are broadcast to all nodes on the network. Each node on the network inspects the destination address of the signal as it travels along the bus – or the communication link. If the address does not match that of the node, the node will take no action and the signal is bounced along the communication link – in sequence, from network node to network node – until it reaches the destination address. Once the signal reaches the destination address, the destination node processes the signal.

Ring topology

A ring topology is a topology in which a network node is connected to two other nodes, thus creating a closed loop ring. It is a topology in which every network node has two connections to it, and in which only two paths between any two network nodes exist. See Figure 5.4.

In a ring topology there are no terminated ends, and each network node on the ring network topology has equal rights and access, but only one network node can talk at any time.

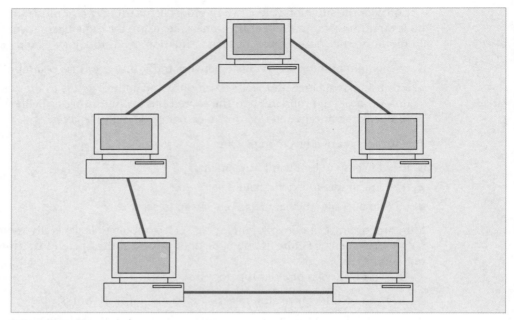

Figure 5.4 Ring topology

When a network node issues a message, the sending network node passes the message to the next network node. If this network node is not the destination node, the message is passed to the next network node, until the message arrives at its destination node. If, for whatever reason, the message is not accepted by any network node on the network, it will travel around the entire network, and return to the sending node.

In a single ring topology, the signal travels around the circle in a single direction – usually a clockwise direction. In a double ring topology (sometimes known as a counter-rotating ring topology) the signal travels in two directions – both clockwise and anti-clockwise – the intention being to provide fault tolerance in the form of redundancy in the event of a cable failure. That is, if one ring goes, the data messages can flow across to the other ring, thereby preserving the integrity of the network.

Unlike a bus topology, a ring topology is an active topology inasmuch as each network node repeats or boosts the message signal before passing it on to the next network node.

The advantages of a ring topology are:

■ High speed of transmission of data is possible because data messages flow in one direction only (for a double ring topology: in the first ring the data message would flow in a clockwise direction, and in the second ring the data message would flow in an anti-clockwise direction – that is, in the opposite direction).

■ Growth/expansion of network employing a ring topology normally has a minimal effect on overall network performance.

■ Each node on the network has equal rights and access.

■ Each node on the network acts as a repeater and allows a ring topology to span distances greater than other hard-type topologies.

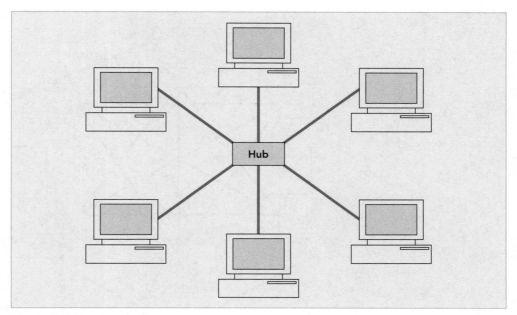

Figure 5.5 Star topology

The disadvantages of a ring network topology are:

- It is often the most expensive topology to implement.

- As a network topology, it requires more connections than a linear bus network topology.

- Perhaps most importantly, the failure of a single network node will impact on the whole network.

Star topology

A star topology is a topology in which all network nodes are connected to a central network node called a hub, which acts as a router for transmitted messages. See Figure 5.5.

Because the central network hub offers a common connection for all network nodes – that is, every network node will have a direct communications connection/link to the central network hub – communication between peripheral network nodes across the network occurs by passing data messages through the central network hub. In essence, peripheral network nodes may only communicate with all other peripheral network nodes by transmitting messages to, and/or receiving messages from, the central network hub only.

The star topology is probably the most common form of network topology currently in use. The advantages of a star network topology:

- It is easy to implement and extend, even in large networks.

- It is simple to monitor and maintain.

- Perhaps most importantly, the failure of a peripheral network node will not have a major effect on the overall functionality of the network.

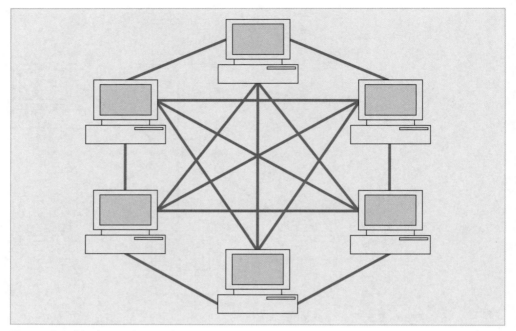

Figure 5.6 Mesh topology

The disadvantages of a star network topology:

■ Maintenance/security costs may be high in the long run.

■ It is susceptibile to infection – if a peripheral network node catches a virus the infection could spread throughout the network.

■ Failure of the central network hubs can disable/cripple the entire network.

Mesh topology

A mesh topology (also known as a complete topology) is a topology in which there is a direct link between all pairs of network nodes within a network, resulting in multiple paths/links connecting multiple network nodes. See Figure 5.6.

In a fully connected network with n nodes, there would be: $n(n-1)/2$ direct links. For example:

■ a mesh topology with 10 network nodes would have 10 $(10-1)/2 = 90/2 = 45$ potential direct links, whereas

■ a mesh topology with 100 network nodes would have 100 $(100-1)/2 = 9{,}900/2 = 4{,}950$ potential direct links, and

■ a mesh topology with 1,000 network nodes would have 1,000 $(1{,}000-1)/2 = 999{,}000/2 = 499{,}500$ potential direct links.

Because of the possible complexity, especially in large mesh topologies, a router is often used to search the multiple paths/links between two network nodes, and determine the best path/link to use for the transmission of data messages. The choice of path/ links between two network nodes will be determined by factors such as cost, time and performance.

The advantages of a mesh topology are:

- Small mesh topologies are easy to create and maintain.
- Such a topology allows for continuous connections and reconfiguration around blocked paths/links by hopping from one network node to another network node until a connection can be established.
- It offers stability, safety and reliability inasmuch as a mesh topology allows communication between two network nodes to continue in the event of a break in any single communication link between them. That is, the redundant connections make the mesh topology very reliable – even in networks with high volume traffic.

The disadvantages of a mesh topology are:

- Larger mesh topologies can be expensive, and costly to install.
- They can be difficult reconfigure.
- They can be difficult to administer, manage and troubleshoot.

Mesh topologies are most often employed in wide area networks (WANs) to inter-connect smaller local area networks (LANs).

Hybrid topology

A hybrid topology is a combination of any two or more topologies and results when two different basic network topologies are connected.

Examples of such hybrid topologies would be:

- star–bus topology (also known as tree topology), and
- star–ring topology,

Star–bus topology

A star–bus topology (also known as a tree topology) is a topology in which a collection of star networks is arranged in a hierarchical relationship and connected to a linear bus backbone (see Figure 5.7).

A star–bus topology has three key characteristics:

1 Individual peripheral network nodes (sometimes referred to as leaves) are able to transmit messages to, and receive messages from, only one other network node.

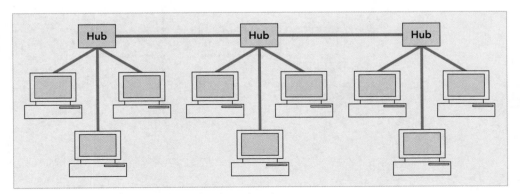

Figure 5.7 Hybrid topology (star–bus topology)

2 Peripheral network nodes are neither able to nor required to act as message repeaters and/or signal regenerators.

3 The function of the central network node (often a network switch,[23] sometimes referred to as an intelligent hub) may be, and indeed often is, distributed along the network.

The advantages of a star–bus topology are that it is:

■ easy to extend,

■ simple to maintain, and

■ resilient – individual peripheral network node failure will not have a major effect on the overall functionality of the network.

The disadvantages of a star–bus topology are:

■ They can be difficult to configure (and physically wire), consequently maintenance costs may be high.

■ Failure of a network switch can disable a large portion of the network.

■ If the network backbone link breaks, an entire network segment may be affected.

Star–ring topology

A variant of a ring topology is a star–ring topology, or token ring network.

A star-wired ring topology functions as ring topology, although it is physically wired as a star topology (see Figure 5.8), with a central connector called a Multistation Access Unit (MAU) which facilitates the movement of messages from one network node to another network node – in a circle or ring fashion.

Within a token passing network, signals are communicated from one network node to the next network node sequentially, using a token or small data frame. When a network

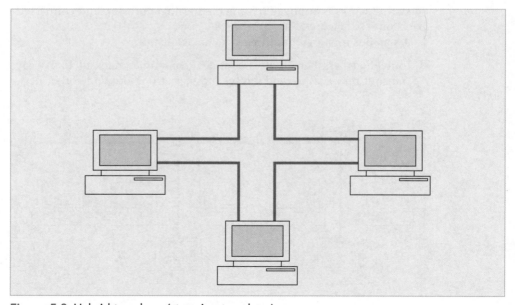

Figure 5.8 Hybrid topology (star–ring topology)

node wishes to transmit a message, it catches the token, attaches the data and a destination address to it, and then sends it around the ring.

Note that each node can hold the token for a maximum period of time.

The token travels along the network ring until it reaches the destination address. The receiving network node acknowledges receipt with a return message – attached to the token – to the sending node. Once the sending network node has received the reply, the sending node releases the token for use by another network node.

In essence token-passing configurations are deterministic inasmuch as it is possible to calculate the maximum waiting and transmission times. In addition such configurations can:

■ use prioritising protocols to permit and prioritise transmissions from designated, high-priority network nodes, and

■ employ fault-detecting protocols to identify and compensate for network fault – for example, selecting a network node to be the active network monitor.

Hard-type networks – protocols

For communications and networking purposes, a protocol can be defined as a convention or standard that controls the connection, and enables the communication and transfer of data and information between two computers and/or network nodes. In a more technical context, a protocol can be defined more specifically as a uniform/formalised set of rules that govern the syntax, semantics and synchronisation of communication.

In hard-type networks, protocols may be implemented by hardware, by software, or by a combination of both hardware and software, with all but the most basic of protocols being layered together, or 'hierarchically arranged', into so-called protocol stacks. A collection of protocols within a protocol stack is known as a protocol suite. Although the terms are often used interchangeably, in a strict technical sense a protocol suite is the definition of the protocols and the protocol stack is the software implementation of them.

There exist many different types/collections of protocols, with the number and variety of protocols continually changing as new ones emerge and old ones are abandoned in the name of information and communication technology development. Clearly, the changing nature of hard-type network protocols makes it very difficult to generalise about different protocols/protocol suites, because of their differences in purpose, sophistication and target audience/technology. For example, some protocols may be defined as proprietary protocols – that is, they are 'dedicated' protocols which are only recognised by, or used in, computer networks or information and communication applications from a particular manufacturer. They are therefore generally not publicly documented – at least not officially! Others may be defined as generic protocols – that is, protocols which seek to provide a common structure, or framework, or platform on which future computing and/or information and communication technologies may be developed.

Nevertheless, despite such differences, because of their underlying raison d'être most protocols/protocol suites, will, at the very minimum, seek to specify at least one (if not more) of the following activities:

■ the detection of network connections (wired or wireless),

■ the existence of other network nodes,

■ the nature of the network connection characteristics,

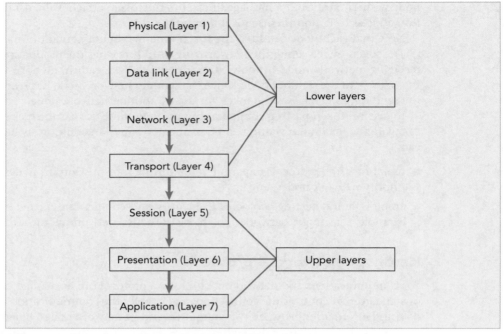

Figure 5.9 OSI reference model (OSI protocol stack)

- the structure and formatting of data/information messages,
- the correction of network and/or data/information transmission problems,
- the detection of unexpected problems and/or network failure,
- the termination of network/session connections.

There are two important generic protocols in contemporary information and communication technologies – applicable to networking and internetworking (or more appropriately the internet).

The first is the 7-layer reference model known as the OSI reference model, or OSI protocol stack (see Figure 5.9).

The OSI reference model is comprised of the following levels:

- **A physical layer (Layer 1)** which relates to the network hardware, and defines the physical characteristics of the transmission medium and the specifications for network devices.

- **A data link layer (Layer 2)** which provides the functional and procedural means for the transfer of data between network entities and is concerned with transferring data across a particular link/medium.

- **A network layer (Layer 3)** which defines the end-to-end delivery of data frames and provides the functional and procedural means for transferring data frames from source to destination using one or more networks while maintaining a required quality of service.

- **A transport layer (Layer 4)** which provides the mechanism for the reliable and cost-effective transfer of data between network nodes/users.

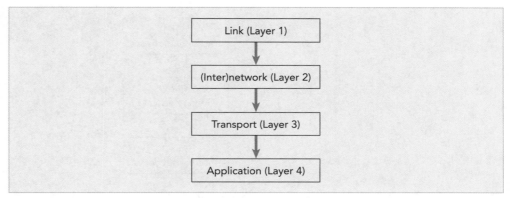

Figure 5.10 Internet model (TCP/IP model)

- **A session layer (Layer 5)** which provides the facilities for managing the dialogue – or, more appropriately, prioritising transmission between application processes.
- **A presentation layer (Layer 6)** which defines the way that data are formatted, presented, converted and encoded, and is responsible for the delivery and formatting of information to the application layer for further processing and/or display.
- **An application layer (Layer 7)** which provides a direct interface with application processes and describes the way that programs interact/communicate with a network's operating system.

The second is the 4-layer reference model known as the internet model or the TCP/IP model (see Figure 5.10).

The TCP/IP model is comprised of the following levels:

- **A link layer (Layer 1)** (also known as the network access layer) which maps to/corresponds with the physical layer and the data link layer of the OSI reference model.
- **An (inter)network layer (Layer 2)** which corresponds to the network layer of the OSI reference model, and manages the movement of data packets across a network and is responsible for ensuring data packages reach their destinations.
- **A transport layer (Layer 3)** which corresponds to the transport layer of the OSI reference model, and provides the mechanism for network nodes/devices to exchange data packets with regards to software.
- **An application layer (Layer 4)** which corresponds to the session layer, the presentation layer and the application layer of the OSI reference model.

Semi-soft-type networks

There are three types of semi-soft-type networks:

1 The internet.
2 An intranet.
3 An extranet.

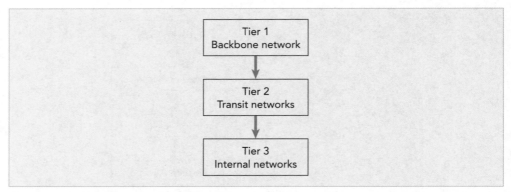

Figure 5.11 The 3-tier network hierarchy

Internet

The internet is the largest internetwork in the world – a network comprised of many thousands of independent hosts/networks that use TCP/IP to provide worldwide communications, an internetwork that operates within a three-tier network hierarchy (see Figure 5.11).

At **Tier 1** is a collection of backbone networks interconnected to form a decentralised mesh network, a collection of core backbone networks that:

■ link the parts of the internet together, and

■ provide the primary data/information carrying lines of the internet.

Many of these backbone networks are now commercially owned, with some of the large multinational companies, including MCI, British Telecom, AT&T, and Teleglobe, acting as backbone network providers, and therefore providing backbone connectivity.

At **Tier 2** (also called downstream tier 1) is a collection of mid-level transit networks,[24] for example:

■ Network service provider (NSP) – an international, national or regional service provider which provides bandwidth and network infrastructure facilities such as transit services and routing services.

■ Internet service provider (ISP) – a local service provider which provides customers with internet access and customer support services.

These mid-level networks connect to the stub networks at Tier 3 (see below), and to the backbone networks at Tier 1.

At **Tier 3** is a collection of stub networks or internal networks (usually a local area network (LAN)) and sometimes referred to as an intranet (see below) which carry data packets between local hosts (that is, nodes within a local area network).

These so-called stub networks include:

■ commercial networks – for example, .com, or .co.uk networks,

■ academic networks – for example, .edu, or .ac.uk networks, and

■ other organisations/networks – for example, .org.uk, or .net networks

. . . and of course many other diverse worldwide physical networks, both wired and wireless.

Put simply, the internet is a packet-switching network[25] with a distributed mesh topology,[26] a client–server architecture and a hierarchical interconnection scheme. That is:

■ National/international NSPs are responsible for developing, constructing, maintaining and managing national or international networks, and sell bandwidth to regional NSPs.

■ Regional NSPs purchase bandwidth from national/international NSPs, and sell on the bandwidth (and other network services/facilities) to local ISPs.

■ Local ISPs sell bandwidth and other internet services/facilities to end users – for example, individuals, companies and other organisations.

However, in order to function as an internetwork, individual networks (as autonomous systems[27]) must interact/communicate with one another, that is, individual networks must exchange data/information. To exchange data/information backbone networks must be connected. Individual networks can be connected using either:

■ an internet exchange point[28] (a convergence of many backbone networks interconnecting at a single point), or

■ a private connection (a convergence of few backbone networks interconnecting at a single point).

The exchange of data/information between individual backbone networks is undertaken using a process known as peering. Peering is the exchanging of internet traffic between networks using different Tier 1 backbone network providers and normally requires:

■ a contractual agreement or mutual peering agreement,[29]

■ a physical interconnection between the different networks (normally called a peering point), and

■ technical cooperation to facilitate the exchange of traffic.

Most peering points (peering via the use of internet exchange points) are located in collocation centres (sometimes called carrier hotels) – data centres where Tier 1 backbone network providers co-locate their points of presence[30] or connections to one another's networks. That is, a peering agreement can only exist between Tier 1 backbone network providers.

However, where individual Tier 1 backbone network providers are interconnected using a private connection it is also possible for a private peering connection between only a few networks to exist.

Intranet

An intranet can be defined as a network based on TCP/IP protocols (essentially an internet) that is contained within, and belongs to, a company and/or organisation – a network which is accessible only by authorised company members, employees and/or agents, although the term intranet is sometimes used as a reference to the visible aspects of a company's/organisation's internal website.

As the fastest growing segment of the internet, secure intranets are increasingly used to:

■ provide secure inter-company/inter-organisational communication – for example, video conferencing;

- facilitate the sharing/dissemination of data and information – for example, policies, procedures, and company announcements; and
- provide access to company resources.

There are two reasons why using intranet is so popular. First, because the development of a secure intranet is simple and inexpensive and, once operational, is easy to manage, maintain and update. Second, because an intranet has three features normally lacking on the internet: speed, security and control. Typically, an intranet will include connections to the internet using a gateway and firewall, to:

- provide access to networks outside the company – for example, the internet;
- allow access to the company intranet from outside the company;
- facilitate the monitoring and controlling of intranet use – for example, websites and/ or other networks accessed using the company intranet.

When (part of) an intranet facility is made available to external agents outside the company, that part of the intranet becomes part of an extranet.

What types of activities are intranets used for?

Today, companies and organisations use intranet facilities, or, more appropriately, intranet portals, to provide a wide variety of resources and services. Whether:

- secured and available to authorised users only, or
- unsecured and available to all users (that is, open access), or indeed
- a combination of both,

intranets have become an essential corporate/organisational tool in:

- reducing operational costs,
- improving organisational efficiency and effectiveness, and
- gaining strategic corporate advantage over competitors.

Some of the main activities for which intranets are used include:

- Information systems and communications management – providing information on:
  - user facilities,
  - technical support and help-desk facilities,
  - network resources,
  - resourcing schedules – for example system updates etc.,
  - information systems security polices and procedures,
  - software training courses,
  - information systems and communications FAQs (frequently asked questions).
- Financial services management – providing information on:
  - financial regulations, policies and procedures,
  - income receipting and expenditure payments procedures,
  - e-commerce facilities,
  - requisitioning systems and asset management procedures and policies,
  - financial reports,
  - budgeting procedures, policies and timetable.

- Human resources management – providing information on:
  - employee conditions of employment,
  - health and safety regulations,
  - organisational/management structure,
  - employee training facilities,
  - recruitment.

  Increasingly companies use intranet facilities to provide a company newsletter.

- Sales and marketing management services – providing information on:
  - marketing data – for example, regional sales, customer demographics etc.,
  - customer feedback,
  - marketing press releases,
  - sales/marketing training facilities,
  - market competitor research.

- Customer services – providing information on:
  - customer order tracking,
  - available products and services,
  - customer FAQs.

- Corporate/organisational management services – providing information on:
  - company history,
  - corporate/organisational strategic plans,
  - management meeting minutes,
  - market analysis – including where appropriate company share price tracking,
  - company calendar tracking/highlighting important events/activities,
  - newsgroup facilities.

Whilst initial set-up costs may be high, for a company the benefits of an intranet cannot be underestimated. Not only does it provide for:

- more effective use of company resources, and
- more efficient communication between internal and external agents,

it also:

- facilitates more effective time management, and
- provides for more secure data/information management.

Extranet

In a broad context, an extranet can be considered part of a company's/organisation's intranet – a part that is extended to authorised external users/agents – and can be defined as a network based on TCP/IP protocols that facilitates the secure sharing of corporate/organisational information and/or resources with external agents such as product/service suppliers, customers, corporate/organisational partners and/or other businesses.

That is, it is an internet-based communication facility designed to support business to business (B2B) activities.

In essence, an intranet provides various levels of accessibility to people who are members of the same company, whereas an extranet provides various levels of accessibility to people who are *not* members of the same company – or, one could say, . . . to outsiders.

In general, for both security and privacy purposes, access to a company extranet is normally controlled using a two-level access protocol – a valid username and password, and/or the issuance of digital certificates. The use of such an access protocol:

■ validates/authenticates the user as an authorised user of the company extranet,

■ determines which elements/facilities of the company extranet the authorised user has right of access to, and

■ decrypts any secured encrypted elements/facilities of the company extranet the authorised user has right of access to.

There is little doubt that since the late 1990s and early 2000s[31] extranets, as a business-to-business (B2B) facility, have become a popular means for companies/organisations to exchange information, information ranging from:

■ generic data/information, such as price lists, inventory schedules and reports, delivery schedules, and ordering/payment facilities, to

■ product/service-specific data/information, such as detailed product/service specification.

The main benefits of an extranet include:

■ better supply chain management by the use of on-line product/service ordering, order tracking facilities and product/service management;

■ reduced costs by providing technical documentation on-line to trading partners and customers;

■ increased operational flexibility by allowing remote access by company and/or organisation staff to core business information/facilities;

■ improved communication and customer service by enabling the sharing of common documentation on-line, and providing customers with direct access to product/service information;

■ improved security of communications – by controlling access to/use of extranet facilities.

Cloud computing

Cloud computing refers to the access to and use of multiple server-based resources through a digital network. It is a form of virtual computing. (Note: the term cloud is used as a metaphor for the internet.)

Applications are provided and managed by the cloud server with data being stored remotely. Users do not download or install applications on their own device or computer; all processing and storage is maintained by the cloud server.

Popular cloud services include, for example, Flickr for on-line photo storage, Hotmail and other web-based clients for email, and Dropbox for on-line document storage.

Cloud computing differs from the traditional client–server model because it provides applications from a server that are managed by a client's web browser. No installed client version of an application is required. Centralisation gives cloud service providers complete control over the versions of the browser-based applications provided to clients, and removes the need for version upgrades.

Put simply, cloud computing service providers deliver applications via the internet, which are accessed from a web browser, while the business software and data are stored on servers at a remote location.

For business organisations, the advantages of cloud computing are that it improves a company's ability to re-provision resources and, as a result, can reduce costs through the use of service level agreements. It also enables the more efficient sharing of resources and increases reliability due to its centralising nature. There, however, some risks/problems, the main issues being:

- information privacy and security,
- possible discontinuity/failure of service, and
- possible problems of integration of cloud-based services with existing IT systems (see Article 5.1).

Article 5.1

An evolutionary approach to cloud computing

Andy Gallagher, Head of the IT advisory service line at Serco Consulting

In the midst of the hype surrounding cloud computing it is sometimes difficult to remember that it is not the panacea, or silver bullet, for all IT service delivery issues. While it will be the right answer in certain, perhaps many, scenarios it will equally be the wrong answer for others.

Cloud computing is essentially just a new delivery model, a 21st century version of the time sharing and bureau functions of the 1980s with a number of commercial, technological and presentational upgrades.

Factors such as speed to market, lack of capital investment, utility/commodity pricing, elastic capacity and financial surety around charging methodologies are prompting many of today's leaders to see cloud as the perfect solution, but there is another group of executives for whom security, resilience, service levels and lock-in are very real concerns, and they are challenging this approach.

IT departments have expended considerable time, effort and cost in evolving from being a back-office function staffed by technologists to an established, business-focused change and delivery partner.

Central to this was the articulation and delivery of technology as a reliable, responsive and enduring service. It is the impact of cloud on these aspects rather than any technology issues that is giving rise to these challenges. Security concerns in a multi-tenant public cloud environment have been raised by a number of experts, but in this case this is not the most significant of the issues raised. Of much more concern are the following:

Even the largest private sector clients will be relatively small players in a public cloud environment, in particular in comparison to the providers. Organisations used to being the number-one customer, or at the very least in the top tier, of their chosen providers will have to adjust to the very different realities of the multi-tenant world.

There is a requirement for a new supplier selection and governance process; it is not just the same old faces as before and the move from in-house or favoured-customer status to the world of commodity will require a major rethink on contracting and governance models.

There is a significant mismatch in service-level agreements (SLAs) between existing systems (tomorrow's legacy) and what is being offered for cloud-based services. Despite supplier promises around availability, standard SLA targets still fall well short of current performance in more traditional delivery models.

Integration with existing applications, such as ERP, has the potential to threaten stability and/or integrity of the existing applications or the performance/functionality/flexibility of the cloud applications.

→

One of the most common concerns with existing delivery models and suppliers is the longer term implications of lock-in; mortgaging the future against short-term benefits. Exit plans in the cloud environment are very much in their infancy and the effectiveness of these embryonic plans has yet to be determined.

It is clear that moving forward, CIOs in large corporations are going to have to manage the expectations of two very different user communities:

Those using, or about to use, the cloud who will 'enjoy' the benefits but possibly unwittingly suffer the concerns and those using legacy applications who will not realise the benefits of cloud, particularly around speed to market and utility pricing, but will continue to receive the reliable, robust services provided today.

These concerns are only on the radar of certain companies and individuals and there is a risk that they will be perceived as dinosaurs, unable to evolve to support the new world. However, it may be that this challenge highlights the last major hurdle for cloud providers to overcome in ensuring an evolutionary rather than revolutionary approach.

17 June 2011

Source: Available at www.computerweekly.com.

To minimise risks involved in using cloud computing it is important for a company to:

- ensure a reputable and reliable provider is chosen;
- agree definitive service level agreements (SLAs) and ensure that they are tailored to the company's specific requirements;
- carefully plan the migration to the cloud, and evaluate the potential risks to maintaining business continuity;
- know where the company data will be stored, because of possible variations in data protection regulations.

Concluding comments

An understanding of how networks operate and how such networks can be managed and controlled has become vital to twenty-first-century market-based companies. The ability to create wealth is no longer solely determined by the quantity of assets possessed but, more importantly, by the networks created and on-line interrelationships used.

Self-review questions

1 In relation to soft-type networks, briefly explain the difference between a bureaucracy and an adhocracy.

2 In relation to hard-type networks, define the term network topology and distinguish between two types of topologies.

3 Explain the advantages and disadvantages of a peer-to-peer network.

4 Describe the advantages and disadvantages of a client–server network.

5 Briefly explain why the internet is often referred to as a 3-tier network.

6 Distinguish between the 7-layer reference model known as the OSI reference model and the 4-layer reference model known as the internet model or the TCP/IP model.

7 What are the major differences between:

(a) an internet,
(b) an intranet, and
(c) an extranet?

8 Define and describe the advantages and disadvantages of:

(a) a bus topology,
(b) a ring topology, and
(c) a star topology.

Notes

1 That is not to say that socio-political and socio-religious groups will not continue to arise, and seek to impose their will, either directly or indirectly, on the fabric of many modern societies. On the contrary – for example, consider the continuing conflicts in Africa, the seemingly ever-present socio-religious confrontation in Afghanistan, the escalating political turmoil in Iraq and the growing unrest in the Middle East, and their impact on the interrelationships between social groups within the UK, the USA, Europe, and indeed all the other Western democracies.

2 The term control is used here in the context of promoting accountability and traceability.

3 ... or semi-hard-type networks.

4 A logical network is concerned with the connection pathways within a network, and is deemed to exist independently of the physicality of the network.

5 Actors within a social network can be a range of entities from an individual, to a small local association, to a large multinational corporate organisation.

6 Such relationships/dependencies may be directed (formal), or undirected (informal), or mixed.

7 ... sound familiar? Of course it does! It's the general systems theory notion that 'all systems are comprised of small subsystems'!

8 A node is a processing location, and can be a computer or some other information/communication device – for example, a printer. Every node in a network will have a unique network address – either a data link control address (DLC), or a media access control (MAC) address.

9 A server is a computer and/or information and communication device that manages network resources – for example:

- a file server is a computer (or collection of computers) that is dedicated to storing files,
- a print server is a computer that manages one or more printers,
- a network server is a computer (or collection of computers) that manages network communications traffic, and
- a database server is a computer dedicated to processing database queries.

10 In a computing context a client is a system/user that accesses a remote service/facility located on another computer within the same and/or related network to the client.

11 As part of a client–server network architecture, a client can be defined as an application that runs on a PC and/or workstation, and relies on a server to facilitate access to, and/or management of the performance of a processing operation(s). For example, an e-mail client is an application which facilitates the sending and receiving of e-mails.

12 Indeed, servers on a client–server network may also perform some of the processing work for client machines – processing which is often referred to as back-end processing.

13 Load balancing is the distribution of processing and communications activity evenly across a network so that no single computer and /or information and communications device is overwhelmed. Such balancing is important for networks where service demand is difficult to predict.

14 . . . as compared to the now ancient and monolithic mainframe computing systems.

15 A router is a computer networking device that forwards data (packets) toward their destinations. In essence, a router acts as a junction between two networks to transfer data (packets) between them. A router differs from a switch, which merely connects network devices (or network segments) to form a network.

16 **Mal**icious **software** that is designed to destroy, disrupt, and/or damage a computer system/network.

17 Spyware is malicious software that covertly gathers user information through an internet connection without the user's knowledge and/or consent.

18 In networking, a bus is a collection of wires that connects nodes within a network, and through which data and information are transmitted from one computer in a network to another computer in the network. While the term backbone is often substituted for the term bus, in a contemporary context it is a term often used to describe the main network connections that comprise the internet.

19 Peer-to-peer networks are often configured as a local bus.

20 Terminator connections situated at the end of the bus – the communication links are designed to absorb the signal once it has reached to end of the network topology, and prevent the signal from being reflected back across the bus.

21 Although most wired networks tend to be regarded as non-passive, almost all wireless networks are regarded as examples of passive bus networks.

22 Carrier Sense Multiple Access (CSMA) is a non-deterministic media access control (MAC) protocol in which a node verifies the absence of other traffic before transmitting on a shared physical medium, such as a bus.

23 A network switch is a computer networking device which connects network segments (a portion of a computer network that is separated by a computer networking device – for example a router, a bridge or switch, and/or a repeater or hub). It is often used to replace a central network hub. A switch is also often referred to as an intelligent hub.

24 A transit network is a network which passes traffic between other networks in addition to carrying traffic for its own hosts, and must have pathways to at least two other networks.

25 That is, data are transmitted in packets across an internetwork that is comprised of multiple interchangeable pathways from source to destination.

26 . . . which facilitates pathway redundancy – that is, if a pathways fails an alternative pathway can be used.

27 Autonomous systems (AS) are the managed networks that comprise the internet. Often operated by an NSP or an ISP, such networks act as both management domain and routing domain, and are identified by a number assigned by ICANN (the Internet Corporation for Assigned Names and Numbers).

28 An internet exchange point (IXP) is a physical infrastructure that allows different ISPs to exchange internet traffic between their respective networks. These were originally known as network access points (NAPs).

29 A mutual peering agreement (MPA) is a bilateral agreement which facilitates the exchange of internet traffic between ISPs and/or NSPs without cost.

30 A point of presence (PoP) is a physical point at which a network meets a higher level or primary data/information carrying line of the internet, and is mainly designed to allow ISPs to connect into NSP networks.

31 Although some academics argue that the term extranet is merely used to describe what companies/organisations have been doing for many years – creating/developing interconnecting private networks for the sharing of data/information, it was during the late 1990s/early 2000s that the term extranet began to be used to describe a virtual repository of data/information accessible to authorised users only, over the internet.

CHAPTER 6

Information management and data processing

Introduction

Commencing with a brief review of the nature of data and data management, this chapter considers a range of issues related to:

- data processing,
- data storage,
- data flow analysis – for example:
    - data flow diagrams,
    - entity relationship diagrams,
    - systems/document flowcharts,
    - decision tables, and
    - organisational coding systems/charts of account,
- databases.

Learning outcomes

By the end of this chapter, the reader should be able to:

- Explain the contextual importance of data management
- Distinguish between and critically evaluate the effectiveness of alternative types of data processing
- Describe the main aspects of a file-orientated approach and a data-orientated approach
- Describe the main components of a database
- Critically evaluate the relevance and usefulness of a range of data analysis techniques

Data management

'Data are worthless . . . but information is priceless!' (Anon.)

To be useful, data require processing. More importantly, they require processing in an organised and controlled manner. Such processing – whether it is manual-based processing, or computer-based processing, or, indeed, a combination[1] (we will look at these in a little more detail later in this chapter) – would normally comprise a number of mutually interdependent stages:

- data selection,
- data conversion,
- data capture,
- data input,
- data storage,
- data maintenance,
- data processing, and
- data output (or more appropriately information generation).

Data selection

The term data selection can be defined as a process of filtering, or, more precisely, a process of determining the appropriateness and relevancy of data. Such data selection would normally be based on predetermined criteria as necessitated by end-user needs/requirements, for example:

- the content of the data,
- the structure/format of the data, or
- the context/relevance of the data.

Data conversion

Data conversion can be defined as a process, or group of processes, which convert(s) data from one data format to another data format. Data conversion is usually necessary where the data is relevant but presented in a structure/format that is inconsistent with the requirements.

Data capture

Data capture can be defined as the acquisition of data. Where data are selected for processing it is important to ensure that all such data *are* processed. Data capture is, therefore, often considered to be a controlling process/function designed to ensure the full and complete processing of all selected data.

Note: In many data processing systems, data selection, data conversion and data capture are viewed as a single stage.

Data input

Data input can be defined as the entry of data into a processing system. Broadly speaking, there are two types of data input: physical data input, and non-physical data input.

Physical input

Physical data input is data input in which the source of the data is a hard copy document. Such input is normally associated with off-line data entry, and is generally used in batch processing – that is, where data are collected perhaps over a period of time, before they are processed.

Examples of such physical input/batch processing would be:

- Time-cards completed by individual employees on a daily basis, which are then collected by payroll personnel and used to calculate individual employee weekly wages.
- Invoices received on a daily basis from product suppliers/service providers, which are collected and processed for payment at the end of a week.

Non-physical input

Non-physical data input is data input in which the source of the data is not a hard copy document. Such input is normally associated with on-line data entry. Such non-physical data input is often referred to as paperless data input or virtual data input.

There are two types of non-physical input: automated non-physical input, and manual non-physical input.

Automated non-physical input

Automated non-physical input is non-physical input which requires no human intervention, an example of which would be digital data input using RFID (radio frequency identification) technologies, and/or chip and PIN technologies.

The benefit of such input systems is that input data can be encrypted at source.

Manual non-physical input

Manual non-physical input is non-physical input which requires human intervention, and can be either:

- manual data capture/data entry – for example, keyboard-based data input,[2] such as using web-based ordering/purchasing, or
- semi-manual/semi-automatic data capture/data entry – for example, optical character recognition (OCR) data input.[3]

Perhaps somewhat unsurprisingly, for many business/accounting related transactions, such manual non-physical data input has become the norm.

Data storage

Data storage can be defined as the structured accumulation of data, in particular secondary data. There are two key issues: *how* are the data stored and *where* are the data stored.

Within manual-based processing systems such data storage would perhaps be limited to physical paper-based systems, for example a hard copy file system. Pre-computer data storage also made use of paper tape and punch cards. Currently, the most commonly used secondary data storage technologies within computer-based processing systems are magnetic storage, semiconductor storage (using semiconductor-based integrated circuits), optical disc storage and magneto-optical disc storage. There are, of course, many interesting future data storage technologies in development, perhaps the most promising being holographic storage and molecular storage.

Where can the data be stored?

Secondary data can be stored internally in-house using for example a network attached storage system (or NAS), or externally using networked on-line storage with the data stored on externally hosted multiple virtual servers – often referred to as 'cloud storage'.

Data maintenance

Data maintenance can be defined as the preservation of data integrity, and generally involves the development of processes and procedures that not only ensure the correctness, accuracy, validity of all stored data, but, more importantly, maintain the relevance of all stored data. Data maintenance processes and procedures are, therefore, concerned with monitoring and controlling access to stored data – in particular authorising access related to the addition, deletion, amendment and/or removal of data from the data store.

Data processing

Data processing can be defined as any process and/or procedure, or series of processes and/or procedures, that converts data into information.

Data output

Data output can be defined as the exit of data out of a processing system. Broadly speaking, there are two types of data output: physical output, and non-physical output.

Physical output

Physical data output is data output produced in the form of a hard copy document – for example, a debtor invoice, or an employee pay slip. Whereas historically, physical data output was regarded as the norm, in contemporary computer-based processing – especially computer-based accounting information systems – such physical data output is perhaps now the exception rather than the rule and is becoming increasingly rare . . . primarily for cost and efficiency purposes.

Non-physical output

Non-physical data output is data output in the form of a virtual (and increasingly) web-based document. For many business/accounting-related transactions, such non-physical output has become more and more the norm – a contemporary example would be providing customer statements/invoices using a secure password-protected website.

Data – the need for structure

In a literal sense, the term datum[4] means that which is given; however, in a more general context, the term data (or sometimes data element) is often used to mean a representation of facts or concepts or instructions in a formal and organised manner, more specifically as a representation of the attributes of an entity.

An entity can be defined as something that possesses a distinct and separate existence, though not necessarily a material or physical existence. For example, an entity can be:

- an object, such as a product or service,
- a person, such as a customer/client or supplier/provider, or
- an event, such as the sale of a product, or the provision of a service.

An attribute can be defined as a characteristic of an entity, that is:

- the value, or cost of a product/service,
- the location of a product supplier/service provider, and/or
- the name of a customer/client.

When data are collected, such data need to be stored and need to be maintained. There are a number of alternative mediums that can be used to store or maintain the data – some more efficient than others. For example:

- in a manual-system/process the storage medium would more than likely be a physical storage medium, such as a paper file-based facility, or a microfiche/microfilm-based facility,[5] whereas
- in a computer-based system/process, use would be made of a virtual storage medium – such as a digital file-based facility,

In terms of storage[6] structure, data storage can categorised as either:

- random data storage, or
- organised data storage.

Random data storage, perhaps unsurprisingly, means data storage without any predictable or systematic pattern. Such data storage is designed to allow data to be:

- stored in any location, and/or
- accessed in any order,

with all storage locations being equally accessible.

Organised data storage means data storage with a predictable and systematic pattern. Such data storage is designed to allow data to be stored and/or accessed in a structured predetermined order – whether sequentially or hierarchically. Although some virtual storage mediums use a random storage structure for the purpose of temporarily storing data and/or processing instructions,[7] the vast majority of storage mediums (both physical and virtual) use an organised storage structure for the permanent storage of data.

Why? Put simply, using an organised data storage structure, whatever the storage medium used, provides for a more effective maintenance of data records/data files – for example, the creation of, deletion of, and/or amendment to, data records/data files – and a more efficient management of data record/data file changes – for example the verification, coordination, validation, integration, and control of data records – whether such records are in data files, or data tables (or indeed data sets).

What types of organised data storage structures are there?

Organised data storage can take several approaches, perhaps the two most common being:

1 Data storage using a file-orientated approach (or the applications approach).

2 Data storage using a data-orientated approach (or the database approach).

File-orientated approach

A file-orientated approach (sometimes referred to as a flat file approach) is based on a simple 'flat structure' (hence the alternative name) in which data files are 'owned' by particular 'application specific' groups within a company, usually with such groups able to dictate for example:

■ the nature and structure of data capture procedures,

■ the content and structure of the data records/data files,

■ the timing of data maintenance issues, and

■ the nature and structure of data retrieval operations.

Have a look at Figure 6.1.

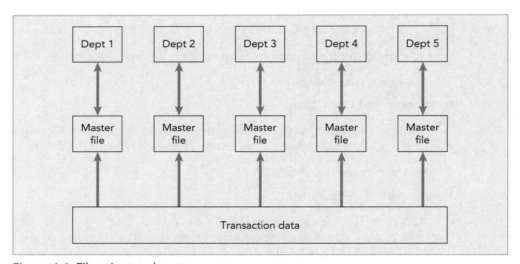

Figure 6.1 File-orientated system

Before we look at the organisation of a file-orientated approach, it would perhaps be useful first to consider how data would be structured using a file-orientated approach.

Within a file-orientated approach, data would normally be stored within data files. A **data file** can be defined as an organised collection of data records, with a data record being a group or collection of data fields/data elements. A **data field** can be defined as a specific area/portion of a data record allocated for a specific data element, and a data element[8] can be defined as a stored attribute, or stored characteristic. It is the term data element that is often abbreviated to the term data.

Consider the following:

LKT plc is a UK-based manufacturing company based in Newcastle. The company sells its products worldwide, and currently has 25,000 customers in 72 countries. The record layout for each customer contains 99 characters, as follows:

Field	Data element	Characters
1	Customer reference number	01–05
2	Customer name	06–21
3	Customer address – street	22–33
4	Customer address – city	34–43
5	Customer address – postcode/zip code	44–50
6	Customer address – country	51–52
7	Opening balance	53–60
8	Transaction type	61–68
9	Transaction date	69–74
10	Transaction reference	75–83
11	Transaction amount	84–91
12	Closing balance	92–99

The current customer record for Potremic Inc is as follows:

Field	Data element	Data
1	Customer reference number	18823
2	Customer name	Potremic Inc
3	Customer address – street	234 35th St
4	Customer address – city	Birmingham
5	Customer address – postcode/zip code	35260
6	Customer country	13
7	Opening balance	1578.90
8	Transaction type	Cr Sale
9	Transaction date	050510
10	Transaction reference	98676
11	Transaction amount	1300.00
12	Closing balance	2878.90

Data element

A data element would have two key characteristics:

(i)   data element name, and

(ii) data element value.

Data element name

The data element name refers to designation of the data. In the above example, the data element name of say field 4 of LKT plc's customer record is: customer address – city.

Data element value

The data value refers to the actual data stored in a data field. In the above example the data element value of field 4 of LKT plc's customer record for the customer Potremic Inc (the customer address – city field) is Birmingham.

Data field

A data field would also have two key characteristics:

(i) field length, and

(ii) data type.

Field length

The field length of a data field refers to the number of continuous positions (or characters) required within a particular data field to store a specific data element type.

In the above example the field length of field 7 of LKT plc's customer record is 8 positions (or characters).

Data type

The data type refers to the class or category of data stored in a particular data field. Such data types can include:

- an alphabetic data type – that is, alphabetic characters only: for example, a name;
- a numeric data type – that is, numeric characters only: for example, a customer reference number;
- an alpha-numeric data type – that is, a combination of alphabetic and numeric characters: for example, a customer address;
- a time and/or date numeric data type – that is, data concerning a point in time: for example, 050510 (5 May 2010);
- value data – that is, numeric values using either fixed or floating decimal point: for example, £1350.00;
- a raw data type – that is, graphic and/or audio/visual data.

In the above example, the data type of each of the 12 fields of LKT plc's customer record is as follows:

Field	Data type
1	Numeric data type
2	Alphabetic data type
3	Combined numeric and alphabetic data type
4	Alphabetic data type
5	Combined numeric and alphabetic data type[9]
6	Numeric data type
7	Numeric data type (fixed decimal point)
8	Alphabetic data type
9	Numeric data type (date type data)
10	Numeric data type
11	Numeric data type (fixed decimal point)
12	Numeric data type (fixed decimal point)

Data record

As suggested earlier, a data record can be defined as a group or collection of data fields/ data elements. In the above example, the data record for Potremic Inc is the complete customer record – containing all 12 data fields, and all 99 data characters.

. . . and a data file?

Data file

A data file is an organised collection of data records. In the above example, one type of data file would be a data file containing all 25,000 records of each of the customers of LKT plc. Such a customer record data file would, as we will see, be considered a master file.

Within a data file, data records can be organised sequentially or non-sequentially. Whereas a sequentially ordered file is a file in which data records are stored in an organised manner – according to a specific data record, for example debtor records in a debtors file may be organised in debtor number order, or debtor name – a non-sequentially ordered file is a file in which data records are stored in a random unorganised manner.

In general, within a file-orientated approach, two specific categories/levels of files would be used:

1 primary files, or source files – because such files contain original source data derived from the system environment, or

2 secondary files, or derivative files – because such files contain duplicate data derived from the transaction file.

Primary files

The main types of primary files within a file-orientated approach would be a master file, a transaction file and a reference file.

A **master file** would contain data related to, or concerned with, a specific entity, or group of entities. In an accounting information systems context, the general ledger, or the creditor ledger, or indeed the debtor ledger, would be regarded as a separate, and individual, master file.

A **transaction file** would contain data related to, or concerned with, specific current events. In an accounting information systems context, such events would include accounting transactions such as sales, purchases, the payment of an invoice, the receipt of payment from a debtor, etc.

A **reference file** would contain data related to, or concerned with, a specific group of attributes – attributes required to complete a transaction event, or group of transaction events. In an accounting information systems context such attributes could be, for example, a product listing, a price listing, a customer/client listing, or a product supplier/ service provider listing.

Secondary files

The main types of secondary files within a file-orientated approach would be a history file, a report file and a backup file.

A **history file**, sometimes referred to as an archive file, would contain data related to, or concerned with, specific past events. In an accounting information systems context, such events would be, for example, completed accounting transactions. Such data would be derived from the transaction file.

A **report file** would contain data derived from the master file and/or the transaction file, and would be generated for a specific purpose. In an accounting information systems context, such reports would include, for example, a stock status report, or a doubtful debt listing, or a creditor payment listing, etc.

A **backup file** would contain data derived from the transaction file, and would be generated for security purposes to ensure that a copy of all source data is available. Because transaction file data are frequently changing, as transactions are processed the backup file would require frequent revision to ensure its contents reflect all processed transactions.

File-orientated approach – data records and data files: design considerations

In designing data files, in particular the arrangement and structure of data records within individual data files, it is important from a data management context to consider:

- who will use the data file(s),
- when the data file(s) will be used,
- what purpose the data file(s) will be used for,
- how the data file(s) will be accessed, and
- where the data file(s) will be accessed.

First, identifying who will use the data file(s) will provide an indication on how data records within individual groups of data files should be organised, for example:

- How should creditor files within the creditor ledger be structured?
- What data records should the creditor file contain?
- How should those data records in the creditor file be arranged?

Second, determining the purpose for which a data file(s) will be used will provide an indication of how long data records and data files should be retained – should data records/files be retained, for example, for 1 month, for 6 months, for 1 year, or for 6 years?[10]

Third, establishing the degree of commonality required between data records in different data files – that is, the extent to which data records in different data files should be capable of consolidation and/or shared by different users – will provide an indication of what security arrangements should be used to maintain the integrity of individual data records/data files, and prevent unauthorised addition, deletion, and/or alteration to data records/data files.

What are the advantages and disadvantages of a file-orientated approach?

The advantages of a file-orientated approach are that they are simple to use and they can be extremely cost-effective – especially if only small amounts of data are stored. In addition, if well designed, such an approach can handle large volumes of data, very efficiently.

The disadvantages of a file-orientated approach are that they can become very cumbersome (lots of duplication of data files), very complex, difficult to manage, overly bureaucratic, and highly politicised often resulting in the limited sharing of data. In addition, they can result in the excessive duplication of data, and high levels of data inconsistency due to the limited enforcement of data standards. More importantly, such systems can be difficult to update and/or change – especially where extensive structural change to data content and/or file organisation is required.

Data-orientated approach/database system

A data-orientated approach/database system is a structural approach in which data are considered a company asset, or, more appropriately 'a shared resource for all authorised organisational users, and their respective applications'. Such a resource is commonly

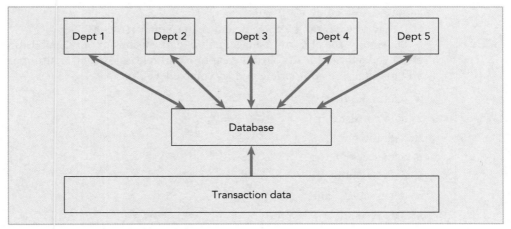

Figure 6.2 Data-orientated system/database system

called a database – an organised collection of data elements, within which the elements are organised into collections of record-like structures often referred to as data tables (or data sets[11]). Have a look at Figure 6.2.

There are a number of alternative structural approaches that can be used within the data-orientated approach, the main alternatives being:

- a flat data model,
- a hierarchical data model,
- a network data model, and
- a relational data model.

What are the advantages and disadvantages of a data-orientated approach/ database system?

There can be little doubt that a database system can provide a powerful centralised coordinating facility to manage the movement of large volumes of data. The main advantages of a data-orientated system/database system are:

- they provide an efficient means of managing data,
- the provide an effective means of controlling data access,
- they promote greater data integration and improved data independence,
- they limit the need for data duplication,
- they provide for efficient data sharing and greater reporting flexibility, and
- they minimise data redundancy and limit data inconsistency.

The disadvantages of a data-orientated system/database system are:

- they can be extremely complex,
- implementation may require substantial change (and so might provoke resistance from some in the organisation),
- there may be a possible vulnerability of data, and
- the cost.

Efficient data management

So, what do we mean by the efficient management of data?

Put simply, the efficient management of data means not only establishing efficient and effective facilities for the accurate capture and release of data, it also means developing and maintaining appropriate and acceptable levels of:

■ data redundancy,

■ data consistency,

■ data integration,

■ data accessibility,

■ data flexibility,

■ data security, and

■ data integrity.

Data capture (entry)/data release (exit)

Perhaps unsurprisingly, whereas data capture is concerned with processes and procedures through which primary data are selected and acquired *from* the real world, data release is concerned with the processes and procedures through which secondary data are issued *to* the real world. Clearly, the more efficient the data capture/data release facilities, the more accurate the data, and the more cost-effective the data capture/data release facilities.

Using a file-orientated approach may require data to be entered more than once – especially where data are duplicated within a company.

Consider the following scenario. PLT Ltd is a UK manufacturing company based in Coventry. The company has six departments. Because PLT Ltd uses a file-orientated approach to store and maintain product/service data, each department holds its own separate master file of product/service details. To update the data record of a particular product/service, it would be necessary to determine on which of the master files a copy of the product/service data is maintained (remember the product/service data may not be held in each master file), access the relevant master file, and then update the relevant master file. This could mean that each of the six master files may need to be updated separately.

Using a data-orientated approach/database system, this multiple updating would not be necessary.

Why? Because only a single product/service master file would be maintained within PLT Ltd – as a company-wide/organisation-wide resource accessible by each of the six departments within the company. To update the product/service master file would therefore only require a single data entry/data update.

Data redundancy

Data redundancy is concerned with the usability of data or, more appropriately, the likelihood that data may become defective and unreliable. Clearly, levels of data redundancy are negatively correlated to levels of efficiency – that is, the higher the levels of data redundancy, the lower the levels of efficiency.

What types of data redundancy are there?

There are two types: direct redundancy and indirect redundancy.

Direct redundancy occurs where data in a data file (using a file-orientated approach), or data in a data table (using a data-orientated approach/database system), are *copies* of data held in another file or database record. **Indirect redundancy** occurs where data in a data file (using a file-orientated approach), or data in a data record (using a data-orientated approach/database system) can be *derived* from data held in another data file or data record.

Using a file-orientated approach creates opportunities for both direct and indirect data redundancy to occur. Indeed, as demonstrated in the PLT Ltd illustration above, using a file-orientated approach can lead to significant levels of direct data redundancy in stored data – that is the existence of many copies of the same data resulting in not only the inefficient use of data storage space but, perhaps more significantly, the possibility of data inconsistencies.

Using a data-orientated approach/database system, data are integrated as an amalgamation of several otherwise distinct data files. While such an amalgamation clearly minimises (but does not eliminate) the possibility of direct data redundancy – that is, the likely existence of multiple copies of the same data within the database system – the possibility of indirect data redundancy nonetheless remains.

Using a data-orientated approach/database system, incidences of data redundancy, whether direct or indirect, can be greatly reduced by a technique known as normalisation. Normalisation is a series of techniques – a process which seeks to convert complex data structures into simple, stable data structures by organising data to reduce the possibility of data anomalies/data inconsistencies emerging.

Data consistency

Data consistency is concerned with uniformity and the standardisation of data, within a file (or series of files) and/or a database.

Clearly, improved levels of data consistency and data uniformity are positively correlated to levels of reliability – that is, the higher the levels of data consistency, the higher the level of data reliability.

Using a file-orientated approach to store and maintain personnel data, the manager of each retail outlet in a chain would hold a separate master file of the staff employed at the retail outlet they manage. In respect of those specialist staff working at more than one retail outlet, such an approach would result in the excessive duplication of personnel data. More importantly, using a file-orientated approach could also result in:

- a high level of data inconsistency – for example changes to specialist personnel staff data may be incorrectly documented or completely omitted, and (perhaps more importantly)
- a low level of standardisation – personnel data may be stored differently by each manager at each retail outlet.

Using a data-orientated approach/database system to store and maintain personnel data centrally in the company's head office would of course not only reduce the opportunity for data inconsistencies to occur, it would also – almost certainly – eliminate any possible standardisation issues.

Data integration

Data integration is concerned with the opportunity to combine two or more data sets for purposes of:

- data sharing between different users (and/or different applications), and/or
- data analysis for information provision purposes.

Clearly, effective data integration not only reduces possible data duplication, it also moderates the requirement for excessive data storage capacity and, of course, improves data availability/accessibility.

Using a file-orientated approach can limit possible levels of data sharing.

Why? Sometimes for economic reasons – for example, the cost/time required to process data for data sharing purposes may be prohibitive; sometimes for technical reasons – for example, data sharing may be difficult because of data inconsistencies and/or a lack of data standardisation between data files; and sometimes for political reasons – for example, a manager may refuse access to, or may make it difficult to gain access to, data which he/she manages/controls.

Using a data-orientated approach/database systems, of course, eliminates some if not all of the above problems, and allows for a higher degree of monitored data sharing and controlled data integration.

Data accessibility

Data accessibility is, of course, concerned with the practicality and suitability of facilities used to provide users with access to data/data files, and whilst there can be little doubt that data use is clearly related to user accessibility, determining the suitability of data access facilities/opportunities can be problematic.

Why? Because when determining the appropriateness of user access facilities/opportunities, issues of data security and data integrity must also be considered. For example, while unrestricted and/or unmonitored access may well promote high levels of user activity, such potentially 'open access' could adversely affect data integrity/security – that is, potential users may steal, fraudulently alter and/or even corrupt data. Conversely, constraining accessibility – for example, imposing severe restrictions on user access – may well help to maintain the integrity and security of the data, but could also adversely affect both the numbers and levels of user activity.[12]

Using a file-orientated approach clearly constrains accessibility inasmuch as data may exist in separate data files, owned by different users/different applications. Conversely, using a data-orientated approach/database system improves accessibility due to the centralisation of data storage.

Data flexibility

Data flexibility is concerned with the ease and cost-effectiveness with which data can be modified. Using a file-orientated approach, flexibility is often very low.

Why? Because, in using a file orientated-approach, data are often defined and organised by the individual (within the company) who effectively *owns* the data. More importantly, because multiple copies of the same data may be owned by different individuals within the company, and stored in different locations within the company, amendment to, or modification of, any such data may be difficult and expensive.

Using a data-orientated approach/database system, flexibility is often very high because the data are held in a single location. Indeed, such flexibility is often seen as the prime advantage of a data-orientated approach/database system.

Data security

Data security is concerned with ensuring that data are kept safe from corruption and that access to them is suitably controlled. Data security is closely related to data privacy and data confidentiality.

Using a file-orientated system, because data may be maintained separately in a number of different locations, there may always be a chance that *some* data may be lost. Using a data-orientated approach/database system, because data are maintained in the same location, *all* or most data may be vulnerable to loss – especially if backup copies are not routinely maintained. Of course, using a data-orientated approach/database systems does allow for the imposition of a comprehensive data security system; however, such security systems can be expensive to implement and difficult to manage/monitor.

Data integrity

Data integrity is concerned with minimising possible data inconsistencies and ensuring that data within a data file (using a file-orientated approach) or data table (using a data-orientated approach) are accurate. Levels of data integrity can be monitored using a range of integrity checks. Such integrity checks can be categorised as follows:

- type checks,
- redundancy checks,
- range checks,
- comparison checks, and
- constraint (or restriction) checks.

Type checks are designed to ensure that the data type within a data field in a data record is correct – for example, checking whether data type within a numeric data field is numeric.

   Redundancy checks are designed to ensure that the data within a data file or data table or data set are useable. (If you recall, we discussed direct and indirect redundancy earlier – see pages 160–1.)

   Range checks are designed to ensure that a data item's value occurs within a specified range of values – for example, in a data field recording an employee's age such a check could ensure that an employee's age is say >16 and <75.

   Comparison checks are designed to compare data within a data field and/or group of data fields with data within another data field and/or group of data fields – for example, checking that the salary of a group of employees is within the salary range/salary scale for those employees.

   Constraint checks are designed to ensure that any constraint, condition or restriction imposed on data within a data field, or data table, or data set, especially data of a personal nature, is complied with – for example legal constraints over the deletion of data within a data field.

   Whereas both the file-orientated approach and the data-orientated approach/database system provide opportunities for the application of all of the above integrity checks, using the data-orientated approach/database system not only helps to centralise the imposition of such integrity checks, but also minimises the cost of such integrity checks while maximising their effectiveness.

File-orientated systems vs. data-orientated systems

File-orientated systems are undoubtedly simple to develop, easy to maintain and, of course, simple to use. However, the lack of integration within such systems often results in a high degree of inflexibility, imposing:

- significant limitations of user accessibility, and
- severe restrictions on data sharing opportunities.

. . . and data-orientated systems/database systems?

While such systems clearly increase user accessibility and promote improved flexibility, they are very costly to develop and can be very complex to maintain.

So, which is the most popular?

Pre-1980s, the file-orientated approach was probably the most popular; however, since the mid/late 1980s (and certainly since the early 1990s), the data-orientated approach/ database system has become the most popular.

Why? There can be little doubt that the increasing availability of information and communication technologies (certainly since the early 1990s), and the ever-reducing cost of database-related technologies has contributed to the growing popularity of the data-orientated approach, its integration into a wide range of information- and communication-related applications, and its widespread adoption – especially in business-related/ accounting-related information systems. Yet, its popularity has perhaps more to do with the increasingly 'in vogue' view that data should be regarded as an organisational resource, whose efficient management (and use) is central to the development and maintenance of shareholder wealth – certainly in today's ever more sensitive, ever more competitive, information-dominated marketplace.

Data processing

As suggested earlier, data processing can be defined as any process and/or procedure, or series of processes and/or procedures, that converts data into information. There are two alternative types of data processing approaches: *manual data processing*, and *computer-based data processing*.

Manual data processing

Broadly speaking, manual data processing can be defined as the processing of data using primarily human-based resources. It does not necessarily signify the complete absence of information and communication technologies, but merely that the use of such resources, while important, is nonetheless of a secondary nature. Such data can loosely be categorised as either:

- routine business-related transaction data, or
- non-routine business-related transaction data.

Manual processing of routine business-related transaction data

Routine business-related transaction data are data relating to, or referring to, socio-economic events/transactions[13] which occur as part of the normal day-to-day wealth-generating activities of a company. Examples would be the purchase of products and services, or the payment of creditor invoices, or the payment of employee wages and salaries.

Although a small minority of companies continue to use manual-based data processing for the processing of routine business-related transaction data, the popularity of such manual-based data processing has declined significantly over the last 20 years.

Why? For a number of reasons – perhaps the most important being that such manual-based processing is:

- generally very slow,
- often very costly, and
- invariably an inefficient use of company resources.

The latter is especially the case where an individual manual-based process becomes politicised and seen as being owned by a group and/or department within a company.

Note: Where manual-based data processing is used for the processing of routine business-related transaction data, such processing would normally involve:

- the collection of transaction data into groups or batches – into a transactions data file, and
- the processing/updating of the master file when either:
  - a predetermined processing limit or batch size has been reached, or
  - a timetabled processing deadline has expired.

How would the updating of the master file – that is, the updating of the master file data with the data accumulated within the transaction file – take place?

There are two alternative approaches:

1 sequential file updating, and
2 non-sequential (or random access) file updating.

Using sequential updating, the data in the transaction file would be validated, the data would be edited where appropriate, and then sorted into the same order as the master file. The master file would then be updated – in master file order.

Using non-sequential updating, the data in the transaction file would be validated, the data would be edited where appropriate, and the master file would then be updated – in transaction file order.

Whichever approach is used, an updating report would be produced – for audit trail purposes.

Although non-sequential updating is much simpler, it can be, and generally does tend to be, much more time-consuming, especially where a large volume of data records require updating. As a consequence, manual-based processing uses the sequential updating approach.

Manual processing of non-routine business-related transaction data

Non-routine business-related transaction data are data relating to, or referring to, socio-economic events/transactions that are not part of the normal day-to-day wealth-generating activities of a company. Such events/transactions are normally characterised as being infrequent and/or unique transactions of a high value, examples of which would be the purchase of fixed assets, or the investment of surplus funds.

Because of the unusual nature of such non-routine business-related transactions, it is likely that any related data would be processed using a non-sequential approach.

Computer-based data processing

Computer-based data processing can be defined as the processing of data using communication and information technologies. Again, it does not necessarily signify the complete absence of human input, but merely that the use of human resources is of a minimal nature.

Such processing is generally used where large volumes of data are regularly processed, in particular where:

- the data processing is routine, continuous, and/or repetitive,
- the data processing involves complex data selection, data capture, and/or data storage procedures,
- the data processing is temporally and spatially separated – that is, it occurs at different times and/or in different places.

Why? Put simply, computer-based processing can process transactions at great speed and with great accuracy. More importantly, it can process transactions at a very low unit cost, and offer a wider choice of secure storage facilities and processing alternatives.

What types of processing alternatives are there?

There are essentially two alternative types of computer-based processing:

1 Computer-based processing in which data are processed periodically (with either sequential updating or non-sequential updating) – usually referred to as **batch processing**.

2 Computer-based processing in which data are processed immediately – usually referred to as **on-line processing** (although it is sometimes referred to as immediate processing, or on-line real-time processing).

Batch processing (or periodic processing)

Batch processing is data processing in which data are collected and processed in groups, or in batches of data, and normally consists of four stages (see Figure 6.3):

1 a collection stage, where individual data are collected into 'controlled' batches of data;

2 an input stage, where the controlled batch of data is input;

3 a processing stage, where the master file is updated – based on the controlled batch of data; and

4 an output stage.

Figure 6.3 relates to the purchase of products/service on credit – in which the supplier's/ provider's credit account, the stock record in the stock ledger, and the debtor's control account in the general ledger are updated as batches of transactions (invoices) are processed.

Companies tend to use batch processing where it is necessary to:

- process and store large amounts of homogeneous data on a regular basis, and
- produce large volumes of output about large numbers of data entities – for example, customers, clients, product suppliers, service providers, employees, etc.

More importantly, it is used where:

- processing consists of the same sequence of pre-established procedures for *all* data, and
- processing response times, whilst significant, are not usually of critical importance – providing the batch processing cycle[14] timetables are adhered to.

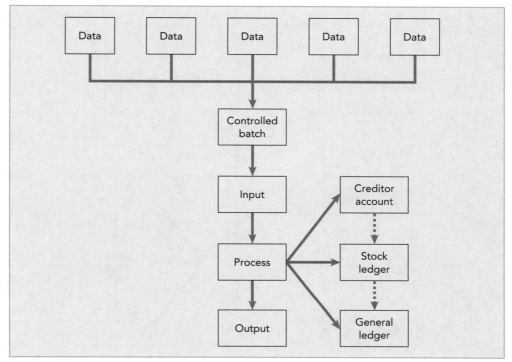

Figure 6.3 Batch processing

It is perhaps unsurprising that batch processing remains popular for the processing of, for example:

■ payroll data for the payment of employee wages and salaries,

■ creditor invoices for the payment of products and/or services received, and

■ debtor invoices for products and/or services provided.

What are the advantages and disadvantages of batch processing?

The advantages of batch processing are:

■ it can provide low-cost processing and, because of the periodic nature of the processing,

■ it can be easy to control.

More importantly, not only can batch processing provide a clear processing audit trail, it can also be very efficient where large volumes of data are processed.

The disadvantages of batch processing are:

■ it can be very time-consuming,

■ processing is often time constrained,

■ it can involve lengthy data preparation,

■ processing response times can be slow, and

■ changes to processing procedures can be difficult to implement.

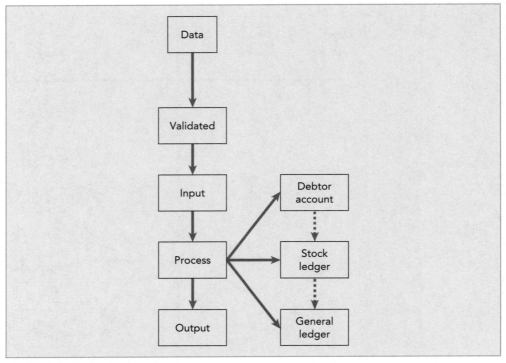

Figure 6.4 On-line processing

On-line processing (or immediate processing)

On-line processing can be defined as data processing in which data are input and processed as soon as complete data become available, and is often used to signify the processing of data immediately upon receipt. The on-line processing of data consists of three stages (see Figure 6.4):[15]

1 an input stage, where individual data are input;

2 a processing stage, where the master file is updated immediately on data input; and

3 an output stage.

Figure 6.4 relates to the sale of products/service on credit – in which the customer's/client's debtor account, the stock record in the stock ledger, and the debtor's control account in the general ledger, are updated immediately, that is, as the transaction occurs.

Companies tend to use on-line data processing where it is not only necessary to support a large and unpredictable number of concurrent users and transaction types and ensure the continuous availability of secure high performance data processing, but more importantly where:

■ the majority of transactions are executed in a short period of time – possibly fractions of a second in some cases, and

■ the majority of interactions between the user and the on-line system are for a short period of time.

More specifically, where:

- a small amount of data is input – per transaction,
- a small number of stored records are accessed and processed – per transaction, and
- a small amount of data is output – per transaction.

On-line processing remains popular for the processing of, for example:

- ATM transactions,
- stock receipts/issues,
- quotations/reservations requests – for example, insurance quotations/airline reservations,
- EPOS transactions, and
- credit card/debit card verification/validation.

What are the advantages and disadvantages of on-line processing?

The advantages of on-line processing are:

- the speed at which data can be input,
- the low cost of data processing,
- immediate error correction,
- all files are updated immediately,
- human interaction/interference is minimised.

The disadvantages of on-line processing are:

- set-up costs can be very high,
- data input and data processing controls can be costly,
- access authority levels may require constant monitoring,
- the system hardware may be costly,
- the system software may require extensive integration,
- data audit trails may be difficult to locate.

Centralised data processing vs. distributed data processing

First, two definitions:

- **Centralised data processing** is data processing performed in one computer or in a cluster of coupled computers – at a single location.
- **Distributed data processing** is data processing performed by several separate computers/computer networks – at several locations, linked by a communications facility.

Historically, in the now dim and distant past when mainframe computers were measured not by the size of their memory capacity/processing capability but by the number of rooms they occupied, centralised processing was the norm. It was the processing approach adopted by the vast majority of companies – an approach in which *all* data were processed at a single head office location. Why?

For three reasons. First, because of the high cost of data processing technologies, centralised data processing was viewed as the most cost-effective means of processing large amounts of data – a way of reducing data processing infrastructure costs. Second, because of the ever-changing complexities of using such data processing technologies, centralising data processing was seen as the most effective means of minimising possible duplication. Third, because of the need for coordination, for control and for accountability, centralising data processing technologies was seen as the most efficient means of ensuring uniformity in the enforcement of processing standards and the imposition of data/ processing security requirements.

Why the demise of centralised data processing?

Put simply, all forms of imposed bureaucracy – all forms of controlled centralisation – inevitably fail, whether as a result of internal pressure generated by ever-increasing inefficiencies[16] and inflexibilities, or external pressure associated with environmental innovation and change. Indeed, it was:

- the increasing demand for faster processing,[17]
- the increasing need for improved mobility, and
- the growing desire for greater flexibility,

excited by the ever changing demands of the business environment, and fuelled by the ever more dramatic advancements in information and communication technologies/ capabilities, that perhaps somewhat inevitably resulted in the demise of centralised processing.

What are the advantages and disadvantages of distributed processing?

The advantages of distributed processing are:

- it promotes greater flexibility in the use of data processing facilities,
- it promotes better resource sharing and greater user involvement,
- it increases location independence, and therefore data processing efficiency, and
- it is more responsive to user needs.

The disadvantages of distributed processing are:

- the initial set-up costs can be very high, and
- the risk of data duplication, possible data incompatibility, processing error, and/or operational/communication failure, can be high where there is an inadequate level of management and coordination.

Centralised data processing vs. distributed data processing – variation in degrees

Although we often discuss notions of centralised data processing and distributed data processing as if they were absolute terms, in reality, such a distinction is perhaps best visualised as a sliding scale on which companies exhibit differing degrees of centralisation.

However, as with all qualitative assessments, measuring/determining degrees of centralised data processing/distributed data processing can be problematic. As a broad principle, where a company operates at a number of geographically dispersed locations the degree of distributed processing utilised by the company would generally be positively correlated with the degree of autonomy exercised at/by each geographically dispersed location. (See Figure 6.5.)

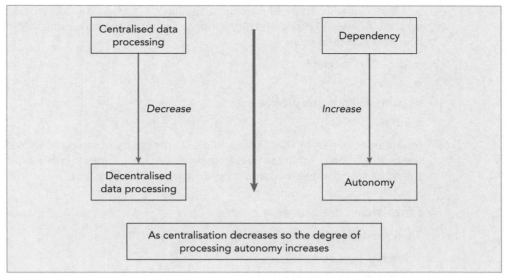

Figure 6.5 Centralised data processing vs. decentralised data processing

Such correlation would of course be affected by:

- the management structure of the company,
- the context type of the company,
- the processing requirements/demands within the company, and
- the connectivity constraints within the company.

Describing data processing systems

Within a company context – specifically within an accounting information systems context – there will always be a need to document and record information on:

- what systems, flows and processes exist,
- how such systems, flows and processes are related,
- what functions such systems, flows and processes perform,
- how each system, flow and/or process is managed/controlled,
- what resources are allocated to each system, flow and process, and
- what added value each system, flow, and/or process produces.

Why? Because accounting information systems and processes are continually changing, continually evolving. Whether such change occurs as a result of internal management policies – for example, the restructuring of organisational activities – or, indeed, as a consequence of external environmental pressure – for example, the development and introduction of new information and communication technologies – such change is inevitable, while its consequences are often unpredictable and uncertain.

There is a wide range of 'documenting' techniques used to describe and analyse the systems, flows, and processes that comprise a company's accounting information system, the most common being:

■ data flow diagrams,

■ flowcharts,

■ entity-relationship diagrams, and

■ decision tables.

In addition, as part of this discussion on documenting techniques, we will also consider the coding system – that abstract framework of alpha-numeric symbols which lies at the heart of every computer-based accounting information system.

Data flow diagrams

There are broadly speaking two types of data flow diagram:

1 Logical data flow diagram.

2 Physical data flow diagram.

Whereas a logical data flow diagram focuses on the content of data flow, a physical data flow diagram focuses on the context of the data flow – that is, a logical data flow diagram describes *what* data flow, and a physical data flow diagram describes *how* the data flow. The emphasis of both types of data flow diagrams is on identifying:

■ the system/process boundaries that surrounded the data flow,

■ the external entities involved in the data flow,

■ the data involved in the data flow,

■ the activities/events that occur within the data flow,

■ the rules used to process the data and manage the data flow, and

■ the data stores/files created and/or maintained as part of the data flow.

What notation is used in data flow diagrams?

Although there are a number of variations concerning data flow diagram notation,[18] for our purposes we will use the following:[19]

■ A square – to indicate an entity.

■ A circle – to portray a process.

■ Two parallel lines – to indicate a data store/file.

■ An arrow – to portray the direction of a data flow.[20]

See Figure 6.6.

A brief description of these terms would be:

■ An **entity** (also referred to as external source/external destination) can be either an object and/or a subject which contributes data to, and receives data from, a process.

■ A **process** is an activity or event and/or a procedure which transforms and/or manipulates data.

■ A **data store/file** is a location at which data are retained either temporarily or permanently.[21]

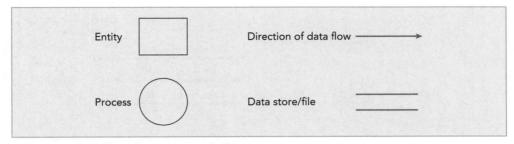

Figure 6.6 Data flow diagram – symbols

■ A named **data flow arrow** depicts the flow of data either to a process or from a process – that is, data flow arrows must either start or end at a process, and cannot occur directly between:
  ■ data stores, and/or
  ■ external entities, and/or
  ■ a data store and an external entity.

Logical data flow diagram

A logical data flow diagram provides, independent of any physical information and communication technology that may be utilised in the data flow, a representation of the flow of data through a transaction system within a company, and documents the relationship between data and data processing.

What does a logical data flow diagram look like?

Broadly speaking, a logical data flow diagram is a component aspect of a data flow model which is merely a hierarchical collection of interrelated logical data flow diagrams, each representing a different level of detail within a data flow of a system/process.

Context level data flow diagram

A context level data flow diagram is a data flow diagram that provides a holistic representation of the major data flows within a system/process. Where the system/process to which the context level diagram relates is composed of lower level subsystems/subprocesses, such a context diagram is sometimes referred to as the *level 0 data flow diagram*.

The main aim of a context level data flow diagram is to provide a simplified *single cycle* overview of the data flow within a system/process.

The context level diagram will generally indicate:

■ the source entity within the data flow,
■ the destination entity within the data flow,
■ the process involved in the data flow, and
■ the direction(s) of the data flow(s).

To construct a level 0 context diagram it is important to:

■ identify all the data flows (for example documents) used in the system/process, and
■ identify all the source entities and destination entities that interact with the system/process.

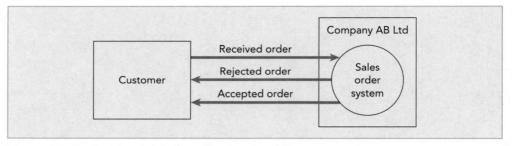

Figure 6.7 Context level data flow diagram (level 0)

Have a look at Figure 6.7. At level 0, the customer order is received by the company and directed into the sales systems, where the order will be accepted or rejected.

Level 1 data flow diagram

Clearly, as an overview diagram, the context level data flow diagram provides very little detailed information. To analyse the system further it is necessary to explode – in a metaphorical sense – or perhaps more appropriately decompose, the system identified in the context level data flow diagram, to provide greater detail on:

- what data flows occur, and
- what processes exist within the system.

This more detailed data flow diagram is known as a *top level* or *level 1 data flow diagram,* and is designed to provide a description of the internal structure of the system, or, more specifically, a description of the component data flows and processes that comprise the system.

Have a look at Figure 6.8. At level 1, the customer order is received by the sales system, where the customer's credit details are checked. Where the customer's credit details are confirmed and validated, the order will be accepted.

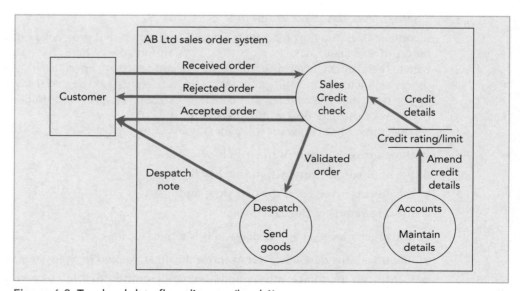

Figure 6.8 Top level data flow diagram (level 1)

Because there are no clear rules to use to determine what is a level 1 process, and what is not a level 1 process, it can be difficult to know where to start.

There are three alternative analytical approaches that can be used to identify a practical starting point:

1 Resource flow analysis.

2 Organisational structure analysis.

3 Document flow analysis.

The resource flow analysis approach is useful when the system consists largely of the flow of resources. Such resources are traced from their input into the system, to their processing, and their output from the system. The rationale behind this method is that data normally flow in the same direction and on the same pathways as such resources.

The organisational structure analysis approach considers the main roles that exist within the organisation, rather than the goods or information – that is, flow around the system – the aim being to identify the key processes and determine which functional areas are relevant and which are not.

Why? Because the data flow between such processes (and relevant external entities).

The document flow analysis approach considers flows of data in the form of documents or computer input and output, the key stages in the approach being:

■ determine the process/system boundary,

■ list the major documents and their sources and recipients, and

■ identify major data flows such as telephone and computer transactions.

Level 2 data flow diagram

Where a process, or a number of processes, identified in a level 1 data flow diagram are composed of lower-level sub-processes, then each such sub-process may itself be decomposed into its component data flows and processes. Such a data flow diagram is known as a level 2 data flow diagram, and is designed to provide a description of the component data flows and processes that comprise the subsystem detailed in the top level (level 1) data flow diagram.

Have a look at Figure 6.9. At level 2, the customer order is received by the sales system, where the customer's credit rating is checked, and the customer's existing account balance is checked. Where the customer's credit rating and account details are confirmed and validated, the order will be accepted.

Clearly, where there is a sub-process at a second level, decomposition is itself comprised of separate data flows and sub-processes; such sub-processes may also be decomposed to a third level, or indeed, a fourth level, or even further, depending on the complexity of the process/processes identified in the level 1 data flow diagram.

At what point will this decomposition process stop?

The sub-process decomposition will only stop when a sub-process can be described using an elementary process description – that is, using a brief textual description of the process. Such an elementary process description would contain for example a description of:

■ the data that are accessed,

■ the business constraints which dictate the process,

■ the circumstances under which the process is invoked, and

■ the constraints imposed upon the use of the process.

Have a look at Figure 6.10.

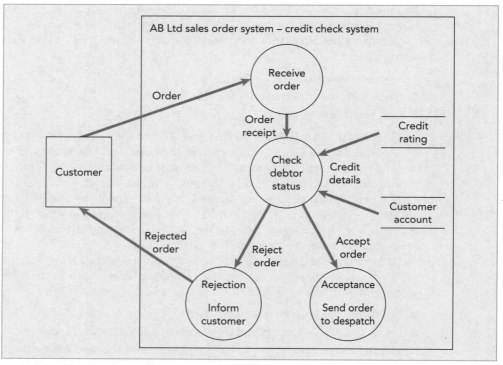

Figure 6.9 Top level data flow diagram (level 2)

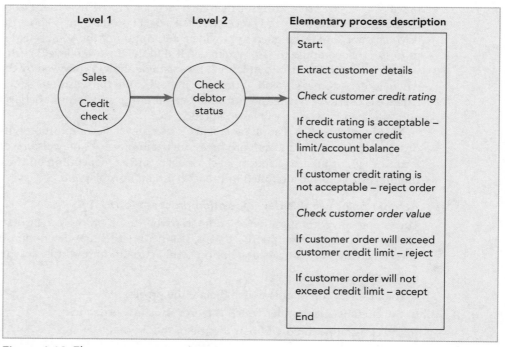

Figure 6.10 Elementary process description

How many levels of decomposition would there be?

That's a difficult question to answer. Broadly speaking:

- a small, simple system/process would perhaps normally contain 2 to 3 levels,
- a medium, fairly complex system/process would perhaps normally contain between 3 and 6 levels, and
- a large, complex system/process would perhaps normally contain 6 or more levels.

However, it is important to remember that decomposition levels within a data flow model (that is, a collection of hierarchically related data flow diagrams) must be consistent with each other – that is, the data inputs and data outputs at a higher level must correspond to the data inputs and data outputs of all the constituent sub-processes at the next, lower level. It is also important to note that while a system may comprise a number of processes, and lower level sub-processes, the number of decomposition levels (that is, levels of sub-processes) may differ, indeed will often differ, between the individual constituent sub-processes of a system.

Physical data flow diagram

A physical data flow diagram seeks to identify, specify and describe the physical environmental context of a data flow, that is, specify within information and communication technology context:

- *what* activities and/or processes occur, and
- *how* such activities and processes are carried out.

Within a physical data flow diagram:

- a process would represent physical programmes and functions, and
- a data store would represent physical data files and databases, both permanent and temporary.

The physical data flow diagram (see Figure 6.11) provides an illustration of a simple payroll system for the payment of weekly wages to factory employees. It is concerned primarily with physical entities and the flow of physical documentation between such entities.
    Physical data flow diagrams are useful in identifying:

- the physical nature of the data flow – for example, manual or automatic;
- the sequence of the data flow process/processes;
- the nature of the data storage – for example, permanent or temporary;
- the names of data files, and
- the names of individuals/departments involved in the movement of data.

However, their use is somewhat limited.
    Why? Because the same information concerning the physical environmental context of a data flow can be provided, often in much greater detail, using a traditional flowchart (see below).

Drawing a data flow diagram

The main stages in drawing a data flow diagram would be:

- Draw a context flow diagram to represent the entire system, and identify and add any external entities, resource flows and/or data flows;

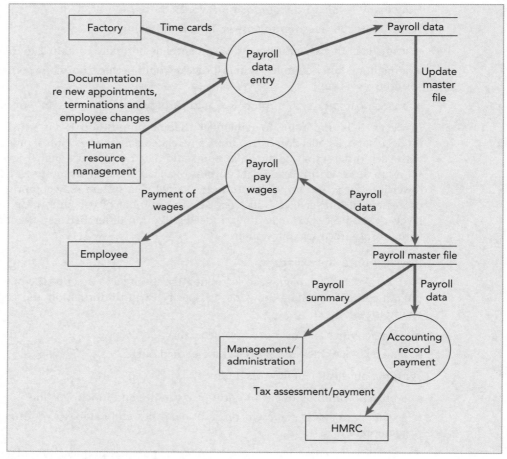

Figure 6.11 Physical data flow diagram

- Draw a level 1 diagram to illustrate the main functional areas of the system under investigation; and where necessary
- Draw a level 2 diagram to illustrate processes not fully explored in the level 1 diagram.

Of course, where appropriate, further decomposition of the level 2 data flow diagram into lower level(s) may be useful.

To ensure data flows are clearly presented, it is important – where possible – to:

- combine processes,[22]
- exclude minor data flows,[23]
- combine external entities, and
- combine data stores.

Are there any general data flow diagram conventions?

Yes, there are essentially five key conventions:

1 The entity rule – that is, an entity must be either a source of data input or a destination for data outputs.

2 The process rule – that is, a process must have both input flows and output flows.

3 The data store rule – that is, data stores must have both input flows and output flows.

4 The data from rule – that is, data flows from a source entity and/or a data store must flow into a process.

5 The data to rule – that is, data flows to a destination entity and/or a data store must flow out of a process.

Remember when drawing a data flow diagram:

■ think logical, not physical, and

■ think data flow, not control process.

Assessing the flow within a data flow diagram

Once a data flow diagram has been prepared, as a representation of a system/process it is, of course, necessary to assess the appropriateness and effectiveness of the data flow.

Why? Put simply, to identify any possible data flow inefficiencies and/or weaknesses. In general, such an assessment would involve posing the following questions:

■ Are all data flows sufficiently analysed?

■ Are all processes decomposed to an appropriate level?

■ Are all processes appropriately labelled?

■ Do all decomposed processes in lower level data flow diagrams portray the same net inputs and outputs as their higher level representations – that is, is there consistency between higher level and lower level data flows?

■ Do all data travelling in the same data flow travel together? If not, why not?

■ Do all data stores have an input data flow? If not, why not?

■ Are there any *black holes* – that is, are there any processes with only input data flows?

■ Are there any *miracles* – that is, are there any processes with only output data flows?

■ Are there any *grey holes* – that is, does every process possess an appropriate/matching level of inflows/outflows?

■ Are all data flows connected to two elements – a process and a terminator or a data store or another process? If not, why not?

■ Do any data flow to a process where they are not used and/or are not required? If so, why?

What are the advantages and disadvantages of data flow diagrams?

The advantages of data flow diagrams are:

■ They are simple and easy to understand.

■ They are a powerful technique for defining the parameters/boundaries of a system/ process.

■ They provide a dynamic representation of a system/process from the viewpoint of data flows/movements.

■ They can be used to represent/analyse a system/process at different levels of detail.

The disadvantages of data flow diagrams are:

- They can be time-consuming to create/develop.
- They can become overly complex.
- They can sometimes be difficult to revise.

Flowcharts

A flowchart is essentially a picture – a map of a process or a flow or a system. More precisely it is a diagrammatic representation of a system, or a computer program, or a document flow, and, as such, can be used for a variety of purposes, for example:

- to identify the logic of a system, computer program, or document flow;
- to identify and/or define a system, computer program, or document flow boundary;
- to identify system, computer program and/or document flow redundancies and/or delays;
- to identify possible areas of improvement; and
- to develop a common understanding about a system, computer program, or document flow.

What symbols are used in flowcharting?

There are a vast number of symbols used in flowcharting, the most common being:

- An oval – to indicate both the start and end of a process, a flow or a system.
- A box – to represent an individual activity within a process, a flow or a system.
- A diamond – to illustrate a decision point.
- A circle – to indicate a connection of a particular activity within a process, a flow or a system to another activity within another process, flow or system.
- A triangle – to indicate a file, or store of data/information.
- A document – to indicate the source of data.
- A flow line – to indicate the directional path of a process, a flow or a system.

But there are many, many more (see Figure 6.12).

What types of flowchart are there?

We can distinguish different types of flowcharts in two ways:

1 by level of detail,
2 by type/category.

Flowcharts distinguished by level of detail

There are essentially three different levels of detail:

1 A macro-level flowchart.
2 A midi-level flowchart.
3 A micro-level flowchart.

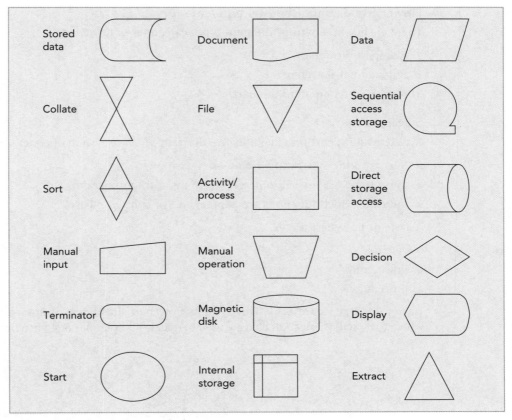

Figure 6.12 Flowchart – symbols

Macro-level flowchart

A macro-level flowchart is, in a management context, a strategic level flowchart. It is designed to show the big picture – or, more appropriately, the organisational context of a system, a process and/or a document flow. For example, such a flowchart may be used to document/record a company's transaction processing system.

Midi-level flowchart

A midi-level flowchart is a tactical level flowchart and typically focuses on a single part/segment of the macro-level flowchart. For example, it may be used to focus on the document flow within the revenue cycle of a company's transaction processing system.

Micro-level flowchart

The micro-level flowchart is essentially an operational level flowchart designed to illustrate/provide a very detailed picture of a specific portion/segment of system, computer program or document flow, its aim being to document/record every action, every flow and every decision. Such flowcharts are commonly used when assessing levels of internal control within a system, process and/or document flow. For example, such a flowchart may be used to focus on the internal controls within the debtors systems of a company's revenue cycle.

Flowcharts distinguished by type/category

There are essentially three different types/categories of flowchart:

1 A systems flowchart.
2 A document flowchart.
3 A program/computer flowchart.

Systems flowchart

A systems flowchart provides a logical diagram of *how* a system operates, and:

- illustrates the system in a step-by-step fashion,
- illustrates the conversion process from input to output, and
- indicates which functions are manual and/or computer-based.

A systems flowchart is:

- vertical,
- linear, and
- procedural.

Have a look at Figure 6.13. This systems flowchart illustrates a transaction process in which (batched) transaction data are used to update a Master file. Such batched transactions

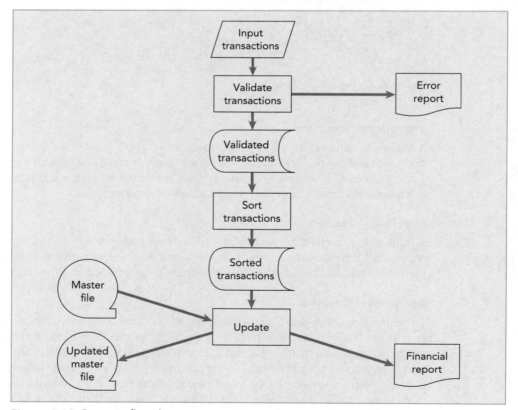

Figure 6.13 Systems flowchart

could be sales transactions used to update a customer (debtor) Master file, or purchase transactions used to update a supplier (creditor) Master file.

Document flowchart

A document flowchart illustrates the flow of documentation and information within a system – from origin to destination – and is concerned with:

- *how* the document flow occurs,
- *what* documents flow, and
- *to and from whom* the documents flow.

A document flowchart is:

- horizontal,
- columnar, and
- documentary.

Have a look at Figure 6.14. This document flowchart (based on a small York-based manufacturing company) illustrates a sales transaction in which:

1 A customer order is received.
2 A sales order is prepared.
3 A customer credit check is performed.
4 A sales invoice is issued (if credit check successful) and authorised.
5 Stock records are updated.
6 A despatch order is issued.
7 A bill of lading is prepared (where necessary).

Program/computer flowchart

A program/computer flowchart provides an illustration of the processing stages within a computer-based system, for example a batch processing system, or an on-line processing, or a real-time processing system.

A program/computer flowchart is:

- vertical,
- linear, and
- procedural.

Have a look at Figure 6.15. This program/computer flowchart shows a transaction process in which transaction data are used to update a Master file record. Such transactions could be detail amendments (address, contact details, etc.) to a customer Master file record.

Which type of flowchart is most commonly used?

In accounting information systems, the most commonly used flowcharts are:

- a systems flowchart (also known as a procedural flowchart), and
- a document flowchart.

Such flowcharts can be used to illustrate/record the flow of resources and/or information within a system and/or process – an important aspect of which is an indication as to

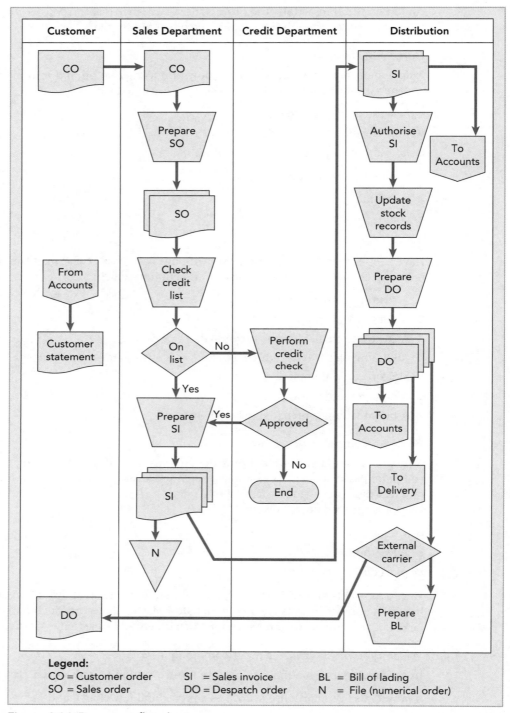

Figure 6.14 Document flowchart

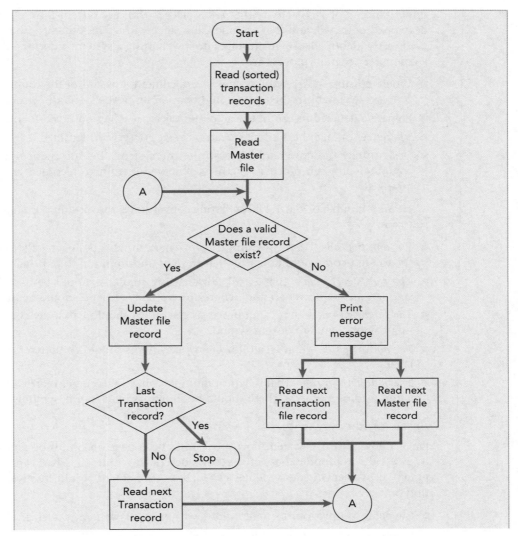

Figure 6.15 Program/computer flowchart

whether a set of procedures or a flow of documents within a system/process incorporate appropriate:

■ authorisation procedures,

■ custody procedures,

■ control procedures, and

■ recording procedures.

Drawing a flowchart

While there are many alternative ways in which a system, a document, and/or a program/ computer flowchart can be constructed, and indeed a vast range of software programs available with which to draw such a flowchart, it is, nonetheless, important that a clear understanding of each activity that takes place within the system/flow and/or process is developed/obtained, and that each decision stage within the system/flow and/or process is correctly identified. The main stages in flowcharting a system, a document flow and/or a computer program/process are:

- Where possible, observe the system, the document flow and/or the computer program/process – to establish the context and boundaries of the system/flow/process.
- Prepare a detailed record of the activities/decision stages observed/identified.
- Sequence/arrange the activities/decision stages observed/identified.
- Design/draw the flowchart, representing the system, the document flow and/or the computer program/process exactly as observed/identified, recorded and sequenced/arranged.

There are a number of general flowcharting conventions; the most important conventions/rules are:

- *The direction rule* – that is, within the flowchart, flows should generally commence on the top left corner and flow from left to right and from top to bottom.
- *The consistency rule* – that is, all flowcharting symbols should be used consistently throughout the flowchart and, where appropriate, a legend should be provided.
- *The sandwich rule* – that is, all processing symbols should be sandwiched between an input symbol and an output symbol.
- *The narrative rule* – that is, all flowcharting symbols should contain a brief descriptive label.
- *The multiple copy rule* – that is, where multiple copies of documents are used in a system, a flow and/or a process, these should be shown as overlapping symbols.

Assessing the flow within a flowchart

Once a flowchart of a system/flow/process has been developed, it is of course important to assess the appropriateness of the flows described within the chart, and identify any potential problems/issues/weaknesses. Such an assessment would involve an examination of:

- the data/information/document flows within the flowchart, to identify:
  - any redundant activities/flows,
  - any processing obstructions and/or weak processing connections,
  - any poorly defined flows, and
  - non-value-adding flows,
- each decision-making event within the flowchart, to identify:
  - any irrelevant decision-making events, and/or
  - non-value-adding decision-making events,
- each activity within the flowchart, to identify:
  - any unnecessary activities,
  - any repeat activities,
  - any poorly defined activities, and
  - any cost only activities, and
- each activity/decision-making loop within the flowchart, to identify any redundant loops.

What are the advantages and disadvantages of flowcharts?

The advantages of flowcharts are:

- they can be drawn with little experience,
- they record the system, program or document flow in its entirety, and
- they eliminate the need for extensive notes.

The disadvantages of flowcharts are:

- they are generally only suitable for standard systems/processes/flows, and
- they are generally only useful for dynamic systems/processes/flows.

Entity-relationship diagram

The entity-relationship diagram is a diagrammatic representation of what is commonly referred to as an entity-relationship model, an approach to data modelling developed in 1976 by Peter Chen, which uses two logical criteria: an entity and a relationship.

An entity

An entity[24] is essentially something that exists – in the form of resources, events, and agents, that is, something that can be identified by means of its *attributes*: the unique characteristics that distinguish one entity (or an entity set/type[25]) from another entity.

An entity can be classified as:

1 an independent (or strong) entity – that is, an entity that does not rely on another entity for identification, or

2 a dependent (or weak) entity – that is, an entity that does rely on another entity for identification, or

3 an associative entity (also known as an intersection entity) – that is, an entity used to associate two or more entities in order to reconcile a many-to-many relationship (see below).

Attributes

An attribute describes the entity to which it is associated – attributes which apply to all occurrences of the entity/entity type. Attributes can be classified as either an identifier, or a descriptor. Whereas an identifier – more commonly referred to as a key – uniquely identifies an entity, a descriptor describes a non-unique characteristic of an entity.

A given attribute belonging to a given entity occurrence can only have one value.

The primary key is the attribute (or group of attributes) that serve(s) to uniquely identify an entity. Where two or more data items are used as the unique identifier this is referred to as a compound key. If several possible primary keys exist, such keys are referred to as candidate keys, and where an attribute of one entity is a candidate key for another entity, it is termed a foreign key.

A relationship

A relationship is an association between two entities and/or entity types. Such relationships are classified in terms of *degree*, *connectivity*, *cardinality*, and *direction*.

Degree of a relationship

The degree of a relationship can be defined as the number of entities associated with the relationship.

A binary relationship exists where an association between 2 entities exists.[26] A recursive binary relationship exists where an entity is related to itself – for example, a company employee may be married to another company employee. An n-ary relationship exists where an association between more than 2 entities exists.[27] Such relationships are generally composed of 2 or more interacting binary relationships.

Connectivity and cardinality

The connectivity of a relationship describes the mapping of an entity relationship. The basic types of connectivity are:

- 1-to-1 – referred to as (1:1),
- 1-to-many – referred to as (1:N),
- many-to-many – referred to as (M:N).

The cardinality of a relationship defines the maximum number of entities/entity types that can be associated with an entity/entity type.

Let's have a look at this in a little more detail.

A **1-to-1 (1:1)** relationship occurs when entity A is associated with entity B, and entity B is associated with entity A. An example of a 1-to-1 relationship would be where the managers of a company are allocated to an individual personal office. For each manager there exists a unique office, and for each office there exists a unique manager.

A **1-to-many (1:N)** relationship occurs when, for entity A, there are 0 or 1 or many instances of entity B, but for entity B there is only 1 instance of entity A. An example of a 1:N relationship would be where a department within a company employs many employees – but each employee can only be employed by/in a single department.

A **many-to-many (M:N)** relationship occurs when for entity A, there are 0 or 1 or many instances of entity B, and conversely for entity B there are 0 or 1 or many instances of entity A. An example of a many-to-many relationship would be where an internal auditor can be assigned to no more than 3 audit projects at the same time, and where individual audit projects are required to have at least 4 assigned internal auditors. That is, an individual internal auditor can be assigned to many audit projects, and an individual audit project can have many internal auditors assigned to it. Here the cardinality for the relationship between internal auditors and audit projects is 3 and the cardinality between audit projects and internal auditors is 4.

Each of the above types of connectivity can be represented diagrammatically (see Figure 6.16).

The direction of a relationship

The direction of a relationship indicates the originating entity of a binary relationship. The entity from which a relationship originates is often referred to as the *parent entity*, and the entity at which the relationship terminates is – somewhat unsurprisingly – often referred to as the *child entity*.

An identifying relationship is a relationship in which the child entity is also a dependent entity, whereas a non-identifying relationship is one in which both entities are independent.

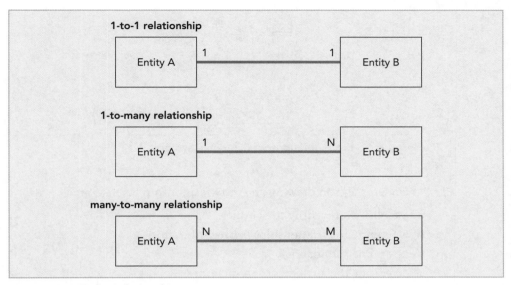

Figure 6.16 Entity relationships

So how is the direction of a relationship determined? The direction of a relationship is determined by its connectivity. For example:

- in a 1-to-1 relationship the direction of the relationship would be from the independent entity to a dependent entity,[28]
- in a 1-to-many relationship, the entity occurring once is the parent entity, and the direction of the relationship would be from the parent entity to the other children entities, and
- in a many-to-many relationship, the direction of the relationship would be arbitrary.

Existence

Existence denotes whether the existence of an entity is dependent upon the existence of another entity. The existence of an entity in a relationship can be defined as either optional or mandatory.[29] For example:

- if an entity must always occur for an entity to be included in a relationship, then the relationship is considered mandatory, or
- if an entity is not required, then the relationship is considered optional.

Drawing an entity-relationship diagram

What notation is used in entity-relationship diagrams?

Although various symbols are used in entity-relation diagrams, the most common are shown in Figure 6.17. These are:

- A square – to indicate an entity.
- An oval – to represent an attribute.
- A diamond – to portray a relationship.
- An arrow – to portray a connection/link.

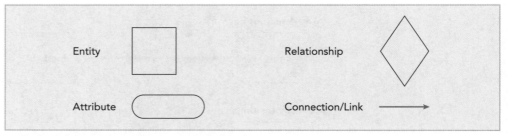

Figure 6.17 Entity-relationship diagram – symbols

The main stages in drawing an entity-relationship diagram are:

- establish and identify the entities,
- determine the relationships between the entities,
- determine cardinality,
- determine the attributes for each entity,
- select and define the primary key for each entity,
- compose an entity-relationship diagram, and
- test the relationships and the keys.

Figure 6.18 provides an illustration of a generic entity-relationship diagram.

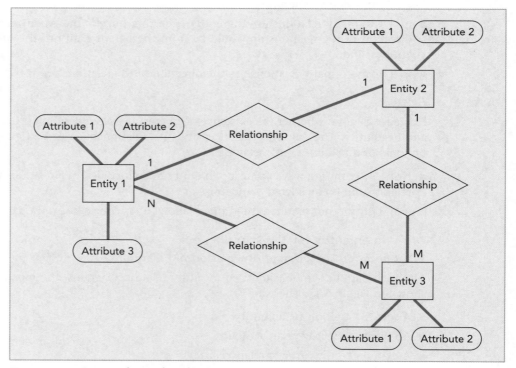

Figure 6.18 Entity-relationship diagram

Test the relationships and the keys

Once an entity-relationship diagram has been drawn, it is of course important to test the relationship and keys, and assess the appropriateness of the entity-relationship diagram. Such an assessment/test would involve an examination to determine if, for example:

- all entities have been correctly identified,
- all attributes have been correctly identified,
- all attributes have been associated with the correct entity, and
- all cardinality pairs are appropriate.

What are the advantages and disadvantages of entity-relationship diagrams?

The advantages of entity-relationship diagrams are:

- they are simple and easy to understand, and
- they are a powerful technique for defining the relationships within a system.

The main disadvantages are:

- they can become overly complex,
- they can be difficult to interpret, and
- they can sometimes be difficult to revise.

Decision tables

As we have seen, while flowcharts – in particular program flowcharts – can be used to provide a representation of a system, procedure or process, such a descriptive technique may not always be suitable, especially when attempting to describe a complex decision process. An accepted alternative to flowcharting a system, procedure or process is to construct a decision table – although, in practice, such tables are often used in addition to, rather than instead of, such flowcharts.

What is a decision table?

A decision table is a table designed to represent the logic of an activity, and illustrate the possible combinations of available outcomes. Such tables are typically divided into four quadrants (see Figure 6.19):

1 Conditions.
2 Condition alternatives.
3 Actions.
4 Action entries.

In the decision table:

- each condition corresponds to a variable whose possible values are listed among the condition alternatives, and
- each action is a procedure or operation to perform with each action entry specifying whether and/or in what order the action is to be performed.

Constructing a decision table

To construct a decision table, it is important to determine the maximum size of the table, eliminate any improbable situations, contradictions, inconsistencies or redundancies, and simplify the decision table as much as possible. That is:

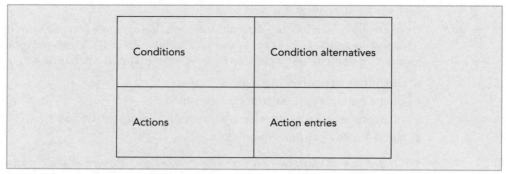

Figure 6.19 Decision table

- Determine the number of conditions that may affect the decision – the number of conditions becomes the number of rows in the top half of the decision table.
- Determine the number of possible actions that can be taken – the number of actions becomes the number of rows in the lower half of the decision table.
- Determine the number of condition alternatives for each condition.[30]
- Calculate the maximum number of columns in the decision table by multiplying the number of alternatives for each condition – for example, if there were 4 conditions and 2 alternatives for each of the conditions (yes or no), there would be 16 possibilities.

Consider the following example:

ABW plc is a UK-based company supplying specialised building materials to the UK building industry. ABW plc allows customers 30 days' credit, and calculates customer discounts and charges as follows:

- If the total value of the order is in excess of £2,500 and the invoice is paid within 10 days of the invoice date a discount of 5 per cent is received – payments made after day 10 do not attract a discount.
- If the total weight of the order is in excess of 500 kg, special delivery containers are used, for which a charge is made – if the value of the building materials order is in excess of £2,500 no charge is made for the special delivery containers.
- If the customer requests delivery outside the UK, an additional charge is imposed – if the value of the building materials order is in excess of £2,500 no charge is made for the overseas delivery.

How is a decision table to represent the above customer policy constructed?

Because this is a simple binary decision table in which the decision rule is yes (Y), or no (N), the number of possible conditions is: [(2 alternatives for condition 1) × (2 alternatives for condition 2) × (2 alternatives for condition 3) × (2 alternatives for condition 4)] or = (2^4) = 16. See Table 6.1.

In Table 6.1:

- The possible conditions are:
  - payment within 10 days,
  - cost in excess of £2,500,
  - weight in excess of 500 kg, and
  - overseas delivery.

Table 6.1 AWB plc decision table (version 1)

	1	2	3	4	5	6	7	8	9	10	11	12	13	14	15	16
Payment within 10 days	Y	Y	Y	Y	Y	Y	Y	Y	N	N	N	N	N	N	N	N
Cost in excess of £2,500	Y	Y	Y	Y	N	N	N	N	Y	Y	Y	Y	N	N	N	N
Weight in excess of 500 kg	Y	Y	N	N	Y	Y	N	N	Y	Y	N	N	Y	Y	N	N
Overseas delivery	Y	N	Y	N	Y	N	Y	N	Y	N	Y	N	Y	N	Y	N
Discount	X	X	X	X												
Delivery charge					X		X		X		X		X		X	
Container charge					X	X							X	X		

- The condition alternatives (of which there are 16 possibilities) are indicated with a Y (yes) or N (no).
- The possible actions are:
  - discount,
  - delivery charge, and
  - container charge.
- The possible action entries are indicated with an X.

To simplify this decision table, first we can eliminate column 8, column 10, column 12, and column 16 – there are no actions to be implemented. Second, we can apply the dash rule to columns where existing pairs can be merged – that is, where an alternative does not make a difference to the outcome. The dash (–) signifies that a condition can be either yes (Y) or no (N), and action will still take place.

The revised decision table would look like Table 6.2.

Table 6.2 AWB plc decision table (version 2)

	1,2	3,4	5,13	6,14	7	9	11,15
Payment within 10 days	Y	Y	–	–	Y	N	N
Cost in excess of £2,500	Y	Y	N	N	N	Y	–
Weight in excess of 500 kg	Y	N	Y	Y	N	Y	N
Overseas delivery	–	–	Y	N	Y	Y	Y
Discount	X	X					
Delivery charge			X		X	X	X
Container charge			X	X			

We can apply the dash rule again to produce a further simplified and final decision table – see Table 6.3.

Table 6.3 AWB plc decision table (version 3)

	1,2,3,4	5,13	6,14	7	9, 11,15
Payment within 10 days	Y	–	–	Y	N
Cost in excess of £2,500	Y	N	N	N	–
Weight in excess of 500 kg	–	Y	Y	N	–
Overseas delivery	–	Y	N	Y	Y
Discount	X				
Delivery charge		X		X	X
Container charge		X	X		

What are the advantages and disadvantages of decision tables?

The advantages of using decision tables are:

■ they provide a simple and understandable summary of the processing tasks/actions for a large number of conditions, and,

■ they can be easily amended when changes in organisation policies/procedures result in the development/emergence of new tasks/action for existing conditions.

The main disadvantages are:

■ they do not provide details of the order in which tasks/actions and conditions can/do occur, and,

■ whilst they can be easily amended, they can become overly complex, and difficult to interpret.

Coding systems

A code can be defined in many ways, for example as:

■ a collection of rules or principles or law (such as a legal code), or

■ an organised collection of instructions (such as a computer code), or

■ an arbitrary compilation of symbols and/or characters (such as a security/access code), or

■ a structured arrangement of alpha-numeric characters (such as an information code).

For our purposes, we will use the latter, and define a code as a system of alpha-numeric characters used to represent a data/information set.

Where such codes are used to facilitate the accumulation, storage and transfer of data and/or information, this is referred to as *encoding*. Where such codes are used to control, protect, or restrict access to data and/or information, the term *encryption* is applied.

In accounting information systems, a code/coding system may be:

■ numeric (or number-based) – for example, a credit card/debit card number, or a network IP address,

■ alphabetic (or letter-based) – for example a computer network username and/or password, and/or

■ alpha-numeric (or letter- and number-based) – for example, a customer reference number and/or an employee's payroll reference number.

In a commercial/business context, coding systems – for encoding purposes – can be classified as either chart-of-accounts-based codes or non-chart-of-accounts-based codes.

Before we look at each of these in a little more detail, it would perhaps be useful to first consider the following question: What are the characteristics of a good coding system?

In general, the characteristics of a good code and/or coding system are:

■ A coding system must have a clearly defined structure.

■ A coding system must be sufficiently flexible to cope with expansion.

■ A coding system must be adaptable to user needs.

■ A coding system should be meaningful.

■ Each individual code within the coding system must have a unique identity.

- Each individual code within the coding system should be sequential.
- Each individual code must be universal and standard (within a company).
- Each individual code should be as short as possible (where human interface is expected).

Chart-of-accounts-based codes

A chart of accounts is the coding system (structure) adopted within a company and/or an organisation for the purposes of processing accounting-related data, the purpose of such a coding system being to provide a means of:

- classifying income and expenditure,
- classifying capital and revenue transactions, and
- managing/controlling the recording of accounting transactions.

More importantly, a chart of accounts should provide a structured framework for:

- the interpretation and analysis of transaction-based/accounting-related information (a financial accounting function),
- the management of transaction-based/accounting-related resources (a financial management function), and
- the determination and allocation of transaction-based/accounting-related responsibilities (a management accounting function).

Who determines the structure of a company's/organisation's chart of accounts?

Although in some countries there is a formally imposed chart of accounts used by all companies[31] – for example, the French *Plan Comptable*, or the Spanish *Plan General de Contabilidad* – in the UK, and many other Anglo-Saxon countries, there is no such imposed formal requirement. In such countries, charts of accounts tend to be developed independently – on a company by company and/or an organisation by organisation basis. As a result, the nature and structure of a company's/organisation's chart of accounts are often be determined by internal management policy – albeit with significant input from the financial accountant – with such charts of accounts generally seeking to match/combine:

- the organisational/operational structure of the company, and
- the regulatory structure of the company's financial statements.

It is for the latter reason that many company charts of account appear to be very similar.

Consider the following:

All companies within the European Union are bound by, and required to adopt, extant directives which comprise the EU company law regulatory framework. In particular, all countries within the EU have adopted the EU 4th directive, which provides prescribed formats for company Profit and Loss Accounts and Balance Sheets. For example:

- In the UK, the required formats were adopted via the UK company law framework.
- In Germany, the required formats were adopted via the German commercial code (the German *Handelsgesetzbuch (HGB)*).
- In France, the required formats were adopted via the French accounting plan (the French *Plan Comptable*).

Furthermore, as of 2010, listed companies on many of the largest stock exchanges (including all the major EU-based exchanges) are required to adhere to additional reporting requirements as prescribed by IASC International Financial Reporting Standards – in particular IFRS 1.

Non-chart-of-accounts codes

Of course, companies use a range of codes other than those we have referred to above for a variety of different purposes. For example, a company may use a code:

■ as a unique identifier – for example, a product bar code, or an employee's payroll number; and/or

■ for the compression data – for example, an abbreviated product/service name; and/or

■ for the classification of data/collection of transactions – for example, a debtor/creditor reference; and/or

■ for the communication of a special meaning – for example access/security codes.

Databases

Although a database can, broadly speaking, be defined as an organised collection of data, or perhaps, more appropriately, a logical and systematic collection of interrelated data that is managed and stored as a single unit, in general a collection of data is only considered to constitute a database if:

■ the data are *managed* to ensure data integrity and maintain data quality,

■ the data are *organised* into an accepted and agreed schema,

■ the data can be *accessed* by a shared community of approved users/user applications, and/or

■ the data can be *interrogated* using an appropriate query language.[32]

Why have databases become so important in the management of transactions-related data?

There are many reasons, perhaps the most important being:

■ the increasing volumes of transactions-related data,

■ the complexity and interconnectedness of such data,

■ the inherent business value of accurate transactions-related data, and

■ the security and privacy restrictions imposed on the management of transactions-related data.

First, a (very) brief history!

Databases – a (very) brief history

Although the collection of data in the form of lists and/or tables can be traced back to the Sumerians of Mesopotamia, the earliest known use of the term data base (as two words) was in the early 1960s,[33] and use of the term database (as a single word) did not become commonplace in the UK and Europe until the early 1970s.

During the latter part of the 1960s, two key data models arose:

1 The network model – based on the work and ideas of Charles Bachman.[34]
2 The hierarchical model – used and developed by Rockwell Industries.

It was at about the same time that Charles Bachman began development of the first database management systems.

The relational model was first proposed by Edgar F. Codd in 1970,[35] and although research prototype databases using the relational model were announced as early as 1976,[36] the first commercial products did not appear until the early 1980s.[37]

During the latter part of the 1980s research activity focused on distributed database systems, with the 1990s seeing attention shift toward object-oriented databases. The early twenty-first century has witnessed a consolidation of database technologies, together with extensive development research in the increasingly fashionable area of XML[38] databases.

Databases – alternative data models

As suggested above, there are a number of alternative data models developed for, and used to structure, data within a database. A data model is simply an abstract description of *how* data is represented/related in a database. Such alternatives include:

- the flat data model,
- the hierarchical data model,
- the network data model,
- the relational data model, and
- the object-oriented data model.

Flat data model

Using the flat data model, data in a database are stored in a two-dimensional table: a single database record per line, with data divided into fields using delimiters or fixed column positions, with no relationships or links between records and fields except the database table structure.

Although databases using the flat data model are simple and easy to maintain, and ideal for small amounts of data, it can be difficult to use them to store complex data, with often multiple copies of the same data being stored, and costly to process and collate large amounts of data.

An example of a flat file database would be a table and/or list of debtor names and addresses.

Hierarchical data model

Using the hierarchical data model, data within a database are organised into a tree-like structure using a parent/child arrangement inasmuch as data are related to each other using a 1-to-many (1:N) relationship. Although the hierarchical data model was widely used in early database systems, it is now rare, mainly because of its inability to accurately model real-world relationships.

Consider the following example:
GHK Ltd is a small Manchester-based retail company specialising in children's games and toys. The company maintains personal records on all employees. In addition the

company also maintains records of any children the employee may have. That is, there is:

- a collection of employee details as a record type called Employees, and

- a collection of children details as a record type called Children.

Using a hierarchical data model, the Employees would represent the parent segment of the hierarchy, and the Children would represent the child segment of the hierarchy. That is, an employee may have many children, but each child can have only have one parent. But . . . what if both the mother *and* the father of the child were employees of GHK Ltd? That would mean the 1-to-many (1:N) relationship central to the hierarchical data model would be violated.

Why? Because not only can an employee have more than one child, a child can have more than one parent! The relationship is therefore a many-to-many (M:N) relationship and, effectively, the hierarchy becomes a network.

Network data model

Conceived and developed by Charles Bachman (the standard specification was published in 1969 by CODASYL,[39] the network model[40] allows an entity type to have multiple parent and child relationships – that is, many-to-many (M:N) relationships, forming what is often referred to as a lattice-type structure. At the foundation of the network model is the so-called 'set construct' – a set consists of an owner record type, a set name and a member record type, with a member record type able to belong to more than one set, hence the multi-parent concept.

An owner record type can also be a member or owner in another set.

Although the network data model was widely implemented, it failed to gain popular support and become the dominant data model – perhaps for two reasons. First, many companies elected to use the hierarchical model in their products rather than the network data model (for example, IBM Inc., and their Information Management System) and, second, the capabilities of the network model were eventually surpassed by development and widespread acceptance of the relational data model.

Relational data model

Using the relational data model, data within a database are organised and accessed according to the relationships between data. Such relationships are expressed by means of two-dimensional tables,[41] which can be used to store data without reference to and/or consideration of any other physical orientation and relationship.

We will look at the relational data model and its use/application in relational databases in a little more detail later in this chapter.

Object-oriented data model

A key problem with each of the above data models is their limited ability to store only alpha and/or numeric text-based data. Using the object-oriented data model, complex data types such as video graphics, pictures, and three-dimensional representations can be stored, often using a traditional hierarchical arrangement in which lower class objects (called sub class objects) are related to, and can inherit attributes from, higher class objects (called super class objects).

Understanding databases – elements of a database environment

Within a database environment, there are five separate elements:

1 The database schema.
2 The database audience.
3 The database management system (DBMS).
4 The database administration system (DBAS).[42]
5 The physical database.

Database schema

A database schema is essentially a structural narrative describing the logical structure of the database – that is:

■ the type of data held within a database – in other words, the objects/facts represented in the database, and

■ the structure/organisation of data stored within a database – that is, the relationships between each of the objects/facts represented in the database.

While there are, as suggested earlier, a number of alternative approaches (or data models) that can be used to structure/organise data within a database, there are essentially three levels to any data model/schema:

1 The external level schema.
2 The conceptual level schema.
3 The internal level schema.

Database audience

There are three broad classes of users within the database audience:

1 The application programmer – responsible for creating, altering, amending and managing the database.
2 The database administrator (via the database administration system) – responsible for controlling all operations within the database.
3 The end-users, who access the database via the database management systems using either:
    (a) a predefined user program, and/or
    (b) a direct query using an appropriate query language.

Database management system (DBMS)

The database management system is the interface which coordinates the various data transactions between the database and users/user applications. The database management system provides a link between the way data are physically stored and each user's/user application's logical view of the data, and as such, is responsible for:

■ controlling the organisation of data[43] within the database,

■ monitoring the storage, and retrieval, of data from the database,

- managing the transfer/movement of data between the database and authorised users/ user applications, and
- applying appropriate authorisation checks and validation procedures to maintain the security and integrity of the data within the database.

Database management system – as a control facility

The database management system provides two types of control often referred to as *transaction control* and *concurrency control*.

Transaction control

One of the key control functions of a database management system is to enforce a database transaction model/processes that possess appropriate data integrity properties.

Concurrency control

In a database management system, concurrency control is concerned with the management of database transactions and is used to:

- ensure transactions are executed in a safe and secure manner,
- ensure transactions are not lost when recovering failed and/or aborted transactions,
- ensure transactions follow the ACID[44] rules, and
- ensure simultaneous users cannot edit/amend/delete the same data record at the same time.

Database administration system (DBAS)

The database administration system is responsible for the overall control of the database system/resource. Where there is sharing of a common database between communities of multiple users, the database administration system – in particular the database administrator – plays a vital role in:

- the planning, the design, and the implementation of the database environment,
- the maintenance of all database facilities, and
- the management and coordination of database-related activities.

Why? Because such sharing requires control – more specifically, to protect the integrity and ensure the security of the database resource, such sharing requires:

- the establishment of rules and regulations for the supervision of user/user application access,
- the development of operational guidelines and procedures for the coordination of user/user application access, and
- the creation of appropriate processes and protocols for the management of database change.[45]

Physical database

While it is of course necessary for a database to possess an identifiable physicality, it is important to note that, in reality, the physical database will often bear little relation to the logical structure of the database.

Why? Because, as new and more efficient storage technologies develop, as new and more effective storage media becomes available, so the physical structure/physical nature of the database will change. Such change will not necessarily affect the logical structure of the database.

What would comprise the physical database? It would have two components:

1 A physical structure in which to store the data – for example, sequential, non-sequential, indexed, etc.

2 A physical medium on which to store the database – for example, disc, tape etc.

Concluding comments

In a twenty-first-century business context, data have become a vital resource, with their acquisition and management now dominated by technologies that regularly facilitate the accumulation, processing and transfer of volumes of data that were unimaginable a generation ago. Indeed, there can be little doubt that the increasing availability and use of computer-based data capture, on-line processing, and computer-based data management (in particular database systems) has revolutionised contemporary understanding of the economic and political value of data.

Self-review questions

1 Distinguish between physical data input and non-physical data input.

2 Describe the main advantages of the data-orientated approach to data storage.

3 Define data redundancy, and distinguish between direct redundancy and indirect redundancy.

4 Distinguish between a data flow diagram and an entity-relationship diagram.

5 What are the main stages involved in constructing a decision table?

6 In an accounting information systems context, what is the purpose of a coding system/chart of accounts?

7 Explain the difference between a flat file data model, a hierarchical model, a network data model and a relational data model.

8 Describe and explain the role of a database management system.

References

Chen, P.P. (1976), 'The entity-relationship model: toward a unified view of data', in *ACM Transactions on Database Systems*, vol. 1:1, pp. 9–36.

Coad, P. and Yourdon, E. (1991), *Object-Oriented Systems Analysis*, Prentice Hall, New Jersey.

Codd, E.F. (1970), 'A relational model of data for large shared data banks', in *Communications of the ACM*, vol. 13(6), pp. 377–87.

Gane, C. and Sarson, T. (1979), *Structured System Analysis*, Prentice Hall, New Jersey.

Notes

1 Such processing is sometimes referred to as hybrid processing.

2 Using an appropriate GUI (Graphical User Interface).

3 Source data could include:

- text-based documents (printed or handwritten) – for example, internal memoranda, letters, surveys, reports, instruction manuals, business cards, index cards, etc.
- number-based documents – for example, financial statements, payroll records, time sheets;
- forms-based documents – for example, questionnaires, application forms of any kind (credit cards, loans, product registration, etc.);
- image-based documents – for example, photographs, charts and graphs; and
- mixed-format documents – for example, bank statements, credit card statements.

4 Data is the plural of the term datum.

5 Microfiche/microfilm are both compact analogue storage media that are still used in many research/library institutions.

6 The term storage is sometimes used (somewhat incorrectly in the author's opinion) interchangeably with the term memory. Where both terms are in used, the term memory is generally used for the faster forms of storage, and the term storage is generally used for the slower forms of storage.

7 For example RAM or random access memory.

8 In a limited sense, the terms 'attribute' and 'data element' can be, and indeed often are, used interchangeably.

9 Although the example data value is purely numeric, it is also possible that the data value could be a combination of numeric and alphabetic characters – for example a UK postcode.

10 Remember for some types of data, specific legal requirements may apply – for example the Data Protection Act 1998, and the Limitations Act 1980.

11 Data set can be defined as a set of data elements bearing a logical relationship, which is organised in prescribed manner.

12 Indeed, a number of anecdotal studies on users of computer-based information systems have suggested that severe access restrictions can also adversely affect data integrity – as users often attempt to find alternative means of access and/or alternative sources of data.

13 These are usually in the form of an exchange of economic consideration.

14 The processing cycle can be defined as the throughput processing period – from input to output. Such a throughput processing period can commence when:

- a specified batch content limit has been reached – for example, a batch of say 100 invoices;
- a specific time period has expired – for example every 7 days, or every 14 days;
- a specific date/time has been reached – for example the 19th day of each calendar month.

15 While it is of course possible for on-line processing to consist of four stages, for example:

(i) an input stage where individual data are input,

(ii) a collection stage where individual data are collected into a secure temporary data file,

(iii) a processing stage where the master file is updated, based on input of the controlled data file, and

(iv) an output stage,

the use and popularity of such on-line processing has declined significantly over recent years.

16 For example, the inefficient/inequitable allocation of resources and/or distribution of information.

17 Because distributed systems provide dedicated resources for user processes, response times can be greatly reduced.

18 Two common variations to data flow diagram notation are for example, (i) the Gane and Sarson notation (see Gane, C. and Sarson, T. (1979), *Structured System Analysis*, Prentice Hall,

New Jersey), and (ii) the Coad and Yourdon notation (see Coad, P. and Yourdon, E. (1991), *Object-Oriented Systems Analysis*, Prentice Hall, New Jersey).

19 This notation is based on the Coad and Yourdon (1991) data flow diagram notation.

20 Alternatively, the Gane and Sarson data flow diagram notation provides the following:

- A square – to indicate an entity.
- A rounded square – to portray a process.
- An open box – to indicate a data store/file.
- An arrow – to portray a the direction of a data flow.

21 In a physical data flow diagram there can be a number of alternative types of data stores, for example:

- permanent computerised data store/file,
- temporary (or transient) computerised data store/file,
- permanent manual data store/file, and
- temporary (or transient) manual data store/file.

22 As a general rule no business process diagram should contain more than 12 process boxes.

23 For example, where data are to be retrieved from a data store, it is not necessary to show the selection criteria used to retrieve them.

24 A regular entity is an entity of independent existence – that is, any physical object, event and/ or abstract concept on which factual data can be obtained. A weak entity is an entity of dependent existence – that is, an entity whose existence is dependent on another entity.

25 An entity set (or entity type) is a collection of similar entities.

26 This is the most common type of relationship.

27 Often referred to as a general entity relationship model (GERM).

28 Where both entities are independent, the direction of the relationship is arbitrary.

29 These are often referred to as a relationship's *ordinality*.

30 In the simple decision table, there would be two condition alternatives – that is a yes or a no for each condition. In an extended-entry decision table, there could be many alternatives for each condition.

31 Such a chart of accounts is often imposed for macro-economic purposes – for the collection of statistical data by national governments.

32 A query language is computer language used to make enquiries into databases and/or information systems. Such query languages can, broadly speaking, be classified as either database query languages, or as information retrieval query languages. For example:

- SQL (Structured Query Language) is a well-known query language for relational databases, and
- DMX (Data Mining eXtentions) is a query language for data mining models.

33 For example in the early 1960s the System Development Corporation (based in California, USA) sponsored a conference on the development of a computer-centred database. See *http://www.cbi. umn.edu/collections/inv/burros/cbi00090-098.html*.

34 Charles W. Bachman was a prominent computer scientist/industrial researcher in the area of databases. He received the Turing Award in 1973 for his work on database technologies, and was elected as a Distinguished Fellow of the British Computer Society in 1977 for his pioneering work in database systems.

35 Codd, E.F. (1970), 'A relational model of data for large shared data banks', in *Communications of the ACM*, vol. 13(6), pp. 377–87. This paper is available at *http://www.acm.org/classics/nov95/ toc.html*.

36 For example, the System R project at IBM.

37 For example, Oracle and DB2.

38 eXtensible Markup Language – a special purpose markup language capable of describing many different kinds of data.

39 CODASYL, or Conference on Data Systems Languages, was an IT industry consortium formed in 1959 to guide the development of a standard programming language that could be used on many computers. Their discussions eventually resulted in the development of COBOL. Although some derivative CODASYL committees continue to the present day, CODASYL itself no longer exists, with interest in CODASYL fading in the early 1980s due to growing interest in relational databases.

40 As defined by the CODASYL specification.

41 Using the relational data model, a table can be defined as a collection of records, with each record in a table containing the same fields.

42 In some smaller companies database administration is sometimes undertaken by a single individual, the database administrator, whereas in larger companies it is often undertaken by a department of technical personnel.

43 Including data fields, data records and data files.

44 ACID (atomicity, consistency, isolation, durability) is a set of properties that guarantee database transactions are processed reliably.

45 Such change could of course relate to:
- structural change – that is, change to the database schema, and/or
- technological change – that is, change to the physical database, and/or
- definitional change – that is, change to either user access to the database resource and/or user rights to use the database resource.

CHAPTER 7

Accounting information systems – a cyclical perspective

Introduction

This chapter analyses the key features of contemporary transaction processing. It provides a contextual typology for the analysis and categorisation of contemporary transaction processing, and an analysis and extended discussion on how such a contextual typology can be used both to understand and to control the increasingly complex and dynamic operations of such companies.

Learning outcomes

By the end of this chapter, the reader should be able to:

- Describe the main features of contemporary transaction processing

- Distinguish between different transaction processing categories, types (and sub-types), cycles and systems

- Critically comment on the importance of such a contextual typology for understanding wealth-maximising organisations

- Describe and critically evaluate the key transaction processing factors that both enable and constrain wealth-maximising organisations

- Consider the implications of the Data Protection Act 1998 for contemporary transaction processing – especially transactions which result in the generation and storage of information covered by the requirements of the Act

Contemporary transaction processing

Clearly there can be little doubt that today's 'global' society is sustained through and increasingly dominated by the global priorities of capital: a marketplace in which the company as a created entity can and often does exercise both enormous power and enormous influence. Just think of the power and influence exercised by companies such as Microsoft Inc., Time Warner Inc., HSBC plc, Shell plc, and many other multi-listed, multinational companies.

And yet while companies (as created entities) have clearly become an important servicing component of the increasingly speculative logic of the competitive marketplace – and thus inseparable from the social, political and economic interests they serve – they are neither isolated nor protected from the international mobility of capital and temporal and spatial consequences of globalisation. Their priorities are constantly reupholstered, reconfigured and redistributed not only by the complex territoriality of inter-state politics or the social pressures of the labour market processes but, more crucially, by the competitive and often chaotic global priorities of an ever-changing marketplace.

There can be little doubt then that companies are increasingly conditioned by a vast array of competing social, economic and political constituencies. Indeed, whereas companies have undoubtedly become central to the globalising logic of capital as a vehicle through which once established social and economic sovereignties are reconfigured, redesigned and reinstalled, they have also – perhaps more importantly – become a mirror of the dominance of the socio-cultural baggage associated with Western capitalism and the marketisation of wealth, its desire to forge interrelationships and interdependencies and impose norms consistent with a self image. Furthermore, this is a self image founded on a distinctive historical geography in which social technologies are increasingly developed subordinate to the needs of a marketplace which is constantly changing, constantly evolving, constantly in a state of instability and unrest: a marketplace which, as a competitive forum for trade and exchange, remains the primary mechanism through which profits are generated and shareholder wealth is maximised – a mechanism whose inherent volatility continues to ensure its outcomes are random, chaotic and unpredictable. But always entertaining!

What has all this got to do with contemporary transaction processing?

Clearly, for purposes of growth, and indeed survival, companies (as semi-open systems) need to/have to interact with other companies, with other organisations, with other semi-open systems, within the environment or, more appropriately, within the marketplace. No matter how chaotic, how unstable, how unpredictable the market may be, such interaction is fundamental and lies at the very heart of market-based competition, wealth creation and profit maximisation. This interaction is more often than not achieved through a company's operations – through a company's market-based activities – through a company's transaction processing systems, and through the movement and/or exchange of both tangible and intangible assets and resources. How?

Consider the following:

A company acquires products, services and resources through a process of exchange, for:

■ other products, services and/or resources, or

■ legal title to other products, services, and/or resources, or

■ a legally enforceable promise to transfer legal title of other products, services, and/or resources (for example a promise to exchange assets) at a future agreed date.

When a company acquires products, services and resources:

■ sometimes such acquired products, services and resources are consumed internally to create other products, services and resources that can be exchanged externally (sold to other external organisations),

■ sometimes such acquired products, services and resources are converted and exchanged externally without any internal consumption, and

■ sometimes such acquired products, services and resources are merely stored (without any conversion – without any change) and then exchanged externally.

Clearly, the acquisition, consumption and/or disposal of such products, services and resources results in a present and/or future flow of funds. This flow of funds inevitably impacts on either:

■ short-term financing such as working capital, and/or

■ long-term financing such as equity or debt.

Sounds familiar? Of course it does! Contemporary transaction processing cycles and their related systems are merely a contextual representation – a physical expression – of:

■ what company accountants have for many years commonly referred to as the corporate financing cycle or corporate funding cycle, and

■ what company managers have for many years commonly referred to as the value cycle and/or the value chain.

See Figure 7.1.

Before we consider the relationship between the corporate funding cycle, value chain, value cycle and a company's transaction processing cycles and systems, it would perhaps be useful to a consider a few generic, albeit extremely important, characteristics of contemporary transaction processing cycles and systems – characteristics often regarded as the 'fundamentals' of transaction processing cycles and systems.

Such characteristics include:

■ flexibility,

■ adaptability,

■ reflexivity,

■ controllability, and

■ purposive context.

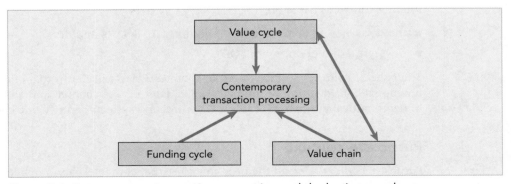

Figure 7.1 Contemporary transaction processing and the business cycle

Flexibility, adaptability and reflexivity

In a marketplace that is rarely constant, rarely stable, rarely predictable, the achievement of any objective/goal – for example increased market share and/or increased profitability and/or increased shareholder wealth – almost certainly requires not only flexibility and adaptability but, more importantly, reflexivity. Whereas flexibility can be defined as the ability of a company's processes and systems to respond quickly to changes in the business environment, adaptability can be defined as the ability to alter corporate structure, function and/or processes in response to changes in the environment. In relation to contemporary transaction processing cycles and systems, reflexivity can perhaps be best defined as movement, activity and/or change performed automatically and without conscious decision.

For contemporary transaction processing cycles and systems, such flexibility – such adaptability – such reflexivity – should seek to ensure that:

■ changes to operating structures, function and/or processes are relevant and appropriate, but more importantly,

■ fundamental functions and processes continue to cope with, and operate within, an increasingly unstable and uncertain environment.

Controllability

There can be little doubt that a central feature of success, a key component to continued survival – in a corporate context at least – is control. Contemporary transaction processing systems should contain, within their operational arrangements, appropriate structures to ensure:

■ the safe custody of products, services and resources,

■ the proper authorisation of exchange transactions,

■ the correct recording and accounting for exchange transactions,

■ the accurate execution and proper completion of exchange transactions, and

■ the appropriate control and management of exchange transactions.

Clearly, while flexibility, adaptability and reflexivity are essential prerequisites for continued survival, the importance of managing and controlling the impact of resource movements and exchange transactions is perhaps beyond question, with such control often operationalised as internal control within a company's transaction processing system. Such internal control is based on:

■ the separation of administrative procedures (or SOAP), and/or

■ the segregation of duties (or SOD).

The issue of control was introduced in Chapter 3. We will return to a brief, albeit more functional consideration of internal control later in this chapter, and will have a more in-depth critical evaluation of internal control and systems security in Chapter 10.

Purposive context

Purposive context refers to the need to ensure that contemporary transaction processing cycles and systems remain not only *input focused* but more importantly *output orientated*.

That is, contemporary transaction processing cycles and systems should not be process driven – their present functions should not be determined solely by the histrionics of past activities/successes. In a commercial context, such a dependency on past glories/successes would be tantamount to long-term economic suicide.

In terms of contemporary transaction processing cycles and systems, purposive context means inherent corporate structures, functions and/or processes must be purposeful. They must exist and function for reasons other than the bureaucracy of self survival or self propagation.

Okay – so now that we have a broad understanding of the fundamentals of contemporary transaction processing cycles and systems, what about the relationship between contemporary transaction processing cycles and systems and:

- the funding cycle,
- the value chain, and
- the value cycle?

The funding cycle

Corporate funding can be divided into:

- short-term sources and applications of funds (or working capital), and
- long-term sources and applications of funds.

While this division may not always be as clear as some business commentators and finance academics would suggest (some sources/applications of funds may well be categorised as both short-term and long-term), the aim of any corporate funding policy is to ensure that a company possesses an adequate level of funds (both cash and non-cash funds) appropriate to its level of activities, and suitable to the supply and demand requirements for such resources within the business.

Clearly, on a day-to-day basis, working capital is essential, and the importance of balancing levels of stocks, debtors, creditors and, of course, cash is beyond question. However, working capital, or short-term funding, is not the only aspect of funding that has an impact on a company's operational capabilities and its abilities to generate shareholder wealth. Long-term funding, or long-term sources and applications of funds, also have a major impact, mainly because of their size and timing – that is, many of these 'non-working capital' sources and applications tend to be large value items that either:

- occur/reoccur regularly, say weekly, monthly or even annually (for example, tax payments, lease payments, dividends, interest and, possibly, the acquisition and disposal of fixed assets), and/or
- occur irregularly as a one-off event (for example, new equity and loan finance and/or redemption of old equity and loan finance).

At the heart of the corporate funding cycle is, of course, contemporary transaction processing – that is, the *practice of business* and the *activity of commodity exchange* through which funds are acquired, profits are generated and wealth is created. Indeed, any redefining of a company's funding/financing policies and/or objectives – for example:

- decreasing the level of investment in stocks to increase cash flow, and/or
- amending sales and debtors policies to increase cash flow, and/or
- the acquisition of additional resources to increase production – to increase sales and consequently cash flow,

will require (at the very least) perhaps a reconfiguring of a company's contemporary transaction processing systems and activities, and/or a redefining of its management/administrative control procedures.

The value chain

The value chain is a model which analyses an organisation's strategically relevant activities – activities from which competitive advantage is derived. Porter (1985) suggested a value chain model composed of two distinct groups of activities – primary activities and support activities. Porter suggested that primary activities could be divided into:

- *Inbound logistics* – the receiving and warehousing of raw materials, and their distribution to manufacturing as they are required.
- *Operations* – the processes of transforming inputs into finished products and services.
- *Outbound logistics* – the warehousing and distribution of finished goods.
- *Marketing and Sales* – the identification of customer needs and the generation of sales.
- *Service* – the support of customers after the products and services are sold to them.

He divided support activities into:

- *Infrastructure* – organisational structure, control systems, company culture.
- *Human resource management* – employee recruiting, hiring, training, development and compensation.
- *Technology development* – technologies to support value-creating activities.
- *Procurement* – purchasing inputs such as materials, supplies and equipment.

See Figure 7.2.

Clearly, the stages and components within the value chain should not be viewed in isolation but considered in a holistic systemic sense – that is, considered within a wider context to include the interactions and relationships not only within processes but between stages. Indeed, for Porter (1985), competitive advantage, profitability and shareholder wealth maximisation could only be achieved through the effective and efficient performance and management of not only primary value chain activities but, more importantly, value chain support activities.

What is the relevance of the value chain to contemporary transaction processing?

The value chain model continues to remain a useful (if often criticised) analytical model for:

- articulating a company's core competencies,
- defining a company's fundamental activities, and
- identifying essential relationships and processes.

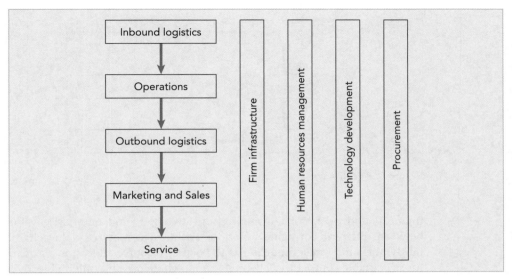

Figure 7.2 Porter's generic value chain

With this analysis, the company can plan its pursuit of competitive advantage and wealth maximisation through cost advantage, by either reducing the cost of individual value chain activities or by reconfiguring the value chain and/or differentiation by either changing individual value chain activities to increase product/service uniqueness or by reconfiguring the value chain.

Clearly, there are many ways in which a company can reconfigure its value chain activities to reduce costs and/or create uniqueness – all of which rely fundamentally on a redefining, rearranging and/or reconfiguring of the contemporary transaction processing activities within relevant value chain activities.

The value cycle

There can be little doubt that the responsibility for value management and for wealth creation is no longer merely the responsibility of the financial manager. The obligation to pursue and adopt wealth maximising strategies and procedures now extends to all levels of tactical and operational decision making. And yet, for:

■ the operational manager concerned primarily with day-to-day service delivery and short-term performance measurements, and

■ the tactical manager concerned primarily with resource management and accountability,

the notion and indeed importance of shareholder value can be an elusive, vague (some would say irrelevant), and often distant concept to adopt and/or even comprehend.

The value cycle model (see Figure 7.3) seeks to address this shortfall.

The value cycle is an inductive model that in essence seeks to provide a 'systems view' of the company, and adopts a holistic view of a 'value creating' organisation/company. In doing so, the value cycle model seeks to establish connections/linkages between strategic,

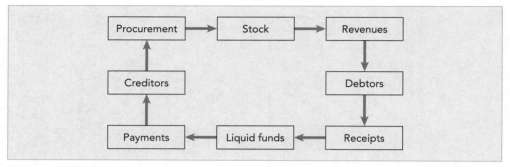

Figure 7.3 Value cycle

financial and operational thinking and activities, and emphasise value relationships between different corporate functions within a company's value chain. More importantly, the value cycle model seeks to balance resource allocation across the value chain for sustainable competitive advantage and, where possible, align objectives and performance measures across a company's value chain.

In a contemporary context the value cycle and value cycle management has become synonymous with efforts to:

- introduce and integrate more technology into transaction processing activities and procedures, and
- synchronise processes and procedures across corporate transaction processing activities.

More importantly, its *systemic approach* has resulted in an increasing acknowledgement of the cyclical nature of wealth creation, and a movement away from the notion of *linear* value chain activities. That is, a rejection of the notion that business activities follow a linear path in the form of a supply/value chain of goods and services – a chain with a beginning and an end – and the adoption of a more dynamic, more holistic, non-linear approach embracing the idea of business (and indeed value creation) as a continuous cycle, a cycle of interrelated systems and activities – of exchange processes and procedures – of management and administrative control devices and mechanisms.

While clearly this is nothing new – it is really just a repackaged version/a restructured application of systems thinking – it does provide a suitable functional context, incorporating the funding cycle and the value chain into a framework within which the holistic nature of contemporary transaction processing activities and related systems and procedures can be appropriately considered.

Contemporary transaction processing – toward a classification

All companies possess something distinctive – a particular corporate disposition based on a vast range of interrelated and interconnected characteristics and qualities peculiar to the company. There are characteristics and qualities founded upon an ever-changing chronicle of past, current and future events and occurrences that reveal themselves in the existence of differences, for example in:

■ degrees of geographical diversification,

■ management hierarchies and decision-making processes,

■ financing and funding policies,

■ levels of organisational technology, and/or

■ operational policies and procedure.

Clearly, because of the vast number of trading, registered public and private companies, and, indeed, the varied nature of their activities (for plcs just look at the variety of companies included in the FTSE 100, FTSE 250 and FTSE 350 indices[1]), it is important to provide a rational context/framework – a general classification – if only to bring some sense of order and understanding to what superficially appears to be an infinite array of chaotic variety and diversity: a classification of company types and sub-types – of transaction processing cycles and systems – into an ordered arrangement based on a defined range of characteristics, relationships, and/or distinctive differences/similarities.

The purpose of any such classification of transaction processing systems is:

■ to enable a description of their structure and relationship to other similar transaction processing systems, but (more importantly)

■ to simplify such relationships in order to facilitate discussion and the construction of general statements about such classes of transaction processing systems.

Adapted and extended from Davis *et al.* (1990) (after Starreveld *et al.* (1998), Wilkinson *et al.* (2001) and Vaassen (2002)), this typology of transaction processing systems (see Figure 7.4) is an *inductive* classification. An inductive approach is when specific observations are used to determine a rule and/or relationship. Consequently, an inductive approach to classification is often also called a 'bottom-up' approach – the classification being derived from specific observations. A *deductive* approach, on the other hand, is when the rule is given first and is then followed by examples of the rule. A deductive approach to classification is often called a 'top-down' approach because the classification is developed from generalised assumptions.

Indeed, inasmuch as its foundation is empirical observation, this taxonomy of transaction processing systems is a generalised hierarchical classification (see Figure 7.5) – a hierarchical classification developed from specific facts and observations over many years by many academics (certainly too many to identify individually). Nevertheless, despite its celebrated history, it is perhaps important to recognise that this classification is

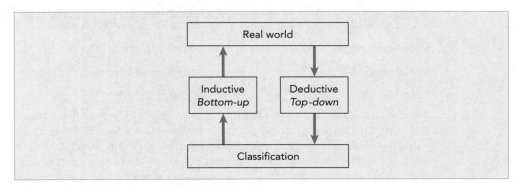

Figure 7.4 Classification – inductive/deductive

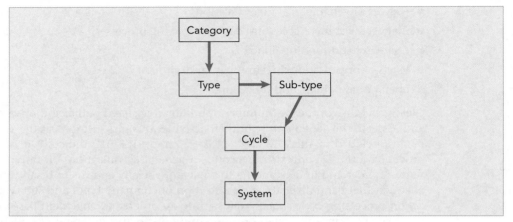

Figure 7.5 Hierarchical classification of transaction processing systems

neither neutral nor unbiased. It is a classification developed upon a number of classic liberal economic assumptions, assumptions such as:

- commodity/service exchange is the foundation of corporate wealth generation,
- all companies are wealth maximising, and
- all (or at least most) companies are free to enter (and exit) markets without constraint and/or penalty.

For the purposes of this typology, the following terminology will be used:

- the term *categories* will be used to refer to a group/subset of companies possessing common characteristics and/or sharing common attributes,
- the term *types* will be used to refer to the company business type/sub-type within a category,
- the term *cycles* will be used to refer to the cycles of operation within the company business type/sub-type, and
- the term *systems* will be used to refer to the systems within a company's cycle of operations.

Contemporary transaction processing – categories

In general, two broad categories of companies[2] can be identified:

- **Category 1** – companies with a dominant flow of commodities, and
- **Category 2** – companies with no dominant flow of commodities.

Clearly, this initial stage classification is intuitive, which perhaps accounts for its rather vague superficiality and simplicity. Nevertheless, it is an appropriate starting point – but it is also important to recognise that while in an empirical context such a distinction exists (or appears to exist), the two categories are by no means definitive and/or exclusive. A company may well diversify its functions/activities and undertake transactions within both of the above categories and/or within different types within a single category.

Contemporary transaction processing – types

Within the above two categories, a total of five types of contemporary transaction processing structures can be identified (each with two sub-types):

- *Category 1 Companies with a dominant flow of commodities*
    - *Type 1(a) Retail and distribution companies*
        - (i)   Consumer-based retail
        - (ii) Non-consumer-based retail
    - *Type 1(b) Manufacturing and production companies*
        - (i)   Continuous production
        - (ii) Non-continuous production
- *Category 2 Companies with no dominant flow of commodities*
    - *Type 2(a) Companies with a limited flow of commodities*
        - (i)   Limited owned commodities
        - (ii) Limited non-owned commodities
    - *Type 2(b) Time/space-based companies*
        - (i)   Specific time/space
        - (ii) Non-specific time/space
    - *Type 2(c) Knowledge/skills-based companies*
        - (i)   Time-based specific knowledge/skills
        - (ii) Supply-based non-specific knowledge/skills.

Category 1 Type 1(a) Retail and distribution companies

(i) Consumer-based retail and distribution companies are companies that *mainly* sell to high street customers and clients, and would include, for example:

- supermarkets and food retail based companies – for example Asda plc, Tesco plc, and Sainsbury plc,
- generic commodity retail companies/groups – for example Marks and Spencer plc, and Boots plc,
- specific commodity retail companies – for example Comet plc and Dixons Retail plc (electrical retail) and United Utilities plc (energy and water management),
- on-line retail stores – for example Amazon.co.uk[3] (on-line entertainment and educational goods and services).

(ii) Trade-based retail companies are retail companies that *mainly* sell to other companies and organisations – that is, the majority of their trade activities is trade-to-trade business within the so-called *product supply chain*. Although many large manufacturing companies may well act as wholesale retailer – for example, Associated British Foods plc (food manufacturer), such companies are included in Category 1 Type 1(b) below. Companies in this category/type would not normally manufacturer/produce the goods/commodities they sell, but would merely facilitate the product exchange process – that is from manufacturer to supplier to retailer to customer. Such companies would include wholesale retail companies in all market sectors, from groceries to electrical commodities to household utilities.

Category 1 Type 1(b) Manufacturing and production companies

(i) Continuous production companies are mass production companies (normally supply focused) that manufacture commodities, extract resources and/or produce energy for either the trade (corporate) markets and/or the retail (consumer) markets. These would include, for example, companies based on:

- Constructive industry – such as Volkswagen AG (car manufacturer), MG Motors UK Ltd (car manufacturer), Hitachi Ltd (electrical goods manufacturer), Vodafone Group plc (mobile phone manufacturer), Carlsberg UK Ltd (brewery), Diageo plc (drinks manufacturer), Associated British Foods plc (food manufacturer), and British American Tobacco plc (cigarette manufacturer).
- Extractive industry – such as BP plc (oil extraction and petroleum production), UK Coal plc (coal mining and extraction).
- Agrarian industry (farming and agriculture).
- Energy production and distribution – such as Npower plc (energy supplier) and BG group plc (gas production/distribution).

(ii) Non-continuous production companies are contract production companies (normally demand focused) that develop/construct/manufacture commodities 'on demand' or more appropriately 'on contractual agreement', and would include for example:

- House building/property development companies – such as Barrett Developments plc and George Wimpey plc.
- Aircraft development and construction companies – such as BAE Systems plc.
- Engineering manufacturing companies – such as Wolseley plc.
- Shipbuilding companies – such as Harland and Wolff Heavy Industries Ltd.

Category 2 Type 2(a) Companies with a limited flow of commodities

(i) Limited owned commodity companies are companies that are services orientated, but nevertheless have a limited flow of owned (either purchased and/or manufactured) commodities – commodities whose legal title (property) and ownership resides with the company. Such companies would include:

- Restaurants – from fast food outlets to the traditional high street brasserie to the Michelin Star restaurants: for example, McDonalds, Burger King and TGI Fridays (fast food); Brasserie Gerard and Loch Fyne (traditional high street brasserie); Aubergine, Le Gavroche, and Fat Duck (Michelin Star restaurants).
- Public bars and night clubs – for example, Scottish and Newcastle plc public bars (52 throughout the UK), Stringfellows (night club).
- Publishing and media – for example, Guardian Newspapers Ltd (newspaper publishing), Pearson Publishing plc (book publishing) and BSkyB plc (satellite broadcaster).

(ii) Limited non-owned commodity companies are companies that are essentially services-based but have a limited flow of commodities whose legal title (property) and ownership resides with a third party. Such companies would include for example repair and/or retail orientated companies:

- Repair companies – companies that provide services related to the repair and maintenance of specific commodities/assets (for example, local garage and/or local electrical repairs).

- Retail companies – companies that provide retail facilities (for example, auction houses such as Sotheby's, and/or estate agencies).

Category 2 Type 2(b) Time/space-based companies

(i) Specific time/space companies are companies that provide identifiable and specific time facilities and/or space capacity for customers and clients. Such business types would normally provide an individualised service and would include for example:

- Hotel services companies – such as Intercontinental hotels plc and Hilton hotels plc.

- Airline services companies – such as BA plc and KLM Royal Dutch Airlines.

- Rail services companies – such as Virgin Rail Group Ltd.

- Postal services companies – such as DHL plc, Interlink plc and Post Office Ltd (owned by Royal Mail Group plc).

- Security services companies – such as Group 4 Securicor plc.

(ii) Non-specific time/space companies are companies that provide non-specific time facilities and/or space capacity for customers and clients. Such business types would generally offer fee-based services 'en masse', and would include for example:

- Cinema services – such as Odeon Cinemas Ltd, UGC.

- Leisure and sport facilities – such as David Lloyd Ltd.

- Localised public transport operators – such as London Underground Ltd.

- Generic (UK-wide) public transport operators – such as Stagecoach Group plc.

Category 2 Type 2(c) Knowledge/skills-based companies

(i) Time-based knowledge/skills companies are companies that provide specific *profession-based* knowledge/skill services – services that are normally time orientated and fee-based (usually by the hour). Many of these business types tend to be Limited Liability Partnerships (LLP), for example Gosschalks (legal services), KPMG PriceWaterhouseCoopers, Ernst and Young (accounting and accounting-related services), and Gelder and Kitchen (architectural and engineering consultants).

(ii) Supply-based knowledge/skills companies are companies that provide non-specific knowledge/skill services for customers and clients. Such services would normally be facilities/services orientated and would generally be offered on a fee and/or subscription basis 'en masse', and would include a wide range of service/business types, for example:

- Internet service provider companies – such as Pipex communications plc.

- Telephone service provider companies – such as BT plc, Motorola Ltd and Orange plc.

- Banking and financial services companies – from high street banking services (for example, NatWest plc, LloydsTSB plc and Barclays plc), to merchant banking (for example Morgan Stanley International Ltd).

- Insurance and related assurance services companies – such as Aviva plc.

- Pension services companies – such as Legal and General plc.

Contemporary transaction processing – cycles

Whatever the company business type/sub-type, within that company a number of transaction processing cycles or cycles of operation will exist, although the exact nature and character of such cycles of operation will differ from company to company – mainly due to structural and/or functional issues.

Structural issues emerge from differences in:

■ management practices,
■ decision-making procedures,
■ operational processes, and
■ levels of technology.

Functional issues emerge from differences in degrees of integration. For example, whereas in some companies the cycles of operation may be distinct and clearly identifiable, in other companies such cycles of operation may be combined and/or merged/amalgamated together for:

■ operational reasons – for example, to make the cycles more efficient by reducing processing procedures and increase processing effectiveness, and/or
■ financial reasons – for example, to reduce costs and promote financial efficiency (and of course maximise shareholder wealth).

Clearly, whatever the precise nature and character of a company's transaction processing cycles and/or systems, its underlying rationale will remain the same – to ensure the expedient, efficient and effective processing of transactions and (as a consequence) the maximisation of shareholder wealth!

So, exactly what are these cycles of operation?

Within a company, four functional cycles of operation (see Figure 7.6) can exist:

1 The revenue cycle.
2 The expenditure cycle.
3 The conversion cycle.
4 The management cycle.

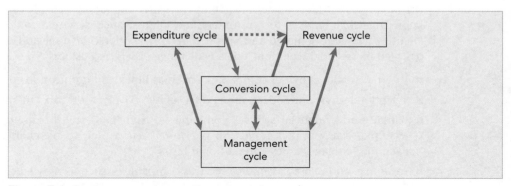

Figure 7.6 Contemporary transaction processing cycles

The revenue cycle

The term revenue means the earnings of a company before any costs or expenses are deducted. It includes all net sales of assets, commodities, services and/or facilities of the company together with any other revenue associated with the main operations of the business. (For our purpose we will not include dividends, interest income and/or non-operating income.)

Such revenue will result in an increase in net current assets – that is:

■ an increase in non-cash-based assets (debtor-based revenue cycles), and/or
■ an increase in cash-based assets (non-debtor-based revenue cycles).

In general, two types of revenue cycles can be identified:

1 Debtor-based revenue cycles which would include company-to-company credit sales and company-to-individual credit sales.

2 Non-debtor-based revenue cycles, which would be normally concerned with either web-based transactions (nPoS EFT) or retail outlet card-based transactions (pPoS EFT).

The expenditure cycle

The term expenditure (whether revenue or capital) is synonymous with the term cost – its purpose being to acquire an asset, commodity, or service and/or obtain access to a facility.

Such expenditure requires the commitment of current and/or future net current assets – that is:

■ the incurrence of a liability (creditor-based expenditure), and/or
■ the reduction of current assets (non-creditor-based expenditure).

In general the majority of corporate expenditure will be creditor-based expenditure.

The conversion cycle

The term asset conversion means any process, procedure and/or event that results in a transformation and/or a change in the use, function, purpose, structure and/or composition of an asset to another use, function, purpose, structure and/or composition. In this definition an asset can be defined simply as anything owned by a company that has commercial (that is, it can produce a stream of current and/or future incomes) or has a current and/or future exchange value.

The asset conversion cycle of operation is associated with physical modification – with a production process, with the conversion of unrelated raw materials into finished saleable products/commodities.

Such conversion/modification may of course take a variety of forms, for example:

■ the refining of oil and the production of petroleum-based products (as with BP plc and Shell plc);
■ the production/manufacture of cars (Ford Inc.);
■ the construction of houses (Barrett Developments plc and George Wimpey plc);
■ the production of brown goods (LG plc, Hitachi Ltd); and
■ food and drinks manufacturing (Associated British Foods plc, Cadbury Schweppes plc, Diagio plc).

The management cycle

The management and administrative cycle is concerned with the designing, developing, planning, programming, evaluating and – most importantly – the control of, business processes and procedures to ensure:

■ the efficient implementation of company policy,
■ the competent operation of company practices, and
■ the effective utilisation of company resources.

Although the precise nature and context of systems to ensure the above will depend on the company type, they will mainly be concerned with:

■ fund management,
■ finance management,
■ asset management, and
■ general ledger management.

Contemporary transaction processing – systems

Revenue cycle systems

Within a (debtor-based) revenue cycle the following systems would normally exist (see Figure 7.7):

■ a retailing system,
■ a distribution and delivery system, and
■ a payment management system.

Retailing system

The purpose of the retailing (customer/client ordering) system is to ensure the acceptance of only authorised orders, to maintain adherence to company credit policies and to ensure adherence to company pricing policies.

A retail system would generally function as follows:

1 Receipt of authenticated and validated customer/client order;
2 Validation of customer's/client's available credit/credit limit;
3 Issue of customer/client order confirmation;

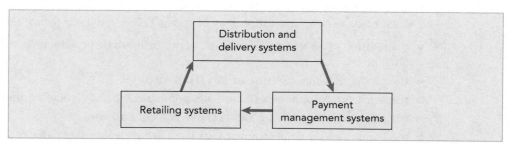

Figure 7.7 Revenue cycle

4 Generation of a stores requisition, or a production order, or a service/knowledge requisition.

The key documentation of such a retailing system would be:

- an approved customer/client order;
- a credit limit approval/amendment;
- an approved customer/client order confirmation;
- an approved stores requisition, or a production order, or a service/knowledge requisition.

Distribution and delivery system

The purpose of the distribution and delivery system is to identify any transportation requirements and, where necessary, initiate, monitor and manage the transportation and routing of the products and the delivery of services.

A distribution system would generally function as follows:

1 Receipt of stock issue request, or production order request, or service/knowledge provision request;
2 Issue of a distribution/delivery order (for products), or issue of a service provision order (for services);
3 Selection of product delivery/service provision mechanism;
4 Issue of a bill of lading (where required).

The key documentation of such a distribution and delivery system would be:

- an approved stock issue request, or production order request (where a product requires manufacturing), or service/knowledge provision request (where a service requires scheduling for delivery;
- an authorised distribution/delivery order (for products);
- an approved distribution/delivery schedule (or transportation schedule); and, where necessary,
- an authorised bill of lading.

Payment management system

The purpose of the payment management system is to ensure:

- the correct assessment of cost of products/services provided to customers/clients,
- the correct invoicing of *all* sales,
- the accurate management of customer/client accounts, and
- the adequate management of customer/client credit facilities and the recovery of outstanding debts.

A payment management system would, for internal control purposes, be divided into two subsystems: the debtor creation (invoicing) subsystem and the debtor management subsystem.

A debtor creation (invoicing) subsystem would generally function to:

- generate the customer/client invoice,
- document all transactions in the company's/organisation's accounting records, and either:
  - create a debtor account for the customer/client, or
  - amend an existing customer's/client's account.

The key documentation of such a debtor creation subsystem would be the invoice and the debtor account.

A debtor management sub-system generally comprises four activities:

1 Collection and recording of payments made by customers/clients.

2 Reconciliation of customer/client account balances.

3 Assessment of doubtful debts.[4]

4 Writing-off bad debts/irrecoverable debtor accounts.[5]

The key documentation of such a debtor management subsystem would be:

- the debtor account,
- a debtor account adjustment,
- the debtor statement of account,
- a debtor account payment reminder, and
- an application to write-off.

Expenditure cycle systems

Within a (creditor based) expenditure cycle (see Figure 7.8) the following systems would normally exist:

- a supplier selection/approval system,
- a product/service ordering system,
- a receiving system,
- a payment management system, and
- a payroll system.

Note: For the purchase of non-current assets additional procedures would exist. (See assets management systems within the management cycle below.)

Supplier selection/approval system

The purpose of the supplier selection/approval system is to identify an appropriate supplier/provider for the product/service required, and to determine an appropriate level

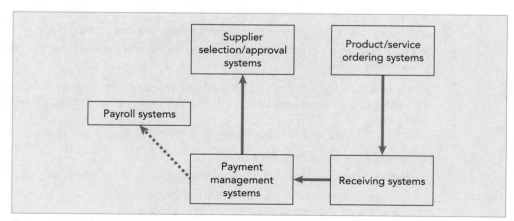

Figure 7.8 Expenditure cycle

of relationship with that supplier/provider. The key documentation of such a supplier selection/approval system would be:

- a supplier approval/registration document,
- an approved supplier/provider register (database),
- a supplier/provider amendment document, and
- a supplier/provider assessment and review document.

Product/service ordering system

The purpose of the product/service ordering system is to ensure that products and services relevant to the business process are ordered by authorised employees only, and obtained from/purchased from appropriately approved suppliers/providers. The key documentation of such a product/service ordering system would be:

- a purchase requisition,
- a purchase order, and (where appropriate)
- a purchase confirmation.

Most companies separate the purchase/ordering system into three key stages:

1 the purchase acquisition stage,
2 the purchase requisition stage, and
3 the purchase order stage.

Receiving system

The purpose of the receiving system is to ensure that:

- all authorised purchases of products/services are appropriately receipted,
- all purchased products are securely stored,
- all purchased services are used in accordance with the purchase requisition/purchase order, and
- all purchases are appropriately accounted for.

The key documentation of such a product/service receiving system would be:

- a delivery note – generated by the supplier, and
- a goods received note – or receiving report.

Payment management system

The purpose of the payment management system is to ensure the correct payment of invoices and the adequate management of creditor accounts. Such a payment management system would, for internal control purposes, be divided into two subsystems:

1 a creditor creation subsystem, and
2 a creditor management subsystem.

The creditor creation subsystem is designed to ensure:

- the verification and validation of the supplier's/provider's invoice, and
- the documentation of all transactions in the company's/organisation's accounting records – that is, either the creation of a creditor account for the supplier/provider or the amendment/updating of an existing supplier's/provider's account.

The key documentation of a creditor creation (invoice receipting) system would be:

- an invoice, and
- the creditor account.

The creditor management subsystem is designed to ensure:

- the processing of approved outstanding invoices,
- the payment of approved outstanding invoices,
- the recording of invoice payments,
- the adjustment/amendment of creditor accounts, and
- the effective and efficient management of creditor accounts – including the reconciliation of supplier/provider account.

The key documentation of such a creditor management system would be a payment document and, where required, a debit memorandum (or refund note) – also known as a creditor account adjustment.

Note: Cash-based non-creditor-based expenditure is often referred to as petty cash expenditure and would be concerned with small value purchases. Card-based non-creditor expenditure may also occur and would normally relate to employee-based expenditure concerned with, for example, business-related accommodation costs, or business-related travel expenses, or, where appropriate, customer/client entertainment expenses.

Expenditure cycle – payroll[6]

Payroll is concerned with ensuring the timely and appropriate compensation of company employees and would include procedures, process, and controls associated with:

- the recruitment of new employees,
- the training of current employees,
- the assignment of work-related tasks,
- the evaluation of employee performance, and
- the voluntary and/or involuntary discharge of employees.

The major sources of inputs would be:

- Company departments (for example human resource management department and the employee employing department) – information on recruitment/appointments, employee conditions of employment, employee terminations, details on employee deductions, details of hours worked and/or products produced.
- Government agencies – information on income tax deductions/payments, National Insurance deductions/payments, employment laws, rules and regulations (including health and safety).
- Other non-statutory bodies (for example, trade unions) – information on conditions of employment, rates of pay, etc.
- Employees – information on/authorisation of voluntary deductions (for example, savings schemes, charitable donations, and/or pension contributions).

The major destination of outputs would be:

- Company departments (including human resource management department) – information on staffing/employment levels and budget commitments.

- Company departments (in particular accounting and finance) – information on both employee payments and payments to other statutory/non-statutory agencies.
- Employees – payment of net pay.
- Government agencies – payment of tax, National Insurance and the provision of statutory payroll information.
- Insurance companies/pension funds – payments of employee and, where appropriate, employer contributions.

In general, the company departments that would more than likely be involved either directly or indirectly in:

- the maintenance of payroll data/information,
- the preparation of the weekly/monthly payroll, and
- the payment of wages and/or salaries to employees,

would include:

- the personnel (or HRM) department,
- the production department (or employing department),
- the payroll department,
- the (management) accounting department – cost control/budgeting,
- the treasury department/cashier,
- the (management) accounting department – cost control/budgeting, and
- the (financial) accounting department – general ledger control.

For control purposes, the payroll procedure would normally be divided into three main stages:

1 The pre-payment stage, which would include:
   - the maintenance and updating of payroll master file data, and
   - the validation and allocation of departmental payroll budgets – including the determination of employee staffing levels.
2 The payment stage, which would include:
   - the collection and validation of time/attendance data, or goods produced data (depending on how employees are remunerated), and
   - the preparation of the payroll, and the validation of payroll deductions (both statutory and voluntary deductions).
3 The post-payment stage, which would include:
   - the disbursement of payments to employees,
   - the accounting for, and reconciliation of payroll payments, and
   - the disbursement of statutory and voluntary deductions.

Conversion cycle

Within a conversion cycle (see Figure 7.9) the following systems would normally exist:

- a product development system,
- a production planning/scheduling system,
- a manufacturing operations system,

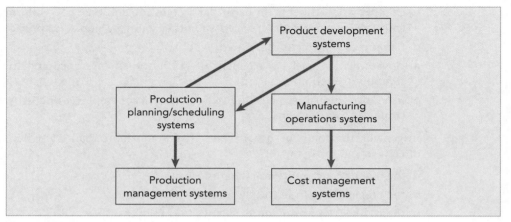

Figure 7.9 Conversion cycle

- a production management system, and
- a cost management system.

Product development system

The product development system is concerned with the conception, development, design and realisation of a new product. It is not only concerned with the identification of new development opportunities and the generation of new product ideas, but is also concerned with establishing the feasibility/plausibility of any new product.

Broadly speaking, the product development system would involve at the very least, three key stages: a design stage, a development stage and a launch stage.

Production planning/scheduling system

A production planning system deals with the planning of human and non-human resources for the purpose of producing products to accommodate customer/client requirements, to ensure that an appropriate quantity of products is manufactured as efficiently and as economically as possible.

A production scheduling system deals with the allocating of resources and the sequencing of activities to ensure the efficient production of goods and services, the aim being to manage and coordinate resource flows within the manufacturing process and identify (and where possible eliminate) possible resource conflicts.

Manufacturing operations

The key part of any conversion cycle is, of course, the actual manufacturing process – that is, the physical creation of the product. Although the specifics of the manufacturing process/processes would differ from product to product, from company to company, from organisation to organisation, in general such manufacturing processes can be classified either by *type* or by *orientation*.

- *Classification by type*: from a functional perspective, manufacturing operations can be classified as either continuous manufacturing[7] (or flow manufacturing), batch manufacturing[8] (or intermittent manufacturing), or on-demand manufacturing.[9]
- *Classification by orientation*: from an orientational perspective, manufacturing operations can be classified as either push-based[10] or pull-based.[11]

Production management system

The production management system – sometimes referred to as operations management – would be concerned with the coordination and controlling of all the activities required to make a product, and encapsulates a range of *strategic*, *tactical* and *operational* issues. For example:

- At a *strategic* level production management would be concerned with:
  - determining the size and location of manufacturing operations,
  - deciding the structure of service or telecommunications networks, and
  - designing technology supply chains.
- At a *tactical* level production management would be concerned with:
  - plant layout and structure,
  - project management methods,
  - equipment selection, and
  - resources replacement cycles.
- At an *operational* level production management would be concerned with:
  - production scheduling and control,
  - stock management,
  - quality control and inspection,
  - traffic and materials handling, and
  - equipment maintenance policies.

Put simply, the aim of production management is to ensure all production-related processes and activities are organised efficiently, performed effectively and managed competently.

Cost management system

The cost management system would be concerned with recording and controlling product cost, and with providing performance information concerning the performance of the conversion cycle systems.

Management cycle systems

Within a management cycle (see Figure 7.10) the following systems would normally exist:

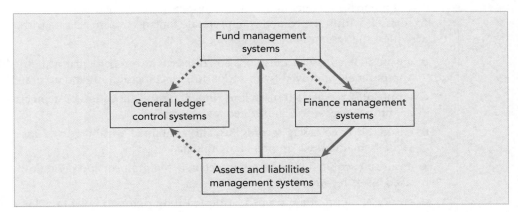

Figure 7.10 Management cycle

- a fund management system,
- a finance management system,
- an asset management system,
- a liabilities management system, and
- a general ledger control system.

Finance management system

The finance management system is concerned with the management of all forms of non-transactional financing including, for example, equity financing, debt (loan) financing, convertible securities, derivative instruments and transferable warrants. Its aim is to:

- ensure the safe custody of all non-transactional finance-related deeds/legal documents,
- ensure the appropriate authorisation of all acquisitions, transfers and/or disposals for all debt- and equity-related financial instruments,
- maintain accurate accounting records for all acquisitions, transfers and/or disposals, and
- ensure the accurate monitoring of all debt-related commitments – including commitments related to convertible securities, derivative instruments and transferable warrants.

Fund management system

The fund management system is concerned with the management of all forms of transactional financing – that is, financing that is directly related to or associated with the revenue cycle activities of the company (inflows of funds) and the expenditure cycle activities of the company (outflows of funds). The aim of the fund management system is to:

- ensure the proper management of all fund-related balances – for example, cash balances, bank balances;
- ensure the adequate maintenance of all fund-related accounting records – including the periodic reconciliation of all fund balances; and
- ensure the accurate supervision of all receipts and disbursements (including small cash receipts and disbursements).

Assets management system

The **non-current assets** management system is concerned with maintaining a level of fixed assets within the company appropriate for, and commensurate with, its operational activities, the system's objectives being to:

- ensure all fixed asset acquisitions and disposals are properly planned, suitably evaluated, appropriately approved (with supporting documentation) and accurately recorded;
- ensure all fixed asset transactions (including the allocation of depreciation expenses) are properly recorded, monitored and controlled;
- ensure all fixed assets records (usually contained within a fixed assets register) are securely maintained, and regularly updated;
- ensure all acquired fixed assets are securely maintained, and periodically reconciled to fixed assets records; and
- ensure all appropriate property titles/custody rights to both tangible and intangible fixed assets are securely stored.

The **current assets** management system is concerned with the management of *stock* (inventory) and *debtors* (receivables).

The *stock* management system is concerned with the insulation and, as far as possible, protection of product/service-related transaction processes from adverse changes in the external environment. That is, the stock management system is concerned with ensuring that:

■ appropriate levels of stock are available within the company to meet anticipated production requirements, possible legal requirements, and/or predicted customer/client demands, and

■ excessive working capital is not tied up in unwarranted/unnecessary stocks – stocks that are surplus to transaction processing requirements.

The *debtor* management system is concerned with ensuring that all debtor-based sales are promptly and correctly invoiced, and all income relating to such debtor-based sales is efficiently collected. In a practical context, this means establishing effective company-wide internal controls to ensure the efficient management and administration of all debtor-related sales.

Liabilities management system

The *debt* management system is concerned with ensuring levels of long-term borrowing and securitisation, and the number of debt covenants is carefully monitored. The *creditor* management system is concerned with ensuring that all creditor-based purchases are correctly invoiced, and all payments relating to such creditor-based purchases are efficiently disbursed.

General ledger management system

As we have seen, the primary objective of a contemporary accounting information system is to generate reliable and relevant information for:

■ controlling and monitoring of business-related activities,

■ safeguarding of company assets,

■ accounting for company liabilities,

■ preparing annual financial statements, and

■ ensuring adherence to/compliance with extant statutory/regulatory requirements.

From an accounting information systems context, the main functions of the general ledger are to provide a framework for the recording of accounting adjustment entries – a data processing/recording function; to provide a control mechanism for the management of accounting data – a controlling function; and to generate appropriate financial reports – an information-generation function.

Contemporary transaction processing – control

Clearly, the importance of operational efficiency and effectiveness within a company's transaction processing systems cannot be overstated; nor can the need for control – more specifically for internal control. Internal control can be defined as management processes designed to provide reasonable assurance that the objectives of reliable financial reporting, effective and efficient operations, and compliance with laws and regulations are achieved.

Such internal control includes all procedures, processes and protocols, financial and otherwise, established by the management in order to ensure:

- business activities of the company are undertaken in an orderly and efficient manner;
- compliance with management policies, and adherence to extant regulatory requirements;
- the safeguarding of all assets; and
- as far as possible, the accuracy and completeness of accounting records and financial information.

Securing effective internal control requires:

- an understanding and appreciation of the *control environment*;
- an understanding of relevant *control activities*;
- an understanding, identification and *analysis of the risk*;
- an assessment of *information and communication* channels both within the company and within the environment; and finally
- an appreciation and understanding of *monitoring* transaction processes.

We will discuss/evaluate each of the above issues in more detail in Chapter 10.

The Data Protection Act 1998

Finally – some legal requirements! The Data Protection Act 1998[12] protects personal information held about individuals, and regulates the processing of data relating to individuals – or, more appropriately – data subjects.[13]

The Data Protection Act 1998 applies to information held on or obtained from computers, and to certain manual records. It gives rights to the individual data subject and imposes responsibilities on:

- the individual data subjects,
- the organisations holding the data, and
- the employees of those organisations who use the information.

The Data Protection Act 1998 implements part of the European Convention on Human Rights. It applies only to information about individuals (such as names, addresses, personal reference numbers, income, entitlement to benefits). It does not apply to non-personal data such as those relating to businesses and limited companies.

Remember the Data Protection Act 1998 only protects personal data about people who are alive.

The Data Protection Act 1998 applies to every company that maintains lists, databases or files (paper or electronic) containing personal details of:

- *Employees* – for example, personnel information such as home address, date of birth.
- *Clients* – for example, account details, agreements, contact details, BACS payment details.
- *Customers* – for example, account details, contact details, credit card details.
- Other related parties.

All companies are required to be registered with the Information Commissioner and to comply with the provisions of the Data Protection Act 1998 and the guidelines and interpretations issued by the Information Commissioner. Failure to do so can result in:

- the imposition of substantial fines, and

- if deemed appropriate by the Information Commissioner, closure of the company.

The Data Protection Act 1998 gives effect in UK law to EC Directive 95/46/EC. The 1998 Act replaces the Data Protection Act 1984 and was brought into force on 1 March 2000. The Data Protection Act 1998 provides the following definitions:

- *Data subject*: an individual who is the subject of the personal information (data). The data subject must be living for the provisions of the Act to apply.

- *Data controller*: a person who determines the purposes for which, and the manner in which, personal data are, or are to be, processed. This may be an individual or an organisation, and the processing may be carried out jointly or in common with other persons.

- *Data processor*: a person who processes data on behalf of a data controller. However, the responsibility for correct processing under the Data Protection Act 1998 remains with the data controller.

The Data Protection Act 1998 also contains eight data protection principles which are designed to ensure data are properly handled. The data protection principles are:

- Principle 1 – personal data shall be processed fairly and lawfully.

- Principle 2 – personal data shall be obtained only for one or more specified and lawful purposes, and shall not be further processed in any manner incompatible with that purpose or those purposes.

- Principle 3 – personal data shall be adequate, relevant and not excessive in relation to the purpose or purposes for which they are processed.

- Principle 4 – personal data shall be accurate and, where necessary, kept up to date.

- Principle 5 – personal data processed for any purpose or purposes shall not be kept for longer than is necessary for that purpose or those purposes.

- Principle 6 – personal data shall be processed in accordance with the rights of data subjects under this Act.

- Principle 7 – appropriate technical and organisational measures shall be taken against unauthorised or unlawful processing of personal data and against accidental loss or destruction of, or damage to, personal data.

- Principle 8 – personal data shall not be transferred to a country or territory outside the European Economic Area, unless that country or territory ensures an adequate level of protection of the rights and freedoms of data subjects in relation to the processing of personal data.

The Data Protection Act 1998 also gives rights to individuals in respect of personal data held about them by others. The rights are:

- right to subject access,[14]

- right to prevent processing likely to cause damage or distress,[15]

- right to prevent processing for the purposes of direct marketing,[16]

- rights in relation to automated decision taking,[17]
- right to take action for compensation if the individual suffers damage by any contravention of the Act by the data controller,[18] and
- right to take action to rectify, block, erase or destroy inaccurate data.[19]

It should be noted that the approach to data protection in Europe differs from that in the USA where a more fragmented sectorial approach is used, relying primarily on a combination of legislation, regulation and self-regulation, rather than governmental regulation alone. As such, the USA has no single data protection law comparable to the EU's Data Protection Directive.

Further details on the UK Data Protection Act 1998 can be found at *www.ico.gov.uk*.

Concluding comments

Contemporary transaction processing systems are socially, politically and economically significant. Not only do they play a leading role in ensuring that the exchange process at the heart of contemporary wealth maximisation is efficient and effective, they are without doubt a crucial factor in the search for corporate sustainability and, indeed, future success.

While the nature, structure and functional efficiency of a company's transaction processing systems will invariably be the product of an enormous diversity of interrelated and interconnected characteristics and qualities, some commonality between the vast range of wealth-maximising companies does nonetheless exist – as suggested by the inductive typology present in the main discussion.

Self-review questions

1 What are the key features of contemporary transaction processing?

2 Distinguish between transaction processing cycles and transaction processing systems.

3 What is meant by, and what are the key differences between, each contemporary transaction processing type/sub-type?

4 What transaction processing systems are normally found within a company's expenditure cycle?

5 What transaction processing systems are normally found within a company's revenue cycle?

6 Explain the main requirements for the securing of effective control within a transaction processing system.

7 In relation to the Data Protection Act 1998, define the following terms:
   (a) data subject,
   (b) data controller, and
   (c) data processor.

8 Describe the eight key principles contained within the Data Protection Act 1998.

References

Davis, J.R., Alderman, C.W. and Robinson, L.A. (1990), *Accounting Information Systems: A Cycle Approach*, Wiley, New York.

Porter, M.E. (1985), *Competitive Advantage: Creating and Sustaining Superior Performance*, The Free Press, New York.

Starreveld, R.W., De Mare, B. and Joels, E. (1998), *Bestuurlijke Informatieverzorging*, Samson, Alphen aan den Rijn.

Vaassen, E. (2002), *Accounting Information Systems – A Managerial Approach*, Wiley, Chichester.

Wilkinson, J.W., Cerullo, M.L., Raval, V. and Wong-On-Wing, B. (2001), *Accounting Information Systems*, Wiley, New York.

Notes

1 The FTSE 100 is made up of the UK's 100 largest companies by market capitalisation, representing approximately 80 per cent of the UK market. It is used extensively as a basis for investment products, such as derivatives and exchange-traded funds, and is the recognised measure of the UK financial markets. The FTSE 250 is made up of mid-capitalised companies, representing approximately 18 per cent of UK market capitalisation. The FTSE 350 is made up of the UK's large capitalisation and mid-capitalisation companies (FTSE 100 + FTSE 250 indices).

2 Although the term company is used throughout this discussion on contemporary transaction processing categories, types, cycles and systems, such discussion may well also apply to other organisational configurations.

3 Amazon.co.uk is the trading name for Amazon.com International Sales, Inc. and Amazon Services Europe SARL. Both companies are subsidiaries of Amazon.com, the on-line retailer of products that inform, educate, entertain and inspire. The Amazon group now has on-line stores in the United States, Germany, France, Japan and Canada. Amazon.co.uk has its origins in an independent on-line store, Bookpages, which was established in 1996 and acquired by Amazon.com in early 1998.

4 In a business context, a debt becomes doubtful where a customer fails to make the appropriate payment within an agreed period, and efforts to determine the reason(s) for such a failure to make payment (for example, telephone calls and/or e-mails to the customer/client) have been unsuccessful. Prudence would suggest that such an outstanding debt should be considered doubtful, and action to recover the outstanding debt commenced, including where necessary County Court action, the issue of a Warrant of Execution for the seizure of debtor assets by bailiffs appointed by the County Court.

5 An outstanding debt should only be written off where – based on available evidence – the outstanding debt (or part of the outstanding debt) is considered to be irrecoverable. Such a decision should be a management decision, taken and approved by members of staff not directly involved in the debt collection and debtor management.

6 Mainly for financial reasons many companies now outsource some or all of their human resource management/payroll activities, using either a payroll bureau or a professional employer organisation.

7 Continuous manufacturing is a method of manufacture in which homogeneous products are continuously produced through a series of standardised procedures. It is generally defined as the complete and uninterrupted manufacture of a product from the raw material components to the final product.

8 Batch manufacturing is a method of manufacture in which products are produced in discrete groups (or batches) which require the same raw materials and production processing/operations. It is generally defined as the intermittent manufacture of a product.

9 On-demand manufacturing is a method of manufacture in which discrete products are produced in accordance with a customer's instructions/requirements.

10 Continuous manufacturing and batch manufacturing are sometimes referred to as push-based manufacturing inasmuch as such manufacturing is normally supply-orientated – that is, the lower the levels of stock of a finished product the company/organisation possesses, the greater the levels of manufacture. A push-based manufacturing system possesses two key features:

(i) all products are manufactured in accordance with a predetermined demand forecast, and

(ii) all information flows in the same direction as the production – that is, from the company/organisation to the customer.

11 On-demand production is normally referred to as pull manufacturing inasmuch as such manufacturing is normally demand-orientated – that is, the manufacture of a product only commences when a sales order is received from a customer/client. In a pull-based manufacturing system, information flows in the opposite direction to production – from the customer to the company/organisation.

12 Details of the Data Protection Act 1998 are available on-line from the UK Information Commissiones at *http://www.ico.gov.uk/for_organisations/data_protection.aspx*.

13 See below for a definition of a data subject.

14 Data Protection Act 1998 s.7, s.8, and s.9.

15 Data Protection Act 1998 s.10.

16 Data Protection Act 1998 s.11.

17 Data Protection Act 1998 s.12.

18 Data Protection Act 1998 s.13.

19 Data Protection Act 1998 s.12(a), s.14 and s.62.

CHAPTER 8

Information technology and the virtual world

Introduction

This chapter considers the practical aspects of e-commerce, in particular the uses of e-commerce innovations and technologies and the problems and opportunities presented by the integration of e-commerce facilities into corporate accounting information systems. It also considers the regulatory issues related to the use of e-commerce in general, and e-money in particular, and the potential problems associated with www-based finance/commerce.

Learning outcomes

By the end of this chapter, the reader should be able to:

- Describe the impact on e-commerce of innovations enabled by information and communication technology

- Explain the major aspects of business-to-business (B2B), business-to-consumer (B2C) and customer-to-customer (C2C) based e-commerce

- Describe the advantages and disadvantages of e-commerce-related technologies

- Assess the implication of legislative and regulatory pronouncements on e-commerce and related activities/services

E-commerce and the changing world of business – toward a self-service economy!

We are constantly reminded, day after day after day, that the world of business and commerce has changed . . . or is changing . . . or indeed, will change! Whatever timeline you may choose to believe, there can be little doubt that the world of business and commerce of the late twentieth century is but a dim and distant memory of what used to be – of a time long ago! Why? Put simply:

■ the rapid development of ever more powerful information and communication technologies,

■ the growing interconnectivity afforded by such technologies, and

■ the increasing importance of the internet and World Wide Web in almost all business-related commercial activities,

has, some would say with growing ease, promoted the development of an increasingly customer-centric self-service e-commerce economy – in which the conservative tradition-alisms of contemporary capitalism and the historical conventionalities of wealth accumu-lation that dominated the world of business and commerce for more than 150 years continue to be swept away, and replaced by a postmodern demand-orientated customer-led *virtual* world of business and commerce.

E-commerce: the success factors

While the success of a company's/organisation's e-commerce facility will of course depend on the demand for its products/services, in many cases it will, more importantly, depend on two groups of interrelated factors: (i) factors based on organisation/structure, and (ii) factors based on function/process.

Organisation/structure factors

Factors based on organisation/structure are those that have a direct influence on the business infrastructure of the company. Clearly, it is important for a company to ensure that there is an adequate level of activity, coordination of activities, and an appropriate level of resource(s) management within the company to ensure that the demands of the customer are met in full. Such factors would include for example:

■ the existence and adequacy of the company's/organisation's long-term strategy,

■ the appropriateness of the company's/organisation's business model and value chain,

■ the knowledge/resource capabilities within the company,

■ the use of technologies within the company, and

■ the adaptability/flexibility of the company.

Function/process factors

Factors based on function/process are those that influence the functionality of a company's/organisation's website.

Clearly, it is also important for a company to ensure that the e-commerce provision provides an enjoyable and rewarding experience for the customer. It is, for example, important for the customer to own the purchasing experience, and be able to direct their purchasing experience.

Therefore, it is important that the customer receives not only a responsive, personalised and user-friendly service, but, more importantly, a secure, reliable and value-for-money experience – an experience which the customer may want to repeat in the future. For example:

- by offering incentives to customers – by providing discount schemes and/or loyalty programmes, and/or
- by creating a sense of community – by developing affinity programmes, and/or
- by providing access to information – by developing/creating social networks.

What makes a good website, and what makes a bad website?
That's difficult to say but, broadly speaking, a good website would be one in which:

- presentation is clear and consistent,
- navigation is simple,
- navigation tools are easy to use,
- features/page layouts are clearly designed,
- video and audio is used in a relevant and appropriate manner,
- information is grouped/arranged consistently and logically, and
- language options are available where necessary/appropriate,

. . . and a bad website would be one in which:

- colours are used in an inconsistent and unhelpful manner,
- audio/video imagery/presentation is poor,
- technology is used in a limited/ineffective manner,
- navigation is difficult, and/or navigation tools do not function adequately,
- page layouts are confusing and inconsistent, and
- presentation limits/restricts audience access.

What are the key rules to good website design?
Put simply – manageability and functionality.

It is not only important to ensure that what is promised on the website is delivered (for example, if the website indicates/promises daily updates will be available then it is important to ensure that such updates are available, but also important to ensure that the website is useable by customers/users!

Remember, just because it can be done does not mean it has to be done! Sophisticated state of the art graphics may look good at the development stage, but if a large proportion of customers/users cannot access them properly, they are – to all intent and purpose – useless.

E-commerce: the failure factors

There are of course many companies whose e-commerce facilities have failed to produce the results initially expected. The most common reasons for such a failure are:

- an inadequate appreciation of the needs and requirements of customers,
- an overestimation of company skills and competence,

- an inadequate understanding of the competitive situation,

- an ineffective coordination of business-related e-commerce activities,

- an inability to manage the impact and consequences of change,

- a lack of organisational commitment, and/or

- a lack of organisational security.

In addition to the above, an e-commerce facility may fail because the product(s) and/or service(s) for sale simply may not be suitable for e-commerce.

For example, products that are generally considered suitable for e-commerce are:

- products that have a high a high value-to-weight ratio,

- digital products/services,[1]

- component products – for example, spare part components for products, and

- products that have a high personal/erotic content – for example, pornography and other sex-related products.[2]

So, what products are generally considered unsuitable for e-commerce? In general:

- products that have a low value-to-weight ratio,

- products that have a smell, taste or touch component – for example, perfume,

- products that need trial fittings – for example, clothing, and

- products where colour appears to be important.

Categories of e-commerce

As we saw earlier, e-commerce is essentially a sub-category of e-business, the principal activity of e-commerce being (somewhat unsurprisingly) commerce (that is, market-related retail and distribution activities or, put simply, the sale and/or purchase of goods and/or services) using digital communications, including also all inter-company and intra-company functions that enable such commerce.

Such e-based retail activities can be categorised into a number of alternative application types:

- business-to-consumer (B2C) e-commerce,

- business-to-business (B2B) e-commerce,

- business-to-business-to-consumer (B2B2C) e-commerce,

- consumer-to-business (C2B) e-commerce,

- consumer-to-consumer (C2C) e-commerce, and

- customer-to-business-to-consumer (C2B2C), e-commerce,

with each of the above types using a *portal* interface to provide access to a *retailing resource*.[3]

In an internet/web context, a *portal* is essentially a virtual doorway – a gateway that provides the customer/user with information on, and access to, a range of company goods, services, and facilities. While the format of an access portal will depend primarily on the nature and image of the company (for example, market location, market branding, corporate/organisation image/colour scheme), the structure of a portal will depend primarily on the range and diversity of the business activities undertaken by the company. A portal – as an access platform – can therefore vary, from:

■ a vertical platform on which specific information on, and/or access to, a single service/ facility or single portfolio of services/facilities is provided, to

■ a horizontal platform on which aggregate information on, and/or access to, a diversified portfolio of services/facilities, is provided.

In addition portals can be, and indeed increasingly are, used as security filters requiring customers/users to input a username and password before access to a retailing resource is permitted. This is especially the case for business-to-business e-commerce portals.

The *retailing resource* provides the facilities/resources for the customer/user to either:

■ purchase goods and/or services, or

■ sell goods and/or services,

depending of course on the e-commerce application type, varying from:

■ a static price platform in which the prices of goods, services and facilities are non-negotiable and determined by the retailer, to

■ a dynamic price platform in which the prices of goods, services and facilities are negotiable – using either:

   ▪ a bid (or auction-based) facility, or

   ▪ a discount (or activity-based) facility.

A bid (or auction-based) facility is a facility in which a customer/user can play a dual role, as either seller (offering to sell goods and/or services) or purchaser (bidding to buy goods and/or services), and the prices of goods, services and facilities are dependent upon the levels of interest shown (or bids made) by potential purchases.

A discount (or activity-based) facility is a facility in which the prices of goods, services and facilities are dependent upon the actions of customers/users – for example, prices discounting for large volume purchases, or free delivery for large value purchases.

Before we look at each of the above application types . . . some definitions!

A dot com company (or a single channel company)

A company that undertakes business activities primarily on-line using a URL that ends in '.com', although it also applies to URLs that end in '.co.uk'. Such companies have no high street presence. Such companies are also referred to as *single channel companies*, or *pure e-tailers*.

A dot bam company (or a dual channel company)

A company that undertakes business activities in both the 'real world', using a physical retail outlet, and on-line; the 'bam' component of the name being an abbreviation of 'bricks and mortar' as a reference to the real physical world environment. Such dot bam companies or *dual channel companies*[4] are also referred to as 'clicks and mortar' companies and/or 'clicks and bricks' companies, and/or *mixed e-tailers*.

A dot bam+ company (or a tri-channel company)

A company that undertakes business activities using three alternative retail channels:

1 on-line retailing facilities,

2 physical 'real world' retail outlets, and

3 retail catalogues – for example, mail order catalogues.

Business-to-consumer (B2C) e-commerce

Business-to-consumer (B2C) e-commerce (often called on-line trading or e-tailing) is the selling of goods, services and/or information by a company to a single individual customer. The most common example of such a business-to-customer (B2C) application is the retail website featuring/advertising/offering for sale a company's/organisation's goods and services which can be purchased by the consumer – usually using:

■ an imaginary 'shopping cart' facility,

■ a virtual 'checkout' facility, and

■ a payment processing facility.

We will discuss business-to-consumer (B2C) e-commerce later in this chapter.

Business-to-business (B2B) e-commerce

Business-to-business (B2B) e-commerce is the selling of goods, services and/or information by a company to another company, and is now popular in a wide range of industries – from traditional so-called 'bricks and mortar' economy companies (for example manufacturing, wholesale distribution and retailing), to the increasingly important information society services based companies.

The majority of business-to-business (B2B) e-commerce occurs between dot bam companies.

Business-to-business-to-consumer (B2B2C) e-commerce

Business-to-business-to-consumer (B2B2C) e-commerce is the selling of goods, services or information by a company to a single individual customer, using a company as an intermediary – or a middleman company.

Consumer-to-business (C2B) e-commerce

Consumer-to-business (C2B) e-commerce is the purchasing of goods and/or services by an individual customer (or a collective of individual customers acting as a buying cartel) from a company.

Consumer-to-consumer (C2C) e-commerce

Consumer-to-consumer (C2C) e-commerce is the selling of goods/services and communication/transfer of information by a single individual/customer to another single individual customer. Such e-commerce is normally associated with the retail of 'second hand' or 'nearly new' products/commodities.

Consumer-to-business-to-consumer (C2B2C) e-commerce

Consumer-to-business-to-consumer (C2B2C) e-commerce is the selling of goods/services and/or the communication or transfer of information by a single individual customer to another single individual customer, using a company as an intermediary. As with the above, such e-commerce is also associated with the retail of 'second hand' or 'nearly new' products/commodities.

Other activities related to e-commerce

There are of course many other activities related to e-business and/or e-commerce, for which a company could use its website, the most common of these being:

■ product/service advertising activities,
■ prospect generation activities, and
■ customer support activities.

Product/service advertising activities

Advertising products/services using a website differs from traditional advertising inasmuch as the website is in effect hidden from the customer. That is, to access a website the customer needs to find it, using:

■ a web link from a search engine,
■ a web link on an existing web page, and/or
■ a web address.

In the first instance, most customers would find a website by surfing – that is, scanning available websites using a search engine (for example, *www.google.co.uk*) until the site is located. Because of the obvious limitations of such an approach, some companies use other company websites for advertising purposes. For instance it is increasingly common for a company to advertise its products/services on the website of another company within the same group of companies (for example, see *www.virgin.com/uk*), or indeed on the website of an unrelated company on a reciprocal quid pro quo[5] basis. Indeed, where retail outlets occupy a single or geographical area it has become increasingly common for such companies to advertise on so-called geographical 'shop front' sites.

The advantages of using a website for product/services advertising activities are:

■ it is a low overall cost alternative – compared to other available alternative media (for example TV), and
■ such advertising can reach a global audience and it not regionally and/or geographically restricted.

The disadvantage of using a website for product/services advertising activities is that such websites are hidden and, therefore, need to be 'found'.

Prospect generation activities

Prospect generation activities relate to websites designed to:

■ provide information to prospective customers – for example, by the use of on-line brochures, promotional material, company newsletter, catalogues, etc., and/or
■ collect information on prospective customers – for example, by the use of on-line data capture forms to collect names, addresses, phone numbers, e-mail addresses, etc.

The advantages of using a website for prospect generation activities are:

■ it is cost-efficient – for example, it saves on printing, manufacturing and distribution costs, and
■ it can be very effective – for example, an on-line brochure can reach hundreds/thousands of potential customers that may never have been reached using traditional hard copy prospect generation activities.

The disadvantage of using a website for prospect generation activities is that restrictions may exist on the collection and storage of personal data – see, for example, the Data Protection Act 1998 (discussed in Chapter 7).

Customer support activities

In addition to prospect generation activities, another growth area in e-commerce has been the increasing use of websites for information provision purposes – that is, for example, using web-based facilities to provide:

■ technical product/service specifications,
■ support facilities – for example, on-line diagnostic tools for troubleshooting purposes,
■ repair/maintenance manuals,
■ customer enquiry pages – for example, FAQ (Frequently Asked Questions) pages, and
■ customer discussion forums.

The advantages of using a website for customer support activities are that it is a cost-efficient, highly effective method of providing product/service information, and may offer a source of competitive advantage for a company.

The disadvantage of using a website for customer support activities is the potential generic nature of support service activity made available to customers – in other words 'one service for all enquiries'.

Barriers to e-commerce

While it would be very easy to believe the media rhetoric that now appears to surround almost every aspect of e-commerce – all, in fact, is not well! Indeed although activities related to e-commerce have grown substantially over the last few years (as we have seen), in general consumers continue to be unwilling to accept the on-line self-service e-commerce business model – in numbers greater than many companies (and indeed many regulatory authorities) would have liked.

Why? There are perhaps several key reasons that may explain this slow uptake, the main reasons being concerns over control, concerns over issues of access, and concerns over issues of privacy, safety, and security.

Control . . . what control?

As we saw in Chapter 4, ICANN (Internet Corporation for Assigned Names and Numbers) continues to retain firm control over the assignment of unique identifiers on the internet, including domain names, internet protocol addresses and protocol port numbers; it is also true to say that there has been, and indeed continues to be very little (if any) control over *what is available* on the internet and the World Wide Web – an issue which continues to be one of great concern for many people. Recent years have seen a growing number of attempts mainly by regional governments (in collaboration with companies such as Google (*www.google.com*)) – some quite successful – to control/manage access to, and use of, the internet. For example:

■ The French government continues to restrict access to websites that stir up racial hatred.

■ The German government continues to restrict access to websites that deny the Holocaust.

- The US government continues to restrict access to websites that infringe commercial copyright agreements.

But the issue of control still continues to worry many users of the virtual highway.

More recently, in the last few years, a number of governments have created task forces to actively pursue control and monitoring policies that enable authorities not only to police and restrict access to, but also identify and locate users of, websites containing inappropriate literature and/or images.[6] See, for example:

- the Virtual global task force[7] at *www.virtualglobaltaskforce.com*, and
- the Internet Content Rating Association at *www.icra.org*.

Although many politicians, social commentators and media groups have welcomed such moves, some critics, while accepting the need for a 'policing of the virtual highway', have suggested that the imposition of excessive restrictions could in an extreme case/scenario lead to excessive political censorship. Many commentators now cite Google's (albeit somewhat reluctant) consent to requests by the Chinese government to severely restrict internet access to a range of websites.

A sign of things to come . . . perhaps! We will have to wait and see!

The world is on-line . . . well part of it!

As we saw in Chapter 4, it is of course a fallacy to presume that the internet is a global phenomenon. There still remain many parts of the world where access to the internet continues to be severely restricted, not only for social and technological reasons but, increasingly, for political and economic reasons. Indeed, far from creating equality, the internet has, as Table 8.1 illustrates, assisted in the creation of an even more divided world – a world in which the structural and technological deficit between those that have access and those that do not have access (or have severely restricted access) continues to become greater day by day. Not so much global integration as imposed fragmentation!

Table 8.1 World internet usage and population (as at 31 March 2011)

World region	Population (millions)	Population % of the world	Internet usage (millions)	Population % penetration
Africa	1,038	15.0	119	11.4
Asia	3,880	56.0	922	23.8
Europe	817	11.8	476	58.3
Middle East	216	3.1	69	31.7
North America	347	5.0	272	78.3
Latin America/Caribbean	597	8.6	216	36.2
Oceania/Australia	35	0.5	21	60.1
Total (world)	6,930	100	2,095	30.2

Source: Internet World Statistics (available at *www.internetworldstats.com*)

Not convinced? Consider the following:

Of a world population of approximately 6.93 billion people, only 30.2 per cent (a little over 2 billion people) use the internet, with the greatest concentration of internet users being found in:

- Asia (approximately 922 million people/users),
- Europe (approximately 476 million people/users), and
- North America (approximately 272 million people/users).

These (approximately 1,670 million people/users) together account for 79.7 per cent of the total of the world population using the internet.

Perhaps more noticeably (and somewhat unsurprisingly) the lowest concentration of internet users is found in:

- Africa (approximately 119 million people/users),
- the Middle East (approximately 69 million people/users), and (more surprisingly)
- Oceania/Australia (21 million people/users).

More importantly, of the top 10 languages used by internet users (as the primary language):

- 27.0 per cent use English,
- 24.3 per cent use Chinese, and
- 7.9 per cent use Spanish

despite the fact that in general usage, only 18.8 per cent of the world population use English as a primary language. The most popular language (in world population terms) is Chinese with 19.8 per cent; Spanish is used as a primary language by only approximately 6.1 per cent of the world population. (See Table 8.2.)

Table 8.2 World internet users by language (as at 31 March 2011)

World language	Internet users by language (millions)	% of all internet users	Population estimate of language use (millions)	% Internet penetration by language
English	565	27.0	1,302	43.4
Chinese	509	24.3	1,372	37.1
Spanish	165	7.9	423	39.0
Japanese	99	4.7	126	78.6
Portuguese	83	4.0	254	32.7
German	75	3.6	95	78.9
Arabic	65	3.1	347	18.7
French	60	2.9	348	17.2
Russian	60	2.9	139	43.2
Korean	39	1.9	71	54.9
Top 10 languages	1,720	82.1	4,477	38.4
Rest of the world languages	375	17.9	2,453	15.3
Total (world)	2,095	100.0	6,930	30.2

Source: Internet World Statistics (available at *www.internetworldstats.com*)

Why the dominance of the English language on the internet?

There are perhaps three reasons:

1 the history/origin of the internet,[8]
2 the management and control of access to the internet (see above), and
3 the composition of the current dominant users of the internet (see Table 8.3).

In respect of (iii) above, it is perhaps worth noting that of the top 20 countries in terms of internet users, a number of countries (for example, the USA, the UK and Australia) use English as a primary language, but a number of other countries (for example, India and Indonesia) also recognise English – though as a secondary language.

Table 8.3 Countries with the highest number of internet users (as at 31 March 2011)

Country/Region	Internet users (millions)	Estimated population (millions)
China	420	1,330
United States	240	310
Japan	99	127
India	81	1,173
Brazil	76	201
Germany	65	82
Russia	59	139
United Kingdom	51	62
France	44	65
Nigeria	44	152
Top 10 countries	1,179	3,641
Rest of the world	916	3,289
Total (world)	2,095	6,930

Source: Internet World Statistics (available at *www.internetworldstats.com*)

E-commerce: is it secure?

While concerns over controllability and accessibility continue to represent a significant barrier to ongoing development of twenty-first-century e-commerce in both the UK and the rest of the world, it is perhaps issues of privacy and security that, in fact, dominate the minds of many companies, organisations, government agencies, regulators and, of course, customers/users. This is a concern only exacerbated by the almost constant media coverage of high-profile security failures and data thefts.

Removing the barriers to e-commerce – protection schemes

Clearly, issues of privacy and security, of customer/user unease, represent an enormous problem to companies engaged in activities related to e-commerce.

There are a number of alternative schemes/technologies that have been, and indeed continue to be, used as a means of improving/enhancing the protection of companies, customers and users. Such schemes/technologies include:

- the establishment of a system/network firewall,
- the use of intrusion detection systems (or intrusion detection software),
- the use of data/information encryption facilities,
- the use of digital certificates, and
- the use of authentication and authorisation software.

B2C (business-to-consumer) e-commerce

Briefly (to recap from Chapter 4), within point-of-service electronic funds transfer (EFT) there are two sub-categories:

- card-based systems, and
- non-card-based systems.

Point of service (EPoS) based EFT card systems can be further sub-categorised as:

- off-line processing using a manual processing system,
- on-line processing using an EFT system – cardholder present, and
- on-line processing using an EFT system – cardholder not present.

On-line web-based e-commerce transactions are essentially classified as on-line processing – cardholder not present transactions. To process on-line cardholder not present transactions, a company has a choice of three alternative methodologies:

1 using an internet merchant account facility, or
2 using a payment processing company facility, or
3 using a shopping mall facility.

In general, the vast majority of private limited companies, and perhaps all public limited companies, use an internet merchant account facility. Alternatives (ii) and (iii) above are typically used by sole traders, small partnerships and/or very small private limited companies.

There are however always exceptions to every rule! To use an internet merchant account facility, a company must have:

- an internet merchant account (and ID), from an acquiring bank, and
- an approved Payment Service Provider (PSP).

What is an acquiring bank?

An acquiring bank is a high street bank that offers debit card and credit card processing services. The acquiring bank acquires the money from the customer, processes the transaction, and credits the company account. If a company wants to take debit card and credit card payment, it will need a merchant service account (and ID) with an acquiring bank. In addition, where a company wants to undertake web-based on-line e-commerce, then the company will also need an internet merchant services account (and ID).

In the UK there are a number of banks that provide both merchant account facilities and internet merchant account facilities – these banks are often referred to as merchant acquirers or acquiring banks.

. . . and a payment service provider?

A payment service provider (PSP) is essentially a payment gateway. It is a virtual service/ system that collects the debit card/credit card details over the web, and passes them to the acquiring bank. A payment service provider acts as an intermediary between the merchant's website (the retailing company) and all the financial networks involved with the transaction. These will include, of course, the customer's debit card/credit card issuer, and the company's/organisation's merchant account.

If a company wants to undertake transactions involving the use on-line of debit card and credit card payments, the company will need a PSP. Examples of current payment service providers include:

- SECpay at *www.secpay.com*,
- Ogone at *www.ogone.com*,

- Universal Gateway Payment at *www.securehosting.com*,

- Worldpay at *www.worldpay.com*, and

- Protx at *www.protx.com*.

Note: Some PSPs only operate with particular acquiring banks. For example, SECpay (see above) has operating agreements with the following acquiring banks: Ulster Bank, NatWest Streamline, Paymentech, LloydsTSB Cardnet, HSBC, Euro Conex, Barclays Merchant Services, Bank of Scotland, Alliance and Leicester, American Express, and Diners; whereas Protx (see above) has operating agreements with the following acquiring banks: Lloyds TSB Cardnet, the Bank of Scotland, Barclays Merchant Services, HSBC, NatWest Streamline, American Express, and Diners.

What does the payment service provider do?

As a payment gateway, the payment service provider essentially:

- checks the validity of the debit card/credit card,

- encrypts the transaction details and debit card/credit card details,

- ensures that the encrypted details are transmitted to the correct destination,

- decrypts the response(s), and

- confirms the response(s) with the merchant's website or shopping cart/basket either as:
  - an authorised transaction,
  - a referred transaction, or
  - a declined transaction.

Many UK acquiring banks (including those mentioned above) offer PSP services as part of their product range – that is, as part of their internet merchant services account facilities. For example, Worldpay is part of the Royal Bank of Scotland Group. In addition, where a payment processing company facility is used, or a shopping mall facility is used, services related to a payment service would normally form part of their service provision.

Okay, so how does web-based e-commerce actually work?

On-line and open for business

As suggested earlier in this chapter, a company e-commerce website would normally comprise two parts:

1 a portal interface (or access portal), and

2 a retailing resource.

The portal interface used by a company would provide the customer/user with information on, and access to, a range of company goods, services, and facilities.

The retailing resource would provide the customer/user with facilities to undertake a range of commercial transactions – in particular the purchase of products and/or services. Such a retail resource would normally comprise (see Figure 8.1):

1 an electronic order-taking facility – using, for example, an imaginary 'shopping cart/basket',

2 a virtual 'checkout' facility, and

3 a payment processing facility.

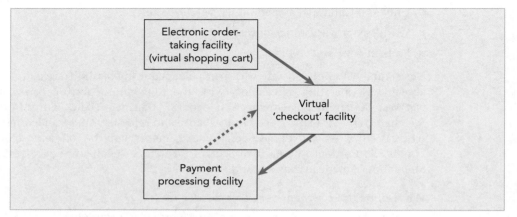

Figure 8.1 E-commerce retailing resource

Electronic order-taking facility

Most on-line retailers use the notion and image of a shopping cart/basket to both typify the electronic order-taking facility, and exemplify the on-line shopping experience. Indeed, for a wide range of on-line retailers, the shopping cart/basket is now considered to be a standard component of the on-line shopping process. But exactly what is a shopping cart/basket, and what purpose does it actually serve?

In essence, the shopping cart/basket is simply a collection facility. It is an interface between the customer, and the company's/organisation's product/services database. That is, every time the customer selects a product/service to purchase, the item/items are added to the shopping cart/basket.

In an information technology context a shopping cart/basket is simply a software program. However, in an operational e-commerce context a shopping cart/basket merely records the ongoing results of the customer's ordering process, and is designed to allow the customer to view the details of all ongoing transactions or purchases, on request, and at any time up to checkout.

When customers have completed all their transactions, they are invited to proceed to the virtual checkout facility to complete the purchasing process.

Virtual checkout facility

An e-mail address is required so that confirmation can be e-mailed to the customer once the order process and payment procedure have been completed. Where the customer is an existing customer all that is required is a customer password (which is linked to the e-mail address).

A new customer, as well as having to supply an e-mail address, will be asked for payment details (credit card and/or debit card details). Once the payment details have been verified, approved and authorised, a confirmation e-mail (containing an order number) is e-mailed to the customer's e-mail address . . . and the transaction (at least the on-line component of the transaction) is complete.

All that is then required is delivery of the product purchased by the customer!

Although a small number of products and services may/can be distributed digitally, most products will need to be physically delivered. Once a commitment to purchase has been made, some on-line retailers allow customers to select alternative delivery modes.

Some retailers advertise the offer of 'free delivery' of products when the total value of a purchase exceeds a predetermined limit or where delivery is required within a particular geographical area, but impose an additional charge where special distribution and delivery mechanisms are requested – for example next day delivery. Other retailers may impose a small nominal charge for all types of delivery irrespective of the purchase order value. In reality, however, whatever the marketing/advertising rhetoric . . . nothing is for free. The cost of any 'free' delivery is merely absorbed within the cost overheads of the product. The distinction between 'free' or 'unpaid for' delivery and 'paid for' delivery is merely a creative marketing tool designed to attract the interest of prospective customers/ clients. In a marketing/advertising context, think of the word 'free' when used in relation to product delivery as a linguistic metaphor – a metaphor used to signify a hidden cost.

Payment processing facility . . . accepting on-line payments

As suggested earlier, there are three alternative methodologies that can be employed to process/receive on-line payments:

1 using an internet merchant account, or
2 using a payment processing company, or
3 using a shopping mall facility.

Let's have a look at these three alternatives.

Using an internet merchant account

Where a company currently accepts debt card/credit card payments, that is face-to-face transactions or, more appropriately, on-line processing pPoS EFT (on-line cardholder present electronic funds transfer (see Chapter 4)), then the company will already possess a current merchant account. To accept on-line credit card/debit card payments, as we have seen, a company would need to acquire an internet merchant account facility. Such an account is useful where a company expects to undertake a high volume of fairly simple, low risk on-line transactions.

The advantage of using an internet merchant account is that debit card/credit card payments are available for use by the company within three to four working days after the transaction.

The disadvantages of using an internet merchant account are:

■ Application procedures can be complex – that is, often merchant banks impose severe information requirements on companies applying for internet merchant account facilities.

■ The technology costs – for example, secure socket layer (SSL) technology is required to encrypt transaction data and to transmit the necessary customer and debit card/credit card details to the acquiring bank for the transaction to be authenticated.

■ The administrative costs – for example, all acquiring banks impose a set-up fee, and day-to-day transaction charges.

In addition, the costs of any fraudulent transactions are borne by the company, not by the merchant bank. That is, if a fraudulent transaction occurs, the value of the transaction is recovered by the merchant bank from the company account – in full.

Using a payment processing company

Where a company:

- does not process a large number of on-line transactions,
- does not currently accept credit card/debit card payments – that is, the company does not currently possess a merchant account, and perhaps
- does not have an established trading history,

the company may consider using the facilities of a payment processing company (sometimes referred to as a payment bureau). Such payment processing companies obtain payment from the customer's credit card and/or debit card issuer on behalf of the company. The advantages of using a payment processing company are:

- Reduced technology costs – that is, there is no need to invest in a costly secure payment system.
- Reduced administrative costs – that is, the payment procedures are managed by the payment processing company.
- Reduced application procedures – that is, information requirements are less severe than the information requirements for an application for an internet merchant account.

The disadvantages of using a payment processing company are:

- The payment processing company may hold payment receipts from customers for a minimum settlement period (the period depends on the payment processing company) before they are transferred to the company account.
- Customers are aware that their payment is being directed through a payment processing company.

In addition (as with an internet merchant account), the costs of any fraudulent transactions are borne by the company, not by the payment processing company.

In general, payment processing companies offer a useful and relatively cheap alternative for companies that have limited debit card/credit card transactions or who, for whatever reason, do not/cannot open a merchant account with an acquiring bank.

An example of such a payment processing company would include Paypal (*www.paypal.com*). For further examples, see *www.electronic-payments.co.uk*, an information website sponsored by a UK government agency.

Using an on-line shopping mall

An on-line shopping mall can be a good alternative for a small company which has a limited turnover of standardised products/services and does not currently offer debit card/credit card sales facilities but is seeking to establish an on-line presence.

What is an on-line shopping mall?

Essentially, an on-line shopping mall is a collection of on-line retail outlets on a single website, in which:

- individual retailers are responsible for maintaining and updating their own retail outlets, and
- the shopping mall provider is responsible for managing the shopping mall facility – including, for example, payment processing facilities.

Such shopping mall facilities are offered by many trade and industry associations. Indeed, some internet service providers (ISPs) also offer on-line shopping mall facilities.

What are the advantages and disadvantages?

For a small company, the advantages of an on-line shopping mall facility are:

- such shopping malls provide an immediate on-line presence, and
- there is no need for the company to arrange/set up an internet merchant account or separate payment processing facilities.

The disadvantages of an on-line shopping mall facility are:

- the company joining the shopping mall will often be limited to a standard format presentation – usually with limited facilities, and (perhaps more importantly)
- such shopping mall facilities can be very expensive – for example, a company joining a shopping mall may have to pay not only an arrangement/set-up fee but also a percentage charge for each transaction undertaken through the shopping mall facility, and, in some instances, a monthly or annual management fee.

B2C (business-to-consumer) e-commerce . . . behind the screen!

Here is a brief step by step guide to an on-line transaction using an internet merchant account and a payment gateway service provider.

Stage 1 The customer visits the retailer's website.

Stage 2 The customer selects purchase items within the retailer's purchasing pages.

Stage 3 The customer's selection is added to the retailer's shopping cart.

Stage 4 Once at the 'checkout', the customer's personal and financial details are recorded on a secure form – using a Secure Socket Layer mode. It is at this stage that the retailer's website should switch to the Secure Socket Layer (SSL) mode. As you may recall, SSL is a widely used encryption technology which allows encrypted information to be transferred between the retailer's checkout page and the payment gateway service server. Usually a padlock symbol will appear on the web page/web browser (lower left-hand corner) to show that the page is secure.

Stage 5 The customer's details are transmitted to a payment gateway service, which is often separate from the shopping cart.

Stage 6 The gateway service securely routes the information through the relevant financial networks to gain authorisation.

Stage 7 The payment gateway service will provide notification of transaction status (authorised, referred or declined) to the retailer, and then process the transaction through the banking system. If the transaction is successful, the customer's account is credited and the retailer's merchant account is debited with the value of the transaction, less the acquiring bank's commission and/or fees.

Stage 8 Once all funds have cleared, the retailer is able to transfer the money to their ordinary business bank account.

Stage 9 The payment gateway service would normally collect fees/charges for the transactions processed on a monthly basis – usually by direct debit.

B2B (business-to-business) e-commerce

Whereas variants of business-to-business e-commerce have existed for many, many years – for example EDI (electronic data interchange) and, more recently, EFT (electronic funds transfer) – such activities were, in a business context, considered peripheral to the main supply chain activities of a company, and therefore often existed as fragmented and disjointed 'stand alone' processes/procedures, divorced from key retail and distribution activities. Although such fragmented processes/procedures did play, and indeed in some instances continue to play, a key role in retail-related business activities, it was perhaps the emergence of web-based information and communication technologies and capabilities that enabled the development of the infrastructure that we now know as business-to-business e-commerce.

What is business-to-business e-commerce?

In a contemporary context, business-to-business e-commerce has become synonymous with supply chain integration and the use of extranet-based[9] facilities to provide access to a range of supply chain facilities, the aim being to improve the efficiency and effectiveness of business-related retail and distribution activities by integrating a customer's network directly to a supplier's network.

Clearly, the precise nature of the business-to-business e-commerce provision will differ from supplier to supplier; however, in broad terms a B2B e-commerce provision would normally include secure access to:

- on-line product/service catalogues,
- product/service synopses,
- product/service availability profiles,
- on-line (real-time) ordering facilities,
- real-time order-based tracking and transportation facilities,[10] and
- customer payment facilities.

Using e-money

Although the term e-money is often used interchangeably and somewhat incorrectly with terms such as electronic cash (eCash), or digital cash, the term e-money has a specific meaning/definition. An e-money scheme is a scheme, regulated by the FSA (Financial Services Authority), that involves the creation of digital value based tokens (in a single currency or multiple currencies) that are stored on either:

- an electronic device – for example a PC and/or computer network, or
- a smart card[11] (also known as e-purse),

that can be transferred from one person/company to another person/company – for example a consumer/buyer to a retailer/seller.

Consequently, e-money can be defined as monetary value which is stored on an electronic device, issued on receipt of funds, and accepted as a means of payment by persons other than the issuer,[12] and can – as an electronic means of payment – be used to pay for goods and services purchased in the high street, by mail order, or via the web/over the internet.

Structurally, there are two types of e-money: identified e-money and anonymous e-money. *Identified e-money* is e-money in which the identities of the parties to the transaction – in particular the payer (or consumer/purchaser of the goods/services) – are revealed in the payment operation. *Anonymous e-money* is e-money in which the identity of the payer (or consumer/purchaser of the goods/services) is not revealed in the payment transaction.

Anonymous e-money essentially operates like a cash exchange and can more accurately be described as eCash or digital cash.

In addition, each of the above types of e-money exists in two varieties:

1 On-line e-money – that is, an e-money transaction in which a transaction can only be completed with a payer/customer once interaction with the originator of the e-money (or an appointed authorised institution) has occurred and the validity of the transaction verified (for example, sufficient funds are available etc.).

2 Off-line e-money – that is, an e-money transaction that can be completed with a payer/customer without interaction with the originator of the e-money (or an appointed authorised institution).

Who can issue e-money?

Banks and building societies that are already authorised by the FSA to provide high street banking services can issue e-money as a component part of their portfolio of banking-related activities. However, specialist e-money issuers[13] have to apply for FSA authorisation to issue e-money and provide e-money-related services.

At the heart of the regulatory framework surrounding e-money lie two EU Directives:

1 Directive 2000/46/EC (the e-money Directive), relating to the taking up, pursuit of, and prudential supervision of the business of electronic money institutions (September 2000).

2 Directive 2000/28/EC amending Directive 2000/12/EC (the Banking Co-ordination Directive), relating to the taking up and pursuit of the business of credit institutions.

Their aim is:

■ to protect consumers and ensure confidence in e-money schemes through the implementation of rules for safeguarding the financial integrity and stability of e-money institutions, and

■ to facilitate/provide for licensed e-money institutions to offer/provide cross-border services/facilities.

The above e-money Directives were introduced into the UK regulatory systems through a number of regulatory provisions/amendments:

■ The Financial Services and Markets Act 2000 (Regulated Activities) (Amendment) Order 2002.

■ The Electronic Money (Miscellaneous Amendments) Regulations 2002.

■ The Financial Services Authority's ('FSA') Handbook of Rules and Guidance.

Consequently:

■ the issuing of e-money is classified as a regulated activity under the Financial Services and Markets Act 2000 (as amended),[14] and,

■ the issuers of e-money (including specialist issuers who are not an existing bank and/or building society) are regarded as credit institutions, and are regulated in a similar way to banks and building societies – although with less stringent requirements.

Who might want to use e-money?

There are of course many alternative potential uses for/potential users of e-money, for example:

■ persons who feel more secure using e-money rather than debit and/or credit cards to purchase goods on the web/over the internet,

■ persons who feel more secure carrying e-money on a plastic smart card, rather than a wallet/purse full of notes and coins,

■ persons/travellers who may need to carry multiple currencies, and (perhaps most importantly)

■ persons who for whatever reason do not have access to a bank account/debit card, or credit card.

What are the advantages and disadvantages of e-money?

The main advantages of e-money are:

■ it is a secure payment methodology,

■ it is very portable,

■ it has growing acceptability, and

■ it is regarded as user-friendly.

The main disadvantage is that, as a payment system, e-money is still in its infancy stage and may take a number of years to fully develop.

M-commerce

M-commerce or mobile commerce can be defined as electronic commerce undertaken with the use of a mobile device such as, for example, a mobile phone. The development and growth of m-commerce was perhaps inevitable given:

■ the increasing growth in internet and web use over the last 25 years,

■ the establishment and continuing development of web-based e-commerce technologies, and

■ the continuing development of portable WAP[15] communication technologies and devices.

However, as business and commerce tread warily into the twenty-first century, m-commerce still remains in its infancy (certainly at the end of 2011). Is it perhaps a technology whose time has yet to arrive?

M-commerce applications

The term m-commerce was first used in the late 1990s during the so-called dot com boom – the idea being to use broadband mobile telephony to provide on-demand services and applications.[16] Unfortunately the idea(s) in many cases disappeared gently into the twilight zone – along with many of the dot com companies.

Why? Put simply, the technologies available during the 1990s were insufficiently evolved to be able to deliver many of the applications and services promised. It was not, therefore, a lack of demand from customers/users – it was an inability to supply on the part of the companies!

In general m-commerce applications can be categorised as either:

■ *active* m-commerce applications – m-commerce in which the customer/user is proactive in the initiation of a service/application, such as in the use of transaction processing facilities and/or digital services; or

■ *passive* m-commerce applications – m-commerce in which the service/application is self-initiating, and the customer/user is merely a reactive recipient.

Currently, the most popular services related to m-commerce include:

■ mobile ticketing;

■ mobile vouchers, coupons and loyalty cards;

■ content purchase and delivery (including film and music);

■ location-based services, for example local discount offers, local weather;

■ information services, for example news, share prices, sports scores, financial records, traffic reporting;

■ mobile banking;

■ hotel and accommodation services;

■ mobile store front advertising;

■ auctions;

■ mobile web browsing;

■ e-catalogues;

■ mobile marketing and advertising.

M-commerce: the regulations

Although m-commerce is a relatively new technology, certain aspects – especially m-commerce services utilising micropayments[17] – are regulated within the framework provided by the European Union e-money Directive, although its implementation (perhaps unsurprisingly) does differ between member states.

Why is this directive of relevance to m-commerce? Put simply, m-commerce micropayments are considered a form of e-money, and are therefore subject to its regulations.

As we saw earlier in our discussion of e-money, in the UK the Financial Services Authority is responsible for the regulation of e-money and related schemes.

What are the advantages and disadvantages of m-commerce?

For companies, the advantages of m-commerce include better targeted service/application delivery, and as a consequence improved cost-efficiency, and a more effective use of business resources. For mobile device users, the advantages include greater portability of, and increased accessibility to, services and applications – perhaps the reason why m-commerce devices are often referred to as 'anytime, anywhere' devices. In addition to such convenience, m-commerce provides increased personalisation of service/application provision – that is, m-commerce transactions are often perceived as 'one-to-one' transactions.

For companies, the disadvantages of m-commerce include the possibility of slow/interrupted data transmission, often resulting from a lack of (inter) network uniformity. For mobile device users the processing demands of the facilities offered can sometimes exceed the capability of the devices they possess – for example, not all mobile device users possess a 4G-enabled device, resulting in slow connectivity and reduced usability. In addition, there are only a limited number of payment methods available to pay for services used/applications purchased, the main methods being:

- use of premium-rate numbers,
- charging to the mobile device user's account and/or deducting the cost from the mobile device user's calling credit, either directly or using a reverse-charged SMS,
- using micropayment services,
- using stored-value cards with, for example, a mobile-device application store or music store.

Contactless commerce

Commerce using contactless payment systems (also known as 'touch and go' or 'wave and pay') essentially involves the use of credit cards, debit cards, key fobs, smart cards or other devices which utilise RFID (Radio Frequency Identification) to make secure payments. The embedded chip and antenna enable consumers to wave their card, fob or device over a reader at the point of sale. No signature or PIN entry is required.

The version of the contactless applications used in the UK (and the rest of the world) currently differs from the USA inasmuch as the UK version has the capability of transacting off-line based on the limit stored in the application.

The first contactless cards in the UK were issued by Barclaycard in 2008. At December 2010 there were approximately 12.9 million contactless-enabled cards, representing 9 per cent of all cards in circulation in the UK, with Barclaycard and Barclays leading the roll-out of contactless-enabled cards in circulation, and having 52,700 terminals.[18]

As with all payment devices, contactless cards have a number of security features. For example:

- the contactless payment systems use the same chip and PIN network used for normal credit and debit card transactions,
- there is a payment limit on single transactions,
- there is a limit on the number of transactions the card can be used for before the card holder is asked for a PIN.

In addition, contactless debit and credit card transactions are protected by the same fraud guarantee as standard chip and PIN based debit and credit card transactions.

Telecommunication operators are also beginning to get involved in contactless payments via the use of near field communication (NFC) phones. In 2009, Barclaycard partnered with mobile phone operator Orange (now Everything Everywhere), to launch a mobile phone with contactless payment technology,[19] integrating m-commerce with contactless payment. (See Article 8.1.)

Article 8.1

Orange and Barclaycard set date for UK's first commercial NFC service

Sarah Clark

British consumers will be able to use NFC phones to make payments at stores across the country from the second quarter of this year, Barclaycard and Everything Everywhere have announced.

Barclaycard and Everything Everywhere, the recently created merger between the UK arms of mobile network operators Orange and T-Mobile, have announced that the UK's first commercial NFC service will go live during the second quarter of 2011.

The long-awaited launch will see consumers able to purchase NFC phones from Orange and then use them to make payments from a new MasterCard PayPass prepaid account stored on their mobile phone.

'When you get your new handset, you need to activate it and link it to your existing Barclaycard, Barclays debit or Orange Credit Card,' Orange has told NFC World. 'Using your handset, you then simply download (or transfer) funds from your card, to your phone . . . Loading your account could not be easier and it can also be done online via MyBarclaycard. The mobile phone can then be used to make payments of £15 or less wherever contactless payments are accepted, by simply tapping the phone itself against a contactless reader.' Orange and Barclaycard first formed a long-term strategic partnership to bring mobile payments to British consumers in March 2009 and a commercial launch was originally expected to take place in late 2010. Last month, Orange revealed it would begin introducing NFC services in the majority of countries in which it has a presence in 2011.

No brand name for the new service has yet been agreed upon, according to Orange, but the official announcement does mention a 'forthcoming contactless Orange Cash prepaid payment card' and explains that 'contactless mobile phone payments will feature as part of the wider Orange portfolio of products, developed in conjunction with Barclaycard', indicating that the new service will see Orange rather than Barclaycard as the lead brand. Currently, there are 42,500 points-of-sale equipped to handle contactless payments in the UK but contactless transaction volumes have been very low to date. In September 2010, for instance, a total of 150,000 contactless Barclaycard transactions were conducted – an average of just over three transactions per point of sale.

'We're making something that's been talked about for many years a reality.'

London's commuters, however, are likely to provide the key to driving adoption of the new service. Transport for London (TfL) is committed to converting the city's buses as well as the London Underground to accepting payments via contactless payment cards and NFC, with work due to begin from the middle of this year. And, last week, MasterCard signed a multimillion pound deal with TfL that will see MasterCard branding appear on turnstiles on the underground as well as some six million of the plastic wallets issued to new Oyster cardholders this year.

Rival mobile network operator O2 is also expected to announce a commercial NFC launch in the near future. O2 Money, the operator's financial services arm, is currently on the hunt for a number of NFC, card and payments specialists to 'help establish the newest name in financial services.'

'This is the beginning of a revolution in how we pay for things on the high street,' says Gerry McQuade, Everything Everywhere's chief development officer. 'It's a cultural shift that is as important as the launch of the personal credit card or ATMs. We're making something that's been talked about for many years a reality and very soon using your mobile to buy a sandwich, a cinema ticket or, in time, even something bigger like a computer will simply be the norm.'

'I believe that future generations will find it surprising that early this century we were still carrying separate items to buy goods and to communicate with each other,' added David Chan, CEO of Barclaycard Consumer Europe. 'As payment experts, our role is to make it easier, more convenient and incredibly secure for people to make purchases and manage their money while on the move.'

Both Orange and Barclaycard have called on the services of Gemalto for the technology underlying the new service. The company is providing Orange with the NFC SIMs that will be issued to subscribers and is supplying Barclays with trusted service management (TSM) services, enabling the secure deployment and management of the mobile contactless payments.

27 January 2011

Source: Available at www.nearfieldcommunicationsworld.com/

Benefits of e-commerce

The benefits of e-commerce can be categorised as follows:

- provider-related benefits, and
- customer/user-related benefits.

Provider-related benefits

For a company providing the e-commerce facility – whether they are a dot com company, a dot bam company, or a dot bam+ company – the benefits include:

- immediate access to a global customer base – products and services supplied anytime, anyplace, anywhere;
- immediate access to non-stop retailing – buying and selling 24 hours a day, 7 days a week, 365 days a year;
- improved opportunity to enter/create new markets;
- improved communications with customers;
- improved inventory control;
- more efficient customer order processing, and customer order tracking;
- reduced operational costs;
- reduced transaction costs; and
- more efficient information and resource management.

Customer/user-related benefits

For a customer using the e-commerce facility, the main benefits of e-commerce include:

- greater competitive pricing of products and services;
- increased access to a 'world of stores';
- increased choice;
- greater availability of a larger and broader selection of products and services;
- increased flexibility;
- greater convenience, increased availability of more in-depth and up-to-date information on products and services;
- increased speed; and
- increased ease of use.

So, what about the problems?

Problems of e-commerce

Although the benefits of e-commerce are significant, such benefits have not come without consequences – that is, without longer-term problems/costs.

Such problems/costs can be categorised as follows:

1 *social costs* of e-commerce,

2 *political consequences* of e-commerce, and

3 *economic costs* of e-commerce.

Social costs of e-commerce

The social costs of e-commerce would include for example:

- a reduction in (local) employment opportunities,
- the closure of local retail facilities, and
- a possible increase in social poverty and deprivation,

as customers migrate from local retail facilities to on-line self-service shopping.

In addition, such costs could also include the social costs associated with the socio-economic/socio-demographic division between those that have access to, and are able to use, web-based services, and those that do not have access to, and are therefore unable to use, web-based services.

Political consequences of e-commerce

The political consequences of e-commerce would include, for example, the need to:

- monitor and ensure the legality of e-commerce operations, and
- regulate the quality and safety of products supplied using e-commerce facilities – for example medical supplies, etc., and
- control the purchase of restricted/banned products using e-commerce facilities – for example pornography, restricted drugs/narcotics etc.

The economic costs of e-commerce

The economic costs of e-commerce would include, for example, the costs associated with:

- an increasingly competitive marketplace,
- an increasingly uncertain business environment,
- a continuing reduction in business margins, and
- a continuing change in customer expectations.

Inasmuch as web-based e-commerce has provided and increased access to global markets, such web-based e-commerce has also increased competition – increased global competition – resulting in ever-growing pressures to maintain a low cost base while at the same time remaining flexible, adaptable and open to change – to ever more increasing change!

E-commerce . . . and the matter of regulation!

It is perhaps not surprising that the continuing proliferation of e-commerce (and of course m-commerce), and the escalating use of e-commerce transactions (both web-based and non-web-based) during the latter part of the twentieth century and the early part of the twenty-first century has not evaded the eagle eyes of European/UK legislators and regulators.

Indeed, the last few years (certainly since 1998) have seen an enormous increase in regulatory pronouncements and the imposition of rigorous (some would say somewhat authoritarian) requirements – more specifically, legislation-based pronouncements.

So, what are the main legislative pronouncements/regulatory requirements? For our purposes we will restrict our discussion to:

- The Data Protection Act 1998[20] and
- The Consumer Protection (Distance Selling) Regulations 2000.[21]

The Data Protection Act 1998

Where a company uses a website merely as a web-based facility to provide advice and/or information or advertise goods and services, the provisions and requirements of the Data Protection Act 1998 do not apply.

Examples of such websites would include:

- a community site – for example, *www.leven-village.co.uk*,
- an archive website – used to preserve valuable electronic content threatened with extinction,
- an information website – a website that contains content that is intended merely to inform visitors, but not necessarily for commercial purposes (for example, *www.dti.gov.uk*),
- a news website – a website dedicated to dispensing news and commentary (for example, *www.ft.com*, and *www.timesonline.co.uk*,
- a search engine – a website that provides general information and is intended as a gateway to other websites (for example, *www.google.co.uk* and *www.yahoo.com*) and
- a web portal – a website that provides a starting point, a gateway, or portal, to other resources on the internet or an intranet.

. . . and many, many more!

However, if a company uses a website as an interactive web-based facility – that is, a facility which provides for/allows for the exchange of personal information (for example, user details and information such as name, address, credit/debit card details), then the provisions and requirements of the Data Protection Act 1998 apply – in full!

Examples of such websites would include:

- a company/business website – a website used to promote a company, business and/or service (for example, *www.tesco.com*, *www.marksandspencer.com* and *www.lloydstsb.com*),
- a download website – a website used for downloading electronic content, such as computer software,
- a professional website – a website designed specifically for members of a professional association (for example, *www.accaglobal.com* and *www.icaew.co.uk*), and
- a game website – a website that is itself a game or 'playground' where many people come to play,

. . . and again – many, many more!

Essentially, all interactive e-commerce websites operated by, and/or owned by, UK-based companies *must* comply with the eight Data Protection Act principles outlined in Chapter 7. Such companies must ensure that personal data acquired as a result of web-based activities must be:

- fairly and lawfully processed,
- used for specific purposes,
- adequate, relevant and not excessive,
- accurate and where necessary kept up to date,
- kept for no longer than necessary,
- used in accordance with the rights of individuals under the Data Protection Act 1998,
- kept secure, and
- *not* transferred to another country outside the EEA without adequate protection.

Essentially, the provisions of the Data Protection Act 1998 require that companies and organisations adopt appropriate technical and organisational measures to minimise the possibility of:

- unauthorised access to, or unlawful processing of, personal data,
- accidental loss of personal data,
- malicious corruption of personal data, and/or
- destruction of or damage to personal data.

So, what would these technical and organisational measures comprise? They would comprise a range of internal controls based measures within three main areas:

1 System security measures – including the use of:
   - hardware and/or software firewalls,
   - encryption procedures,
   - audit trails, user-based password/security protocols,
   - anti-virus software,
   - data backup facilities, and
   - physical location security.
2 Policy and procedures – including the use of:
   - up-to-date and relevant policies and procedures on internet use/abuse, and
   - appropriate separation of duties within data processing activities.
3 Employee training – including the use of compliance training/testing.

Remember: companies engaging in e-commerce activities must ensure:

- the reliability of employees who have access to client/customer personal data where personal data are processed in-house, or
- the compliance of the data processor with the requirements of the Data Protection Act 1998 where data processing is outsourced.

In general, to comply with the provisions and requirements of the Data Protection Act 1998, companies and organisations should:

- appoint a data controller,
- identify and document how the company collects, processes and stores personal data, and
- produce a company-wide data protection/privacy policy.

In terms of web-based activities, companies should produce a detailed website policy (which should be available on-line):

- specifying the terms and conditions associated with use of the company website, and
- detailing company data protection/privacy[22] in relation to the company website.

The company's/organisation's data protection/privacy policy should contain details of:

- what data/information is collected,
- how the data/information is collected,
- how the data/information is stored,
- for what purpose the data/information is used, and the purposes for which the data/information will not be used,[23]
- who the data/information will be shared with,
- whether the data/information collected will be transferred outside the EU,
- how a website user/visitor can verify (and if necessary update) the personal data stored, and
- how the website user/visitor can object to your use of covert data collection (for example the use of cookies).

The Consumer Protection (Distance Selling) Regulations 2000[24]

The Consumer Protection (Distance Selling) Regulations 2000 were brought into force in October 2000 to implement the EC Distance Selling Directive in the UK, and imposed specific obligations on suppliers of goods and services, in particular – for our purposes – web-based suppliers.

The Consumer Protection (Distance Selling) Regulations 2000[25] give consumers certain rights and protection when they shop for goods or services 'at a distance'.

A distance contract[26] is one where there has been no face-to-face contact between the consumer and a representative of the company selling the goods and/or services, or someone acting indirectly on the business's behalf, such as in a showroom or a door-to-door salesperson, up to and including the moment at which the contract is concluded.

Key features of the regulations[27] are:

- the consumer must be given clear information about the goods or services offered,
- after making/agreeing to purchase goods and/or services, the consumer must be sent confirmation, and
- the consumer must be granted a 'cooling-off' period of seven working days.

The Distance Selling Regulations apply to companies if they sell goods or services without face-to-face contact using an organised scheme, for instance via:

- the World Wide Web (e-commerce),
- text messaging,
- phone calls,
- faxing,
- interactive TV,
- mail order catalogues, and/or
- mail order advertising in newspapers or magazines.

The Distance Selling Regulations do not apply to business-to-business (B2B) transactions, and do not apply to:

■ financial services,

■ the sale of land or buildings,

■ purchases from a vending machine or automated commercial premises,

■ the use of a public pay phone,

■ auctions, including internet auctions, and/or

■ rental agreements that have to be in writing (for example a lease for 3 years or more).

(See Consumer Protection (Distance Selling) Regulations 2000 s.5(1).)

In addition, the following types of transactions are exempt:

■ accommodation, transport, catering or leisure services,

■ package travel and timeshare,

■ food and drink or other goods for everyday consumption delivered to the consumer's home or workplace by regular roundsmen (for example, a milkman).[28]

(See Consumer Protection (Distance Selling) Regulations 2000 s.6(2).)

In brief, the Distance Selling Regulations provided that a company must 'always give clear and unambiguous information to customers', to allow prospective customers to make an informed decision as to whether or not to undertake a purchase.

The information a business must give must include details about:

■ the business,

■ the goods or services,

■ payment arrangements,

■ delivery arrangements, and

■ the customers' right to cancel their orders.

Companies must also provide customers with confirmation of the above details in writing or, where appropriate, by some other 'durable' medium.[29]

Web Accessibility Initiative

The World Wide Web Consortium (W3C) was founded in October 1994 to oversee the development of the World Wide Web. However, by 1997 the consortium had identified a core problem: as the World Wide Web expanded so did the amount of inaccessible Web content.[30] Pursuant to W3C's commitment to 'lead the web to its full potential . . . [including] the promoting of a high degree of usability for people with disabilities', the Web Accessibility Initiative (WAI)[31] was launched in 1997 to 'work with organisations around the world to develop strategies, guidelines, and resources to help make the Web accessible to people with disabilities'.

The Web Accessibility Initiative, through its working groups,[32] and in partnership with organisations from around the world,[33] pursues its core objective of accessibility through five primary activities:

1 Ensuring that core technologies of the web support accessibility.

2 Developing guidelines for web content, user agents, and authoring tools.

3 Facilitating development of evaluation and repair tools for accessibility.

4 Conducting education and outreach.

5 Coordinating with research and development that can affect future accessibility of the Web.

Web Content Accessibility Guidelines version 1.0 (WCAG 1.0)

Published by WAI, the Web Content Accessibility Guidelines version 1.0 (WCAG 1.0) is a definitive set of international guidelines to be used for building accessible websites.

The guidelines comprise 65 checkpoints categorised into three levels of priority assigned by the web content working group based on each checkpoint's impact on accessibility, and three levels of conformance, as follows:

- **Conformance level A** is a basic standard of accessibility. To achieve this standard company websites must comply with all of the priority 1 checkpoints.

- **Conformance level AA** is a medium level of accessibility. To achieve this standard, company websites must comply with all priority 1 and 2 checkpoints.

- **Conformance level AAA** is the highest standard of accessibility. To achieve this standard, company websites must comply with all priority 1, 2, and 3 checkpoints.

Where a company and/or organisation claims conformance – at whatever level – such conformance MUST be indicated on the company web page.[34]

Web Content Accessibility Guidelines version 2 (WCAG 2.0)

WCAG 2.0 addresses a wide range of accessibility issues, and is comprised of 13 guidelines categorised under four principles of accessibility:

1 Perceivable – that is, all content must be perceivable; for example, providing text for non-text content.

2 Operable – that is, interface elements in the content must be operable; for example, access via a keyboard or keyboard interface.

3 Understandable – that is, content and controls must be understandable; for example, text should not be confusing or ambiguous.

4 Robust – that is, content must be robust and sufficiently adaptable to operate with current and future technologies; for example, the content will work with old, new and potential future technology.

In additions WCAG 2.0 offers a number of recommendations for making web-based content more accessible.

Concluding comments

Disregarding the many myths that continue to surround e-retailing and e-commerce there is, perhaps as one would expect, a range of opinions regarding the costs, the consequences and the potential future impact of e-commerce on society.

While many of these opinions (perhaps unsurprisingly) reach very different conclusions on the social, political and economic costs and benefits associated with e-commerce and the emergence of the self-service economy, they all nonetheless agree that as a society – as an increasingly interrelated and interconnected global marketplace – we are, at the start of the twenty-first century, in the midst of an ongoing virtual revolution: a revolution whose final outcome has yet to be determined (. . . or even invented).

Why yet to be determined? Put simply, technologies – especially information and communication technologies associated with web-based activities are (contrary to the naivety of popular belief) developed in a fragmented and often disjointed manner. While we can speculate (perhaps with some degree of certainty) that future technologies will:

- improve internet security,
- increase user freedom and mobility,
- enhance internet usability, and (hopefully)
- improve accessibility,

we have no way of knowing how such future technologies will impact on the demand for, and use of, e-commerce and m-commerce related services (see Article 8.2). We will, I suppose, just have to wait and see!

Article 8.2

Mobile phones bring the cashless society closer

Miles Brignall

Get ready to start paying for sandwiches, magazines and pints down the pub with nothing more than a swipe of your mobile phone as a payment revolution hits Britain's high streets.

The idea is that your mobile phone will be embedded with a chip that contains your credit and debit card details. For low-value items, selling for no more than £15, all you will have to do is wave the phone in front of the shop's sales terminal. For higher priced goods, you'll have to punch a pin number into the phone as well.

Orange last week unveiled its Quick Tap service, while rival O2 says it is lining up for a major launch in the autumn. Meanwhile, Google this week launched Google Wallet for Android phones which might soon make the traditional wallet stuffed with cards, notes and coins a thing of the past.

The UK Payments Council – which represents banks and card companies – also announced it was undertaking a major project into how to make paying by mobile 'as easy, efficient and secure as any other way to pay'.

The transformation is going to happen with extraordinary speed, according to one thinktank, The Future Foundation, which, in a report this week,

predicted that the 'majority' of Britons will be using their mobile phone to purchase goods, pay bills and manage their bank accounts by 2015.

Will the revolution really take place? Will it make your phone even more of a target for thieves? And does it mean that every purchase you make, from a bar of chocolate and a newspaper upwards, will be logged and tracked? Money tried to find some answers.

Orange is the first company out of the blocks. Its Quick Tap system will let you buy goods up to £15 at 'wave and pay' contactless readers already installed in 50,000 UK stores. But the system will initially only work with one handset – the Samsung Tocco Lite – though more are promised later, and is operated only through Barclaycard.

O2's more advanced offering will let your phone host several bank and credit cards and permit purchases above £15 while inputting a pin. It will also allow you to text money, so if you owe someone a tenner you'll be able to send it from your phone to theirs.

The banks are hoping that the new mobile phones will kick-start contactless payments, which have until now been rather slow to take off.

Outlets such as McDonald's, EAT, Wilkinson, Pret a Manger and Subway, and some Boots stores already allow consumers to use their contactless credit and debit cards to make payments of up to the £15 limit. But so far these tills have yet to grab the public, perhaps a little fearful of security risks.

Orange's Jason Rees says mobile payments are set to take the sector to another level: 'Users will be able to check their balance on the mobile phone's screen to see how much they are spending, which you cannot immediately do when touching your debit or credit card on contactless readers. Feedback from the trials we have done is overwhelmingly positive.'

Alastair Lukies, chief executive of Monitise, which provides mobile banking services to high-street banks, says: 'The driving forces are clear: people wanting to manage their money more closely; the arrival of the smartphone; and the development of 3G networks which transfer all information quickly, plus the creation of new apps and services by banks and retailers.

'Mobile banking has truly come of age as people no longer see the ability to effectively manage their finances by mobile as a novelty or a "nice to have", but increasingly as the norm.'

What about theft or misuse?

If you lose your phone, or it is stolen, the phone companies say you will report its loss in the same way as before, and the card balance is protected. They say you will not be liable for purchases that you can prove you didn't make; in the case of Orange, Barclaycard bears those losses.

Telefonica, O2's parent firm, says mobile phone users, on average, report their handset stolen within 13 minutes of its loss; it takes much longer for bank card users to realise that their purse or wallet has gone.

The O2 system the Guardian saw being trialled in Spain was designed to ask for a pin every few transactions, to prevent a thief making a series of small purchases in quick succession.

Phone companies also argue that smartphones already have a higher level of security, with most requiring a pin to be activated. Orange will require customers to select a new pin when they set up a Quick Tap account. Users can require a pin to be inputted on every purchase, including those under £15, but it is not mandatory.

When will it be on every new phone?

The mobile industry knows that the key to making this a success rests on the ability of the phone suppliers to offer 'near-field' technology in a big range of handsets. Apple is understood to be working on introducing it in its iPhone range. Currently, Samsung is leading the way, but expect a raft of new handsets offering the technology over the next few months.

Google recently launched a Samsung-manufactured smartphone – the Google Nexus S – that contains the technology required to make wireless payments. The new Nokia C7 also has it. O2 says that it will offer a 'range of handsets' when it launches its mobile payments offering, but could not give any details this week.

Where will I be able to use it?

Contactless payments are currently limited to certain food outlets and stores, but the idea is that eventually, the majority of point-of-sale tills will feature the technology. It's ideal for pubs – though many rounds will break the initial £15 barrier which has been set by the card industry. Expect to see that raised in line with prices, and as more stores come online.

In the Telefonica trial in Sitges, Spain, visited by Money last year, around half the contactless items were made in the supermarket. The 2012 London Olympics has been targeted as a major contactless event, and with Visa a major sponsor, expect further announcements soon.

Earlier this year Transport for London announced that customers will be able to make contactless payments (using Visa) for pay-as-you-go journeys on 8,500 London buses from February 2012, with the underground following soon after.

How much will it cost?

Orange customers will have to purchase the Quick Tap-enabled Samsung Tocco Lite phone, available at £59.99 on pay-as-you-go or free from £10 a month on 24-month contracts. There are no additional costs for using the payments service; you will not be charged any data charges for accessing the Quick Tap Wallet or the Barclaycard payment application when you are in the UK. O2 users will also need a new handset, but again these will probably be free to those on longish contracts.

→

The drawbacks

Anyone who has had to report a problem with mobile companies will question if their customer service will be up to this. Guardian Money gets lots of complaints about mobile phones, though the fact that Barclaycard is managing Orange's payments app may create more confidence. Several stories about poor service following a payments problem could set the project back years in the mind of consumers already rather distrustful of changes.

Could this be the end of cash?

Young people who have grown up with mobiles will not think twice about using these systems, but it remains to be seen whether older adults will embrace it in big numbers. Though you are no more at risk of fraud by embedding a bank card in your handset than you are using a traditional card, there are clearly perceived security issues. There's a feeling that there will have to be some benefit – faster-moving queues in shops or a discount to encourage people to go contactless. Also, the industry is going to have to avert concerns among some mobile users that this does not represent an extension of the 'Big Brother' surveillance.

Banks and store chains prefer electronic payments because handling large amounts of notes and coins is expensive and time-consuming. They will be keen to get consumers to switch to contactless payments wherever they can. But any likelihood that notes and coins will disappear altogether is probably a very long way off.

28 May 2011

Source: Available at *www.guardian.co.uk*.

Self-review questions

1 Explain what is commonly meant by the term self-service economy.

2 What are the main factors that contribute to a good website design?

3 Distinguish between a dot com company, a dot bam company, and a dot bam+ company.

4 Describe and explain the three main component facilities of a business-to-business (B2B) e-commerce website.

5 Describe and briefly explain the main stages of a business-to-consumer (B2C) e-commerce transaction.

6 Distinguish between identified e-money and anonymous e-money, and briefly explain the main advantages and disadvantages of using e-money.

7 Distinguish between an active m-commerce service/application and a passive m-commerce service/application.

8 Briefly describe the Web Accessibility Initiative, and distinguish between WCAG 1.0 and WCAG 2.0.

Notes

1 Such products/services would include for example:
   - information and communication services,
   - music,
   - movies,
   - software, and
   - financial transactions.

2 Perhaps unsurprisingly the provision of such products and services has become the largest and most profitable segment of e-commerce.

3 Remember we are only concerned with e-commerce facilities which provide opportunities/ facilities for the exchange of goods, services and resources.

4 It would of course be feasible – albeit highly unlikely – for a dual channel company to operate without on-line facilities, that is with:

- physical 'real world' retail outlets, and
- retail catalogues – for example, mail order catalogues.

5 Quid pro quo is a commonly used Latin phrase meaning 'something for something'.

6 For example literature and images associated with terrorist activities or child pornography.

7 The Virtual Global Taskforce (VGT) was created in 2003 as a direct response to lessons learned from investigations into on-line child abuse around the world. It is an international alliance of law enforcement agencies working together to make the internet a safer place. The mission of the Virtual Global Taskforce is:

- to make the internet a safer place;
- to identify, locate and help children at risk; and
- to hold perpetrators appropriately to account.

The Virtual Global Taskforce comprises:

- the Australian High Tech Crime Centre,
- the National Crime Squad for England and Wales,
- the Royal Canadian Mounted Police,
- the US Department of Homeland Security, and
- Interpol.

(For more information see *www.virtualglobaltaskforce.com/aboutvgt/about.html*.)

8 See Chapter 4.

9 See Chapter 5.

10 Using RFID (Radio Frequency Identification) technology.

11 In essence an e-money card/smart card looks and functions like a debit card; however, the main differences are:

- the user does not need to have a bank account to use it, and
- losing an eMoney card is equivalent to losing cash.

12 Electronic means of payment that:

- can only be used to pay for an issuer's own goods/services, and
- are only accepted by the issuer in payment for such goods and services

are not considered to be eMoney schemes and are therefore not subject to FSA regulations.

13 Small e-money issuers that satisfy a number of strict criteria are not regulated by the FSA, but need to apply for an FSA certificate confirming that they meet the criteria. Such a certificate may be granted to a company/institution (other than a credit institution) with a UK-based head office if one of the following apply:

- the company/institution only issues e-money with a maximum storage of 150 euro on its e-money devices, *and* the company's/institution's total e-money liabilities will not exceed 5,000,000 euro, or
- the company's/institution's total liabilities with respect to its e-money scheme will not exceed 10,000,000 euro, and the e-money issued by the firm is accepted as a means of payment only by other companies/institutions within the issuing company's/institution's group, or
- the e-money issued by the company/institution is accepted as a means of payment in the course of business by not more than 100 persons within a limited local area or all have a close financial/business relationship with the company/institution. (Such a company/institution is often referred to as a local e-money issuer.)

14 See Article 9B of the Regulated Activities Order 2002.

15 Wireless Application Protocol (WAP) is an international standard for applications that use wireless communication – for example, internet access from a mobile phone. WAP is now the protocol used by the majority of mobile internet sites, aka WAP-sites. The Japanese I-MODE system is the other major wireless data/application protocol.

16 Indeed, it was the idea that highly profitable m-commerce applications would be possible through the broadband mobile telephony provided by 3G mobile phone services which resulted in high licence fees (somewhat willingly) paid by mobile phone operators for 3G licences during 2000 and 2001.

17 A micropayment is an on-line financial transaction involving a very small sum of money.

18 See *http://www.contactless.info/Facts-and-Stats.asp*.

19 See 'Barclaycard and Orange unveil pay-by-mobile service' by Garry White, *Daily Telegraph* (09-03-08); *http://www.telegraph.co.uk/finance/newsbysector/mediatechnologyandtelecoms/telecoms/4958655/Barclaycard-and-Orange-unveil-pay-by-mobile-service.html*.

20 Available at *www.hmso.gov.uk/acts/acts1998/19980029.htm*.

21 Available at *www.hmso.gov.uk/si/si2000/20002334.htm*. In addition, the DTI Consumer Protection (Distance Selling) Regulations: Guide for Business is available at *www.dti.gov.uk/ccp/topics1/pdf1/bus_guide.pdf*.

22 For further information, see the Information Commissioner's Data Protection Act 1998 Compliance Advice: Website FAQs, available at *www.informationcommissioner.gov.uk/cms/DocumentUploads/Website%20FAQ.pdf*.

23 A website user/visitor should be given the choice (that is to 'opt-in' or to 'opt-out') on how data/information is to be used – in particularly where the intention is to:
- use such data/information for direct marketing purposes, or
- share such data/information with other third parties.

24 The Consumer Protection (Distance Selling) Regulations (2000) are enforced by:
- the Office of Fair Trading,
- local authority trading standards departments in England, Scotland and Wales, and
- the Department of Trade and Industry.

These bodies are under a duty to consider any complaint received and have powers to apply to the courts for an injunction against any person, company and/or organisation considered responsible for a breach of the regulations.

25 Commonly referred to as the Distance Selling Regulations (2000) or DSRs (2000).

26 The Consumer Protection (Distance Selling) Regulations (2000) define a distance contract as:

> any contract concerning goods and services concluded between a supplier and a customer under an organised distance sales or service provision scheme run by the supplier who for the purposes of the contract makes exclusive use of one or more means of distance communication up to and including the moment that the contact is concluded. (2000: s.3)

27 The regulations do not apply if a business does not normally sell to consumers in response to letters, phone calls, faxes or e-mails and/or does not operate an interactive shopping website.

28 This exception does not apply to the growing market for home deliveries by supermarkets.

29 For the purposes of the distance selling regulations (2000) the term 'durable' medium includes e-mail, post and/or fax.

30 See Dardailler, D. (1997), *Briefing package for project Web Accessibility Initiative (WAI)*, available at *www.w3.org/WAI/References/access-brief.html*.

31 See *www.w3.org/WAI/*.

32 These working groups include:
- Authoring Tools Working Group (AUWG) – develops guidelines, techniques, and supporting resources for Web 'authoring tools', which are software that creates websites.

- Education and Outreach Working Group (EOWG) – develops awareness and training materials and education resources on web accessibility solutions.
- Evaluation and Repair Tools Working Group (ERT WG) – develops techniques and tools for evaluating accessibility of websites, and for retrofitting websites to be more accessible.
- Protocols & Formats Working Group (PFWG) – reviews all W3C technologies for accessibility.
- Research and Development Interest Group (RDIG) – facilitates discussion and discovery of the accessibility aspects of research and development of future web technologies.
- User Agent Working Group (UAWG) – develops guidelines, techniques and supporting resources for accessibility for web 'user agents', which includes web browsers and media players.
- Web Content Working Group (WCAG WG) – develops guidelines, techniques, and supporting resources for web 'content', which is the information in a website, including text, images, forms, sounds and such.

33 These include a wide range of public and private sector organsiations – for example, companies, government agencies, education-based research organisations, and many more.

34 Indication of conformance can be presented in two alternative forms:

1 **Form 1:** Specify on each page claiming conformance:

- the guidelines title: 'Web Content Accessibility Guidelines 1.0',
- the guidelines URI: *http://www.w3.org/TR/1999/WAI-WEBCONTENT*,
- the conformance level satisfied: 'A', 'Double-A', or 'Triple-A',
- the scope covered by the claim (e.g., page, site, or defined portion of a site).

An example of this would be: 'This page conforms to W3C's "Web Content Accessibility Guidelines 1.0", available at *http://www.w3.org/TR/1999/WAI-WEBCONTENT*, level Double-A' or

2 **Form 2:** Include on each page claiming conformance, one of three icons provided by W3C and linking the icon to the appropriate W3C explanation of the claim. Information about the WAI icons, and instructions on how to insert them into a web page, are available at *www.w3.org/WAI/WCAG1-Conformance.html*.

Part 3

RISK, SECURITY, SURVEILLANCE AND CONTROL

Part 3 of this book examines a range of issues associated with risk, security and control.

Chapter 9 explores the social and economic contexts of risk, and considers a range of issues associated with accounting information systems related fraud, cyber terrorism and computer crime.

Chapter 10 looks at the socio-economic contexts of control – in particular internal control – and considers the implications of internal control on information and communication technology enabled transaction processing systems.

Chapter 11 examines the underpinning rationale of audit, and considers the major issues and problems associated with auditing computer-based corporate accounting information systems. It also considers a number of alternative contemporary approaches to auditing computer-based corporate accounting information systems, including auditing through, with, and/or around, the computer.

Chapter 12 explores the major stages of the systems development life cycle, and the socio-political context of corporate accounting information systems development.

CHAPTER 9

Risk exposure – fraud, cyber terrorism and computer crime

Introduction

This chapter considers the alternative sources and types of risk that a company may face, the issues and problems associated with minimising the degree of risk exposure, and the problems and conditions affecting corporate exposure to risk. It also considers the management of risk exposure and, in particular, risk issues associated with fraud, cyber terrorism and computer crime.

Learning outcomes

This chapter presents an analysis of the key features of risk, risk exposure and fraud, and examines issues associated with fraud management and the risks associated with information systems and information technology – in particular computer crime.

By the end of this chapter, the reader should be able to:

- Describe the social and economic contexts of risk

- Distinguish between different types of sources and types of risk and explain the control issues associated with minimising risk exposure

- Describe and critically comment on the problem conditions affecting exposure to risk

- Evaluate the key issues associated with fraud and computer crime

The social and economic context of risk

Risk is the chance or possibility of loss or bad consequence. It arises from a past, present and/or future hazard or group of hazards of which some uncertainty exists about possible consequences and/or effects. Put simply, whereas a hazard or group of hazards is a source of danger, risk is the likelihood of such a hazard or group of hazards developing actual adverse consequences/effects. In this context, uncertainty relates to the measure of variability in possible outcomes – the variability (whether expressed qualitatively or quantitatively) of the possible impact and consequence/effect of such hazards. While such uncertainty can clearly arise as a result of a whole host of complex and often interrelated reasons, it does – in a corporate context at least – more often than not arise as a result of a lack of knowledge or a lack of information and/or a lack of understanding.

What types of risk exist?

As with the never ending variety that is symptomatic of modernity, there are many types of risk – many of which overlap in terms of definition and context.

Have a look at the following definitions/examples of risk:

■ *Social* risk – the possibility that the intervention (whether socio-cultural, political, and/or institutional) will create, fortify and/or reinforce inequity and promote social conflict.

■ *Political* risk – the possibility that changes in government policies will have an adverse and negative impact on the role and functioning of socio-economic institutions and arrangements.

■ *Economic* risk – the risk that events (both national and international) will impact on a country's business environment and adversely affect the profit and other goals of particular companies and other business-related enterprises.

■ *Market* risk – the risk of a decline in the price of a security due to general adverse market conditions (also called systematic, or systemic, risk).

■ *Financial* risk – the possibility that a given investment or loan will fail to bring a return and may result in a loss of the original investment or loan.

■ *Business* risk – the risk associated with the uncertainty of realising expected future returns of the business (also known as unsystematic, or non-systemic, risk), and/or the uncertainty associated with the possible profit outcomes of a business venture.

You will probably recognise most if not all of the above, and clearly while there are many other definitions/examples of risk – many other categorisations of risk, especially within the context of socio-economic activities (see Figure 9.1) – they all possess a singular common feature. Whatever way we seek to perceive or indeed conceptualise risk,[1] however we seek to define or describe it, at the core of any definition – any understanding of risk (including all of the above) – is the notion of uncertainty and the associated possibility of danger, of hazard, of harm and/or of loss from uncertain future events. Such future events may be social, cultural, economic, political, psychological and/or even physiological in origin.

Indeed, whether risk is viewed primarily in a *qualitative* context as:

■ a social construction,[2]

■ a product of reflexive modernisation,[3]

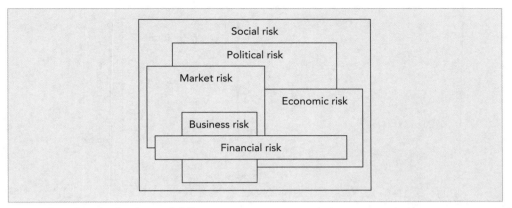

Figure 9.1 Categorisations of risk

- a cultural[4] consequence of the growing economisation of society and polity, and/or
- a product of modern society's increasing interconnectivity but diminishing trust,[5]

or primarily in a *quantitative* context as:

- a quantifiable deviation from the norm,
- a statistical probability, or
- a calculable and determined measurement,

issues of uncertainty and of risk (from wherever they originate) now dominate contemporary understanding of corporate activity and its context and location within the macro-economic framework of the so-called *global village*. Such issues not only influence and determine all forms, all aspects, all levels, of corporate decision making (especially, as we shall see, decisions related to corporate accounting information systems) but continue to be an authoritative influence on, and pervasive (some would say insidious) feature of many (if not all) aspects of contemporary economy, society and polity.

Indeed, in today's ever more risk-averse world – a world bounded by the sociology of commodification, a world constrained only by the politics of marketplace and economics of 'more, more, more' – social, economic and political activities are increasingly influenced by (and indeed organised around) a singular cautionary notion. That notion is that it is better to be safe than sorry or, perhaps more appropriately, that it is better to err on the side of caution.

Enshrined within this cautionary approach (some would say pessimistic approach) is an assumption of the worst-case scenario. That is:

- when the outcomes of present or future actions and events are uncertain or unpredictable or
- when information, knowledge or understanding is incomplete or uncertain,

such an approach provides that:

- where there are significant threats of serious or irreversible damage,
- where substantial uncertainties could result in severe and permanent harm, and/or
- where critical hazards exist which could be potentially fatal,

a lack of certainty should not be used as a reason – as a justification – for postponing measures to prevent such damage and/or such harm.

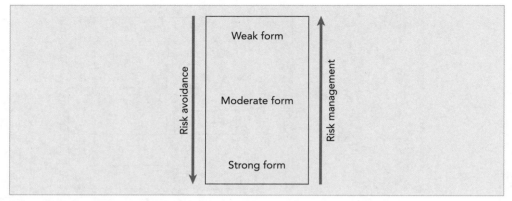

Figure 9.2 Precautionary principle – variants

It is this approach – this assumption of worst-case scenario – that has in recent years become known as the precautionary principle. With origins clearly linked to the German *Vorsorgeprinzip* (foresight principle), the precautionary principle is now increasingly used – and is indeed widely embraced (both formally and informally) at various levels within society, economy and polity (that is, not only at a societal/governmental level but also at economic/market level) – to deal with the various risks and uncertainties arising from:

- the imposition of new technologies,
- the development of new products, and
- the expansion and growth of new markets.

Primarily introduced to regulate and control hazardous environment-based activities, prevent environmental harm and control health-related issues/developments,[6] the precautionary principle with its three variants – the weak form, the moderate form and the strong form (see Figure 9.2) – has subsequently been redesigned, repackaged, exported and indeed adopted into the decision-making processes surrounding a diverse range of socio-economic activities, none more so than corporate risk management – specifically information systems and information technology risk management.

Why is there such interest in this precautionary principle?

Put simply, in today's increasingly complex and uncertain world, for a corporate entity operating in a highly competitive and highly diversified environment, with a diversity of technologies – more importantly a diversity of computer-based information systems technologies whose loss or failure could result in substantial damage, financial or otherwise – the adoption of the precautionary principle, the embracing of such cautionary strategy, not only minimises risk, it also safeguards security, protects future stability, and, in the longer term, (hopefully) maximises shareholder wealth.

As indicated earlier, the precautionary principle operates at three levels. In a general corporate risk context, these three levels can be viewed as follows:[7]

1 Weak form precaution (generic reactive intervention) – intervention only where there is general positive evidence of risk, the possibility for harm/damage, and evidence that such intervention would be effective and cost-efficient. The underlying presumption is one of risk management.

2 Moderate form precaution (specific reactive intervention) – intervention on a case-by-case basis where there is specific positive evidence of risk, the probability of harm/damage, and evidence that such intervention would be effective and where possible cost-efficient. Again the underlying presumption is one of risk management.

3 Strong form precaution (proactive intervention) – intervention where perceived risk of potential harm/damage exists, and there is evidence that such intervention would be effective. Cost-efficiency is not a concern. Because of the nature and severity of the risks, the underlying presumption is one of risk avoidance.

How is the application of each (or any) of the above determined?

While there is no widely accepted formal rule set (or criteria) by which the application of any of the above can be determined, in general and very informally, the potential application of each (separately or in combination) is often determined by:

■ the level of uncertainty in the consequences of the particular hazard, and

■ the level of uncertainty in the likelihood that the particular hazard will be realised.

See Figure 9.3.

That is, the level of uncertainty and therefore the level of risk exposure associated with a particular hazard and/or group of hazards would not only determine the nature, the context and the focus of corporate precautionary activities but, more importantly, the level of:

■ diagnostic monitoring,

■ remedial maintenance, and

■ preventative intervention,

that a company may engage in/undertake.

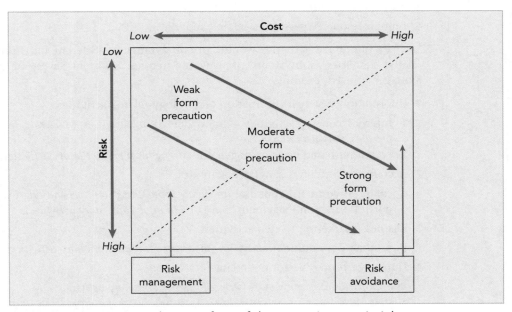

Figure 9.3 Activities at each variant form of the precautionary principle

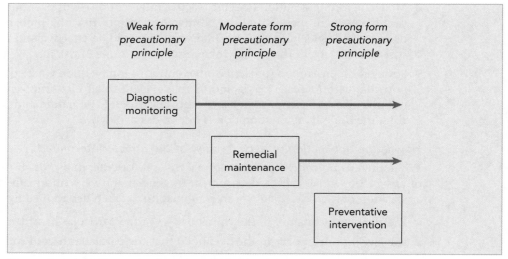

Figure 9.4 Activities at each variant form of the precautionary principle

In other words: different corporate activities are subject to/exposed to different hazards and threats – different risks – different uncertainties. As a consequence, for purposes of efficiency and the effective utilisation of corporate resources, they should be subject to different levels of precautionary activities. See Figure 9.4.

Consider, for example, the following range of corporate activities (systems):

1 information systems/information technology-related activities,
2 accounting and finance-related activities,
3 business/marketing-related activities,
4 human resources/personnel-related activities.

Each of the above activities would contain a range of different but nonetheless risk-related activities (subsystems) that would require different levels of precautionary management. For example:

1 Information systems/information technology-related activities:
   ■ internal control activities – fraud detection activities (*moderate form/strong form precautionary activities*)
   ■ computer-based virus management (*strong form precautionary activities*).

2 Accounting and finance-related activities:
   ■ capital investment appraisal (*moderate form/strong form precautionary activities*)
   ■ portfolio/debt management (*moderate form precautionary activities*).

3 Business/marketing-related activities:
   ■ product development activities (*moderate form precautionary activities*).

4 Human resources/personnel-related activities:
   ■ appointment of new staff (*strong form precautionary activities*)
   ■ staff development activities/staff training (*weak form/moderate form precautionary activities*).

Risk exposure

As suggested earlier, risk can be described in many ways, for example, as a hazard, a chance of bad consequence, or exposure to mischance. And for a company, the measurability of such risk is directly related to the probability of loss.

Indeed, the very existence of uncertainty, of unpredictability, of randomness, of change, of a lack of knowing, means that risk – the risk of loss – cannot be fully eliminated. It cannot be systemised, nor can it be fully controlled. It can only be managed. It can only be minimised by the adoption of appropriate control – of precautionary activities the nature of which are (as suggested above) dependent on three key features:

1 The nature and source of risk.
2 The type of risk.
3 The degree of risk exposure.

Source of risk

As we saw earlier, there are many alternative definitions/examples of risk – many alternative sources of risk – all of which can and, indeed frequently do, affect the socio-economic environment/marketplace within which companies trade.

In an information systems context, in particular, a corporate accounting information systems context, we can distinguish between two primary sources of risk and three associated secondary sources of risk.

The primary sources of risk can be categorised (somewhat subjectively) as:

■ *Event/activity-based* risk – that is, risk associated with a particular event/activity and/or a group or series of events/activities, and a subsidiary primary source,

■ *Resource/asset-based* risk – that is, risk associated with the possession and/or use of a resource/asset or group of resources/assets.

The foundation of all contemporary business activity, of contemporary capitalism, is movement. Capitalism is a *socially constructed event-based process*. That is, all contemporary business activity is based ultimately on the buying and selling of goods and services and/or the transfer of property and ownership in exchange for payment or promise of payment. Indeed at the heart of any business transaction is an identifiable event and/or activity – an event/activity which ultimately results in the temporal and/or spatial displacement of assets and/or resources (the duality of which accountants record using the age-old methodology of double entry bookkeeping).

What are the secondary sources of risk?

Associated with both of the above primary sources of risk are the following secondary sources of risk:

■ *Authorised internal employee and/or external agent based risk* – that is, for example, risk of possible loss that may result from either unintentional mistake/oversight or premeditated, intentional or deliberate error, theft and/or acts of violence.

■ *Unauthorised persons based risk* – that is, for example, risk of loss that may result from possible breaches of security and/or acts of violence resulting in the theft or misappropriation of assets, resources, information, and/or identity.

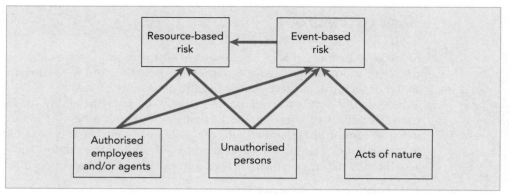

Figure 9.5 Sources of risk

- *Act of nature based risk* – that is, for example, risk of possible loss that may result from geographical disaster, adverse meteorological conditions and/or non-human-created catastrophes.

See Figure 9.5.

Types of risk

Clearly, within the secondary sources of risk identified above, there are many types of risk associated with computer-based/information technology-orientated information systems, in particular, corporate accounting information systems.

- *Unintentional errors* – these relate to inadvertent mistakes and/or erroneous actions attributable to bad judgement, ignorance and/or inattention, and are neither deliberate nor malicious in intent.[8]
- *Deliberate errors* – conscious incorrect or erroneous action designed to damage, destroy and/or defraud a person, group of persons and/or organisation. Such errors are intentional and deliberate.
- *Unintentional loss of assets* – an undesigned loss whose incidence occurs without deliberate purpose or intent. Such (accidental) losses may occur due to bad judgement, ignorance and/or inattention.
- *Theft of assets* – the wrongful and criminal taking of property from another.
- *Breaches of security* – the successful defeat and/or violation of controls which could result in a penetration of a system and allow/facilitate unauthorised access to information, assets and/or system components whose misuse, disclosure, and/or corruption could result in severe financial loss.
- *Acts of violence* – intentional, reckless, and/or grossly negligent acts that would reasonably be expected to cause physical injury and/or death to another person, and/or cause damage to and/or the destruction of valuable tangible/intangible assets.
- *Natural disasters* – events with catastrophic consequences whose origins lie beyond humankind and human activity; events that can result in death, injury, damage and/or destruction to people and/or property; events dependent on many factors which themselves may not be natural in origin but created by human action/inaction.

Degree of risk exposure

Clearly the degree of risk exposure is dependent on many factors, perhaps the most important being:

- the types of events/activities,
- the frequency of the events/activities,
- the vulnerability to potential loss as a result of the events/activities, and
- the possible extent/size of the potential loss as a result of the events/activities.

Minimising risk exposure and ensuring information security

The need to identify security risks/threats and ensure the existence of adequate control procedures is paramount to:

- Ensuring the effectiveness and efficiency of corporate operations, the continuity of business processes, and the survival of the company.
- Minimising unproductive time and effort, and reducing the cost of downtime and service outage.
- Protecting the corporate brand name, the corporate image, any intellectual property rights, and of course the company's market share and underlying share value.
- Ensuring compliance with applicable laws and regulations, and avoiding any penalties and fines that may arise from a failure to comply with extant legislative requirements and regulatory pronouncements.

Minimising risk is indelibly associated with three aspects central to contemporary notions of information security:

1 The maintenance of confidentiality – that is, protecting information from unauthorised disclosure.
2 The preservation of integrity – that is, protecting information from unauthorised modification.
3 The assurance of availability – that is, protecting the availability of information.

Not only in a business context but, more importantly, in a corporate context, maintaining confidentiality, preserving integrity and ensuring availability are dependent upon:

- establishing an appropriate control environment,
- undertaking regular risk assessment,
- developing and maintaining structured control activities,
- ensuring the existence of adequate information and communication systems and protocols,
- ensuring monitoring activities are regularly undertaken, and
- maintaining internal control and the separation of administrative functions.

Although we will consider issues of internal control and systems security in greater detail in Chapter 10, it would perhaps be useful here to provide a brief review of the contemporary regulatory framework of information security management.

British Standard BS 7799 Part 1 (published in 1995) provided a code of practice for information security management. It was revised in 1999. In 2000 British Standard BS 7799 Part 1 became ISO/IEC 17799,[9] an international standard (code of practice) for information security management which provides amongst other things a comprehensive set of security controls/practices currently in use by business worldwide.

British Standard BS 7799 Part 2 (published in 1999) provided/defined a management framework for the identification of security requirements and the application of the best practice controls as defined in ISO/IEC 17799, and specified the key requirements of an Information Security Management System (ISMS). Standard BS 7799 Part 2 was adopted by ISO in 2005 as ISO/IEC 27001.

In 2005, ISO/IEC 17799 was revised and in 2007 it was incorporated in the ISO/IEC 27000 series of standards as ISO/IEC 27002.

British Standard BS 7799 Part 3 (published in 2005) focused on effective information security through ongoing risk management activities, and is consistent with ISO/IEC 27001.

ISO/IEC 27002 applies to all information regardless of where it is located, how it is processed and/or how or where it is stored. It also outlines a number of key principles central to effective information security:

- *Risk assessment* – that is, identifying and evaluating risks, and specifying appropriate security controls to minimise loss or damage associated with these risks.

- *Periodic review of security and controls* – that is, the assessing and identifying of any changes within the company/business activities that may result in new threats and vulnerabilities.

- *Implementation of information security* – that is, the designing, implementing, monitoring, reviewing and improving of information security.

It identifies the following relevant aspects of control:

- *Adoption/development of a security policy* – to provide management direction and support for information security.

- *Organisation of assets and resources* – to assist in managing information security within the organisation.

- *Classification and control of assets* – to assist in identifying and appropriately protecting corporate assets.

- *Provision of personnel security* – to reduce the risk of human error, theft, fraud and/or the misuse of corporate systems, networks and/or facilities.

- *Existence of physical and environmental security* – to prevent unauthorised access, damage and/or interference to or with business premises and information.

- *Appropriate communications and operations management* – to ensure the correct and secure operation of information processing facilities.

- *Installation of access control* – to manage and control access to information.

- *Existence of systems development and maintenance procedures* – to ensure that security is built into information systems.

- *Appropriate business continuity management* – to counteract interruptions to business activities and to protect critical business processes from the effects of major failures or disasters.

■ *Regulatory compliance* – to avoid breaches of any criminal and civil law, statutory, regulatory or contractual obligations, and any security requirements.

Key to the effective implementation of the above principles is of course the development and implementation of an information policy – a corporate-wide information security policy. Although such a policy would clearly vary from business to business, from company to company, in general such an information security policy should include most (if not all) of the following:

■ A definition of the nature of 'corporate' information security – its scope, objectives and importance to the company.

■ A statement of intent, and an explanation of standards, procedures, requirements and objectives of the policy.

■ A detailed explanation of the consequences of security policy violation, and the legal, regulatory and possible contractual obligations for compliance.

■ A definition of the general and specific roles and responsibilities, in terms of promoting security awareness and information security training and education, and ensuring the prevention and detection of viruses and other malicious software.

■ A statement detailing the processes and procedures for reporting/responding to security incidents.

■ A statement detailing the location and availability of information security supporting documentation – for example, corporate policy, operational procedures and implementation guidelines.

COBIT

COBIT is a framework created by ISACA.[10] It is a framework for information technology management and information technology governance, providing a toolset that allows managers to bridge the gap between control requirements, technical issues and business risks. COBIT was first released in 1996; the current version, COBIT 4.1, was published in 2007[11] and is currently being updated (COBIT 5 is expected in late 2011/2012).

The aim of COBIT is to develop, publicise and promote an authoritative, up-to-date, international set of generally accepted information technology control objectives for day-to-day use by business managers, information technology professionals and assurance professionals.

COBIT identifies 34 generic processes to the management of information technology. Each process is defined together with process inputs and outputs, key process activities, process objectives, performance measures and an elementary maturity model. The framework supports information technology governance by defining and aligning business goals with information technology goals and processes. It is focused on what is required to achieve adequate management and control of information technology and is consistent with the ISO/IEC 27000 series. The COBIT components include:

■ a framework for information technology governance, objectives and good practices,

■ process descriptions/process maps as reference process models,

■ control objectives – for the effective control of each information technology process,

■ management guidelines for the assignment of responsibility, development of objectives and the measurement of performance,

■ maturity models – for maturity and capability analysis.

Accounting information systems – fraud, cyber terrorism and computer crime

As suggested earlier, there are many sources and types of risk – many types of events/ activities whose occurrences may result in the possibility of danger, of hazard, of harm, and/or of loss. In a corporate accounting information systems context, perhaps the most important problem conditions are fraud, cyber terrorism and computer crime (or more specifically computer assisted crime).

Fraud

Originating from the old French word *fraude* and the Latin *fraus* meaning deceit and/or injury, the word fraud is defined[12] as criminal deception, the use of false representation to gain unjust advantage, or a wrongful or criminal deception intended to result in financial or personal gain, or (perhaps more appropriately to our needs) the use of deception with the intention of obtaining an advantage, avoiding an obligation or causing loss to another party.

Whilst there exists no single statutory offence of fraud in the United Kingdom, the UK government (the Home Office) in its publication *Counting Rules for Recording Crime* (2004), provides examples of offences that would be classified as fraud (or fraudulent):

- false statements by company directors (Theft Act 1968 s.19),
- fraudulent trading (Companies Act 1985 s.458),
- false accounting and failure to keep proper accounting records (Theft Act 1968 s.17 and Companies Act 1985 ss.221 (5) and (6)),
- obtaining property by deception (Theft Act 1968 s.15),
- obtaining services by deception (Theft Act 1968 s.1),
- insider dealing (Criminal Justice Act 1993 s.52),
- carrying on business with intent to defraud (Companies Act 1985 s.458),
- unauthorised access to computer material (Computer Misuse Act 1990 s.1),
- fraudulent misappropriation of funds (Proceeds of Crime Act 2002),
- evasion of liability by deception (Theft Act 1978 s.3),
- conspiracy to commit cheque or credit card fraud (Theft Act 1987 s.12),
- obtaining pecuniary advantage by cheque or credit card fraud (Criminal Justice Act 1987 s.12),
- misconduct in the course of winding up (Insolvency Act 1986),

. . . and many, many more!

The term fraud clearly encompasses an array of irregularities and illegal acts – illegal acts which include:

- *deception* – providing intentionally misleading information to others;
- *bribery* – offering something (usually money) in order to gain an illicit advantage;
- *forgery* – the making or adapting of objects or documents with the intention to deceive (fraud is the use of objects obtained through forgery);

- *extortion* – forcing a person to give up property in a thing through the use of violence, fear or under pretence of authority;
- *corruption* – the unlawful or improper use of influence, power, and other means;
- *theft (of assets and/or identity)* – larceny or the act of taking something from someone unlawfully;
- *conspiracy* – undertaking secret agreement(s) to perform and/or carry out some harmful or illegal act;
- *embezzlement* – the fraudulent appropriation of funds or property entrusted to your care but actually owned by someone else;
- *misappropriation* – the illegal taking of property (includes embezzlement, theft, and fraud);
- *false representation* – the fraudulent concealment of material facts; and
- *collusion* – agreeing (with others) to defraud another of his property and/or rights, and/or obtain an object and/or property forbidden by law.

The more serious of the above illegal acts may be subject to possible SFO investigation (UK Serious Fraud Office),[13] and such illegal acts can loosely be categorised as follows:

- An intentional perversion of truth, misrepresentation, concealment or omission of material fact perpetrated with the intention of deceiving another which causes detriment and/or injury to that person.
- A deceitful practice or device perpetrated with intent of depriving another of property, and/or other rights.
- A dishonest act designed to manipulate another person to give something of value.

Although there are many types of fraud, the following, although not exclusively restricted to technology-based issues, nevertheless rely heavily on remote communication (often the internet) to further the aim of the fraud – that is, they are what is sometimes referred to as computer *assisted* fraud (rather than computer *related* fraud).[14]

Examples of computer assisted fraud would include:

- false billing,
- financial (funds) fraud,
- advance fee frauds,
- identity theft, and
- phishing.

False billing

This type of fraud is usually aimed at large corporate organisations with large, often automated, payments systems/subsystems. It often involves an attempt to obtain funds/payments for goods and/or services that have never been provided.

Many variants exist, including for example:

- fraud which attempts to obtain funds for placing an advert in a non-existent publication,
- fraud which attempts to sell space in a false and/or limited-distribution business directory, and,
- fraud which attempts to gain payment for false invoices for non-existent goods and/or services.

Financial (funds) fraud

Examples can range from financial theft and the illegal transfer of funds from a company bank account, to ATM-based frauds, to credit card/electronic fund related crimes that normally involve obtaining goods/services for payment using stolen and/or illegally obtained financial information.

The most common types of financial (funds) frauds are:

■ card-not-present fraud – that is, using a stolen or cloned debit or credit card to buy goods and services, and

■ cash-back money transfer fraud.[15]

Advance fee frauds

These often (but not exclusively) originate from parts of Africa. In particular, Nigeria is infamous as a source of this type of fraud. Indeed, advance fee frauds are often referred to as '419 schemes' after section 4:1:9 of the Nigerian government penal code.

The common characteristics of such advance fee frauds are:

■ a company receives a communication (e-mail, letter or fax) from a purported 'official' representative of a foreign government agency;

■ the communication offers to transfer millions of pounds into the company's bank account (for a 'pay-off fee' which the company will receive on completion of the transfer), normally claiming that the funds are from over-invoiced projects or unaccounted excess funds from a previous political regime, or funds related to property transfers/low cost oil transfers; and

■ the targeted company (or more appropriately victim company) is nearly always asked to provide blank company letter-headed paper, bank account details/information, confidential telephone/fax numbers and, sooner or later, the payment of an up-front or advance fee payment to cover various taxes, legal costs, transaction costs and/or bribes.

A variety of such advance fee frauds is the dead relative variety, or the current affairs/disaster variety. For example the January 2010 earthquake in Haiti produced a plethora of fee fraud e-mails.

Identity theft

Identity theft is the deliberate assumption of another's identity (either person and/or company), usually:

■ to fraudulently obtain goods and/or services using that identity,

■ to gain access to a source of finance and/or credit using that identity,

■ to allocate/apportion guilt for a crime and/or fraud to that identity,

■ to enable illegal immigration using that identity, and/or

■ to facilitate terrorism, espionage, blackmail and/or extortion.

There are many ways in which an identity can be assumed, from scouring local press/ media to 'web spoofing' – that is, setting up websites to elicit information as part of a seemingly legitimate transaction.

To assist in the prevention of card-related identity fraud, there is an increasingly large range of anti-fraud measures available. Some of the more popular involve the use of:

- forced on-line protocols,[16]
- floor limits,[17]
- '1-in-n'checks – that is, sample random transactions checks,
- multiple transaction checks,
- hot card files,[18]
- encryption,
- Secure Socket Layer (SSL),[19]
- card security codes (CSC),[20]
- address verification services (AVS),[21] and
- payer authentication.[22]

Phishing

Phishing (and pharming) is the fraudulent acquisition, through deception, of sensitive personal information such as passwords and credit card/finance details by:

- masquerading as someone (either a person or company) with a legitimate need/ requirement for such information, and/or
- using malicious/invasive software programs (for example, a Trojan horse – see later in this chapter) to obtain covertly confidential and highly sensitive information.

Phishing is in essence a form of social engineering attack – an attack designed to deceive users and/or managers/administrators at the target site or location. Historically, such social engineering attacks were typically carried out through conventional telecommunication channels – for example, telephoning users and/or operators and pretending to be an authorised user, to attempt to gain illicit access to systems. In terms of contemporary business activity, however, in particular in terms of computer-based information systems and computer security, a social engineering attack can be defined as: the practice of using information technology to deceive people into revealing sensitive information and/or data on a computer system – that is, to gain personal and/or confidential information for the purposes of identity theft and/or funds fraud.

It is perhaps not surprising that the term is often associated with e-mail fraud in which an e-mail is sent to an end-user with the intent of acquiring personal and/or corporate information from the end-user. It is perhaps worth noting that such phishing (and pharming) is no longer the sole domain of the external hacker/cracker – internal hackers/ crackers are increasingly regarded as a primary threat to corporate information security.

Fighting fraud and minimising loss

There can be little doubt that the twenty-first century has seen an enormous increase in the number of frauds and illegal scams directed at both companies and individuals. While the greater availability of information technology and the increased accessibility and use of the internet are often cited as the key reasons for this increase, such reasons clearly represent only part of the answer.

In recognising the increasingly complex threat posed by the use of improved technology by both national and international criminal elements in:

■ the modifying and adapting of existing corporate frauds – that is, supporting traditional crimes with the use of internet and information technology: crimes such as fraud, blackmail, extortion, identity theft and cyber-stalking, and

■ the developing, designing and executing of new corporate frauds – that is, using the internet and information technology to not only develop new crimes and further present new opportunities to both national and international criminal elements, but also challenge contemporary law enforcement: crimes such as hacking, virus transmission, denial of service (DoS) attacks, and spoof websites,[23]

the UK government created the National Hi-Tech Crime Unit in April 2001 to combat national and transnational serious and organised hi-tech crime which either impacts upon and/or occurs within the United Kingdom. In April 2006, however, the National Hi-Tech Crime Unit was disbanded, and some of its staff and duties were transferred to the e-Crime unit of the UK Serious Organised Crime Agency. The remaining duties and responsibilities were transferred to the Police Central E-Crime Unit (PCeU) which was established in October 2008 to centralise the efforts of all police forces in the UK (excluding Scotland) to fight all forms of e-crime.

The Police Central E-Crime Unit (PCeU) is a part of the Specialist Crime Directorate of the Metropolitan Police and is a dedicated service designed to combat e-crime in England, Wales and Northern Ireland.

The stated mission of the Police Central E-Crime Unit (PCeU) is:

■ to improve the police response to victims of e-crime by developing the capability of the police service across England, Wales and Northern Ireland;

■ to coordinate the law enforcement approach to all types of e-crime; and

■ to provide a national investigative capability for the most serious e-crime incidents.

The Police Central E-Crime Unit (PCeU) is active within Europol and Interpol's cyber workstreams, and works closely with the new National Fraud Reporting Centre (NFRC) and other international agencies including the US FBI and CIA. (See Article 9.1.)

Article 9.1

UK police charge suspected CIA hacker

Simon Mundy and Joseph Menn

British police have filed charges against a suspected computer hacker in connection with a slew of online security breaches, including attacks on the websites of the UK's Serious Organised Crime Agency and the CIA.

Ryan Cleary, 19, had been charged with five offences under the Computer Misuse Act, police said. He was arrested in Wickford, 30 miles east of London, on Monday night, as part of a joint operation with the US Federal Bureau of Investigation and is due to appear in court on Friday.

One of the charges relates to bringing down the website of Soca – the UK's FBI equivalent – using a flood of traffic, in what is known as a 'distributed denial of service' attack.

'The arrest follows an investigation into network intrusions and distributed denial of service [DDoS] attacks against a number of international business and intelligence agencies by what is believed to be the same hacking group,' the police said.

The arrest came after a DDoS attack forced Soca to take down its website on Monday. Such attacks cripple websites by overloading them with traffic, and have been compared by hackers to peaceful 'sit-in' protests.

Responsibility for the breach was claimed by LulzSec, a hacker group that called DDoS its 'least powerful and most abundant ammunition'. The group was formed after a split in the group Anonymous, which last year attacked organisations that co-operated with a US crackdown on WikiLeaks, the whistleblowing website. Other attacks claimed by LulzSec include those on the CIA public website and Sony servers.

All three attacks are being investigated as part of the operation that led to the arrest, a Scotland Yard spokesman said. Security experts assisting the FBI identified the suspect as Mr Cleary, whose details were published last month on an Anonymous-run site. A post on the group's blog accused Mr Cleary of organising a 'coup d'état' against Anonymous, in protest against its 'leaderless command structure'.

LulzSec said this week that the two organisations had joined forces for a new campaign, Antisec, which would steal and leak information from governments, banks, and 'other high-ranking establishments'.

On Tuesday, LulzSec mocked the idea that Mr Cleary was the organisation's 'mastermind'. 'Seems the glorious leader of LulzSec got arrested, it's all over now? . . . wait? . . . we're all still here!' it wrote on Twitter.

The security researchers admitted that Mr Cleary's role in LulzSec was unclear. Graham Cluley, a technology consultant at computer security group Sophos, said that LulzSec had been 'playing a dangerous game'. 'Their Twitter account, which has more than 220,000 followers, has become increasingly vocal,' he said.

23 June 2011

Source: Available at *www.ft.com*.

So what can a company do to minimise the possible occurrence of fraud?

There are a number of key practical steps that can be adopted.

First, the company could seek to identify potential reasons as to why the company may/may not be susceptible to fraud. Possible reasons could, for example, include:

- a lack of internal control,
- a lack of internal audit,
- inadequate fraud risk management skills,
- poor data integrity and security,
- inappropriate authority levels,
- ineffective employee recruitment procedures, and/or
- a continuous and unrestricted abuse of separation of duties.

Secondly, it could undertake a company-wide risk assessment and establish a fraud management strategy group to:

- identify the key risk areas,
- assess the potential scale of risk,
- develop a (workable) fraud management protocol,
- allocate responsibilities to all management levels, and
- regularly monitor the effectiveness of corporate internal controls and fraud management protocols.

Finally, the company could develop a fraud management control system, by:

■ adopting and implementing a corporate code of conduct,

■ implementing regular employment checks for potential and current employees,

■ ensuring the regular rotation of staff employed in risk areas,

■ implementing appropriate internal control procedures,

■ undertaking regular fraud audit,

■ promoting regular ethics training to employees, and

■ undertaking appropriate surveillance of employee activities.

Perhaps on a more functional computer-based transaction level, as part of a fraud management control systems, a company may also, where appropriate, seek to:

■ adopt a suitable level of cryptography to safeguard information,[24] and

■ promote the use of electronic signatures for e-based transactions.[25]

The Electronic Communications Act 2000 (together with the Electronic Signatures Regulations 2002 and the Electronic Commerce (EC Directive) Regulations 2002) provides a regulatory framework for the use of cryptographic service, and clarifies the legal status of electronic signatures.[26]

Cyber terrorism

Historically, the term cyber terrorism was used to refer to attacks that threatened property or lives, and was therefore defined as any threats and/or disruptive activities against a computer-based information system, particularly via the internet, with the primary aim of causing physical real-world harm and/or severe disruption. In a contemporary context, however, cyber terrorism is used to refer to any planned and premeditated use of threats and/or disruptive activities against a computer-based information system, designed to cause harm and/or further social, ideological, religious, political and/or financial objectives or beliefs.

Essentially, cyber terrorism is the use of information technology by a group or an individual for the organisation and execution of attacks against computer networks, information systems and telecommunications infrastructures to further their agenda. Where that agenda is primarily financial it is often referred to as cybercrime.

Examples of cyber terrorism would include:

■ sabotage of computer-based information systems,

■ introducing malicious viruses to vulnerable computer networks,

■ website defacing,

■ denial-of-service attacks,

■ terrorist threats made via electronic communication.

While many companies claim to have been the target of cyber terrorism – the most recent being the 2011 cyber attack on Sony's PSN and its on-line entertainment network – in general, cyber terrorists' activities are often 'macro' in nature and designed to do damage to the integrity of critical infrastructure systems such as water supply, the electrical supply grid, transportation infrastructure systems, telecommunications systems and, of course, financial systems/financial organisations. (See Article 9.2.)

Article 9.2

IMF targeted in big cyber attack

Alan Beattie and Joseph Menn

The International Monetary Fund has launched an investigation after its computer network was hacked by an unknown outside agent. The Federal Bureau of Investigation is leading the probe into the breach of security, news of which was reported in The New York Times after a warning to IMF staff last week.

David Hawley, an IMF spokesman, said: 'I can confirm that we are investigating an incident.' He declined to give details, but said the IMF was fully functional. The IMF has private information that could be valuable to investors in the financial markets, possibly including details of rescue plans for crisis-stricken west European economies. The perpetrator, target or method of the hacking have yet to be pinpointed although there is as yet no evidence that anything sensitive has been taken.

An e-mail from an IMF officer to staffers on June 8 alerted them to the breach but said the Fund did not believe the hackers wanted information as part of a fraud, prompting some experts to suggest the most likely culprit was a national government. States could use IMF information in negotiations or to profit in the markets.

However, people familiar with the investigation told the Financial Times that such conclusions were premature. 'It's still too early to say,' one of them said. The IMF's link to the World Bank computer system was taken down as a precaution. The fund said the only linked parts of the two systems were the organisations' intranets which contain administrative information of little value.

A hackers' grouping called Anonymous has threatened to infiltrate the IMF's network in protest at its participation in the rescue lending to Greece, which demands cuts in public spending and higher taxes in return for assistance. But the organisation does not appear to be behind this particular attack.

The IMF has been under increased public scrutiny since the resignation of Dominique Strauss-Kahn, its managing director, after he was arrested and charged with the sexual assault of a New York hotel maid last month.

12 June 2011

Source: Available at www.ft.com/.

Fighting cyber terrorism

The threat of cyber terrorism is similar to the threats of other types of internet-based exploitation. Unfortunately the internet was not designed to promote confidentiality or integrity. It was designed for availability and resiliency by providing a packet switched mesh network. As a consequence security against cyber terrorism must be implemented at the user application level by:

- implementing strong access control systems to ensure that only authorised individuals can access internet-based systems;
- using strong encryption to ensure confidentiality and integrity of information stored, processed, and transmitted on and through cyberspace;
- closely monitoring all cyber activity by using log files and log analysers;
- maintaining up-to-date policies and ensuring such policies are strictly enforced;
- implementing effective detection systems to recognise cyber attacks quickly;
- appointing active cyber security leadership to implement a real-time defence strategy.

Computer crime

Computer crime can be defined as a deliberate action to gain access to, and/or steal, damage or destroy, computer data without authorisation. It involves/includes:

■ the dishonest manipulation of computer programs and/or computer-based data,

■ the fraudulent use/abuse of computer access and resources for personal gain, and/or

■ the deceitful use of computer-based data/computer-based resources in the perpetration of fraud.

There are many reasons advanced by both academics and practitioners in seeking to explain the exponential growth in computer crime over the last 15–20 years. Perhaps the most common of these are:

■ the increasing access to and concentration of contemporary computer processing in business (and in society),

■ the increasing necessity for and use of highly integrated computer systems/networks in business and commerce, and

■ the increasing dependency on computer-based decision-making processes in both personal and business/corporate activities.

Nearly all UK companies regularly use the internet and/or possess a website. During 2009:[27]

■ 83 per cent of UK businesses (for larger UK businesses the figure was 92 per cent) had a malicious security breach within the last 12 months,

■ The average number of security breaches within the last 12 months was 14 (for larger UK businesses the figure was 45).

Yet, in the UK, businesses (in particular corporate businesses) still only spent an average of 10 per cent of their information technology budget on security (for larger UK businesses the figure was 6 per cent) with only 60 per cent of UK businesses possessing a formally defined and documented information security policy (for large UK businesses the figure was 90 per cent.)[28]

Clearly, the number of UK businesses that possess a security policy has continued to increase over the past 10 years:

■ 67 per cent of UK businesses (for larger UK businesses the figure is 90 per cent) now possess a formally documented security policy.[29]

■ 75 per cent of UK businesses (for larger UK businesses the figure is 82 per cent) undertake periodic risk assessments.[30]

■ 51 per cent of UK businesses (for larger UK businesses the figure is 68 per cent) have fully or partially implemented the information security standard ISO/IEC 27001.[31]

Nevertheless, as long as companies (or more importantly company managers) fail to recognise the importance of computer systems/networks as a fundamental/core wealth-creating resource in contemporary corporate activity, and fail to invest in:

■ better staff education,

■ enhanced security protocols,

■ improved security and protection procedures,

- better management control systems/security audits, and
- more effective contingency planning,

the army of potential threats that now exists within the socio-economic marketplace, the army of potential threats ready to expose and indeed exploit any computer system/network security weakness, will only continue to grow – as will computer crime!

How common is computer crime?

Here are some facts. For 2009:[32]

- 33 per cent of UK businesses suffered a systems failure or data corruption (for larger UK businesses this figure was 14 per cent).
- 40 per cent of UK businesses suffered an infection by malicious software (for larger UK businesses this figure was 34 per cent).
- 1 per cent of UK businesses suffered from physical theft of computer equipment (for larger UK businesses this figure was 5 per cent).
- 5 per cent of UK businesses suffered from fraud or theft using computers (for larger UK businesses this figure was 13 per cent).
- 1 per cent of UK businesses suffered from theft or unauthorised disclosure of confidential information (for larger UK businesses this figure was 9 per cent).
- 9 per cent of UK businesses suffered from the misuse of the internet and e-mail (for larger UK businesses this figure was 12 per cent).
- 3 per cent of UK businesses suffered an infringement of laws or regulations (for larger UK businesses this figure was 6 per cent).
- 8 per cent of UK businesses suffered an attack or unauthorised access by outsiders (for larger UK businesses this figure was 7 per cent).

The average cost to UK businesses of their most serious security breach was between £27,500 and £55,000 (for large UK businesses it was between £280,000 and £690,000).

Clearly, then, there can be little doubt that computer crime represents a contemporary (and likely continuing) socio-economic problem not only for business in general and for business organisations, but for corporate organisations in particular. But who actually commits this so-called computer crime (including of course computer assisted fraud), and, perhaps more importantly, why do they do it?

While any demographic would clearly be an over-generalised and grossly simplified classification of those involved in computer crime, those identified or found guilty of committing computer crime often (but not always) tend to present one or more of the following characteristics:

- They are often white Caucasian male, usually aged 19–30 years old (computer crime), and 25–45 years old (fraud).
- They are often intelligent, generally well educated, and like a challenge.
- They tend to be first-time offenders with what is often described as 'a modified robin hood syndrome'.
- They identify with technology, and are often employed in an information technology role and/or a financial/accounting role.
- They generally feel exploited, under-paid and dissatisfied with their employer, but do not (generally) intend harm, seeing themselves as borrowers, and not as thieves.

Table 9.1 Types of computer crime/security breach suffered by UK businesses in 2009

Type of computer crime	Major incident (%)	Minor incident (%)
Inappropriate use of information systems	14	20
Theft of computer hardware	3	28
Unauthorised access and information theft	36	20
Computer fraud or confidentiality breach	4	27
Systems failure	49	41
Virus infection and disruptive software	29	38

Source: Information Security Breaches Survey 2010 Technical Report (April 2010), PriceWaterhouseCoopers and and InfoSecurity Europe (available at *www.infosec.co.uk/.../isbs_2010_technical_report_single_pages.pdf*)

The main reasons perpetrators of computer crime offer as a defence for their actions/ activities generally fall into one (or more) of the following areas:

■ personal financial pressure,

■ personal vices (drugs/gambling etc.),

■ personal lifestyle,

■ personal grievances – due perhaps to increased stress/pressure related to employment conditions,

■ personal vendetta against the business/company or one or more of its managers/owners.

What are the main types of computer crime?

There are many types, many differing categorisations of computer crime, of which the following are perhaps typical examples (see Table 9.1):

■ inappropriate use of corporate information technology,

■ theft of computer hardware and/or computer software,

■ unauthorised access and information theft,

■ fraudulent modification of data/programs,

■ sabotage of computing facilities, and

■ premeditated virus infection and disruptive software.

Fighting computer crime

Inappropriate use of corporate information technology

Inappropriate use is not inadvertent misuse. Inadvertent means not on purpose, or accidental and without intention. Inadvertent misuse of corporate information technology generally occurs as:

■ a one-off/accidental event, and

■ a consequence of a series of breaches of protocol and/or procedural controls which are not the responsibility of the person guilty of inadvertent misuse of corporate information technology facilities.

Such inadvertent misuse of corporate information technology facilities is often minor in consequence, and generally results in little or no loss of assets and/or resources.

Clearly, however, where such inadvertent misuse occurs repeatedly with increasing/ escalating consequence, then such inadvertent misuse may indeed become inappropriate.

Table 9.2 Types of inappropriate use of computer information technology suffered by UK businesses in 2009

Type of inappropriate use of computer information technology	Small businesses (%)	Large businesses (%)
Misuse of web browsing facilities	34	80
Misuse of e-mail facilities	29	75
Unauthorised access to systems and/or data	13	58
Infringement of laws and/or regulations	10	45

Source: Information Security Breaches Survey 2010 Technical Report (April 2010), PriceWaterhouseCoopers and InfoSecurity Europe (available at *www.infosec.co.uk/.../isbs_2010_technical_report_single_pages.pdf*)

What is inappropriate use?

Clearly such a term can cover a very wide range of activities – activities including:

- The use of corporate technology for personal reasons, for example, employees shopping on-line during work hours, and/or employees sending personal e-mails to internal and/or external individuals).

- The abuse of corporate information technology, for example, the viewing, downloading and/or distribution of pornographic material and/or the viewing, downloading and/or distribution of racist material.

- The misuse of corporate information technology for malicious criminal purposes, for example, employees disclosing confidential corporate information and/or employees selling sensitive and confidential corporate information.

See Table 9.2.

The impact of such use, abuse and misuse of corporate information technology can have many consequences. Not only can external knowledge of such abuse and/or misuse be extremely embarrassing for the company, particularly where such abuse and misuse is widespread, it can also severely, and in some circumstances irreparably, damage a company's social/market reputation.

More importantly, such activities could potentially result in:

- an increased risk of possible virus infection and/or the downloading of other invasive and potentially damaging software programs,

- a potential loss of revenue especially where such abuse and misuse of corporate information technology results in a reduction in overall productivity,

- a severe reduction and/or even loss of network bandwidth where significant inappropriate activities are occurring, and

- an increased risk of liability and legal action where such inappropriate activities result in for example:
  - racial or sexual discrimination and harassment,
  - misuse of personal information in breach of the Data Protection Act 1998,
  - the propagation of libellous literature, and/or
  - the loss of goods, services and/or information.

What can be done to prevent/minimise inappropriate use?

Clearly, prevention is better than any cure and a number of measures can be employed:

- The development of active employee screening and vetting procedures.
- The development of a clear policy/definition of what is and is not acceptable.

- The installation of an active and up-to-date virus defence.
- The use of e-mail content checking.[33]
- The adoption of usage filtering and monitoring.[34]

However, while all the above can assist in minimising inappropriate use, where inappropriate use of corporate information technology is detected, a corporate recovery strategy must be adopted. The form that such a strategy might take would depend largely on a range of interconnected variables, for example:

- the nature and context of the inappropriate use,
- the period over which inappropriate use may have occurred,
- the extent to which potential losses may have been incurred,
- the degree (if any) to which the inappropriate use may have exposed the company to legal liability, and finally
- the extent to which the inappropriate use may have been detected by and/or impacted on other (external) parties.

Nevertheless, while the precise nature of the strategy may differ, the basic process would involve:

- qualifying the exact nature of the inappropriate use incident(s),
- establishing the potential threat posed to the company by the inappropriate use incident,
- assessing the impact of the inappropriate use incident, and determining the extent of the inappropriate use incident,
- containing the impact of the inappropriate use incident, and
- adopting appropriate countermeasures, for example:
  - adopting software upgrades and/or installing software patches,
  - increasing network protection/security,
  - reviewing intrusion detection protocols and policies,
  - adjusting network server access,
  - reviewing outsourcing agreements (as appropriate),
  - revising and/or negotiating liability clauses and warranties,
  - managing publicity issues, and
  - where appropriate, involving relevant regulatory and/or investigatory external parties.

Theft of computer hardware and computer software

There can be little doubt that where the opportunity arises, due to negligent security controls and/or infrequent and ineffective security monitoring/surveillance, theft will occur. Not may occur, not can occur, but *will* occur!

With 28 per cent of UK businesses reporting that the physical theft of computer equipment was the most disruptive of all security breaches – and the most costly to the business[35] – the prevention of theft of computer hardware and/or software is clearly an important issue. Such prevention requires a commitment to security and investment in the provision of a wide range of measures and controls that can be categorised as follows:

- *Preventative* controls – that is, controls designed to minimise and/or prevent opportunities for theft to occur.
- *Detective* controls – that is, controls designed to detect theft attempts.

■ *Recovery* controls – that is, controls designed to trace/track down stolen items and facilitate the recovery of such items and/or the possible prosecution of any individual/individuals responsible for the theft/misappropriation.

Such controls would normally operate on three distinct hierarchical layers:

1 Physical security control layer.

2 Technical security control layer.

3 Human security control layer.

Physical security control layer

Physical controls can generally be divided into two types:

(i) physical controls designed to prevent/restrict resource access, and

(ii) physical controls designed to prevent/restrict asset movement.

Physical controls preventing/restricting resource access are generally designed to prevent/restrict access to a secure area/facility, and invariably exist on a number of levels or at a number of different layers. For example, secure areas (such as those areas/buildings in which corporate computer facilities are located) may be monitored using closed-circuit television cameras (CCTV) recording access to and from such secure areas. In addition, access may be restricted to authorised personnel only, by the use of entry control facilities. Such entry controls could range from:

■ the use of ID badges, to

■ the use of hardware/software tokens, to

■ the use of smart cards, to

■ the use of security passwords, to

■ the use of personalised biometric measurements.

A combination of such entry controls may of course be used in concert – especially where the consequences of any theft or misappropriation of computer hardware/software may result in substantial financial distress. For example, primary perimeter controls may be used to restrict access to a secure area/facility, whereas secondary internal controls may be used to restrict movement/access within the secure area/facility.

Physical controls preventing/restricting asset movement are generally designed to minimise the possibility of unauthorised misappropriation of assets, and facilitate the traceability of stolen items of computer hardware/software. These controls can range from:

■ the security tagging of both computer hardware and computer software, to

■ the registration and regular audit of computer hardware, to

■ the secure storage of software programs and applicable registration licences and security passwords, to

■ the use of radio frequency identification (RFID) technologies.

Clearly, security tagging and registration and audit are of major importance where computer assets are sited in remote locations (not necessarily networked), away from the company's main computing facilities – for example, where employees are geographically dispersed and use portable computing facilities as part of their daily activities/duties.

The history of **radio frequency identification (RFID)** technologies is a disputed one. While the origins of RFID can be traced back to Leon Theremin (1945),[36] for many, the modern precursor of current RFID technologies is Mario Cardullo's (1973) development of a passive radio transponder . . . with a memory.

In a contemporary context, RFID technologies are often referred to as automatic identification technologies, that is, technologies which rely on the storing and remote retrieval of data/information using transponder devices. Such transponder devices are often referred to as RFID tags.[37]

What is an RFID system?

An RFID system would consist of several components, for example:

- RFID tags,
- RFID tag readers,
- processing hardware, and
- application software.

It would be designed to:

- enable data/information to be transmitted from an RFID tag,
- enable such data/information to be read by an RFID reader, and
- facilitate the processing of such data/information according to the needs of a particular application/system.

What type of data/information can be transmitted by an RFID tag?

In general, the data/information transmitted by an RFID tag can be categorised into three types:

1 Location information – that is, information about the geographical location of a subject and/or an object.
2 Object information – that is, information on object-related characteristics, for example product price, product colour, product date, etc.
3 Subject information – that is, information on the identity of a subject and/or the location of a subject.

There are essentially three types of RFID tags. They can be:

- passive,
- semi-passive (or semi-active), or
- active.

A *passive* RFID tag is an RFID tag that does not possess an internal power supply. Such passive tags operate using a process often referred to as 'backscattering' – that is, the RFID tag antenna is not only designed to collect power from the incoming signal (the carrier signal from the reader), but also to transmit an outgoing signal to the reader. Passive RFID tags are often referred to as dumb tags.

A *semi-passive* RFID tag is very similar to a passive tag except for the addition of a small battery. The battery allows the RFID tag to be constantly powered, and therefore removes the need for the RFID tag antenna to collect power from the incoming signal. Semi-passive RFID tags are generally faster and stronger compared to passive tags.

Unlike passive and/or semi-passive RFID tags, *active* RFID tags possess their own internal power source – usually an internal battery – to 'generate and transmit an outgoing signal to the reader'. Active RFID tags are often referred to as beacon tags because such tags broadcast their own signal.

The current areas in which RFID tags are now used include:

- supply chain management,
- product tracking and distribution management,
- product/asset security,
- transport management,
- revenue collection, and
- personal identification.

Technical security control layer

Whereas physical security controls are designed to prevent/restrict resource access and asset movement, technical security controls are generally designed to restrict/control the user privileges.

There are of course a number of possible security controls available, of which the most common appear to be:

- the use of access controls to define profile user rights and prevent the unauthorised appropriation, or accidental removal, of software programs and data files; and
- the use of cryptographic facilities to encode sensitive software programs and data files, to restrict access and ensure the security and integrity of any such programs and files.

Technical security controls may also be used to monitor use and survey access by:

- the use of penetration testing[38] to evaluate the effectiveness of the technical security of a computer system or network in protecting software programs and data files – often by simulating an attack by an unauthorised and malicious hacker/cracker, and
- the use of intrusion detection systems/programs designed to detect inappropriate use and/or unauthorised access. (These are discussed in greater detail below.)

Human security control layer

Within any business system – especially within a computer-based information system – people-based controls, or what can be called the human security control layer, are perhaps the most important control feature.

Why? No matter how virtual the commercial business process becomes, no matter how computerised business information systems become, indeed, no matter how fictitious payment methodologies become – at some point in the business process (however fleeting and/or insignificant it may appear to be), the physical world becomes an important and relevant feature, and human interaction becomes inevitable. Indeed, while technologists would have us believe that humankind is now a redundant or at least a less active participant in the contemporary business process, the human touch still remains a key feature of the materiality that lies at the heart of contemporary capitalism.

What do we mean by human security controls?

Such controls can range from informal control in terms of promoting security consciousness and creating a control culture through awareness training, education programmes and in-house training, to the imposition of formal contractual obligations that enforce restrictions on the activities employees can undertake.

Unauthorised access and information theft

As indicated earlier, 8 per cent of UK businesses in 2009 suffered an attack or unauthorised access by outsiders (for larger UK businesses this figure was 7 per cent), with nearly 22 per cent of UK businesses reporting some form of probing attempt – that is, an attempt to:

- probe, scan or test the vulnerability of a system, server or network and gain access to data, systems, servers or networks, and/or
- breach security or authentication measures and gain access to confidential information (see Article 9.3)

without express authorisation of the owner of the system, the server and/or the network.

Article 9.3

Tesco's call centre staff sacked for massive online fraud

Kurt Bayer

Fourteen staff at Tesco's main UK call centre in Dundee have been sacked or suspended after auditors uncovered a massive fraud involving false discount vouchers used to buy groceries, alcohol, cigarettes and DVDs over the internet. Last week investigators removed computers to search hard drives in a bid to discover the true extent of the fraud, which is believed to run well into six figures.

Instead of answering calls from customers, crooked employees spent hours on the office internet purchasing thousands of pounds' worth of groceries, drink, cigarettes and DVDs for pennies by inputting codes for VIP discount vouchers into online orders – which were then delivered to their home by Tesco deliverymen.

Some internet shopping bills were slashed from £200 to just £10 and it is understood that a manager at one of the large Dundee Tesco superstores has been suspended for not spotting the transactions.

One woman involved is said to have defrauded more than her £13,000-a-year salary. Another is understood to have offered to repay the value of the goods stolen.

According to the company, four workers have been sacked and ten have been suspended pending disciplinary action following the discovery of fraud by auditors.

27 February 2006

Source: Available at *http://business.scotsman.com*.

The Information Security Breaches Survey 2010 (see earlier) also found that 32 per cent of UK businesses who had suffered an unauthorised access breach regarded the breach as major and extremely disruptive (compared with 20 per cent who regarded the unauthorised access breach as minor).

There can be little doubt that twenty-first-century connectivity has proved to be a vivid paradise not only for those vain cavaliers of the virtual highway – the world's hackers – but also for the criminal rogues of the virtual highway – the world's crackers.

Hackers and crackers?

Confused? Let me explain. Originally, the term hacker was used to describe any amateur computer programmer seeking to make software programs run more efficiently and computer hardware perform more effectively. However, in a contemporary context the term hacker is often used misleadingly (especially by the media) to describe a person who breaks into a computer system and/or network and destroys data, steals copyrighted software, and/or performs other destructive or illegal acts – that is, a computer vandal.

This is perhaps unfortunate, since such definition is more appropriate for a person known as a cracker[39] – that is, someone who breaks (or cracks) the security of computer systems in order to access, steal or destroy sensitive information. In essence, a cracker is a malicious hacker and – contrary to popular belief – the term cracker is not synonymous with the term hacker.

What damage can a cracker do?

There are many reasons why an individual would attempt to breach a computer system/network security protocols – that is, attempt to gain unauthorised access to a computer system and/or network – and the damage caused by such a breach could include, for example:

- the theft of confidential and sensitive corporate information, and/or
- the theft of protected information, and/or
- the disruption of a corporate service and/or facilities (for example payment systems), and/or
- the infestation of a computer system and/or network.

There are, of course, a number of strategies that a company can adopt in order to prevent and/or manage unauthorised access to a computer system/network and/or data:

- the development and adoption of a corporate defence protocol,
- the ensuring of user vigilance,
- the adoption of appropriate training and education, and (perhaps most important of all)
- the use of information and communication technologies.

There are many security tools and computer-based technologies that can be used to manage access, control use and, where appropriate, prevent unauthorised entry. Such tools and technologies include use of:

- system/network firewalls,
- intrusion detection systems/software,
- data encryption facilities,
- digital certificates,
- authentication and authorisation software, and
- scanners, patches and hotfixes.

Firewalls

Often referred to as border protection devices, firewalls are essentially system gateways – system gateways designed to prevent unauthorised access to or from a personal computer and/or a private network. They are frequently used to prevent unauthorised internet users from accessing private networks connected to the internet, especially intranets. They can be in the form of:

- a hardware appliance and/or network device,
- a feature of another network device – for example, a network router,
- a software package installed on a server/host system,
- a combination of some or all of the above.

A firewall is designed to ensure that only approved network traffic of:

- an authorised nature and/or type, or
- from a prescribed application,

is allowed to move in and between a network or networks according to an approved security protocol, thereby preventing unauthorised access and the possible risk of a security breach.

The basic task of a firewall is to control traffic between areas or regions of different levels of trust;[40] that is, to provide controlled connectivity through the enforcement of a security/access policy on the least privilege principle,[41] and so can be used to:

- control and record network connection attempts and network traffic,
- authenticate users trying to make network connections,
- inspect network packets,
- monitor network connections,
- inspect application traffic, and
- protect internal networks.

How does a firewall work?

There are essentially two access denial criteria used by firewalls:

1 to allow all traffic unless it meets certain criteria, or
2 to deny all traffic unless it meets certain criteria.

The criteria used by a firewall to determine whether traffic should be allowed through will depend on:

- the type of firewall,
- the concern of the firewall (for example, control/restrict access by traffic type, or source address types, or destination address type), and
- the network layer/operational location of the firewall – that is, the layer within the OSI and TCP/IP network model.

What different types of firewalls are there?

Firewalls can be broadly classified into four categories:

1 a packet filter,
2 circuit level gateway,
3 an application level gateway, and,
4 a multilayer inspection firewall.

A **packet filter** firewall operates at the network layer of the OSI model, or the IP layer of TCP/IP, and is usually part of a router. In a packet-filtering firewall each packet is compared to a set of criteria before it is forwarded. Depending on the packet and the criteria, the firewall can reject the packet, forward the packet, or send a message to the packet originator. Rules can include source and destination IP address, source and destination port number, and protocol used. Packet filtering firewalls are a low-cost firewall option that tend to have a relatively low impact on the performance of the system/network on which they are used.

A **circuit level gateway** operates at the session layer of the OSI model, or the TCP layer of TCP/IP, and monitors TCP handshaking between packets to determine whether a requested session is legitimate. While circuit level gateways are also a relatively inexpensive option, such gateways cannot be used to filter individual packets.

Packet filtering and circuit level gateways are often referred to as network layer firewalls.

Application level gateways – also referred to as proxies – are essentially application specific circuit level gateways that filter packets at the application layer of the OSI model: that is, incoming and/or outgoing packets will be denied access to services for which there is no proxy. For example, an application level gateway configured as a web proxy will only allow web-based traffic through. All other traffic will be rejected.

Because application level gateways can be used to filter application specific commands, to record logins and log user activity, they offer a high level of security, but can have a significant impact on system/network performance.

Multilayer inspection firewalls generally combine aspects of each of the above types of firewalls, inasmuch as they:

- filter packets at the network layer,
- determine whether session packets are legitimate, and
- evaluate contents of packets at the application layer.

Multilayer inspection firewalls are often referred to as state-full firewalls (as opposed to state-less firewalls[42]). Because such a firewall can monitor/track the state of a system/network connection, and distinguish between legitimate packets and illegitimate packets for different types of connections, they can provide a high level of security and transparency. However, they can be expensive and insecure if inappropriately managed.

Intrusion detection system (IDS)

An intrusion detection system (IDS) acts as a system/network security service, its primary aims being to monitor and analyse system events for the purpose of detecting, identifying, and providing real-time warning of, attempts to access system/network resources in an unauthorised manner.[43] IDS can be used to:

- protect key internal network servers,
- identify internet-based attacks, and
- monitor network access points.

An example of an open-source network intrusion and detection system is Snort – a system which combines signature-based, protocol-based and anomaly-based inspection methods.[44]

An intrusion detection system is composed of three key components:

1 a sensor(s) which monitors activity and generates security events,

2 a console which monitors the security events and controls the sensors, and

3 a control device which records the security events recorded by the sensor(s) in a database and uses pre-established rules to generate alerts from security events received.

An IDS can also be categorised by location, by nature, or by type.

By *location*, intrusion detection systems can be classified as either:

- network-based systems – where the intrusion detection system monitors the network to monitor traffic, identify malicious packets, prevent network intrusion, and report on suspicious and/or atypical activity, or
- host-based systems – where the intrusion detection system is installed on network servers to identify activity and anomalies and report on server-specific problems or activity.

By *nature*, intrusion detection systems can be categorised as either:

- passive detection systems – where the intrusion detection system detects a potential security breach, logs the information and signals an alert, or
- reactive detection systems – where the intrusion detection system responds to the suspicious activity by either:
  - logging off a user to prevent further suspicious activity, or
  - reprogramming the firewall to block network traffic from the suspected malicious source.

By *type*, intrusion detection systems can be categorised as either:

- misuse detection systems – where the intrusion detection system analyses the information it gathers and compares it to large database of attack signatures (that is, the intrusion detection system monitors for specific known attacks – attacks that have already been documented), or
- anomaly detection systems – where the intrusion detection system uses a pre-defined baseline, or normal, state of a network's traffic load, breakdown, protocol, and typical packet size, and monitors network segments to compare their state to the normal baseline and look for anomalies.

Encryption

Cryptography[45] is the study of alternative means of converting data/information from a comprehensible format into an incomprehensible format, the aim being to render the data/information unreadable to anyone without a special knowledge of the conversion process. It is this conversion process that is known as encryption – a process designed not only to ensure secrecy but, in a contemporary context, to ensure and maintain security, especially in the communication of confidential, sensitive and highly valuable data/information where it is important to be able to verify both the integrity and authenticity of a message.

In a contemporary context, there are two different types of encryption:

1 symmetric key algorithm[46] (or secret key cryptography), and

2 asymmetric key algorithm (or public key cryptography).

In a *symmetric* key algorithm (or secret key cryptography), both the sender of the message/communication and the receiver of the message/communication possess a shared secret key – the same shared secret key. The sender uses the secret key to encrypt the message/communication, whereas the receiver uses the secret key to decrypt the message/communication. Many of the early classical ciphers[47] used a symmetric key algorithm (or secret key cryptography), examples of which would include:

- a substitution cipher,[48]
- a transposition cipher,[49]
- a product cipher,[50]
- block cipher,[51] and/or
- a stream cipher.[52]

In an *asymmetric* key algorithm (or public key cryptography) there are two separate keys:

1 a public key which is published and available to the public and therefore enables any sender to encrypt a message/communication, and

2 a private key which is kept secret by the receiver and enables only the receiver to decrypt the message/communication.

Companies encrypt a wide range of data types, for example:

- laptop hard disks,
- desktop hard disks,
- wireless network transmission,
- web-based customer transactions (using Secure Socket Layer (SSL) encryption),
- employee remote access to systems (via virtual private network, or VPN),
- data transfers to other companies/organisations,
- data backups,
- sensitive data fields held in databases,
- data held on virtual storage (for example, the cloud).

Digital certificates

Digital certification is a security technique that encrypts a digital certificate containing a unique key onto a client computer system/network.

A digital certificate is an electronic file that can be used as a means of identification and authentication. Such certificates are the digital equivalent of positive identification and are based on public key cryptography which, as we have seen, uses a pair of keys (private and public keys) for encryption and decryption.

In essence, the digital certificate contains the public key linked to the personal identification (ID) of the certificate holder (Slay and Koronios 2006: 149). To be valid, such digital certificates require the digital signature and the endorsement of a Certification Authority, for example:

- Verisign Ltd (*www.verisign.co.uk*), or
- Comodo Group (*www.comodogroup.com*).

Authentication and authorisation systems

Authentication can be defined as the process of proving an identity – for example of a user – that is, determining who they are. *Authorisation* can be defined as the process of permitting or denying access to a system and/or a resource and/or a facility to an authenticated user – that is, determining what they are allowed to do.

There are many alternative methods of authentication – these can be categorised as:

- attribute-based – that is, authentication based on something the user is, for example a biometric characteristic/identifier (DNA sequence/fingerprint/retinal scan), or a biological trait (voice pattern recognition);

■ possession-based – that is, authentication based on something the user possesses, for example an identification card or a security token/card;

■ knowledge-based – that is, authentication based on something the user knows, for example, a password, or phrase, or a personal identification number (PIN).

Such authentication procedures/systems are increasingly used where it is important to control user access. For example, authentication systems are commonly used for controlling ATM transactions and/or managing/controlling access to internet banking facilities, with many authentication systems often involving a combination of attribute/possession/knowledge-based authentication methods.

Scanners, patches and hotfixes

Scanners remain a popular type of virus/hacking defence software.

Virus scanners (see also later in this chapter) are software programs designed to identify and eradicate 'known' viruses. They are simple to install and generally easy to use. However, they require constant maintenance inasmuch as they need to be frequently updated (using approved patches and/or hotfixes) with the latest virus information in order to remain effective.

Vulnerability scanners are software programs designed to test for 'known' security defects. Because such scanners can only test for existing and 'known' faults – much like virus scanners – they require constant updating with the latest version.

The Computer Misuse Act 1990

The Computer Misuse Act 1990 provides for three distinct offences:

1 Unauthorised access to computer material.

2 Unauthorised modification of computer material.

3 Unauthorised access with intent to commit or facilitate the commission of further offences.

Issues related to the unauthorised modification of computer material and unauthorised access with intent to commit or facilitate the commission of further offences will be discussed later.

In relation to unauthorised access to computerised material, the Computer Misuse Act 1990 (s.1) makes it an offence for any person and/or persons to cause a computer to perform any function with intent to secure unauthorised access to any program or data file held in a computer. That is, the Act makes it a criminal offence to access a computing system/network unless authorised to do so. The Act clarifies the term 'unauthorised access' as including the altering, erasing, copying and/or moving of programs and/or data files to another storage medium other than that in which it is held (s.17(2)).

The Computer Misuse Act 1990 (s.1) (as amended by the Police and Justice Act 2006) makes the activity of hacking and/or cracking a criminal offence, and a person found guilty of such an offence is liable:

■ on summary conviction, to imprisonment for a term not exceeding six months or to a fine not exceeding the statutory maximum or to both, and

■ on conviction on indictment, to imprisonment for a term not exceeding two years or to a fine or to both.

Fraudulent modification of data/programs

In an information technology/information systems context, the fraudulent modification of data/programs means the dishonest and deceitful variation, alteration, and/or adaptation of software programs and/or data files. Examples of such actions would include:

■ the destruction of data files,

■ the creation and/or introduction of a virus, and/or

■ the deliberate generation of data/information to promote a computer system/network malfunction.

The Computer Misuse Act 1990 (s.3) makes it an offence for a person and/or group of persons to undertake the unauthorised modification of computer programmes and/or computer based data files that will:

■ impair the operations of a computer system/network,

■ prevent or hinder access to computer programs and/or data files, and

■ impair the integrity of any computer program and/or data file.

This offence also covers the introduction of harmful worms and viruses to a computer network/system.

The Computer Misuse Act 1990 further provides (s.17(7)) that a modification occurs if by the operation of any function of any program on a computer system/network:

■ any program or data file held in the computer system/network is altered or erased, or

■ any program or data file in the computer system/network is added to.

In addition, the Computer Misuse Act 1990 (s.17(8)) provides that a modification is unauthorised if the person and/or group of persons promoting the modification is:

■ not entitled to determine whether the modification should be made, and/or

■ does not possess the requisite consent/authority to undertake the modification.

For the Computer Misuse Act 1990 (s.3) to apply there must be:

■ intention to cause and/or promote modification, and

■ knowledge and understanding that the intended modification was/is unauthorised.

And any person or persons found guilty of an offence under The Computer Misuse Act 1990 (s.3) is, following the 2006 amendments, liable:

■ on summary conviction, to imprisonment for a term not exceeding six months or to a fine not exceeding the statutory maximum or to both, and

■ on conviction on indictment, to imprisonment for a term not exceeding five years or to a fine or to both.

Sabotage of computing facilities

In its broadest sense, the term sabotage means the wilful, malicious and/or deliberate destruction or damage of resources, assets, and/or property to hinder the legal activities of a person, group of persons and/or organisations, and adversely affect the reputation and/or safety of a business and its employees.

In an information technology context or, more specifically, an information systems context, the term sabotage means the interference with computer processes by causing deliberate damage to a processing cycle and/or to computer equipment. That is, any invasive, deliberate and/or malevolent act motivated by either revenge and/or malicious intent that results in:

■ the loss and/or destruction of data files, and/or

■ the corruption/destruction of software programs, and/or

■ the theft/misappropriation of resources/assets, and/or

■ the complete failure of a computer system/network.

Clearly, sabotage (whether promoted by an employee, an ex-employee and/or an external agent) can take many different forms, including:

■ damaging key computer hardware,

■ damaging network activity,

■ altering or deleting data files,

■ theft of computer hardware and/or software,

■ distribution of unauthorised and/or abusive and/or offensive literature, and

■ unauthorised disclosure of confidential information to competitors.

At a corporate level, the consequences of any invasive act of sabotage can be extremely damaging and financially costly. Yet, at an industry/market sector level, detecting sabotage and/or collecting empirical evidence of its occurrence and/or estimating with any degree of accuracy the frequency of such attacks against corporate computer-based information technology systems continues to be almost impossible.

Why? Put simply – many corporate victims choose not to disclose such events/occurrences because:

■ companies often see very little benefit for themselves (as the victim company) inasmuch as the damage is done and the law is often unlikely to be able to undo the damage caused by the saboteur(s);

■ companies often view the possible cost of collecting evidence and launching possible legal action against the saboteur(s) as prohibitive (although recently this is increasingly not the case); and finally

■ companies often believe the potential adverse publicity surrounding the disclosure of such events/occurrences could have disastrous commercial consequences and harm the future prospects of the company.

There are, however, legal remedies available should a company choose to pursue the matter. The Computer Misuse Act 1990 (s.2) makes it a criminal offence for any person and/or persons to gain unauthorised access to a computer system, network, program and/or data file held in a computer with the intention to:

■ promote a denial of service, and/or

■ commit or facilitate the commission of further offences.

Any person or persons found guilty of an offence under The Computer Misuse Act 1990 (s.2) is, following the 2006 amendments, liable:

■ on summary conviction, to imprisonment for a term not exceeding six months or to a fine not exceeding the statutory maximum or to both, and

■ on conviction on indictment, to imprisonment for a term not exceeding two years or to a fine or to both.

Premeditated virus infection and disruptive software

For our purposes we will categorise computer infections and disruptive software/programs into five main categories:

1 Viruses.

2 Worms.

3 Trojan horses.

4 Spyware.

5 Adware.

Before we look at each of the above in a little more detail, it would perhaps be worthwhile noting that the DTI Information Security Breaches Survey (2010) found that 43 per cent of UK businesses (for larger UK businesses the figure was 14 per cent) had been infected by a virus.

Viruses

A computer virus is a computer program that invades, replicates and/or attaches itself to a program file or data file. It is essentially a software program capable of unsolicited self-reproduction/self-replication, that can disrupt, modify and/or corrupt data files and/or other program files without human assistance, and cause substantial damage to a computer system.

There are two key aspects of a virus:

1 self-execution, and

2 self-replication.

What types of virus/infections exist?

Although many types of virus exist, they can be categorised into perhaps six main types (although these categories are by no means definitive):

1 A macro virus: this normally attaches itself to features within standard computing applications to perform unexpected tasks – for example, moving data and/or inserting text and numbers (recent examples include DMV, nuclear, word concept).

2 A file virus/program virus: this normally attaches itself to files and affects the operation of program files. The virus infects executable program files[53] which are stored in the computer memory during execution. It becomes active in memory, making copies of itself and infecting files in the system memory (recent examples include Sunday, Cascade).

3 A boot sector virus: this normally lies dormant and becomes active only when a particular system/computer operation is commenced (recent examples include form, disk killer, michelangelo, and stone virus).

4 A multipartite virus: this is a hybrid of program and boot viruses, and initially infects program files which when executed infect the boot record (recent examples include invader, flip, and tequila).

5 A stealth virus: this virus actively seeks to conceal itself from discovery, or proactively defends itself against attempts to analyse or remove it (recent examples include frodo, joshi, whale).

6 A polymorphic virus:[54] this is a virus that alters its codes to avoid being detected by anti-virus programs. Polymorphic viruses encrypt themselves differently every time they infect a system/network, making it harder to track and prevent them (recent example include stimulate, cascade, phoenix, evil, proud, virus 101).

Worms

A worm is a virus-like program that is designed to replicate and spread throughout a computer system/network. Such programs usually hide within application-based files (for example, Word documents/Excel files), and can:

■ delete and/or amend data, and/or

■ migrate rapidly through a computer system/network, and/or

■ incapacitate particular data files and software programs.

Their presence normally results in a significant drain on computer resources, memory availability and, in some cases, network access.

Because this type of infection/infestation is self-propagating, worms can have a devastating impact on a computer system/network.

Trojan horses

A Trojan horse is a malicious program (often hidden and/or disguised), which when activated can result in the loss, damage, destruction and/or theft of data. Unlike a worm (or indeed any other virus) a Trojan horse cannot self-replicate. However, such impotence, such inability to procreate, does not minimise the destructive impact a Trojan horse can have on a computer system/network. Some common features/consequences of Trojan horse program infection include:

■ amending payments (changing payment values),

■ initiating unauthorised payment (causing illicit payments to be activated),

■ instigating network/system-wide configuration changes,

■ distributing confidential security information to external third parties (for example, usernames and access passwords),

■ providing unauthorised access pathways to external third parties (usually known as backdoors and trapdoors).

Perhaps worthy of note here is the term *logic bomb* (a term derived from the malicious actions such a program can prosecute when triggered). A logic bomb is in effect a type of Trojan horse – a Trojan horse which is placed within a computer system/network with the intention of it executing a predetermined set of actions when some triggering condition occurs. Such a triggering condition could be for example:

■ a change in the content of a file,

■ the input of a particular data sequence,

■ the execution of a particular computer program, or

■ the input of a particular time and/or date.

How are these viruses and infections transmitted?

Usually viruses/infections are disguised as, and/or attached to, something else. For example:

■ a software update/release,

■ an e-mail or e-mail attachment, and/or

■ an internet download.

What can a virus/infection do?

The impact of any virus and/or any infection can and will vary – depending on:

■ the origin of the virus and/or infection, and

■ the nature of the virus and/or infection.

The consequences of any infestation can range from:

■ mild system irritation – for example, computer crashes and/or unauthorised move-ment of data and/or files, and/or overloaded network servers, to

■ temporary loss of data integrity – for example, changing data fields and file content, and/or the unauthorised release of data files, to

■ complete loss of computing resource – for example, loss of systems partitions (organ-isation of disc space), to

■ significant loss of corporate assets – for example, theft of financial resources.

Can an infestation be prevented?

There are many ways a company can seek to minimise the potential risk of virus infec-tion; strategies can include:

■ the promotion of environment security and user vigilance, and

■ the adoption and use of appropriate and up-to-date virus defence software and, where appropriate, software security patches and/or hotfixes.

It is also important for a company to possess a clear and definitive virus defence strategy detailing:

■ the deployment of anti-virus software,[55]

■ procedures/mechanisms for updating virus defence software,[56]

■ isolation procedures/policies for if an infection event occurs,

■ the post-event recovery procedures.

While the above can represent a substantial cost, there can be little doubt that whatever cost may be incurred for virus prevention, in the long-term this will be small compared to the possible costs and associated consequences of dealing with, and recovering from, a virus infection. Recovery would include costs related to:

■ the eradication of the virus and/or infection,

■ the organisation of any clean-up operation, and

■ the installation of procedures to ensure no potential re-infestation.

Spyware

Spyware can be defined as any malicious software that covertly gathers user information through an internet connection without the user's knowledge and/or consent. It is similar to a Trojan horse inasmuch as it is usually packaged as a hidden component of, for example:

- a downloaded freeware and/or shareware program,[57] and/or
- a downloaded peer-to-peer file.

Once downloaded and installed, such spyware can:

- monitor keystrokes,
- scan files on a computer hard drive,
- invade and/or monitor other software applications,
- install other spyware programs,
- read cookies,[58]
- use internet bandwidth and computer memory,
- monitor internet activity and change the user settings,
- amend web browser specifications, and
- transmit confidential information to a third party – information which could include for example:
  - e-mail addresses,
  - security usernames and passwords, and
  - credit card/debit card numbers.

Can the presence of spyware be detected?

Indirectly yes! For example:

- the frequent malfunction of computer processes – including computer crashes,
- the occurrence of unauthorised changes to a web browser specification,
- the appearance of extra toolbar facilities,
- the frequent appearance of pop-up advertisements – usually adult related advertisements, and
- the failure of established internet links (hyperlinks),

all suggest (although not conclusively) the presence of spyware.

. . . and the solution?

Anti-spyware software! Indeed, like a firewall and/or other anti-virus program, anti-spyware software is now crucial to maintaining the security of a system/computer network.

Anti-spyware software essentially searches for evidence of spyware within a computer/network, and deletes any spyware detected. A wide range of anti-spyware software is now available.

Adware

Adware (or **ad**vertising-supported soft**ware**) is a software program which automatically plays, displays, or downloads pop-up advertising material to a computer/computer system.

There are essentially two types of adware:

1 passive adware – that is, adware attached to a legitimate software program, the purpose being to promote and advertise other legitimate software programs and/or related products, and

2 active adware – that is, adware which takes the form of either:

- spyware which tracks user activity, often without consent, or
- malware which interferes with the function of other software applications.

. . . and the solution?

As with spyware, the solution is to use anti-adware software.

Botnet

Botnet is a term used to describe a collection of software robots, or bots, that run autonomously and automatically. The term is often associated with malicious software but it can also refer to the network of computers using distributed computing software – a collection of compromised computers (called Zombie computers) running software, usually installed via worms, Trojan horses, or backdoors, under a common command-and-control infrastructure.

Botnets are now a significant part of the internet, albeit increasingly hidden and often including a variety of connections and network types. They are used for various purposes, including:

- denial-of-service attacks,
- the creation or misuse of SMTP mail relays for spam (Spambot[59]),
- click fraud,
- adware,
- spyware,
- spamdexing,[60] and
- the theft of application serial numbers, login IDs, and financial information such as credit card numbers.

Concluding comments

There can be little doubt that as society treads wearily into the early part of the twenty-first century and as businesses (in particular corporate businesses) seek to employ a growing arsenal of computer-based technologies in the name of corporate efficiency, the never-ending search for greater profitability and increased competitive advantage, the potential risk of fraud (especially computer-assisted fraud) and the threat of computer crime in terms of:

- the increasing incidence of security breaches, virus infection and disruptive software,
- the growing occurrences of information systems misuse,
- the increasing frequency of unauthorised access attempts,
- the growing incidence of theft and fraud involving computer systems/networks, and
- the increasing levels of systems/network failure/data corruption,

remain both a growing and ever-present danger (see Article 9.4).

Article 9.4

If Google can be hacked, is anyone safe?

Seth Berman and Lam Nguyen

Businesses pour millions of dollars into a never-ending 'virus-antivirus' arms race, all the while wondering: 'If the technology titans can be hacked, what are the chances that my own data is secure?'

IT sophistication means we can now watch individual data packets as they enter and exit systems; we can scan files for known viruses, as well as those yet to be written; we can examine corporate networks to see who's online, what they are doing and how they are doing it. Yet we are still vulnerable. At the heart of this insecurity is the 'zero-day exploit'. It is derived from a programming concept that refers to day one of a software development project; known as the zeroth day.

Thus, a zero-day exploit takes advantage of the window of time between when developers are made aware of a problem and when the complete software fix can be developed and distributed. Zero-day exploits, by definition, are vulnerabilities that have not been addressed by hardware and software manufacturers. Thus, there are no virus signatures to be downloaded or software patches to be updated, leaving the bad guys with the upper hand. Add to this the complexity and sophistication of today's attacks and it becomes easier to understand why industry giants such as Google can be hacked.

Recent reports indicate the Google attacks started on social networking sites. The attackers watched key Google employees to identify their friends and associates and hacked these accounts.

Then they used information gained to contact other employees and, appearing legitimate, lured unsuspecting victims to nefarious websites, which provided the doorway through the company's firewall.

These attacks have become known as chained exploits, a series of vulnerabilities and weaknesses that, when used in tandem, can break even the most secure systems. In another example, a corporation detected a calamitous virus infection which plagued more than 500 computers in its network. It thought it had dealt with it successfully but six months later the company identified suspicious traffic indicating the presence of another virus. After forensic analysis, it was discovered the 'new' malware had been installed during the earlier attack. Once the second virus was in place, it didn't matter to the hackers that the first virus had been destroyed.

Chained exploits not only create new vulnerabilities, they can lead to a false sense of reassurance by allowing the first virus to serve as a decoy, leaving the impression that efforts to destroy the first virus have solved the problem.

So what can you do mitigate this risk? First, assume that no matter how good your firewalls, infections will happen from time to time. Maintaining diligent and timely patch management of applications, operating systems, and network devices is a must – but not sufficient. Where possible, restrict access to sensitive information to as few people in the company as possible – that way a breach of one person's computer won't open the keys to the kingdom. You also need an emergency response plan in place before a virus attack to assess whether it is the sort of attack that can be dealt with using commercially available virus detection software (which will be true in most cases), or if the infection is systemic or is affecting an especially sensitive system that constitutes a breach of your central infrastructure. In that case you might need to decompile the virus's code to understand exactly what it did, how it operated, and seek expert advice on finding and containing the damage.

The recent cyber attacks also reveal a changing motive – the hackers wanted to steal intellectual property or corporate secrets. Indeed, some recent hacks involved viruses that automatically copied every e-mail sent or received by key individuals to a shadow address, giving the hackers a clear view of company secrets.

In short, this new wave of hacking is corporate espionage. The implication is clear: previously, the financial risk of hacking was primarily of damage to a network and perhaps reputation. Now the risk is far greater – the new target is the business information upon which a company relies.

5 March 2010

Source: Available at *www.ft.com/*

As we have seen, the consequences of fraud, cyber terrorism and computer crime can range from:

- minor business disruption and damage to business reputation, to
- substantial data corruption, major loss of business capabilities, and significant direct financial loss.

So, what is the solution? Perhaps there is no single solution – no single correct strategy but merely a series of alternative (some would say common sense) practices and procedures that can be adopted to protect and secure assets, resources and technologies from abuse and/or misuse.

Clearly, the ever-changing demands of the business environment/marketplace require an increasing understanding of technology and technology management, but, more importantly, a greater awareness of the importance of security and, of course, willingness to react quickly and to invest in system/network security.

Implicit in each of the above requirements is the need for businesses, and in particular companies, to ensure that:

- adequate employee training regarding fraud and computer crime is available/undertaken,
- appropriate updated anti-virus software, and other hardware and/or software protection technologies are used,
- appropriate write/protect procedures and protocols are adopted,
- data/file back ups of all essential data and programs are maintained,
- access to computer systems/networks is appropriately monitored and controlled.

Perhaps most important of all is the need to use common sense! Indeed, even the most elaborate frauds/business scams have been revealed by nothing more than employee intuition and basic common sense.

Self-review questions

1 Briefly explain the precautionary principle, and distinguish between weak form precaution, moderate form precaution, and strong form precaution.

2 Distinguish between event/activity-based risk and resource/asset-based risk.

3 What are the three main factors that determine the degree of risk exposure a company may face?

4 What is the purpose of BS 7799 Part 1 and IOS/IEC 17799?

5 Define the term fraud and describe/explain the illegal acts normally associated with the term.

6 Briefly explain the main differences between a virus, a worm, and a Trojan horse.

7 Distinguish between preventative controls, detective controls, and recovery controls.

8 What are the main categories of computer crime?

References

Abercrombie, N., Hill, T. and Turner, B. (1984), *Dictionary of Sociology*, Penguin, Harmondsworth.

Beck, U., Giddens, A. and Lash, S. (1994), *Reflexive Modernization: Politics, Tradition and Aesthetics in the Modern Social Order*, Stanford University Press, Stanford.

Beck, U., Bonss, W. and Lau, C. (2003), 'The theory of reflexive modernization: problematic, hypotheses and research programme', in *Theory, Culture and Society*, vol. 20(2), pp. 35–48.

Berger, P.L. and Luckmann, T. (1966), *The Social Construction of Reality: A Treatise in the Sociology of Knowledge*, Anchor Books, New York.

Department of Trade and Industry and PriceWaterhouseCoopers LLP (2004), *Information Security Breaches Survey 2004 Technical Report*, DTI, London.

Slay, J. and Koronios, A. (2006), *Information Technology Security and Risk Management*, Wiley, Milton, Queensland.

Weyman, A. and Kelly, C. (1999), 'Risk Perception and Communication: a review of the literature', Health and Safety Executive, Research Report 248/99.

Notes

1 There is a range of approaches used to conceptualise risk. For example, whereas the actuarial approach would seek to use past data to extrapolate and forecast future trends, the epidemiological approach would use modelling to explore causality and attempt to identify and quantify the relationship between exposure to a hazard and outcome. Whereas the engineering approach would seek to use probabilistic analysis to identify cause and consequence, the economic approach would use cost-benefit analysis and seek to balance possible gains with possible risks while assuming that participants are rational, economic actors interested solely in maximising gains. And, finally, whereas the psychological approach would use heuristics (rules of thumb) to focus on personal preferences and seek to identify alternative perceptions of risk, the cultural approach would seek to view risk as a social construct and explore responses to and perceptions of risk as determined by cultural belief patterns and/or social imposed filters.

2 Social constructionism is an idea/notion that reality is constructed uniquely by each person and/or group of persons – that reality is an invention or artifact of a particular culture or society (see Berger and Luckmann 1966).

3 The theorists of reflexivity suggest that modernity has begun to modernise its own foundations. It has become directed at itself (see Beck *et al.* 2003), thus the term reflexive modernisation means: 'the possibility of a creative (self-) destruction for an entire epoch – that of industrial society . . . [with] the subject of this creative destruction not the revolution, not the crisis, but the victory of western modernization' (Beck *et al.* 1994: 2).

4 The term cultural is used here to define the symbolic and learned processes which generate and sustain norms and values between members of a social group (for example, see Abercrombie *et al.* 1984: 59).

5 In a contemporary context, trust has emerged as an area of major significance in understanding risk perceptions and responses – and as suggested by Weyman and Kelly (1999) serves as a zone of convergence between psychological and socio-cultural approaches to risk.

6 See UNEP (United Nations Environment Programme), Declaration on Environment and Development, Rio de Janeiro, June 1992.

7 Adapted from Annex 1 Precautionary Principle: Policy and Application, United Kingdom Interdepartmental Liaison Group on Risk Assessment (UK-ILGRA), available at *www.hse.gov.uk/aboutus/meetings/committees/ilgra/pppa.htm*.

8 Where unintentional errors occur regularly, then such unintentional errors may well hide a deliberate intention to defraud and/or cause harm or damage.

9 The full text of ISO/IEC 17799 Code of Practice for Information Security can be obtained at *www.iso.ch*.

10 ISACA is an international professional association that deals with IT Governance. Previously known as the Information Systems Audit and Control Association, ISACA now goes by its acronym only, to reflect the broad range of IT governance professionals it serves.

11 COBIT has had several major releases:
  • in 1996, the first edition of COBIT was released;
  • in 1998, the second edition added 'Management Guidelines';
  • in 2000, the third edition was released;
  • in 2003, an on-line version became available;
  • in December 2005, the fourth edition was initially released;
  • in May 2007, the current 4.1 revision was released.

12 *Oxford English Dictionary* (1991), Edmund, S., Weiner, E.S. and Simpson, J. (eds), Oxford University Press, Oxford.

13 In the United Kingdom the Serious Fraud Office (SFO) is an independent government department responsible for investigating and prosecuting serious or complex fraud. The key criterion used by the SFO in deciding whether to accept a case is that the suspected fraud should appear to be so serious or complex that its investigation should be carried out by those responsible for its prosecution. The factors generally considered are:
  • does the value of the alleged fraud exceed £1 million?
  • is there a significant international dimension?
  • is the case likely to be of widespread public concern?
  • does the case require highly specialised knowledge, e.g. of financial markets?
  • is there a need to use the SFO's special powers, such as Section 2 of the Criminal Justice Act?
The SFO does not have jurisdiction over Scotland, the Isle of Man or the Channel Islands.

14 Although the distinction is by no means widely accepted, in a broad context, a computer *assisted* fraud is a fraud and/or fraudulent act in which the use of a computer, and/or a computer system/network is central to the fraud, whereas a computer *related* fraud is a fraud and/or fraudulent act in which the use of a computer, and/or a computer system/network is coincidental.

15 This is popular where a sale of an asset is taking place – especially on-line. It is a sale where the buyer (usually an overseas buyer) offers payment by a cheque or banker's draft – often for more than the asking price of the asset. The seller is then requested to send all or some of the difference to the 'buyer', a third party or a 'shipping agent', by way of money transfer (irrespective of whether their cheque or banker's draft has already entered your account). Typically the cheque or banker's draft will not clear – it will 'bounce' or it may be recalled by the bank (because it was stolen) – even after the funds have gone through the clearing cycle and are showing on your account. Any money transferred by you cannot be recalled and result in a loss.

16 Where a merchant is unsure about the validity of a customer/cardholder's identity or has suspicions about the transaction, the merchant can force the transaction to be authorised on-line.

17 A floor limit is an agreed limit between the merchant and acquirer. If the transaction amount exceeds the floor limit, the transaction is forced on-line for authorisation.

18 Hot card files contain details of lost and stolen cards. Where hot card checking is installed, each time a merchant accepts a card as payment for a transaction, the system checks the card number against entries in the hot card file. Obviously if the card number is listed, the merchant *must* decline the transaction and retain the card.

19 SSL provides a secure method of transmitting and authenticating data over a network via TCP/IP. Developed to enable the secure transmission of information over the Internet, SSL can be used to reduce the risk of credit card information being intercepted.

20 Card security codes (CSCs) were introduced as an anti-fraud measure for customer/cardholder-not-present transactions (nPoS EFT) where objective verification/validation is not possible. A CSC is a 3-digit number (4-digit number for American Express) that is generated automatically on manufacture. The CSC is printed on the signature strip on the back of the card.

21 Address verification services (AVSs) were also introduced as an anti-fraud measure for customer/cardholder-not-present transactions (nPoS EFT) where objective verification/validation is not possible. AVS entails checking information about the customer/cardholder's address.

22 Specifically to reduce the incidence of fraudulent internet-based transactions, payer authentication enables on-line merchants to authenticate customers/cardholders in real time.

23 Denial of service (DoS) attack is a type of cybercrime – it prevents a target computer, computer systems and/or computer network from accessing a network resource. See *www.mynetsec.com/html/security.htm*.

24 Cryptography encrypts documents or messages and seeks to ensure they remain confidential, and such encryption can be used as a basis for an electronic signature.

25 An electronic signature is associated with an electronic document and seeks to confirm the authenticity of the document/communication.

26 See Information Security: Guide to Electronic Communications Act 2000 (2004), Department of Trade and Industry (available at *www.dti.gov.uk*).

27 See Information Security Breaches Survey 2010 Technical Report (April 2010), PriceWaterhouseCoopers and and InfoSecurity Europe (available at *www.infosec.co.uk/.../isbs_2010_technical_report_single_pages.pdf*).

28 The Information Security Breaches Survey 2010 Technical Report (April 2010) categorises UK businesses as follows:

- a small UK business is a business with 1–49 employees,
- a medium UK business is a business with 50–249 employees, and
- a large UK business is a business with 250+ employees.

29 See Information Security Breaches Survey 2010 Technical Report (April 2010), PriceWaterhouseCoopers and and InfoSecurity Europe (available at *www.infosec.co.uk/.../isbs_2010_technical_report_single_pages.pdf*).

30 Ibid.

31 Ibid.

32 Ibid.

33 A content checker filters incoming and outgoing e-mail messages and attachments for specific words and phrases to ascertain whether given file types are present. Messages can also be filtered to limit the size of e-mails.

34 Monitoring staff usage of corporate information technology is a controversial issue, with a fine balance between the corporate need to prevent crime and the employees' human rights. The following legislation must be considered where the monitoring of employee e-mails is being considered:

- the Human Rights Act 1998,
- the Data Protection Act 1998 (specifically the Data Protection Monitoring at Work section and Part 1 (Vetting & Personnel),
- the Regulation of Investigatory Powers Act 2000,
- the Telecommunications (Lawful Business Practice) (Interception of Communications) Regulations 2000.

35 See Information Security Breaches Survey 2010 Technical Report (April 2010), PriceWaterhouseCoopers and and InfoSecurity Europe (available at *www.infosec.co.uk/.../isbs_2010_technical_report_single_pages.pdf*).

36 And his invention of a covert listening device for use by the Russian government during the 1940s and 1950s.

37 An RFID tag is a small object that can be attached to, or indeed incorporated into, an object (for example a product), or a subject (for example a person, or an animal). Such tags generally contain digital chips and antennae to enable them to receive and respond to radio frequency queries from an RFID transceiver.

38 Penetration testing is often characterised by simulating an attack by an unauthorised and malicious hacker/cracker to identify security weaknesses.

39 Crackers often like to describe themselves as hackers. Cracking normally relies on persistence and repetition of a handful of fairly well-known tricks to exploit security weaknesses of target computer systems/networks. See *www.infosec.gov.hk/engtext/general/glossary.htm*.

40 For example, an external network such as the internet may be regarded as a region of little or no trust, whereas an internal network may be regarded as a region of high trust.

41 In an information and communication technology context, the principle of minimal privilege (also known as the principle of least authority) requires that in granting privileges, authority, and/or access, only that level of privileges, authority and/or access which will permit legitimate and effective action to occur should be granted. That is, excessive privileges, authority, and/or access should not be granted to an individual, and/or group of individuals where such privileges, authority, and/or access are not required for that individual and/or groups of individuals to undertake their duties and activities effectively and efficiently.

42 A state-less firewall is a firewall that treats each packet in isolation, and as such is not able to determine if a packet is part of an existing connection, or part of an attempt to establish a new connection, or merely an illegitimate rogue packet. Modern firewalls are state-full firewalls inasmuch as they are connection-aware (or state-aware).

43 See for example Honeynet (available at *http://www.activeworx.org/programs/hsc/index.htm*).

44 Snort (available at *www.snort.org*) is the most widely deployed intrusion detection and prevention technology worldwide and has become the de facto standard for the industry.

45 From Greek *kryptós* meaning: 'to hide', and *gráphein* meaning 'to write'.

46 An algorithm is a procedure or a finite set of instructions for accomplishing a particular task/procedure.

47 A cipher is an algorithm for performing the encryption and decryption process – that is, the series of defined procedures that must be followed during the encryption and decryption process.

48 A substitution cipher is a cipher in which data (for example, a word or character) are replaced with other data (for example, another word or character) in a prearranged manner (Slay and Koronios 2006: 133).

49 A transposition cipher (sometimes known as a route cipher) is a cipher in which plaintext is first written out in a grid of given dimensions, then read off (or transposed) in a predetermined pattern. Variants include columnar transposition, double transposition and disrupted transposition.

50 A product cipher is a cipher in which a combination of other kinds/types of ciphers is used.

51 A block cipher is a cipher in which the data are divided into defined blocks each of which is then encrypted independently of other blocks – although in reality often there is some commonality in the encryption of blocks of data.

52 A stream cipher is a cipher in which data items are encrypted as single data items – one data item at a time. A substitution cipher is an example of a steam cipher.

53 Such as those with extensions like .BIN, .COM, .EXE, .OVL, .DRV (driver) and .SYS (device driver).

54 See *www.antivirus-software.net/glossary.shtml*.

55 In a contemporary context the deployment of virus defence software normally occurs at three distinct levels: the internet gateway level; the network server level, and the desktop/workstation level.

56   There are three common types of virus defence software: scanners, check-summers, and heuristics.

57   Although not all freeware and/or shareware is infected with hidden spyware!

58   A cookie is a message given to a web browser by a web server which is then stored by the web browser as a text file.

59   A spambot is an automated computer program designed to assist in the sending of spam. Spambots harvest e-mail addresses from material found on the internet in order to create mailing lists for sending unsolicited e-mails (also known as 'spam'). Such spambots are web crawlers that can gather e-mail addresses from websites, newsgroups, special-interest group (SIG) postings, and chat-room conversations.

60   Spamdexing can be defined as the deliberate manipulation of search engine indexes using, for example, repeating unrelated phrases.

CHAPTER 10

Internal control and accounting information systems security

Introduction

This chapter explores the socio-political issues associated with internal control and systems security, and the alternative types/forms of internal control procedures and processes that a company may adopt to minimise systems risk and ensure the physical security of resources, data/information and system networks. It also considers the ongoing reciprocal relationship between information and communication technologies and internal control (and system security), and the problems and issues associated with information and communication enabled business processes and procedures.

Learning outcomes

By the end of this chapter, the reader should be able to:

- Describe the socio-economic contexts of control

- Distinguish between alternative classifications of control and the issues associated with systems security

- Describe and critically comment on the impact of information and communication technologies on internal control and systems security

- Evaluate the implications for internal control and systems security of business processes enabled by information and communication technologies

Internal control and information systems security – a contemporary context

Internal control comprises the processes and/or procedures designed to provide reasonable assurances that a company's business objectives – primarily the maximisation of shareholder wealth – will be achieved, and any undesired events, unwelcome occurrences and/or unfavourable incidents will be prevented and/or detected and corrected.

Internal control is of course closely related to:

- **Management control** – which can be defined as a diverse range of activities designed to conduct, direct and control business activities and ensure consistency with corporate business objectives;

- **Information control** – which can be defined as a diverse range of activities undertaken by or on behalf of a company's management, designed to ensure the proper and appropriate operation of underlying information systems, and the consistency, reliability and relevance of information provision for both internal and external use; and, of course,

- **Information and communication technology (ICT) control** – which can be defined as all those activities, employed by or on behalf of a company's management, designed to ensure the reliability of a company's information systems.

See Figure 10.1.

As an enclosing definition, the term internal control includes all those imposed management procedures and processes designed to ensure:

- the reliability and integrity of both financial and non-financial information;
- the economic, effective and efficient use of business resources;
- compliance with management policies and adherence to extant regulatory requirements;
- the safeguarding of all business assets and resources; and
- the accomplishment of established corporate/organisational goals and objectives.

The provision of effective internal control requires:

- an understanding and appreciation of the *control environment*,
- an understanding of relevant and appropriate *control activities*,
- an understanding of *(internal and external) risk*,

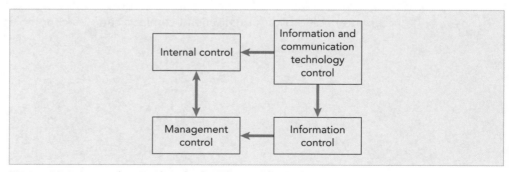

Figure 10.1 Internal control and related control types

- an assessment of the efficiency and effectiveness of *information and communication* channels used both internally within the company and externally within the environment, and

- an appreciation and understanding of the need for effective and appropriate *monitoring* of transaction processes and procedures.

We will return to these issues and discuss each of them later in the chapter. For the moment . . . what about systems security?

For our purposes we will classify systems security as a specific (increasingly important) component aspect of internal control and, as such, we will define systems security as the deployment of a range of procedures, processes, policies and protocols to protect assets, resources, data and/or information against:

- unauthorised access,

- loss,

- misappropriation, and/or

- improper modification, deletion and/or alteration.

Clearly, there is a close, often symbiotic, relationship between a company's internal control procedures and the security of a company's operational systems inasmuch as such systems security procedures and processes are designed not only to ensure:

- the security of tangible/non-tangible resources,

- the security of data/information, and

- the security of company/organisational networks,

but also to ensure proper and adequate protection from possible systems failures/disasters. Indeed, as a legitimate and (some would say) necessary corporate expense, systems security procedures should seek to maintain:

- the integrity of corporate operations,

- the confidentiality of corporate data and/or information, and

- the protection of corporate assets and resources.

Internal control – a composed framework

In September 1992, the Committee of Sponsoring Organizations of the Treadway Commission (COSO), a voluntary private sector organisation established in the USA, published a four-volume report entitled *Internal Control – Integrated Framework*.[1] It was later re-published with minor amendments in 1994. It established a common internal control model against which companies can assess their control systems, and is a framework which involves four key concepts:

1 Internal control is a process. It is a means to an end, not an end in itself.

2 Internal control is affected by people. It is not merely policy, manuals, and forms – but *people* at every level of an organisation.

3 Internal control can be expected to provide only reasonable assurance, not absolute assurance, to an entity's management and board.

4 Internal control is geared to the achievement of objectives in one or more separate but overlapping categories.

The COSO internal control framework consists of five interrelated components which together provide an effective framework for describing and analysing the internal control systems implemented in a company:

1 The control environment.

2 Control activities.

3 Analysis of (internal and external) risk.

4 Information and communication.

5 Monitoring.

It is the combination of these five interrelated components that is commonly referred to, using the generic and enclosing term, as 'internal control'.

Control environment

The imposition/identification of a control environment is the foundation for all other components of internal control within the company. It provides:

- discipline – within business procedure,
- structure – within business processes.

The term control environment refers to the (imposed) norms and values – or, in other words, the actions, the policies and the procedures imposed by the company management – and seeks to reflect the overall attitudes of the company management, the company directors and the company owners (shareholders) about control (specifically internal control) and its importance to the company.

The creation/determination of a control environment in effect seeks to impose, within an operational environment, a control consciousness: a control consciousness imposed by, but derived from, the norms and values that form the central character of the company's organisational culture. Such norms and values would include:

- ethical values enshrined within company procedures,
- the company management commitment to competence and best practice,
- company management operating philosophy,
- company structure and organisational accountability,
- assignment of authority and responsibility within the company, and
- company human resources policies and procedures.

An effective control environment is an environment within which individuals and participants are aware of:

- the activities/procedures and/or processes for which they are responsible,
- the limits of their authority and role(s) within the company, and
- the controls imposed upon them and their activities within the company.

It is clearly within the context of the control environment that control activities exist.

Control activities

These are the policies and procedures used by management to meet its objectives – within the framework of the norms and values imposed by the control environment.

They are the activities and actions which when undertaken in a proper and considered manner and supported by appropriate and relevant policies and procedures facilitate the management (and hopefully reduction) of risk.

Such control activities can be categorised into the following groups:

- adequate segregation of duties,
- appropriate separation of administrative procedures,
- relevant and appropriate authorisation procedures,
- appropriate documentation and records,
- appropriate physical security of assets and records, and
- relevant and proper direct and indirect supervision of business procedures and business performance.

Within a control environment such control activities must be implemented/applied consistently and, of course, cost-effectively.

What if control activities fail?

Whereas minor lapses in control activities could result in:

- possible loss of assets/resources, and/or
- possible interruption/suspension of business activities and the financial losses associated with such disturbance,

substantial failure of such control activities could lead to:

- significant adverse publicity, and/or
- significant fluctuations in share values (and ultimately collapse of the company).

Clearly, central to the existence of adequate control activities is:

- an understanding of the risk associated with a failure of internal control,
- the existence of adequate communication channels and flows of information, and
- the effective monitoring of both company processes and procedures . . . and control activities.

Analysis of internal and external risk

The analysis of risk, or risk assessment/evaluation, is the study of the weaknesses and threats, and:

- the likelihood of such threats materialising,
- the possible impact of such threats, and
- the theoretical effectiveness of security measures/internal control procedures.

That is, a risk assessment is concerned with:

- the identification and analysis of risks relevant to the achievement of operational objectives, financial reporting objectives and/or compliance objectives,
- the determination of expected losses, and
- the establishment of the degree of risk acceptable to system operations.

Such an assessment seeks to answer three simple questions:

1 What can go wrong?
2 How likely is it to occur?
3 What would the consequences be?

The risk assessment is designed to assist in:

■ the formulation of appropriate control strategies/policies that can be incorporated into the company/organisation control environment, and
■ the implementation of relevant procedures and processes that can be incorporated in the company's/organisation's range of control activities.

Information and communication

Appropriate and relevant information, and efficient, cost-effective and well-organised communication channels are, therefore, an essential prerequisite for effecting adequate control. Information about a company's:

■ strategic plans,
■ control environment,
■ internal and external risks,
■ control activities,
■ current operational activities, and
■ current performance

must be communicated up, down and of course across the company's management structure/hierarchy.

Clearly, relevant information must be:

■ appropriately identified,
■ captured,
■ transmitted, and
■ communicated,

not only in an understandable form/context but, more importantly, in a relevant and appropriate timeframe to enable recipients to undertake their activities and associated responsibilities effectively and efficiently.

Clearly, such information (structured and/or unstructured) may be:

■ information concerning internal operations – based primarily on internally generated data, and/or
■ information concerning external conditions and events, and/or external activities operations required to adequately inform internal business decision-making/management processes and procedures.

Such communication channels may be:

■ formal – within a predetermined and regulated hierarchical structure, and/or
■ informal – within an undefined and unregulated social framework.

Monitoring

Monitoring refers to the collection and analysis of financial and non-financial information on a regular basis in order to evaluate performance on control activities. It includes regular management and supervisory activities, and other control-associated actions undertaken by other personnel in the performance of their duties and the exercising of their responsibilities.

It is in essence the assessment of control activities:

- over a period of time, and/or
- over a range of corporate activities.

Such monitoring is usually accomplished through:

- the continuous monitoring/evaluation of all control activities within a control environment, and/or
- the separate evaluation of specific pre-identified control activities/internal control procedures/processes within a control environment through the use of internal self-assessments, internal/external peer reviews and/or internal audits.

Clearly the scope and frequency of separate evaluations will depend primarily on the risks associated with a particular control activity and the effectiveness of continuous ongoing monitoring procedures.

While the monitoring of control activities is often seen as an internal activity – that is, such monitoring is normally concerned with inputs, activities and outputs – it can also be an external activity.

What is the purpose of monitoring control activities?

The purpose of monitoring control activities – whether as a continuous process or a series of separate evaluations – is to assess the quality of such control activities/internal control systems (usually over time), and to:

- ensure the regular collection and analysis of information,
- assist in timely decision making,
- promote accountability, and
- provide the basis for organisation learning.

Internal control

Clearly, internal control – as a framework composed of five interrelated components (see page 324) – is an ever-changing, ever-evolving, ever-developing collection of related processes, procedures and activities. The existence of an appropriate internal control framework can clearly assist a company in:

- ensuring the reliability of its financial reporting,
- ensuring compliance with extant laws and regulations,
- maintaining long-term wealth creation/maximisation,
- minimising all possible losses, and
- ensuring corporate survival.

Nevertheless, it is important to realise that the existence of an adequate internal control framework does not in any way provide any absolute guarantee or any unqualified assurance as to a company's future success.

Why? For a number of reasons!

For example, individual component aspects of internal control may operate efficiently; however, poor and/or faulty management decision-making procedures may reduce the effectiveness of such internal control. In addition, internal control activities, while appropriate, may be circumvented through either

- the conscious collusion of one or more individuals and/or

- inappropriate management activities.

Finally, the effectiveness of internal controls may be adversely affected by management-imposed resource constraints. Remember – the benefit accrued from the imposition of any internal control procedure/process **must** outweigh the cost of imposing that internal control.

Classification of controls

There are many ways of classifying different types of controls that comprise internal control, the most commonly used being:

- Classification of controls by function, for example:
  - preventative controls,
  - detective controls, and
  - corrective controls.
- Classification of controls by type/scope, for example:
  - application controls, and
  - general controls.

Before we look at each of the above in a little more detail, it would perhaps be useful to note that whether controls are classified by function or by type/scope, there is – perhaps somewhat predictably – a degree of commonality, or a degree of overlap, between the types of controls included in each of the two classifications (see Figure 10.2):

- Application controls essentially comprise preventative and detective type controls, whereas

- General controls essentially comprise preventative, detective and, in some instances, corrective type controls.

Classification by function

Preventative controls

Preventative controls are proactive controls designed to prevent and/or deter the occurrence of adverse events and the loss of assets and/or resources. Examples of such controls would be:

- the segregation of management/administrative duties,
- segregation of transaction processing duties,

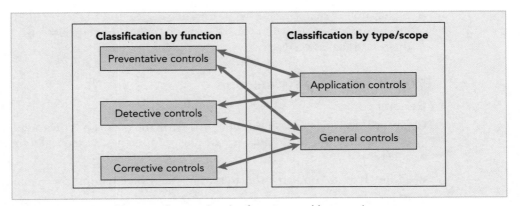

Figure 10.2 Classification of controls – by function and by type/scope

- the existence and use of appropriate and adequate formal documentation,
- the existence and use of proper authorisation procedures/processes,
- the formal controlling of access to assets/resources/facilities, and
- the existence and use of defined policies/procedures/processes.

Detective controls

Detective controls are passive/reflexive controls, or 'after the event' controls. They are designed to detect undesirable consequences of events which may have already occurred. Examples of such controls would be:

- the duplicate checking of calculations,
- the preparation of monthly accounting trial balances,
- the review of policy procedures and controls,
- periodic physical stocktakes,
- periodic reconciliations of balances (for example, debtors, creditors and bank), and
- periodic internal audits.

Corrective controls

Corrective controls are active controls designed to eliminate, and/or remedy the causes of, adverse threats and/or undesirable events. Examples of such controls would be:

- the creation and retention of backup copies of transaction data/information,
- the creation and retention of backup copies of master files,
- adherence to data protection policies, and
- the existence and use of adequate data processing correction procedures.

Put another way – although there is some overlap, in a control context:

- Approvals procedures are generally preventative in nature.
- Reconciliation and review processes tend to be detective in nature.
- Asset/resources management procedures are typically corrective in nature.
- Asset/resource security procedures tend to be both preventative and detective in nature.

■ Segregation of management/administrative duties, and the segregation of transaction processing duties, are often viewed as preventative in nature although they are sometimes regarded as corrective.

Classification by type/scope

General controls

General controls relate to all activities involving the company's/organisation's resources, assets and facilities (including accounting information systems resources). They are designed to:

■ ensure that a company's/organisation's control environment remains stable and secure;

■ maintain the integrity of corporate functions/activities (including accounting information systems processing functions/activities) and associated systems and networks;

■ preserve the ongoing reliability of the company's/organisation's control environment *and* enhance the effectiveness of application controls;

■ maintain appropriate levels of physical security practices and environmental protection measures to minimise the possible risk of vandalism, theft, and/or sabotage; and

■ ensure the adoption of appropriate disaster planning and recovery protocols to ensure continuity of systems, networks and processing procedures.

In an accounting information systems context, general controls seek to ensure that:

■ all appropriate data are correctly processed;

■ all systems applications and network functions and processes are operated in accordance with the established schedules and protocols;

■ all processing errors are identified, traced and resolved;

■ appropriate recovery procedures are established for processing failures;

■ data/information file backups are maintained and updated at periodic intervals;

■ systems/network development and change control procedures are applied; and

■ all related human resources activities are monitored and reviewed.

General controls are generally classified into the following categories:

■ Organisational controls.

■ Documentation controls.

■ Access controls.

■ Asset-management controls.

■ Management practice controls.

■ Information systems controls.

Organisational controls

Organisational controls usually exhibit either a preventative control focus or a detective control focus, and comprise all those controls that are either derived from and/or related to the structural composition of a company. They are inevitably political in nature and are invariably associated with:

- the hierarchical nature of the company, and
- the structural relationship between company personnel – their duties, their activities and their responsibilities.

In a social context, such controls normally manifest themselves in the form of:

- a functional separation of management/administrative processes, procedures and protocols – a preventative control focus,
- a segregation of duties, activities and responsibilities between company/organisation personnel – also a preventative control focus, and
- the independent monitoring/reviewing of processes, procedures and protocols – a detective control focus.

The purpose of organisational controls is to establish *organisational autonomy*, or, more appropriately, *function/activity independence*, with the primary objective being to ensure the complete separation of incompatible functions and activities. Organisational controls, therefore, normally seek to ensure a separation between:

- procedures concerned with the *authorisation* of transactions,
- activities associated with the *custody* of assets/liabilities,
- processes connected to the *recording* of transactions, and
- functions related to the *controlling* of assets/liabilities.

There can be little doubt that the principal activities of the company (and its associated – externally imposed – regulatory requirements) and the internal management/organisational structure of the company/organisation (and its associated internal politics) will clearly influence:

- 'how' such a separation of management/administrative processes and procedures is realised, and
- 'how' such a segregation of duties and/or activities is implemented.

Yet, it is the composition and availability of resources within the company that will, perhaps more importantly, determine the balance between a preventative control focus and a detective control focus.

Consider the following.
First, consider the issue of a small/medium sized company. For such a company – a company with limited financial assets and often limited personnel resources – the existence of organisational controls established upon the separation of management/administrative processes and procedures and the segregation of transaction processing duties/functions may be not only impractical and unrealistic but, more importantly, unfeasible and perhaps inappropriate. Where resource constraints exist that not only impose limitations on the scope of such organisational controls but also restrict the effectiveness of such controls, the emphasis of control activities – as a component of internal control – often migrates from organisational controls with a preventative control focus (separation of processes and procedures and the segregation of duties/activities), to organisational controls with a detective control focus (independent management monitoring/internal audit – usually 'after the event monitoring' of processes and procedures): a short-term, resource-led solution that is – certainly in the longer term – a particularly risky internal control strategy.

Second, consider the issue of information technology and computer-based transaction processing. Companies are increasingly interconnected through the internet, with computer-based transaction processing now the norm. Many companies (as a matter of general business practice) employ a wide range of information systems technologies. For example, in 2010:[2]

- 34 per cent of companies were critically dependent on externally hosted software services accessed over the internet
- 32 per cent considered the use of social networking sites important to their business
- 85 per cent used wireless networking
- 47 per cent used Voice over IP telephony.

The vast majority of UK businesses now also use transactions websites that allow customers to initiate transactions. Within such companies, a number of important transaction processing functions/controls are often integrated/automated – for example:

- customer credit approval (where appropriate),
- customer order authorisation, and
- customer payment approval.

More importantly, information systems technologies have become a key controlling feature in an array of transaction processing systems activities – an array of transaction processing activities in which the apparent complete separation of control activities appears no longer possible! To maintain/ensure some degree of control – some degree of accountability – within such companies, a separation of administrative responsibilities – a segregation of functions and activities – must exist, for example, between:

- information systems development activities,
- data management/processing procedures,
- information and communications services functions, and
- information systems administration activities.

In other words, within such companies, within such transaction processing systems, the preventative control focus remains – integrated within the information systems management, design and implementation.

Documentation controls

Documentation[3] controls are all those controls associated with managing the format and content of all corporate documentation utilised in processes and procedures connected to:

- the acquisition and recording of data and/or information,
- the storage of data and/or information, and
- the distribution of data and/or information.

Such data/information can be *permanent* in nature – for example data/information related to:

- established policies and procedures,
- management hierarchy,

- responsibility structures,
- administrative procedures, and/or
- operational protocols.

Or it can be *transactional* in nature – for example data/information related to:

- all source input documentation,
- all documentation related to processing procedures, and
- all output-based documentation.

Documentation controls should ensure that:

- all documentation is controlled,
- all documentation (including changes to existing documentation) is approved prior to use, and
- all (details and examples of) approved documentation is properly secured within a documentation library.

Where information systems technologies are used extensively in transaction processing, in addition to the above permanent and/or transaction data/information-related documentation, additional documentation controls would exist – for example:

- System documentation – including documentation related to:
  - systems management and development policies,
  - information technology operations procedures and policies, and
  - security and disaster recovery procedures and policies.
- Systems application documentation – including documentation related to:
  - application procedures (systems flowcharts and narrative descriptions),
  - data format and file descriptions,
  - input/output documentation (format descriptions and details),
  - charts of accounts (relationship schedules), and
  - control and error correction policies and procedures.
- System program documentation – including documentation related to:
  - program procedures (program flowcharts and narrative descriptions),
  - input/output documentation (format descriptions and details),
  - change procedure and policies,
  - program content and listings,
  - test procedures and policies, and
  - error reporting policies and procedures.
- Data documentation – including documentation related to:
  - data elements/format descriptions, and
  - data element relationships.
- Operating documentation – including documentation related to:
  - performance and management instructions,
  - setup policies and procedures,
  - recovery and restart policies and procedures, and
  - report distribution lists and procedures.

- User documentation – including documentation related to:
  - data input/entry policies and procedures,
  - input accuracy/completeness checks,
  - report formats, and
  - error correction policies and procedures.

Access controls

Access controls exhibit a preventative control focus and are all those controls associated with ensuring:

- the security of company/organisation assets and resources,
- the integrity of corporate/organisational operations and activities, and
- the confidentiality of corporate data and/or information,

and minimising the risk of:

- unauthorised/undetected access,
- loss,
- misappropriation, and/or
- improper modification, deletion and/or alteration.

We will consider access controls later in this chapter.

Asset-management controls

Asset-management controls are all those controls associated with ensuring:

- assets are properly managed, suitably controlled and appropriately valued;
- assets are properly recorded and appropriate control registers/records are maintained of all asset acquisitions, transfers and disposals;
- periodic reconciliations are undertaken to confirm asset values and corroborate asset balances; and
- periodic reviews and assessments are undertaken to determine the ongoing condition of, and relative value of the assets.

Asset-management controls seek to minimise possible financial loss associated with:

- accidental loss/damage,
- deliberate impairment,
- larceny,
- incorrect valuation, and/or
- bad management decision making.

They are closely associated with access controls and their role in maintaining/protecting the security of assets (discussed later).

Management practice controls

Management practice controls are all those controls associated with minimising management-related risks – risks that may arise from:

- inadequate and/or unsatisfactory management decision making,
- deficient and/or incompetent management practices, and/or
- dishonest and/or fraudulent management activities.

Indeed, as history has repeatedly revealed (for example: Maxwell Communication Corporation plc, BCCI plc, Marconi plc, Vivendi plc, Barings Bank plc, Enron Inc., Worldcom Inc., Tyco Inc., Global Crossing Inc., Credit Lyonnais SA, and Parmalat SpA), bad management activities and practices, or perhaps more appropriately *the activities and practices of bad management*, often lie at the heart of many of the most spectacular corporate collapses – certainly many of the major corporate failures during the latter part of the twentieth century and the early part of the twenty-first century.

What are management practice controls?

Management practice controls include not only the general controls discussed so far – organisational controls, documentation controls, access controls and, of course, asset-management controls – but also all controls associated with 'the management, administration and development of application systems', and all those controls associated with systems management and development, in particular:

- amendment/modification controls, and
- development management controls.

Although we will explore the above controls in more detail in Chapter 12 when we discuss issues related to systems development and design, such controls would include all those controls related to the planning, analysis, design, and implementation of new and/or amended application systems.

Information systems controls

Information systems controls are all those controls associated with:

- information technology management, and
- information systems administration.

Information technology management controls seek to ensure the protected custody of computer hardware and related peripheral equipment, and the security and integrity of software programs. Such management controls are clearly related to access issues (and related security issues), and will be discussed later in this chapter.

Information systems administration controls seek to ensure the correct and appropriate processing of data and information through:

- the scheduling of data collection activities,
- the continuous monitoring of data processing activities, and
- the management of data/information output activities.

Application controls

Application controls – sometimes called transaction controls – are controls that relate to specific aspects of a company's/organisation's processes, procedures, resources, assets and/or facilities (including accounting information systems resources). They are designed to:

- prevent and detect transaction processing errors,
- identify transaction processing discrepancies, and
- correct transaction processing irregularities.

In an accounting information systems context, application controls (or application specific controls) seek to ensure that:

- only authorised transaction data appropriate to the specific systems is processed;
- all transaction processing is efficient, effective, appropriate, accurate and completed in accordance with established systems-specific procedures and protocols;
- systems-specific transaction processing procedures and transaction processing programs are secure, and
- all systems-specific transactions processing errors are identified, corrected and accounted for when an error occurs.

Application controls are generally classified into the following categories:

- Input controls (for example, undertaking editing tests).
- Processing controls (for example, ensuring appropriate record counts).
- Output controls (for example, maintaining error catalogues/listings).

Input controls

Input controls are designed to ensure the validity, appropriateness and correctness of system/application-specific input data, for example:

- Payroll input data (for example, hours worked, hourly pay rates) are processed by the payroll system.
- Purchasing input data (for example, payment of invoices) are processed by the purchasing system.
- Sales input data (for example, the issue of sales invoices) are processed by the sales system.

Input controls would, for example, include the use of:

- appropriateness checks (such as data matching checks),
- authorisation procedures checks,
- conversion controls tests (such as batch control totals and/or hash control totals),
- record count checks,
- error identification tests/checks,
- error correction procedure checks, and
- completeness checks (such as sequence totals and/or control totals).

In addition to the above, where input data are transmitted (from a source origin to a processing destination), additional supplementary input controls would normally be required and would for example include:

- transmission tests (for example echo checks and/or redundancy checks),
- security checks (for example verification checks), and
- validation checks.

Processing controls

Processing controls are designed to ensure that:

- only authorised system/application specific input/transaction data are processed;
- all authorised transaction data are processed accurately, correctly and completely;
- all appropriate program files/system procedures are used in the processing of transaction data;
- all processing is validated and verified, and
- an appropriate audit trail of all transaction processing is maintained.

Such controls would, for example, include the use of:

- file maintenance checks,
- file labelling checks,
- verification checks,
- processing logic checks,
- limit checks,
- reasonableness checks,
- sequence checks,
- audit trail controls,
- control totals checks, and
- data checks (for example, checks for duplicate data and/or missing data).

Output controls

Output controls are designed to ensure that:

- all output is validated, verified and authorised;
- all output is accurate, reliable and complete; and
- all output is distributed to approved and authorised recipients.

Such controls would, for example, include the use of:

- distribution controls,
- verification checks,
- reconciliation checks,
- review checks (for example source data/document comparisons),
- reconciliation of totals.

In addition to the above, where output data are transmitted (from a processing origin to a user destination), additional supplementary output controls would normally be required and would, for example, include:

- transmission tests,
- recipient identifier checks,
- redundancy checks,
- security checks, and
- validation checks (for example, continuity checks).

Internal control – consequences of failure

A failure in the processes and procedures associated with internal controls could have significant impact on a company. Such a failure could result in:

- the theft and/or misappropriation of company assets,
- the theft of data/information (see Article 10.1),
- the purposeful corruption/destruction of data/information,
- the loss of customers/clients, and
- the loss of revenue income (and profits).

Article 10.1

ICO fines T-Mobile workers for data theft

David Neal

UK data protection enforcer the Information Commissioner's Office (ICO) has fined two ex T-Mobile employees for having stolen customer data for financial gain.

In a statement the ICO said that the two former employees picked 'select customer data' in 2008 and have been fined for their actions.

The two workers, David Turley and Darren Hames, were ordered to pay a total of £73,700 in fines and confiscation costs and, it added, failure to do so could result in prison time.

Both men pleaded guilty to offences under Section 55 of the Data Protection Act (DPA) in 2010, following an investigation by the ICO that started when T-Mobile noticed that something was awry in 2008.

'Today's hearing marks the final chapter in an investigation that has exposed the criminals behind a mass illegal trade in lucrative mobile phone contract information. It also marks a new chapter of effective deterrents on data

crime where the courts will act to recover the ill-gotten gains,' said information commissioner Christopher Graham as he announced the sentences.

'Those who have regular access to thousands of customer details may think that attempts to use it for personal gain will go undetected. But this case shows that there is always an audit trail and my office will do everything in its power to uncover it. The lifestyle the pair gained from their criminal activities has been short lived and I hope this case serves as a strong deterrent to others.'

This is the first time that the ICO has called on the Proceeds of Crime Act to claw back some of the proceeds of crime. Some of these proceeds will go towards training its own staff, it explained, while the remainder presumably will go to T-Mobile.

13 June 2011

Source: Available at www.theinquirer.net.

Internal control and the revenue cycle

A failure of internal controls within the *retailing system* could result in the acceptance of incomplete and/or incorrect customer orders and/or the acceptance of orders from customers with inappropriate credit ratings. More importantly, it could result in the loss of customer orders and/or a failure to fulfil legitimate customer orders.

A failure of internal controls within the *distribution and delivery system* could result in:

- the despatch of products/services to the wrong customer or wrong location,
- the despatch of incorrect products/services to the customer,

- the despatch of incorrect quantities to the customer,
- the despatch of products/services at the wrong time, and/or
- the loss (or theft) of products/services in transit.

A failure of internal controls within the *payment management system* could result in a failure to invoice customers correctly and/or record transactions correctly (accounting entries). It could also result in the theft and/or misappropriation of payment receipts, the fraudulent management of refunds/reimbursements and/or the improper recording of customer payment receipts.

Internal control and the expenditure cycle

A failure of internal controls within the *supplier selection/approval system* could result in, for example, the approval of inappropriate suppliers, the creation of fictitious supplier profiles and/or the theft of confidential supplier data.

A failure of internal controls within the *product/service ordering system* could result in the issue of unauthorised purchase orders and/or the issue of purchase orders to unapproved suppliers.

A failure of internal controls within the *receiving system* could result in the under/over delivery of products/services, the incorrect delivery of products/services and/or the loss, damage or misappropriation of products.

A failure of internal controls within the *payment management system* could result in the incorrect processing of payments for products/services, and the incorrect processing of transactions including the violation of supplier settlement policies. It could also result in the fraudulent amendment of supplier documentation.

Finally, a failure of internal controls within the *payroll system* could result in:

- the unauthorised deduction of funds from employee payments,
- the violation of statutory HMRC requirements,
- a failure to comply with employee pension requirements,
- the incorrect/fraudulent disbursement of payroll payments,
- the fraudulent duplication and/or alteration of payroll payments,
- unauthorised amendments to the payroll master file,
- the incorrect processing/calculation of payroll payments,
- the theft/misappropriation of payroll payments, and/or
- the loss, alteration and/or unauthorised disclosure of payroll data.

Internal control and the conversion cycle

A failure of internal controls within any systems in the conversion cycle could result in:

- the poor development and design of products,
- the incorrect production of products,
- the inappropriate investment in production resources/assets,
- the theft/loss of raw materials, work-in-progress and/or finished products,
- the loss, alteration and/or unauthorised disclosure of confidential conversion cycle data.

Internal control and the management cycle

A failure of internal controls within the *finance management system* could result in a failure to maintain accurate, up-to-date records of existing levels, types and sources of finance, and a failure to record, document and authorise the transfer of financial instruments. It could also result in the incorrect payments of dividends and/or interest, and/or a failure to comply with legal requirements.

A failure of internal controls within the *fund management system* could result in the theft/misappropriation of funds and/or the fraudulent misuse of cash resources.

A failure to adequately manage the *acquisition, retention, and disposal of assets* could have serious consequences for a company. A failure in internal controls here could result in:

■ the fraudulent misappropriation of assets,

■ the deliberate damage to, or sabotage of, assets,

■ the incorrect valuation of assets,

■ the incorrect disclosure of assets, and/or

■ the inappropriate retention of assets beyond their useful economic life.

A failure of internal controls within the *liabilities management system* could result in the incorrect valuation of liabilities and the fraudulent disclosure of liabilities and debt.

A failure of internal controls within the *general ledger management system* could result in the incorrect updating of general ledger accounts, the unauthorised amendment to general ledger accounts, and/or the generation of incorrect financial statements.

COSO Guidance on Monitoring Internal Control Systems

In January 2009, COSO published its Guidance on Monitoring Internal Control Systems to clarify the monitoring component of internal control. The monitoring guidance builds on two fundamental principles:

1 Ongoing and/or separate evaluations enable management to determine whether the other components of internal control continue to function over time.

2 Internal control deficiencies are identified and communicated in a timely manner to those parties responsible for taking corrective action and to management and the board as appropriate.

The monitoring guidance further suggested that these principles are best achieved through monitoring that is based on three broad elements:

1 Establishing a foundation for monitoring, including:
   ■ a proper management understanding of monitoring,
   ■ an effective structure that assigns monitoring roles to people with appropriate capabilities, objectivity and authority, and
   ■ a starting point or 'baseline' of known effective internal control from which ongoing monitoring and separate evaluations can be implemented.

2 Designing and implementing monitoring procedures focused on operation of key controls that address meaningful risks to company objectives.

3 Assessing the severity of any identified deficiencies and reporting the monitoring results to the appropriate personnel for timely action.

Information systems security – purpose and scope

Systems security is indelibly linked to internal control, the aim of such security measures/ protocols being to provide an appropriate level of protection from:

- unauthorised and/or undetected access to corporate systems;
- unauthorised use and/or acquisition of corporate assets, resources and facilities;
- improper deletion and/or alteration of systems data, information and/or procedures;
- systems breakdown and/or processing interruptions; and
- systems failure.

Such security measures/protocols can be classified into four categories:

1 Internal control procedures and processes designed to maintain the security of tangible/ non-tangible resources.

2 Internal control procedures and processes designed to maintain the security of data/ information.

3 Internal control procedures and processes designed to maintain the security and integrity of company/organisational networks (including computer-based networks).

4 Internal control procedures and processes designed to assist in the retrieval, recovery and/or reconstruction (where necessary) of any:

- lost assets, resources and/or facilities, and/or
- corrupted data/information

lost/corrupted as a result of an adverse incident/event and/or systems failure. Such measures are often referred to as disaster recovery and contingency procedures.

Internal control and the security of tangible/non-tangible resources

Security measures/protocols in this category would normally consist of (internal) controls designed to:

- validate and verify the existence (or otherwise) of all assets and resources,
- monitor and control access to assets and resources, and
- restrict/control the privileges of users who have a legitimate right of access to assets and resources.

The primary aims of any such security measures are to:

- ensure the accountability/traceability of all assets and resources,
- minimise and/or prevent opportunities for the misappropriation and/or theft of assets and resources, and
- facilitate the detection and recovery of any misappropriated assets and resources.

To ensure accountability/traceability, such security measures could include:

- the use of asset registers to record the location/valuation of company assets;
- the use of regular asset audits (including physical stock-checks and, where appropriate, valuation checks);

- the use and maintenance of appropriate control procedures for the acquisition and/or disposal of assets;
- the maintenance of appropriate records of, and procedures for, the movement of assets; and
- the use of security tagging of valuable assets (see Article 10.2).

To minimise and/or prevent opportunities for the misappropriation and/or theft of assets, such security measures could include:

- the use of access controls – for example, ID badges, smart cards, security passwords and/or personalised biometric measurements, to define/restrict access to assets; and
- the use of surveillance controls, for example, the use of intrusion detection systems and procedures to detect inappropriate use and/or unauthorised access.

Article 10.2

Self-destruct laptops foil thieves

FT

Guy Dixon

A 'self-destruct' technology kicks in when a laptop is moved from its designated space

UK firm Virtuity has come up with a 'self-destruct' technology based on Wi-Fi and radio frequency ID tags that kicks into action when a laptop is moved from its designated space.

The BackStopp software monitors the electronic 'heartbeat' of a laptop to determine its location. If the laptop is moved from its permitted zone the software blocks access and ultimately destroys data.

The system is designed to provide an additional layer of protection in conjunction with encryption software. BackStopp offers administrators an 'at-a-glance report' of which laptops contain what data, and their level of security, according to the company.

If a machine is deemed to be 'at risk' following unauthorised movement, Backstopp sends out the self-destruct message. The software will also prompt any laptop featuring an in-built webcam to start taking photographs to help with identification of the thief.

'There are millions of laptops out there that contain valuable data,' said Virtuity chief technology officer Dean Bates. 'The vast majority are not stolen for their data, but the [thief] will often come across the data and use it for criminal purposes. This solution prevents that illicit use.'

Prices start at £10 per laptop per month.

19 February 2008

Source: Available at *www.vnunet.com*.

Internal controls and the security of data/information

Here, security measures/protocols would normally consist of (internal) controls designed to:

- validate and verify the existence of all data and/or information files;
- monitor and control use of, access to, and transfer of, data and/or information files; and

- restrict/control the privileges of users who have a legitimate right of access to data and/or information files.

The primary aims of any such security measures are to:

- prevent the dishonest acquisition of data and/or information files;
- prevent the deceitful misuse of data and/or information files;
- restrict fraudulent variation, alteration, and/or adaptation of, data and/or information files;
- prevent the deceitful infection and/or destruction of data and/or information files; and
- minimise the deliberate and fraudulent reproduction and transfer of data and/or information files.

In addition, for companies whose activities require the collection, storage and use of personal data/information, such security measures should also ensure compliance with the requirements/provisions of the Data Protection Act 1998.

Internal controls and the security of company/organisational networks

In this category, such security measures/protocols would normally consist of (internal) controls (often technology based) designed to:

- validate and verify all access to company/organisational networks, and
- monitor and control the use of company/organisational networks.

The primary aims of any such security measures are to:

- ensure the continued security of company/organisational networks and related programs and files, and/or
- maintain the integrity of company/organisational networks and related programs and files,

and to prevent:

- the unauthorised appropriation of company/organisational network programs,
- the malicious removal (accidental or otherwise) and/or destruction/sabotage of company/organisational network programs,
- the deliberate and/or malevolent infection of company/organisational networks,
- the misappropriation and misuse of confidential and sensitive corporate information,
- the theft of protected information, and/or
- any other adverse events that could lead to the possible disruption of a corporate service and/or facilities.

Such security measures will invariably (although not exclusively) consist of computer-based technologies used to:

- manage access,
- control permission, and (where appropriate)
- monitor usage.

The kind of tools and technologies used would include:

■ ID protocols,

■ hardware and/or software firewalls, and

■ intrusion detection systems.

So, in terms of systems security, especially computer-based systems (including of course computer-based accounting information systems), what are the most vulnerable areas? McClure et al. (2005)[4] suggested the following top 14 key areas:

■ inadequate router access control,

■ unsecured and unmonitored remote access,

■ information leakage,

■ host running unnecessary services,

■ weak, easily guessed and/or reused passwords,

■ excessive user privileges,

■ incorrectly configured internet servers,

■ incorrectly configured firewall and/or router,

■ out-of-date and/or un-patched software,

■ excessive file and/or directory access,

■ excessive trust relationships,

■ unauthenticated services,

■ inadequate logging, monitoring, and detection capabilities,

■ lack of accepted/promulgated security policies.

Enterprise Risk Management – Integrated Framework

In 2004, COSO published *Enterprise Risk Management – Integrated Framework* – a framework which expanded on internal control, providing a more robust focus on the broader subject of enterprise risk management. The eight components of enterprise risk management encompassed the previous five components of *Internal Control – Integrated Framework* but expanded the model to meet the growing demand for risk management, producing the following:

1 *Internal environment* – the internal environment sets the basis for how risk is viewed and addressed by the company, including risk management philosophy and risk appetite, integrity and ethical values, and the environment in which they operate.

2 *Objective setting* – objectives must exist before management can identify potential events affecting their achievement.

3 *Event identification* – events affecting achievement of an entity's objectives must be identified, distinguishing between risks and opportunities.

4 *Risk assessment* – risks are analysed, considering likelihood and impact, and should be assessed on an inherent and a residual basis.

5 *Risk response* – developing a set of actions to align risks with the company's risk tolerances and risk appetite.

6 *Control activities* – policies and procedures are established and implemented to help ensure the risk responses are effectively carried out.

7 *Information and communication* – relevant information should be identified, captured, and communicated in a form and timeframe that enable people to carry out their responsibilities.

8 *Monitoring* – the entirety of enterprise risk management should be monitored and modifications made as necessary.

The Sarbanes–Oxley Act 2002

In 2002, the US Congress reacted to a number of corporate financial scandals, including those affecting Enron, Arthur Andersen, and WorldCom, by passing the Sarbanes–Oxley Act of 2002. The Act, named after Senator Paul Sarbanes and Representative Michael Oxley, who drafted the Sarbanes–Oxley, is often referred to as SOX or Sarbox. The Act was designed to protect investors by improving the accuracy and reliability of corporate disclosures, formalising and strengthening internal controls, and instituting new levels of corporate governance to ensure full transparency. The 2002 Act imposed:

- new levels of auditor independence;
- personal accountability of senior executive and financial offcers;
- collective accountability for corporate boards;
- increased criminal and civil penalties for securities violations;
- increased disclosure regarding executive compensation, insider trading and financial statements; and
- the certification of internal audit work by external auditors.

The Act applies to all public companies in the USA. However it also applies to:

- **all** international companies (including UK companies) that have registered equity or debt securities with the Securities and Exchange Commission in the USA, and
- **all** accounting firms (both US-based and non-US-based) that provide auditing services to them.

Non-compliance can result in a fine of up to $1 million and possible imprisonment for up to ten years. If non-compliance is wilful, the fine can be increased up to $5 million and the prison term can be increased up to twenty years.

Disaster contingency and recovery planning

The term 'systems failure' is a generic term – a term that can be, and often is, used to describe the adverse consequences of a wide range of incidents and events, which may affect a company's ongoing operational capacity. Such incidents/events could range from:

- minor incidents – such as:
  - the failure of a network server,
  - the temporary failure of power supply,
  - the partial flooding of administration offices, to
- major events – such as:
  - the failure of on-line payment/receipting facilities,
  - long-term industrial action by key employees,
  - significant industrial accident, to
- company-wide disaster/crises – such as:
  - the total failure of core facilities (for example, IT services/processes),
  - the complete destruction of key operational assets/resources and loss of personal resources.

All of the above can be caused by, or result from, a wide variety of factors including:

- External environment-based factors – such as earthquakes, floods and fire.
- Socio-economic factors – such as power supply problems, infra-structure failure and industrial action.
- Socio-political factors – such as social unrest, bombings and war.
- Internal environment-based factors – such as corporate sabotage and user error.

. . . and no doubt many others!

In today's highly volatile and decidedly unpredictable environment, in which the only certainty is uncertainty, adverse incidents and events occur all the time. While some of these incidents and events will be minor in nature and their potential impact limited, some will inevitably be major and their potential impact both serious and wide-ranging – perhaps, in extreme situations, even fatal. Clearly, then, it is important for a company to possess an appropriate and up-to-date plan of action to not only manage but also limit the impact of such incidents/events: an appropriate and up-to-date disaster contingency and recovery plan (DCRP) to provide a cohesive collection of approved procedures, guidelines and protocols. Such a formal incident/crisis management framework would assist in:

- minimising the overall impact of any adverse incident/event, and
- ensuring the continuity of business activities and other related operational capabilities.

What would a DCRP consist of?

A comprehensive DCRP (see Figure 10.3) would normally consist of two defined (albeit interrelated) protocols:

1 A prevention protocol.
2 A recovery protocol.

A **prevention protocol** (or 'before the event' protocol) would normally comprise:

- *A DCM system* (disaster contingency management system) designed to maintain the relevance and appropriateness of the company's DCRP (especially where substantial organisational change has occurred).

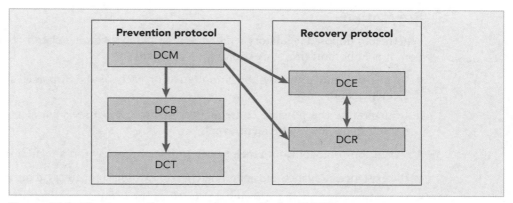

Figure 10.3 Disaster contingency and recovery plan (DCRP)

■ *A DCB procedure* (disaster contingency backup procedure) designed to secure and maintain the safe storage of company, assets, resources, data and information.

■ *A DCT protocol* (disaster contingency testing protocol) designed to test – using mock disaster scenarios – the suitability and effectiveness of a company's DCRP.

A **recovery protocol** (or 'after the event' protocol) would normally comprise:

■ *A DCE protocol* (disaster contingency emergency protocol) designed to provide procedures and guidelines to be followed during and immediately after an incident/disaster.

■ *A DCR protocol* (disaster contingency recovery protocol) designed to restore/re-establish full operational capacity.

Remember, there is no magic answer, no off-the-shelf solution, and no generic step-by-step reference guide to managing such adverse incidents/events.

What is the key to a company's recovery?

The key to a company's recovery from any adverse incident/event and/or corporate-wide crisis/disaster is prioritisation: that is, the *determination of criticality* and the identification of those aspects of the business – its assets, resources, processes and services – which are critical to continued survival, and those which are not.

Why? Put simply, for even the most well-prepared of companies, the ability to recover all affected assets and resources, to restore all affected business processes, services and facilities, immediately after a traumatic adverse incident/event (even a minor isolated event), can be severely impeded by the ambiguity of past events, the uncertainty of future events, and the irrationality of management!

What does criticality mean?

Criticality is the ascertainment of importance (or, perhaps more appropriately, a question of significance), founded on a determination of how long a company can survive without a set of business assets and/or resources, or a collection of processes and/or procedures, or a group of essential services and/or facilities. Clearly, while some assets and resources, some processes and procedures, some services and facilities, may require/necessitate immediate recovery, others may not. It is actually quite surprising what a company can survive without – at least in the short term!

Prevention

Whether an imposed regulatory requirement or merely a commercial/financial consideration, it is important (if not essential) for a company:

- to identify and prioritise the importance of each of its corporate systems/system elements, and
- to determine the possible consequences of such systems/system elements failing as a result of an adverse incident/event.

A prevention protocol would seek to determine and review (on a regular basis):

- the existence, relevance and appropriateness of existing company systems and procedures;
- the existence of any local/regional threats[5] to the company's operational capabilities;
- the existence of any potential single points of failure with the company's system/procedures;[6] and
- the existence of relevant and appropriate licences, warranty agreements and relevant support contracts.

As a consequence, it would need to:

- identify possible adverse changes within the company's environment;
- assess the possible consequences of such environmental changes;
- eliminate, or least reduce, corporate dependency on any single service source, asset and/or resource;[7] and thus
- minimise the disruption that may be caused by any potential adverse incident/event.

How? This could be achieved through the development and existence of appropriate security measures/internal control procedures, that would include, for example:

- the existence of appropriate staff appointment procedures, staff education and crisis awareness training;
- the maintenance of regular backups of data and information and the storage of such backups away from company premises;
- the use of mutual support agreements with other unrelated companies and/or organisations;
- the existence of backup resource facilities and/or incident support premises and equipment; and
- the regular testing of disaster contingency measures and procedures.

Although prevention is better than cure, unfortunately, no matter how well informed the company may be – no matter how up to date, appropriate and effective the company's prevention protocols may be – adverse incidents/events will still occur. Recovery then becomes a priority!

Recovery

A recovery protocol would normally consist of four key stages:

1 Qualification of the incident/event.
2 Containment of the incident/event.

3 Assessment of the impact of the incident/event.

4 Application of countermeasures.

Qualification of the incident/event

For qualification purposes, the key issue is the determination of:

- the size of the incident/event,
- the possible causes of the incident/event, and
- the possible consequences of the incident/event – both short term and long term.

For minor incidents, it is probable that recovery, containment and assessment procedures would take place within the established management hierarchy of the company; countermeasures may well require higher-level management approval. For major incidents, however (including company-wide disasters/crises), most companies would assemble a pre-designated/pre-arranged incident response team which would, for example, include:

- For operational issues – managers from the company areas affected by the incident/event.
- For staffing and employment issues – human resources representatives/managers.
- For asset/resource issues – appropriate facilities/utilities managers and/or representatives.
- For PR issues – public relations/corporate communications managers and/or representatives.

Clearly, the size of the incident response team would depend on the nature and impact of the incident/event.

Containment of the incident/event

For containment purposes, the key issue is damage limitation – the minimising of consequences of any adverse incident/event by ensuring:

- affected systems, services, assets and/or resources are isolated (certainly if the incident is ongoing),
- appropriate human resources policies are implemented, and
- relevant and appropriate internal/external regulatory bodies are informed.

Such containment procedures must be:

- timely,
- relevant,
- appropriate, and of course
- effective.

Assessment of the impact of the incident/event

For assessment purposes, it is essential not only to establish the extent of the potential damage of the incident/event but, more importantly, to determine both the short-term and long-term impact of the incident/event on the company and its business activities – commercially, financially and operationally.

Clearly, an essential aspect of such assessment procedures will be a determination of the source(s)/cause(s) of the incident/event. If malicious intent is suspected then:

- appropriate evidence must be collected, and
- relevant regulatory authorities (including the police) will need to be informed.

Application of countermeasures

Once the nature of any incident/event has been qualified, once containment procedures have been introduced, and once an appropriate assessment of the impact of the incident/event has been performed, appropriate countermeasures need to be determined – a formal active response to:

- alleviate the adverse consequences of an incident/event,
- mitigate any potential undesirable effects of such an incident/event, and
- minimise the possibility of future threats and/or vulnerabilities.

The determination and application of such countermeasures should, of course, be a collective decision made either by the incident response team (if such a team exists), or by management, in consultation with appropriate managers. More importantly, such countermeasures should be applied in risk priority order, and their effectiveness monitored to ensure predicated outcomes are achieved. Where appropriate – where the incident/event is of a major nature and one which may adversely affect the company's future business activities – media and public relations exercises may also be required, as part of the countermeasures, to alleviate any potential unfavourable market reactions resulting from possible speculation regarding the future viability of the company.

Concluding comments

There can be little doubt that:

- the increasingly chaotic realities of the global marketplace,
- the ever more uncertain realities of corporate activities, and
- the increasing demands for greater corporate responsibility and accountability,

have been responsible for promoting the need for more effective corporate governance. Corporate management needs to understand the relevance of corporate control activities and, more importantly, to regulate, monitor and control corporate procedures, processes and activities – to ensure the existence of appropriate control processes and procedures within a company to:

- provide reasonable assurances that business objectives (primarily the maximisation of shareholder wealth) will be achieved, and
- ensure any undesired events, unwelcome occurrences and/or unfavourable incidents will be prevented and/or detected and corrected.

Clearly, while internal control and system security measures cannot directly influence the creative processes of wealth development/maximisation, they nonetheless play an important role in:

- maximising the utility of corporate processes and procedures,
- optimising the utility of corporate assets and resources, and
- sustaining the operational capability of the company.

Self-review questions

1 Describe the five interrelated components that comprise the term internal control.

2 Distinguish between preventative controls and detective controls.

3 Define the term corrective control and describe four examples of such corrective controls relevant to a computer-based accounting information system.

4 Distinguish between general controls and application controls.

5 Define, describe and evaluate the following general controls:

   (a) organisational controls,
   (b) documentation controls,
   (c) access controls, and
   (d) asset-management controls.

6 What are the main purposes of application controls?

7 What are systems security measures designed to ensure?

8 Define and explain the key components of a prevention protocol and a recovery protocol.

Reference

McClure, S., Scambray, J. and Kutz, G. (2005), *Hacking Exposed: Network Security, Secrets and Solutions*, McGraw-Hill, San Francisco.

Notes

1 Available at: *http://www.coso.org/IC-IntegratedFramework-summary.htm.*

2 See Information Security Breaches Survey 2010 Technical Report (April 2010), PriceWaterhouseCoopers and InfoSecurity Europe (available at *www.infosec.co.uk/.../isbs_2010_technical_report_single_pages.pdf*).

3 The term documentation does not relate solely to *physical documentation* but includes all formatted media (including virtual media – for example, computer screen, web page, database page, etc.) through which data/information can be collected, stored, analysed, and communicated.

4 See McClure *et al.* (2005), Appendix B (p. 657).

5 Such external threats would include, for example, the existence of:

   • adverse environmental conditions, or
   • neighbouring companies that may be a source of high risk, or
   • neighbouring companies that may be the source of civil unrest.

6 Such single points of failure would include, for example:

   • communication links,
   • source of accommodation,
   • power supply,
   • transport links/facilities, and
   • computer system/network.

7 Such as using possible alternative service providers/supplementary resources suppliers or seeking insurance against the failure of such providers/supplies.

CHAPTER 11

Accounting information systems audit

Introduction

This chapter explores the underpinning rationale of an audit – in particular an accounting information systems audit – and evaluates the role of the internal and external auditor. It also considers the major issues and problems associated with auditing computer-based corporate accounting information systems and explores a number of alternative approaches to auditing such systems, including the use of computer-assisted audit techniques (CAATs).

Learning outcomes

By the end of this chapter, the reader should be able to:

- Define the term audit and describe the main alternative types of audit a company may be or may choose to be subject to

- Distinguish between CAAT-based and non-CAAT-based auditing

- Critically comment on the importance of accounting information systems audits to contemporary capitalism, and to the management and shareholders of wealth-maximising organisations

- Describe and critically evaluate from a systems perspective the key features and aspects of a corporate accounting information systems audit

The role of the auditor

'In god we trust. Everyone else we audit!'[1]

Like much of the English language, the word audit has its roots in Latin – *audire* meaning to hear or to perceive a sound. Consequently, an auditor is, literally, one who hears, or someone who listens attentively – because audits were originally presented orally.

What is an audit?

The term audit can be defined in many ways. In a broad context, an audit is an inspection, examination and verification of a company's financial and accounting systems, supporting documents, records and financial statements.

This rather broad definition of an audit can be further divided (somewhat subjectively) into two separate albeit highly interrelated definitions. An audit is either:

1 A review and examination of records and activities to assess the adequacy of system controls to ensure compliance with established policies, procedures and pronouncements, and recommend appropriate changes in controls, policies, and procedures

   or

2 A professional assessment and verification of a company's accounting documents and supporting data for the purpose of rendering an opinion as to their fairness and consistency, and of the conformity of the company's financial statements with UK GAAP.[2]

The former would normally be associated with the role of an *internal auditor*, whereas the latter would normally be associated with the role of an *external auditor*.

We will revisit the relevance of this distinction in a moment.

What exactly does an auditor do?

For our purposes – that is, from an accounting information systems perspective – we will define an audit as an independent examination[3] that seeks to evaluate the reliability of corporate accounting information and the efficiency and effectiveness of corporate accounting information systems. It is an independent examination by a competent and authorised auditor (a qualified accountant[4]), whose role – in a contemporary corporate context – can accordingly be defined as:

■ the inspection of the accounting systems, records and practices of a company,[5] and (where required and/or appropriate)

■ the provision of an independent report to a company's members as to whether its financial statements have been properly prepared.[6]

Okay, so what about the different types of auditors? There are in essence two types of auditor:

■ an internal auditor, and

■ an external auditor.

Types of auditor

Internal auditor

An internal auditor is an employee of the company. Responsible and accountable to the senior management within the company, and independent of any functional activity/ procedure within the company, the role of an internal auditor in:

■ appraising the efficiency of operational activities of the company,

■ assessing the effectiveness of internal administrative and accounting controls, and

■ evaluating conformance with managerial procedures and policies,

would generally involve undertaking a wide range of audits/examinations/reviews, including:

■ systems-based audits,

■ internal control evaluations,

■ risk appraisals,

■ governance reviews, and

■ security audits (especially in computer-based information systems).

The Institute of Internal Auditors suggests that the primary function of an internal auditor is:[7]

■ To examine and evaluate how organisations are managing their reputational, operational or strategic risks.

■ To provide the company (audit committee and/or the board of directors) with information about whether risks have been identified and how well such risks are being managed.

■ To offer an independent opinion on the effectiveness and efficiency of internal controls (extant operation protocols, policies and procedures).[8]

■ To review accounting information systems developments to ensure that appropriate internal controls policies and procedures are maintained.

■ To provide (where appropriate) consultancy services and/or undertake special reviews at the request of management.

And there can be little doubt that:

■ issues of corporate governance and the development of the Combined Code of Practice (2000),[9]

■ the increasing role and influence of non-executive directors in company affairs,

■ the growing use of corporate audit committees, and

■ the increasing occurrence of large corporate failures/collapses (not only in the UK but worldwide), have all contributed to:

- enhancing the prominence of internal audit within corporate activities, and

- ensuring its continued presence in twenty-first-century corporate activities.

External auditor

An external auditor is independent of the company (or organisation)[10] and is appointed /re-appointed annually at the company (or organisation) AGM (Annual General Meeting).

The role and duties of an external auditor are – in the UK – regulated by provisions of UK corporate legislation. The external auditor's primary functions/duties are provided in the UK Companies Act 2006 (s.495). Under these provisions, an external auditor is required – as part of a statutory annual audit – to report to the company shareholders stating whether in their opinion:

- the company's financial statements provide a true and fair view[11] of the company's state of affairs as at the end of the financial year, and its profit and loss accounting for the year, and

- that such financial statements have been properly prepared in accordance with the requirements of the Companies Act 2006.

An external auditor is required prima facie to ensure that the company has maintained proper underlying accounting records and that the financial statements are in agreement with the underlying accounting records.

Specific requirements exist regarding the appointment, removal and/or replacement of an external auditor: for example, s.385 (for private companies) and s.489 (for public companies) (Companies Act 2006) provide for company shareholders to appoint an external auditor on an annual basis. Failure to do so can result in a default appointment by the Secretary of State (s.486 for private companies and s.490 for public companies). Similarly resolutions to remove and/or replace an external auditor must also be made at a company's AGM.

How effective are external auditors in discharging their statutory duties?

Although the evidence on the effectiveness of external auditors in discharging their statutory duties is contradictory and inconclusive, it is perhaps worth noting that, in 2010, of the FTSE 100 companies:

- 40 were audited by PricewaterhouseCoopers,

- 24 were audited by KPMG,

- 20 were audited by Deloitte, and

- 16 were audited by Ernst and Young.

While PricewaterhouseCoopers, KPMG, Deloitte, and Ernst and Young audited 95 per cent of the FTSE 350 and nearly 63 per cent of all listed companies, this dominance is soon to be questioned (see Article 11.1).

Article 11.1

OFT to act on 'Big Four' audit firms

Helia Ebrahimi

The Office of Fair Trading (OFT) said it saw clear problems with competitiveness in the audit market, meaning referral to the Competition Commission is almost certain. The OFT said the dominance by so few firms – PricewaterhouseCoopers, Ernst & Young, Deloitte and KPMG – made it hard for rivals to compete and didn't allow for companies to switch auditors, creating what critics have described as a dangerous dependence on too few firms. 'The OFT been concerned for some time that the market for external audit services to large firms in the UK is highly concentrated, with substantial barriers to entry and switching,' the regulator said.

Policy-makers have criticised accountancy firms for giving banks a clean bill of health just before they needed to be rescued as the financial crisis hit. The OFT's decision is the latest development as regulators focus on the accountancy industry as they work to tackle systemic risks to the financial system. Michel Barnier, the European markets commissioner, has spearheaded Europe's investigation into anti-competitive dominance of the accountancy industry. Draft legislation is due next year.

Senior auditors at the top firms warn referral to the Competition Commission will take two years to complete and is likely to be overtaken by events in Europe. The referral could also provoke the EC to push for harsher measures to outpace the UK regulator.

Although institutional shareholders attacked the Big Four's stranglehold over audits of public companies, those within the industry say increased transparency in reporting could allay many of the concerns.

The OFT will have a series of round-table discussions before making a final decision at the end of June which will be open for public consultation. It will then decide whether there are reasonable remedies the Commission could enforce before it decides on the referral. Remedies such as mandatory tendering or rotating, which would force companies to change their accountants every three years, risk creating instability in capital markets and damaging the quality of service for clients, warn the accountancy firms. One senior partner at a top four firm said: 'Forcing companies to switch auditors puts them on a merry-go-round of endless pitching that will be hugely costly for companies and auditors alike and make us more salesmen than auditors.'

18 May 2011

Source: Available at www.telegraph.co.uk.

Porter *et al.* (2008: 4) have suggested that: 'Based on primary audit objective, 3 main categories of audits may be recognised, namely financial statements audit, compliance audit and operational audit.' They define each of these as follows:

- A financial statement audit is: 'an examination of an entity's financial statements, which have been prepared [. . .] for shareholders and other interested parties outside the entity' (Porter *et al.* 2008: 4).

- A compliance audit is: '[designed to] determine whether an individual or entity has acted (is acting) in accordance with procedures or regulations established by an authority such as the entity's management or a regulatory body' (Porter *et al.* 2008: 6).

- An operational audit is: 'The systematic examination and evaluation of an entity's operations which is conducted with the view to improving the efficiency and/or effectiveness of the entity' (Porter *et al.* 2008: 6).

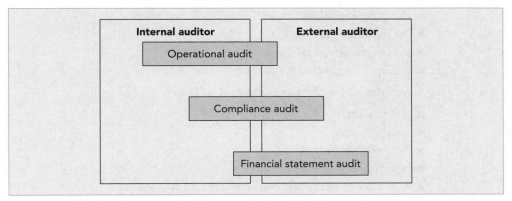

Figure 11.1 Role of the internal auditor and external auditor

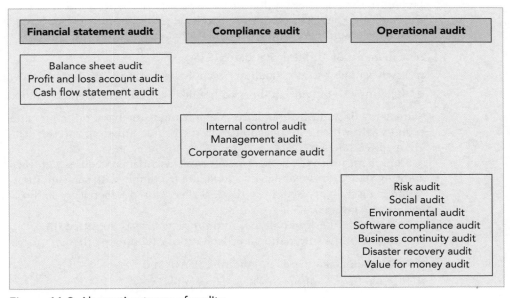

Figure 11.2 Alternative types of audits

While the above does provide an insight into the alternative categories of audit, and a basis on which to distinguish between the role of an internal auditor and the role of an external auditor (see Figure 11.1), we can – in a more functional context – further sub-divide each category and identify and distinguish between a number of alternative types of audit[12] (see Figure 11.2).

What types of audits exist within each category?

Types of audit within the *financial statement audit* would, for example, be:

- a balance sheet audit,
- an income statement audit, and
- a cash flow statement audit.

Types of audit within the *compliance audit* would, for example, be:

- an internal control audit
- a management audit, and
- a corporate governance audit.

Types of audit within the *operational audit* would, for example, be:

- a risk audit,
- a social audit,
- an environmental audit,
- a software compliance audit,
- a disaster recovery and business continuity audit, and
- a value for money audit.

Before we have a look at each of these types of audit in a little more detail, it would perhaps be useful to note that in the UK since 1991, it has been the responsibility of the Auditing Practices Board (APB)[13] to issue pronouncements (see Scope and Authority of APB pronouncements (Revised) 2004), that can be categorised as follows:

- Statements of Auditing Standards (SASs).
- Practice notes – to assist auditors in applying Auditing Standards of general application.
- Bulletins – to provide auditors with guidance and new or emerging issues.

Statements of Auditing Standards (SASs) contain the basic principles and essential procedures with which external auditors in the United Kingdom and the Republic of Ireland are required to comply.

Compliance with the basic principles and essential procedures identified within extant auditing standards is mandatory and failure to comply with such auditing standards may result in disciplinary action by the RSB (Recognised Supervisory Body) with which the auditor is registered.

In addition, the International Auditing Practices Committee (IAPC), a committee of the council of the International Federation of Accountants (IFAC),[14] issues:

- International Standards on Auditing (ISAs), and
- International Auditing Practice Statements (IAPSs),

to improve the degree of consistency, uniformity and homogeneity in auditing practices throughout the global marketplace.

Before we look at the various types of audit, it is important to note that small UK private companies can prepare abbreviated financial statements in accordance with the special provisions of Part 15 of the Companies Act 2006 as applicable to small companies, and exempt themselves from a financial statement audit providing the directors of the company formally acknowledge their responsibilities in:

- ensuring the company maintains accounting records which comply with s.386 and s.387 of the Companies Act 2006, and
- preparing financial statements which give a true and fair view of the state of affairs of the company as at the end of financial year and of its profit or loss for each financial year in accordance with the requirements of s.394 and s.395, and which otherwise comply with the requirements of the Companies Act 2006 relating to financial statements, so far as is applicable.

Purpose of an audit

As we have seen, an audit is an inspection, examination and verification of a company's financial and accounting systems, supporting documents, records and financial statements. It is perhaps due to:

- the growing complexity (and ever-increasing virtual nature) of transactions and transaction processing,
- the increasing temporal and spatial remoteness of transactions and transaction processing,
- the escalating possibility and consequence of error, fraud,[15] loss/theft of assets, and breaches of security/acts of violence, and
- the increasing possibility of conflicts of interest, resulting from transactions and transaction processing

that accounting information systems audits are often purposefully viewed as being designed primarily to promote greater functional efficiency of capital markets, through:

- increased information transparency,
- greater information accuracy,
- increased transaction/transaction processing security, and
- enhanced corporate management accountability.

What does the auditor (external and/or internal) seek to do?

The auditor will seek to obtain sufficient appropriate audit evidence to be able to draw reasonable conclusions on which to base an audit opinion. In this context:

- *sufficiency* is the measure of the quantity of audit evidence,
- *appropriateness* is the measure of the quality or reliability and relevance of audit evidence, and
- *audit evidence* is the facts and impressions that auditors acquire which help them in forming an opinion.

Sufficiency of audit evidence – the quantity of audit information required – will be both influenced and determined by, for example

- the consequences, risk and materiality of any potential error and/or misstatement,
- the nature of existing internal control systems, and
- the source and reliability of evidence.

Appropriateness and dependability of audit evidence – the quality or reliability and relevance of audit evidence – will be determined by the origin/basis/foundation of the audit evidence: for example, whether such audit evidence has been obtained from:

- the inspecting of financial and accounting systems, supporting documents, records and financial statements; and/or
- the undertaking of appropriate computational analysis; and/or
- the making of enquiries and the obtaining of confirmation of the existence, ownership, and valuation of assets/liabilities; and/or

- the observing of company procedures and processes, and the determining of the existence and effectiveness of internal controls.

Clearly, whilst such audit evidence needs to be:

- relevant,
- reliable,
- appropriate,
- timely, and
- cost-effective,

from an (all encompassing) accounting information systems audit context, such audit evidence should seek to ensure the existence of adequate/efficient/effective internal controls. These should include, among other things:

- appropriate levels of segregation of duties in company procedures and processes,
- adequate physical controls in the acquisition, management and disposal of assets and liabilities,
- relevant and proper authorisation procedures in the acquisition, management and disposal of assets and liabilities,
- adequate management and supervision procedures in the acquisition, management and disposal of assets and liabilities,
- an established and defined organisational/management/control structure,
- adequate arithmetic and accounting procedures in company procedure and processes, and
- approved personnel procedures for the recruitment, appointment, promotion, management and dismissal of staff members.

Types of audit

Types of financial statement audit

A financial statement audit (also referred to, somewhat misleadingly, as a year end audit, and/or a statutory audit, and/or financial audit) is an examination (by an external auditor) of the records and reports of a company, and an examination/assessment (by an external auditor) of the degree to which a company's financial statements are in accordance with generally accepted accounting principles and practices.

As suggested earlier, a financial statement audit can – if so required – be sub-divided between:

- *A balance sheet audit* – which would include:
    - determination of both existence and ownership of all assets and liabilities,
    - confirmation that all assets and liabilities have been correctly and properly valued in accordance with UK GAAP,
    - confirmation that all assets and liabilities have been measured in accordance with UK GAAP,

- verification that the presentation and disclosure of all assets and liabilities is complete and consistent with the requirements of UK GAAP, and in particular the provisions of the Companies Act 2006.

- *An income statement audit* – which would include:

  - verification that all income and expenditure has been correctly determined in accordance with UK GAAP,
  - confirmation that all profits and losses have been properly assessed in accordance with UK GAAP,
  - confirmation that all transactions have been appropriately measured in accordance with UK GAAP,
  - verification of the completeness of disclosure of all income and expenditure and all profits and losses, and
  - verification that the presentation and disclosure of information is consistent with the requirements of UK GAAP, and in particular the provisions of the Companies Act 2006.

- *A cash flow statement audit* – which would include:

  - confirmation that all transactions have appropriately measured in accordance with UK GAAP, in particular FRS 1 (as amended),
  - verification of the completeness of disclosure of all income and expenditure, and,
  - verification that the presentation and disclosure of information relating to:
    - company operating activities,
    - returns on investments and servicing of finance,
    - taxation,
    - capital expenditure and financial investment,
    - acquisitions and disposals,
    - equity dividends paid,
    - the management of liquid resources, and
    - corporate financing,

    is consistent with the requirements of UK GAAP, and in particular the provisions of FRS 1 (as amended).

Clearly, the key features of such a financial statement audit are:

- primarily financial in orientation,
- principally concerned with historical/static created representations, and
- orientated to/designed for external corporate stakeholders.

As such, the audits are designed to substantiate/validate/verify and/or confirm the information contained within a company's financial statements, and facilitate the formulation of an opinion on whether the financial statements of a company provide a true and fair view of the company's state of affairs as at the end of the financial year, and on its profit and loss accounting for the year.

Types of compliance audit

Internal control/systems audit

Mainly systems based, an internal control audit is an objective examination and evaluation of the effectiveness of a company's internal control procedures in the prevention and detection of potential security threats and/or other financially damaging events/occurrences.

Such an audit would also seek to assess the adequacy of management feedback processes and procedures in identifying and eliminating potential threats and risks to the company's governance, present well-being and future survival.

An internal control audit is essentially an objective assurance/review process designed to:

■ identify system requirements, procedures, processes and protocols;

■ determine current compliance with existing system requirements, procedures, processes and protocols;

■ determine areas of potential internal control weakness;

■ provide a quantifiable risk assessment of any such internal control weaknesses; and

■ recommend possible improvement to internal controls to eliminate possible financial/non-financial loss;

and as a consequence not only improve, but also add value to the company's activities and operations.

Undertaken as part of a company's ongoing internal audit function, such an internal control audit would:

■ be mainly system based, and

■ aim to support the work of the company's external auditor.

Management audit

A management audit is an evaluation of performance and compliance in relation to regulatory, process, economic and efficiency-based accountability measures at all management levels. Such an audit focuses on outputs and results (rather than merely process) and evaluates the effectiveness and suitability of controls by contesting the validity of extant processes and procedures, systems and methodologies. A management audit is not designed merely to test and identify conformity and/or non-conformity with existing system requirements, procedures and protocols.

The key objectives are to validate the need for existing system requirements, procedures and protocols, and identify key problem areas – or cause-and-effect patterns.

Management audits are generally performed internally – by internal auditors – and are essentially systems-based compliance audits.

Corporate governance audit

The term corporate governance describes (for our purposes) the processes by which a company is directed and controlled, and complies with relevant legislation, current rules and codes of practice. It is in essence a broad framework of rules and relationships, systems, processes and procedures by which authority is exercised and controlled within a company, with the generally accepted contemporary principles of corporate governance including:

■ the rights of shareholders,

■ the interests of other stakeholders,

■ the role and responsibilities of the company directors and board members (including non-executive directors), and

■ company disclosure policies and procedures.

A corporate governance audit would include:

- an examination of the general procedures involved in the preparation of a company's financial statements;
- an examination of company internal controls procedures;
- an assessment of the independence of the company's external auditors;
- a review of corporate remuneration arrangements for all executive directors, non-executive directors and senior managers;
- an examination of corporate procedures for the nomination of individuals on the board;
- a review of the level of resources made available to directors in pursuance of their fiduciary duties; and
- an examination of the company procedures for the management of risk.

The key objectives of a corporate governance audit are:

- to ensure openness and transparency,
- to promote integrity and honesty and trust, and
- to encourage responsibility and accountability.

Corporate governance audits are generally undertaken by external auditors.

Types of operational audit

Risk audit

A risk audit is an examination of the effectiveness of company processes, procedures and protocols in:[16]

- identifying the nature and contexts of risk (risk identification),
- constructing an effective understanding of its origin and nature (risk assessment),
- developing an appreciation of its implications (risk evaluation), and
- designing effective strategies to manage its consequences (risk management).

Such a risk audit may relate to:[17]

- a category/group/subset of companies possessing common characteristics and/or sharing common attributes,
- a company and/or business type/sub-type within a category/group/subset,
- a cycle of operation within the company and/or business type/sub-type, and
- a system within a company's cycle of operations.

A risk audit may, for example, consider:

- the nature of company/cycle/system transactions (for example, the volume of transactions, the value of transactions and the complexity of transactions);
- the adequacy of the company/cycle/system internal controls;
- the nature of the company/cycle/system operating environment;
- the nature of the company/cycle/system regulatory environment; and
- the level and adequacy of company/cycle/system resources (including human resources and tangible and non-tangible assets).

Social audit

A social audit is an examination of the extent to which the operations of a company have contributed to social goals of the wider community. Social audits are concerned more with effectiveness rather than efficiency, and can be seen as a means of assigning some influence over corporate activities to relevant external stakeholder groups such as employees, consumers and the local community. They provide a framework through which a company can:

- identify and qualitatively measure its social performance,
- account for its impact on the community, and
- report on that performance to its key stakeholder groups.

In a corporate context, social audits remain at a very early stage of development and remain difficult to perform because there is no generally accepted measure of social performance.

Environmental audit

An environmental audit is an independent assessment of the current status of a company's compliance with applicable environmental requirements and/or an evaluation of a company's environmental policies, procedures, practices and controls. In essence, an environmental audit is an examination of a company's environmental friendliness, and is concerned primarily with a company's environmental management systems.

Such an audit would review the company's:

- environmental policies,
- objectives and targets,
- performance procedures and monitoring protocols,
- management review processes.

Where a company is registered with the European 'eco-management and audit scheme' (EMAS),[18] the company is required to appoint an external verifier – usually an external auditor – and to publish, annually, an externally verified (or audited) environmental statement.

For a company, the benefits of EMAS registration[19] and of an environmental audit may include:

- possible development of marketing opportunities by demonstrating corporate awareness of environment issues and concerns,
- possible access to new markets by demonstrating greater internal efficiencies through the active management of environmental risks, and
- enhanced use (where the company or organisation is registered) of ISO 14001.[20]

Software compliance audit

A software compliance audit involves the the identification of software assets, the verification of software assets including licences and rights of usage, and the identification of differences between existing installations, licences and acquired rights of usage.

Such an audit can be a useful means of controlling software installations and lowering the costs of licensing.

Disaster recovery and business continuity audit

Disaster recovery and business continuity refers to a company's ability to recover from a disaster and/or unexpected event and continue operations. An audit of a disaster recovery and business continuity plan would consider for example:

■ how often the disaster recovery plan is updated,

■ the appropriateness of hot sites/cold sites,[21]

■ the frequency of data and systems backups,

■ the location of data and system backups,

■ the frequency of disaster recovery procedure tests and drills,

■ the composition of the disaster recovery committee,

■ the frequency of systems and documentation updates, and

■ the availability of hardware and software providers.

Value for money audit

A value for money audit is an examination of the manner in which assets and resources are allocated and utilised within the business and, as such, is concerned primarily with three interconnected and interrelated concepts: economy, efficiency and effectiveness.

Although retrospective in nature, the primary objectives of value for money audits are to provide an independent assessment and examination of how economically, efficiently and effectively resources and assets are being utilised, and to offer independent information and advice to companies on how to improve corporate services and competitive performance by adopting value for money policies and procedures.

Such a value for money audit may relate to:

■ an identifiable cycle of operation within the company and/or business type/sub-type (for example, the corporate expenditure cycle), or

■ an identifiable system within a company's cycle of operations (for example, the purchasing system within the corporate expenditure cycle), or

■ an identifiable activity within a system (for example, the use of consultants in the purchasing systems within the corporate expenditure cycle).

Auditing techniques

While an important aspect of an audit is the testing of transactions processes and procedures, using both compliance tests[22] and/or substantive tests,[23] there are a range of audit techniques that auditors (both internal and external) regularly employ to gather data/information, obtain audit evidence, communicate findings and, of course, formulate and develop an opinion on:

■ a system (or subsystem),

■ a group of procedures,

■ a cluster of processes,

■ a collection of regulations/protocol/controls, and/or

■ a set of financial statements,

to determine the existence, adequacy, efficiency and effectiveness of internal controls – many of which are now IT-based.

Such auditing techniques would (within the context of an audit plan/programme[24]) include:

- the use of narrative reports/descriptions,
- the use of flowcharts (including systems, program and document flowcharts),
- the use of internal control questionnaires (ICQs),
- the use of statistical sampling, and
- the use of computer-aided audit techniques (CAATs).

Narrative reports/descriptions

Primarily used as a descriptive tool, an auditor's narrative description is essentially a detailed description of *how* a system/subsystem operates. It would include a detailed explanation and/or review of:

- all the documentation (physical and/or virtual) used in the system/subsystem under review;
- all the processes, procedures and protocols that exist as part of the system/subsystem under review; and
- all the internal control procedures and processes that are present within the system/subsystem under review, including details of relevant segregation of duties, physical controls, and authorisation, management and supervision/control procedures.

The main advantages of narrative reports/description for an auditor are:

- They can be written/prepared with little technical experience.
- They can record/portray a system, a program and/or a document flow in precise detail.

The main disadvantages of narrative reports/description for an auditor are:

- They are language specific and, therefore, lack international mobility.
- They do not readily describe the temporal flow and/or the sequencing of events and/or data/information flow in a system and/or subsystem.
- They can be time-consuming to prepare and to use, especially where excessive detailed narrative is used.

Flowcharts (including system, program and document flowcharts)

A flowchart is merely a diagrammatic representation – a picture – of a system, a (computer) program, and/or a document flow.

The main advantages of flowcharting for an auditor are:

- Flowcharts can be drawn with little knowledge and/or experience.
- They can record/portray a system, a program and/or a document flow in its entirety.
- They eliminate the need for extensive narrative descriptive notes.

The main disadvantages of flowcharting for an auditor are:

■ Flowcharts are only suitable for recording/portraying standard systems.

■ They are only useful when recording dynamic/active systems.

■ Major amendment to flowcharts can sometimes be difficult.

What types of flowcharts are there?

The main types of flowcharts used in auditing are:

■ A system flowchart – which provides a logical diagram/picture of how a system operates, and illustrates the system in a step-by-step fashion, from input to conversion process to output.

■ A document flowchart – which illustrates the flow of documentation and information within a system, from origin to destination.

■ A program flowchart – which describes the processing stages within a computer-based system, for example:
  ■ a batch processing system, and/or
  ■ an on-line processing system, and/or
  ■ a real-time processing system, and/or
  ■ a distributed/remote processing system.

Internal control questionnaires (ICQs)

An internal control questionnaire is a standardised questionnaire comprising a series of questions, each of which seeks to enquire as to the existence, effectiveness and efficiency of internal control procedures within a company's transaction processing cycle, systems and subsystems.

An internal control questionnaire would seek to ascertain/confirm/verify that internal controls established by the company to ensure:

■ adherence to management policies,

■ the safeguarding of assets, and

■ the completeness and accuracy of accounting and financial records,

are functioning in an orderly and efficient manner, in terms of:

■ separation of duties,

■ definition and allocation of responsibilities,

■ documentation of procedures, processes and transactions,

■ authorisation, approval and security protocols, and

■ supervision/management of operational transactions.

Statistical sampling

In an audit context, sampling means:

the application of audit procedures to less than 100 per cent of the items . . . to obtain and evaluate audit evidence about some characteristic of the items selected in order to form or assist in forming a conclusion concerning the population. Audit sampling can be used as part of a test of control or as part of a substantive procedure.

(SAS 430[25] paragraph 4)

Auditors use sampling to formulate conclusions and/or opinions about a population/ universe of transaction data and/or procedures/processes based on the sample – usually because it would be either too costly or too time-consuming (or both) to examine an entire population/universe.

Such sampling techniques include *inter alia:*

- Unsystematic sampling (or unrestricted random sampling) – random sample selection not based on any qualitative/quantitative characteristic.

- Judgemental sampling – subjective sample selection based on a predetermined set of qualitative/quantitative characteristics, for example, size, value, event date, etc.

- Block or cluster sampling – sample selection in which particular groups or jurisdictions comprising groups are randomly identified.

- Statistical sampling[26] – sample selection determined by the application of probability theory and required confidence levels/levels of sampling risk.

- Restricted random or systematic sampling – random sample selection followed by, for example, every nth item.

Computer-aided audit techniques (CAATs)

There can be little doubt that the last twenty-five or so years have seen information technology invade conventional auditing procedures, processes and established audit techniques in an unprecedented, unpredictable and often chaotic way – sweeping aside and replacing years of established custom, convention and tradition with little more than passing concern.

How has computer-based information technology invaded the auditing of accounting information systems?

In terms of *audit procedures/processes*, the invasion of computer-based information technology has been seen in areas such as:

- the creation/amendment/storage of audit working papers,
- the scheduling/monitoring of audit investigations/activities,
- data collection – for example, computer-based ICQs or ICEs (internal control evaluations),
- information analysis/interpretation – for example, computer-based flowcharting and narrative report writing, and
- audit report generation.

In terms of *audit techniques*, the invasion of computer-based information technology has been seen in areas such as:

- the development and facilitation of remote location audit (virtual auditing),
- the development of generic software testing programs,
- the promotion of computer-based statistical sampling techniques,
- the use of analytical review procedures,
- the development of decision support systems, and (perhaps most importantly of all)
- the development of computer-assisted audit techniques (CAATs).

Computer-assisted audit techniques (CAATs) can be defined as any audit technique, any group and/or any cluster of audit techniques that use information technology-based applications as primary investigative tools – such as:

- Generic audit software.
- Embedded audit modules/facilities.
- Utility software.
- Expert audit software.
- Test data.
- Application software.

Generic audit software

Generic audit software is specific purpose-related and/or function-related computer programs (for example, data retrieval programs) designed to:

- examine specific computer files/records;
- select, manipulate, analyse, sort and summarise data held in specified files/records;
- undertake examination and analysis of data held in specified computer files/records;
- select samples of computer files/records/data for analysis; and
- prepare format-specific reports.

Embedded audit modules/facilities

These are audit facilities/modules and/or audit applications permanently embedded within a computer-based processing system. Such embedded audit facilities/modules are generally used in:

- high data volume computer systems/networks, and/or
- high risk computer systems/networks.

Utility software

Utility software/programs are provided by computer hardware/software manufacturers/ and/or retailers. They are usually add-on programs often utilised in the operational functioning of the computer system/network.

Such utility programs can be used to:

- examine processing activity,
- test program activities,
- test system activities and operational procedures,
- evaluate data file activity, and
- analyse file data.

Although these utility programs are not specifically designed for auditing purposes, they can be, and indeed often are, used in pre-processing procedures – that is, for manipulating record data into an auditable format by:

- extracting specific data items from a database, and/or
- sorting, merging or joining files and/or specific data records within them.

Expert audit software

Expert audit software and/or auditing decision support systems/programs are essentially 'automated knowledge systems' of experts in the field. Such expert systems can include, for example:

- risk analysis programs,
- transaction analysis protocols, and
- control objective testing packages.

Test data

Test data can be used to test and assess the validity and efficiency of computer-based processing procedures. It can also be used to test the effectiveness of computer-based control protocols and the accuracy of computer-based analytical and computational processes.

Application software

Application software means specialised programs/tools that can be used to:

- analyse data flow through specified software applications,
- assess the processing logic of specified software applications,
- validate and document the processing procedures, and
- evaluate software application controls, processing logic, paths and sequences.

Application software includes mapping, tracing, parallel simulations and code comparisons.

Auditing computer-based accounting information systems

For an effective and efficient audit of a computer-based accounting information system, an auditor needs to validate/verify the existence of:

- appropriate application controls to ensure the completeness and accuracy of records and the validity of data,
- relevant environmental or general controls to ensure the proper development and implementation of applications and the integrity of program data files.

It is therefore common for auditors to adopt a two-tier approach:

1 A content (or application) audit – to assess the functional/operational processes, procedures and protocols of the computer-based accounting information systems.

2 A context (or environment) audit – assessing the general controls/environment aspects of a company's accounting information systems architecture, for example:
   - organisational controls,
   - development and maintenance controls,
   - access controls, and
   - sundry controls.

Content (or application) audit

Historically, content/application auditing – assessing the functional/operational processes, procedures and protocols of the computer-based accounting information systems – was classified as follows:

- auditing around the computer,
- auditing through the computer, and
- auditing with the computer (using a range of computer-assisted audit techniques, or CAATs).

However, this classification, while still enjoying some popularity in a number of contemporary accounting information systems texts, and indeed some auditing texts, is rather dated and, in a contemporary context, perhaps somewhat naive, since it fails to recognise how current advances in information technologies have not only changed the nature, analytical ability and processing capability of many CAATs, but also increasingly distorted the boundaries between what were historically well-defined, independent and discrete CAATs.

For our purposes, we will adopt a more contemporary classification, as follows:

- Non-CAAT-based auditing (auditing around the computer), and
- CAAT-based auditing (auditing through and/or with the computer using a range of computer assisted audit techniques).

Both of these are very relevant and extremely important to the effective and efficient auditing of accounting information that is computer-based/information technology orientated.

Non-CAAT-based auditing (auditing around the computer)

Audit around the computer refers to an operational approach in which the computer (system and/or network) is considered a black box – a device, network and/or a system whose function and/or activities are known but whose internal design and/or operations/processes are not. As a consequence, only externally identifiable behaviour, outcomes and/or inputs/outputs are visible and therefore measurable.

Such an approach entails circumventing the computer system and/or network and assessing/reviewing input data and output data only. By using such an approach, no review of the computer system/network processing and/or application controls is undertaken.

Clearly, such an approach is only suitable where:

- complete documentation (either physical or virtual) is available, and an audit trail of events, activities and/or procedures is complete and visible;
- audit evidence of the accuracy and occurrence of events, activities and/or procedures is available and verifiable; and
- events, activities and/or procedures are simple and identifiable.

CAAT-based auditing (auditing through/with the computer)

As we saw, computer-assisted audit techniques can be defined as any audit technique or group and/or cluster of audit techniques that use information technology-based applications as primary investigative tools – such as generic audit software, test data, application software, expert audit systems and embedded audit facilities.

Although there are a number of CAATs that can be, and indeed are, used for more than one purpose, in general CAATs can be categorised as follows:

- CAATs used in the analysis of data/information.
- CAATs used in the verification of (internal) control systems.

CAATs used in the analysis of data

Although not necessarily confined to accounting data,[27] these CAATs are/can be used to select, analyse/examine and summarise permanent data and/or transaction data held/stored in specified files/records.

There are essentially two types of CAATs commonly used for the extraction, analysis, and/or reviewing of computer-based file/record data. These are:

1 generic and/or expert audit software to undertake data file interrogation,

2 embedded audit modules/facilities to monitor data file activity.

Data file/record interrogation software/programs can/may be used to perform a variety of audit-related procedures, including:

- selecting files/records for assessment/examination (including the use of sampling procedures);
- testing the content and structure of selected files/records to ensure conformance to required/specified standards/formats;
- analysing file/record content by specified characteristic (called content stratification);
- searching for files/records for the existence of duplicate transactions;
- searching for files/records for the existence of interruptions/variances in processing sequences;
- comparing the content of two or more files/records (that should match/agree) for any inconsistencies, disparities and/or exceptions;
- comparing the content of two or more files/records (that should not match) for content equivalency and/or similarity;
- analysing, categorising, and/or merging files/records for further audit testing; and
- summarising file/record content (including preparing control totals etc.).

Whilst the use of generic audit software for data file/record interrogation is efficient and effective in terms of time and reliability, and generally easy to use, there is a need to ensure the compatibility of the generic audit software with the target system/subsystem and, of course, with the computer system/network.

An **embedded audit module/facility** is an audit application (usually a cluster of related programs) that permanently resides in a processing system/subsystem within a system/network. Such embedded audit modules/facilities are generally employed in:

- processing systems/subsystems that process high volumes of data, and (increasingly)
- processing systems/subsystems that process high risk data (for example, high value data records and/or confidential data records).

Although many variations to the use of embedded audit modules/facilities exist, these can be classified into two distinct approaches:

- embedded data collection, and/or
- tagging.

In the former an embedded audit module/facility essentially monitors and examines all transactions that enter a processing system/subsystem. When a transaction arises that satisfies a pre-selected criterion/parameter, a record (an audit file) of the transaction details is created before the transaction is permitted to continue for further processing.

In the latter, specified records are merely tagged – an extra field is added to each specified/pre-selected data record – to facilitate/enable identification for future audit analysis. Again, a summary audit file would be created recording the details of all data records tagged and processed.

Embedded audit modules/facilities are clearly a very powerful and potent audit technology. However, it is important to ensure that:

- the interception of transactions occurs at the most appropriate processing stage within a system/subsystem stage,
- the operation of the embedded audit module/facility does not degrade system/subsystem performance,
- the audit selection criteria/parameters and created audit files are protected against unauthorised alteration.

CAATs used in the verification of (internal) control systems

These CAATs are designed to examine, assess, and verify a system/subsystem's internal controls, to:

- determine the reliability of controls, and
- assess the accuracy/validity of accounting files and data records, and indeed other associated non-accounting files and data records.

There are (perhaps unsurprisingly!) many alternative techniques that can/may be utilised to review and verify internal controls. Among others, these include:

- the use of test data,
- the use of integrated test facilities,
- the use of parallel simulation, and
- the use of program code comparison.

Test data can be used to test and assess:

- any program/procedure or group and/or cluster of programs/procedures,
- any system/network component, and/or
- any system/network in its entirety.

However, more importantly, test data can confirm the operation of:

- existing programs whose processed output is unpredictable and/or random,
- existing programs whose processed output is irreconcilable with data input, and/or
- new and/or amended programs.

Test data can be either:

- live test data – test data used during normal computer-based processing cycles, or
- dead test data – test data used outside the normal computer-based processing cycle,

and can be used to examine/assess the processing logic of programs and authenticate input protocols, processing procedures, output routines and error detection facilities.

Such test data can also be used to assess any associated non-computer-based processes, procedures and protocols.

The main advantages of using test data are:

- it is simple to operate,
- it is extremely cost-effective, and
- it requires limited technical knowledge/ability.

The main disadvantages/problems, however, associated with using test data are:

- The use of test data only confirms/authenticates the programs tested at the time they are tested.
- Where a new *in development* program is tested, changes (whether authorised or otherwise) may occur/may be allowed to occur after testing but prior to *live* implementation.
- The use of test data (on either an *in development* program and/or a *live* program may not test all the combined unpredictable permutations of circumstances that may arise.

It is, therefore, extremely important to ensure that where test data are used:

- effective configuration management and/or change control protocols exist – to ensure that tested procured and/or developed software/programs are securely protected from any unwarranted and/or unauthorised amendment, and
- efficient test data design protocols exist to ensure that:
  - a wide range of programming functions/processes are appropriately exercised, and
  - a variety of program permutations are adequately assessed,

and confirm that the tested program (whether *in development* or *live*)

  - does/will do what it is meant to do, and
  - does not do/will not do what it is not meant to do.

An **integrated test facility** is sometimes used in the audit of complex application systems. In essence, an integrated test facility provides an inbuilt test facility through the creation of a fictitious system/subsystem (for example, a subsidiary, a department, or a branch) within a company's live accounting information system.

Whilst there are clearly limited operational costs involved (once a test facility has been designed, developed and implemented), the main advantages of using an integrated test facility are:

- it provides comprehensive testing of a live system,
- it facilitates unscheduled, undisclosed and anonymous testing, and
- it provides prima facie and authenticatable evidence of correct and proper program functions/operations.

More importantly, once such an integrated test facility is operational it can be used not only for program testing, but also for user training, etc.

However, there are significant risks involved in using such test facilities!

Where an integrated test facility is created – whether for auditing purposes or training purposes – it is important that any test data created during an audit are not allowed to corrupt the *live* accounting information system.

A **baseline (systems and/or security) evaluation** is the assessment, selection and implementation of systems procedures and/or security measures within a computer-based system based upon systems procedures and/or security measures and protocols used in similar computer-based systems in companies that are generally accepted to be well run.

Such evaluations can take many forms, including the use of test data to validate selected systems procedures/security protocols.

Parallel simulation is the generation of an independent program to simulate/imitate part of an existing application program. It is designed to test the validity and verify the accuracy of an existing program or cluster of programs. The main advantage of using parallel simulation is that since any simulation program will normally be concerned with only a few discrete aspects of a live operational program within the accounting information system, such simulation programs will generally be:

- simple to operate,
- not very complex,
- cheap to design and implement.

However, as with test data (see above), the main disadvantage/problem with using parallel simulation is that the use of such parallel simulation as a test can/will only confirm/authenticate the program(s) tested at the time they are tested.

Code comparators are utility programs that will:

- compare generational versions (definitive and amended versions) of the same computer program,
- identify changes and/or alterations made,
- ascertain and validate the source of such changes and/or alterations, and
- report on the impact of such changes and/or alterations.

For existing live programs, such utility programs are often used as part of an *authorisation audit* – to assess all variations between a definitive version of a *live* program and the amended currently used version of a *live* program to determine an authorisation audit trail.

Alternatively, for newly installed development and/or procured programs, such utility programs can be used as part of a *configuration audit* – to assess the validity of implementation control protocols and procedures by comparing the current version of a *live* program to its predecessor *development and/or procured* program to identify any unauthorised configuration changes that may have been made.

Some guidelines on planning the use of CAATs

Although CAATs can be used for a wide variety of audit purposes (and indeed some non-audit purposes), there is, perhaps not unsurprisingly, no clear definitive guide on *how* to use CAATs.

Why? Because their use and application will vary depending on:

- the nature of the client company being audited,
- the nature and structure of the target system/subsystem being tested,

- the structure and content of the files/data records being tested, and
- the CAAT application(s) being used.

However, in determining whether or not to use CAATs, the main decision factors would include:

- the computer knowledge, expertise and experience of the auditor/audit team;
- the availability of suitable CAATs and information technology facilities;
- the cost-effectiveness of using CAATs;
- the resource implications of using CAATs;
- the possible time constraints imposed on the audit and/or the use of CAATs;
- the integrity of the client's information system and information technology environment; and,
- the level of audit risk associated with the audit.

In a general context, the following can perhaps be regarded as a broad guide:

- Define the aim and objective of the test(s).
- Agree file/data retention protocols with the client company.
- Analyse the client company's target system/subsystems program operations.
- Identify relevant file(s) and data records required.
- Confirm the structure and location of relevant file(s) and data records.
- Determine the criteria for selecting files and data records required.
- Determine sampling routine (if required).
- Determine the level of file/data record interrogation required.
- Identify the position within the processing cycle at which file/data records interrogation will be performed.
- Specify the format of the data file and method of storage.
- Ensure/confirm the correct version of *live* files are interrogated and, where appropriate, arrange for copies of the live files/data records to be taken for your use in the interrogation.
- Present interrogation findings/evidence, and determine an opinion.

Context (or environment) audit

A context (or environment) audit is an assessment of the effectiveness of a company's accounting information systems architecture and related internal controls.

What is an accounting information systems architecture?

In a broad sense, the term accounting information systems architecture means the totality of surrounding conditions – the entirety of all the physical and other factors that can and do affect the effective and efficient operation of a company's system, subsystems and/or network. It is, in essence, the combination of corporate procedures, processes, and protocols which facilitates the interface between the computer system/network – as a physical entity, and the accounting information system – as a virtual construct, and the corporeal reality of the *real world*.

To put it another way, it is the physical design and/or structural arrangements of computer hardware, software and data communications components within a company's accounting information system.

Within a computer environment – in particular within a company's accounting information systems architecture – we can distinguish between four levels of general controls:

1 Organisational controls.

2 System development and maintenance controls.

3 Access controls.

4 Sundry controls.

Organisational controls

The cornerstone of a company's internal control procedures is the existence of adequate and well-defined hierarchical separation of duties. Within a company's computer environment, at a minimum there should be a distinct separation/division between:

■ operational processes and procedures, and

■ systems/network management, analysis and design.

Furthermore, within a company's computer environment/accounting information systems architecture, at a minimum – within computer-associated operations – there should be a distinct separation of duties between:

■ *authorising events* – that is, procedures involved in the authorising and approving of defined phases of processing;

■ *executing events* – that is, procedures involved in the active processing of data;

■ *managing events* – that is, procedures involved in the supervision and administration of data processing activities; and

■ *safeguarding events* – that is, procedures involved with the protection and security of physical assets and non-physical resources (for example, data files, data records and structured output information).

In essence, a separation of duties should exist between:

■ data capture procedures,

■ data entry procedures,

■ data processing procedures, and

■ processing authorisation protocols.

More importantly, sufficient internal controls should exist to ensure that:

■ computer operations staff are **not** involved in or responsible for data capture procedures and/or systems analysis and programming procedures, and

■ systems analysis and programming staff are **not** involved in or responsible for data capture procedures and/or computer operational procedures (data entry and data processing).

Indeed, from a functional/operational aspect, such internal controls should ensure that:

- within the a computer operations department adequate separation of duties exists between:
  - data administration processes,
  - computer operations procedures,
  - data control activities,
  - file library maintenance procedures, and
  - network control processes and protocols; and
- within the systems analysis department adequate separation of duties exists between:
  - systems analysis procedures,
  - systems design processes,
  - systems maintenance and management activities, and
  - programming procedures.

System development and maintenance controls

Within systems management, development and maintenance procedures, sufficient internal controls should exist to ensure that any new system does not:

- compromise existing live systems,
- conflict with existing security protocols, or
- introduce/create additional environment risks.

Sufficient internal controls should exist to ensure that:

- all new systems developments/acquisitions are adequately reviewed, tested and appropriately approved,[28]
- all (internal) control system[29] changes and program alterations are approved,
- all document procedures are regularly validated, and
- all systems and/or program specifications are reviewed, amended as required, and approved by management and user departments.

The existence of such internal controls should ensure that data are processed appropriately, completely and without prejudice; but also, where appropriate and effective validation procedures exists, the efficient detection, location and correction of processing errors will reduce the overall possibility of financial loss.

Access controls

Earlier we explored three distinct hierarchical layers of control:

1 the physical security control layer,
2 the technical security control layer, and
3 the human security control layer.

It is these three layers of control that collectively comprise what are commonly referred to as access controls – inasmuch as:

1 Physical security controls are designed to prevent/restrict resource access and asset movement.
2 Technical security controls are designed to restrict/control the user privileges.
3 Human security controls are designed to enforce *an approved* control culture.

Such internal controls should ensure the active use of appropriate authorisation procedures to:

- control access to computer hardware/resources to authorised and approved personnel only,
- restrict access to software/programs to appropriately authorised personnel/users and control authorised personnel/user rights and privileges, and
- manage/control access to data files and data records,

perhaps through the use (individually or in combination) of:

- personalised ID badges/security smart cards,
- security passwords and/or personalised biometrics,
- hardware/software security tagging and software/program encryption, and
- computer usage/data file access monitoring.

Sundry controls

Sundry/other internal controls relate to:

- the safeguarding of assets and resources, and
- the secure protection of data and information.

These controls should ensure that appropriate systems and procedures exist for:

- the secure protection of data files, transaction data and programs (including protection from theft, breaches of security, acts of violence and/or the impact of natural disasters);
- the regular backup (secure copying) of data files, transaction data and programs; and
- the secure off-site storage of backup data files, transaction data and programs.

A key aspect of such sundry controls would of course be the existence of a disaster contingency recovery protocol – in the unlikely event of a significant and widespread disaster befalling the company.

Auditing computer-based accounting information systems – more issues

There can be little doubt that for the auditing of computer-based accounting information systems, modern advances in technology – in particular information technology – have metaphorically speaking been a 'double edged sword'.

Such advances have revolutionised the *modus operandi* of many aspects of corporate accounting information systems, most noticeably by:

- fundamentally revolutionising data capture/data entry procedures,
- radically transforming data processing procedures,
- drastically expanding data/information storage capacities, and
- significantly enhancing information analysis and data/information transfer/communication.

They have also:

- transformed many of the traditional techniques used in auditing corporate accounting information systems – for example, IT-related/computer-based:

- data collection (ICQs/ICEs),
- data analysis (flowcharting and narrative report writers), and
- narrative report writers, and

- introduced a vast portfolio of new computer-assisted auditing techniques – for example, IT-related/computer-based:

- generic software testing programs,
- computer-based statistical sampling techniques,
- IT-related analytical review procedures, and
- computer-based decision support systems.

Such advances have nonetheless created a number of significant issues for auditors in the auditing of computer systems – in particular computer-based accounting information systems – of which the most important issues areas are *databases, on-line networks* and *real-time systems*.

Databases

As an organised body of information, or an information set with a regular structure, or a collection of related information organised to facilitate complex interpretation and analysis, databases – in particular relational databases – are now a central feature of *all* computer-based accounting information systems.

Problems associated with the use of databases relate to:

- the recognition of inappropriate use,
- the identification of unauthorised access,
- the detection and prevention of unapproved content changes, and
- the detection and correction of improper database processing.

Clearly, a failure to detect/identify inappropriate use, unauthorised access, unapproved content changes and improper processing could compromise the security of the database, the integrity of the data contents and the validity of data records. When personal data are recorded, processed and/or stored, it could compromise the confidentiality of data elements. This is especially relevant in cases where a company's database or databases can be accessed remotely, via either a private network or a public network (for example, over the internet).

Remember, a company has a legal duty under the Data Protection Act 1998 to ensure that any personal data are appropriately processed and securely maintained.

Appropriate internal controls should exist to ensure:

- the use of encryption facilities to securely protect highly sensitive database contents,
- the use of authorisation keys/passwords to restrict access to authorised personnel users only,
- the use of appropriate separation of duties between database administration and database security management, and
- the use of access/performance logs to monitor/record database access/changes, and, where appropriate, prevent unauthorised access/changes to sensitive data elements.

(On-line) networks

As we have seen, a network is essentially a data communications system – a system enabling an organisation and/or company to share information and programs; an on-line network is a computer system/network and/or facility/service that is accessed remotely through a public or private network.

While historically, such communication networks were (indeed some continue to be) hard-wired networks, in the early twenty-first century the major feature in information technology development has been the move toward wireless networking (WLAN) and the reliance on radio waves and/or microwaves to:

- establish network connections,

- maintain communication channels, and

- transmit/transfer data and information.

Wireless networking now offers greater networking mobility and flexible connectivity at an ever-reducing cost, despite problems associated with the possible intrusion by other wireless devices/transmission and potential interference by unauthorised users.

Clearly, for all communication networks facilities which:

- capture (input) finance-related data and information,

- process/record/convert financial data and/or information, and/or

- transmit (output) finance-related data and information,

it is essential that:

- regular vulnerability scans including network perimeter assessments,

- frequent penetration tests including security evaluations/assessments, and

- regular communication tests including network traffic efficiency/effectiveness assessments,

are undertaken, to ensure:

- the verification and validation of all appropriate network traffic,

- the identification and prevention of inappropriate use and unauthorised access/security breaches,

- the prevention of communication disruptions,

- the detection and correction of unapproved network amendments, and

- the correction of inappropriate network traffic.

Real-time systems

A real-time system is a computer system/network and/or facility/service that responds to prescribed environmental events *in the world* as they happen, and in which the time at which output is produced is significant.

That is, for a real-time system, it is the input-to-output response time that is the key identifiable requirement of the system.

Real-time systems can be sub-divided into a number of alternative types, based on:

- the speed of response of the system, and

- the criticality of response of the system.

Using the speed of response, a system can be categorised as either a *fast real-time system*, or a *slow real-time system*. Although there is no clear boundary/distinction between the types, generally:

■ a system with a response time measured in seconds (or less) can be considered fast, and

■ a system with a response time measured in minutes (or more) can be considered slow.

Clearly, this leaves an indeterminate area/period of response times in which a system could theoretically be categorised as either fast or slow!

Using criticality of response, a system can be categorised as a *hard real-time system*, or a *soft real-time system*.

A hard real-time system is a system where the response time is specified as an absolute value, with the response time normally dictated/imposed by the external environment. In such systems, where a response is not generated, the system will be considered to be in error, and will invariably require the performance of some form of error recovery procedure, while operating at either:

■ a reduced level of functionality, or

■ a zero level of functionality (shutdown).

A soft real-time system is a system where the response time is normally specified as an average value, with the response time normally dictated by the company and/or the business/industry within which the company operates. For any single response there is a defined acceptable range/time period for a response. Where a response is not generated within such a defined range/period the system may be considered in error.

In essence, real-time systems can be categorised into a topology containing four system types:

(i)   hard fast real-time systems,

(ii) hard slow real-time systems,

(iii) soft fast real-time systems, and

(iv) soft slow real-time systems.

Examples of hard fast real-time systems would be:

■ embedded computer process control systems, and

■ computer-based intrusion/inflection detection systems.

Examples of soft fast/very fast real-time systems would be:

■ ATM systems,

■ EPOS systems,

■ PIN and chip payment systems, and

■ data streaming and/or on-line network communication systems.

Particular problems faced by auditors when auditing real-time computer-based accounting information systems/subsystems relate to:

■ the verification of appropriate segregation of duties,

■ the confirmation of hardware/software management protocols,

■ the authentication of transaction verification procedures,

■ the validation of data file/data record security,

■ the confirmation of program and communications security, and

■ the verification of system/program update authorisation procedures.

Clearly, testing for the existence of appropriate segregation of duties, system administration and management processes, and security and control protocols within a real-time system will not only depend on:

■ the configuration of the system/subsystems,

■ the purpose of the system/subsystems,

■ the level of activity of the system/subsystem,

■ the criticality of the system/subsystem, and

■ the network relationship (to other systems/subsystems) of the system/subsystem,

but will also require the use of a range of content (application) audit techniques – probably CAAT-based – and a range of context (environment) audit techniques.

Concluding comments

While there can be little doubt that the *nature* of the company audit as an independent inspection and examination of a company's accounting information systems has remained more or less unchanged for many years – certainly over the last 50 years – there can also be little doubt that:

■ the ever-increasing and very often public demise of many highly respected, long established, and once enormously profitable companies, and (perhaps as a consequence)

■ the increasingly risk-averse attitude of many market participants,

has clearly influenced the *emphasis/focus* of contemporary accounting information systems audits.

More important, perhaps, has been the enormous growth in, and availability of, computer-based technologies/IT-related facilities.

With the traditional bureaucratic paper-based processing systems now confined (thankfully) to the tattered and worn pages of corporate history, and replaced by a vast array of increasingly complex and increasingly interactive computer-based processing systems/ networks, it has been the almost overwhelming embrace of such technologies and the use of increasingly sophisticated computer-based/IT-related systems and facilities, that has:

■ revolutionised the *process* of contemporary company audit, and

■ transformed the *role* of the auditor.

A revolution that has catapulted auditors and auditing into a postmodern IT-dominated brave new world!

Self-review questions

1 Briefly explain the role of an auditor and distinguish between the role of an internal auditor and the role of an external auditor.

2 Distinguish between a financial statement audit, a compliance audit and an operational audit.

3 Define and explain the possible use of a non-CAAT-based audit.

4 What factors should an auditor consider before using a CAAT?

5 Define and explain a context (environmental) audit.

6 Identify and describe five alternative auditing techniques.

7 Define and distinguish between each of the following terms:

(a) generic audit software,
(b) utility software,
(c) expert audit software.

8 Briefly explain the main types of controls often used by companies to minimise the risks and problems associated with the use of EDI.

References

Davies, T., Boczko, T. and Chen, J. (2005), *Strategic Corporate Finance*, McGraw-Hill Irwin, London.

Porter, B., Simon, J. and Hatherley, D. (2008), *Principles of External Audit*, Wiley, Chichester.

Notes

1 Attributed to Sam Fleming, President, Third National Bank (1950–70), Nashville, USA.

2 UK GAAP (United Kingdom Generally Accepted Accounting Principles) is the overall body of regulation establishing how company accounts must be prepared in the United Kingdom. This includes not only extant accounting standards, but also applicable UK company law.

3 Undertaken in accordance with extant UK Auditing Standards.

4 In the UK, for auditing purposes the term qualified accountant means an individual or firm that has a current audit-practising certificate and is a member/are members of one of the 5 recognised supervisory bodies (RSB) (as defined and recognised by the Secretary of State), these being:

- the Institute of Chartered Accountants in England and Wales,
- the Institute of Chartered Accountants of Scotland,
- the Institute of Chartered Accountants in Ireland,
- the Association of Chartered Certified Accountants, and
- the Association of Authorised Public Accountants.

Details of the requirements for recognition as an RSB are given in Companies Act 2006 Schedule 10.

5 Not all companies are required to have an annual audit. If a company qualifies for exemption and chooses to take advantage of such exemption, dormant companies and certain small companies do not have to have their accounts audited. To qualify for total audit exemption, a company (other than a dormant company) must qualify as a small company, have a turnover of not more than £5.6 million, and have a balance sheet total of not more than £2.8 million. To qualify for dormant company audit exemption, a limited company (together with a series of other criteria) must not have traded during the financial year.

6 The term 'prepared properly' means 'in accordance with the Companies Act 1985'.

7 Available at *www.iia.org.uk/about/internalaudit*.

8 By ensuring:

- all assets of the company (or organisation) are being securely safeguarded;
- all corporate operations are conducted effectively, efficiently and economically in accordance with internal protocols, policies and procedure;

- all laws and regulations are complied with; and
- all records and reports are reliable and accurate.

9   In May 2000 the original Cadbury Code (1992) and subsequent reports (including the 1998 Hampel Committee update of the Cadbury Code, and the 1999 Turnball Committee report *Internal Control: Guidance for Directors on the Combined Code*, published by the Institute of Chartered Accountants in England and Wales) were all consolidated by the Committee on Corporate Governance (see Davies *et al.* 2005).

10 Following the EU 8th Directive, the Companies Act 1989 introduced a framework for regulating the appointment of external auditors, to ensure that only appropriately qualified and properly supervised people are appointed as company auditors.

11 '. . . the financial statements must present a true and fair view of the company's state of affairs as at the end of the financial year, and its profit or loss for the financial year, and must also comply with the form and content requirements of Schedule 4 of the Companies Act 1985 (CA 1985 s.226)' (Porter *et al.* 2008: 100).

12 This list is by no means exhaustive, and many other alternative industry, sector, and/or company specific types of audit/definitions of audits may exist.

13 See *www.apb.org.uk/apb*.

14 See *www.ifac.org*.

15 While not specifically required to search for fraud, an external auditor undertaking a financial statement audit, SAS 82 Consideration of Fraud in a Financial Statement Audit (1997) places a duty of care on the external auditor to plan and perform their audits to obtain reasonable assurance that such financial statements are free from material misstatement, and to report to the company any evidence that may indicate the occurrence of fraud.

16 See also the discussion on the precautionary principle in Chapter 9.

17 See also the discussion on contemporary transaction processing in Chapter 7.

18 EMAS (Eco-Management and Audit Scheme), a voluntary initiative designed to improve corporate environmental performance, was established by EU Regulation 1836/93 (subsequently replaced by EU Council Regulation 761/01). Its aim is to recognise and reward those companies (and organisations) that go beyond minimum legal compliance and continuously improve their environmental performance. In addition, it is a requirement of the scheme that participating companies (and organisations) regularly produce a public (and externally verified/audited) statement that reports on their environmental performance. For further information, see *www.emas.org.uk/aboutemas/mainframe.htm*.

19 See *www.emas.org.uk/why%20register/mainframe.htm*.

20 ISO 14001 was first published in 1996 and specifies the actual requirements for an environmental management system. It applies to those environmental aspects over which the organisation has control and over which it can be expected to have an influence.
    The standard is applicable to any company (and organisation) that wishes to:

- implement, maintain and improve an environmental management system,
- demonstrate conformance with extant internal environmental policies, procedures and protocols,
- ensure compliance with environmental laws and regulations, and
- seek certification of its environmental management system by an external third party.

    See *www.iso14000-iso14001-environmental-management.com/iso14001.htm*.

21 A hot/cold site is a location to which a company can move after a disaster if the current facility is unusable. The difference between the two is that a hot site is fully equipped to resume operations, a cold site is not.

22 Compliance tests are undertaken by an auditor to gather evidence as to a company's adherence to prescribed processes and procedures and/or control requirements.

23 Substantive tests/procedures are those activities performed by the auditor to gather evidence as to the completeness, validity and/or accuracy of account balances and underlying classes of transactions.

24 An audit programme is a procedural framework, a list and/or plan of audit procedures required to be followed during an audit. It is a series of structured steps necessary to achieve the audit objective. It is, in effect, the functional context of the audit itself.

25 SAS 430 *Audit Sampling*.

26 The most common approaches being sampling for attributes (measuring the frequency a particular characteristic is present is not present, and sampling for variables (measuring/estimating the total value/number with a population/universe).

27 These CAATs can also be used to select, analyse/examine and summarise data held/stored in non-accounting files/records – for example, processing logs and/or access/security logs, which may be created when computer-based files and records are accessed and accounting data are processed.

28 While the auditors should not – in any way – be considered part of any system/subsystem, any process and/or any procedure since that would seriously jeopardise the auditors' independence, the auditor should nonetheless be consulted (as should end-users) when significant new developments/alterations are being considered.

29 Simple integral internal controls should always be preferred – essentially because they minimise bureaucracy and are therefore time-efficient and cost-effective. Such integrated internal controls should be part of a general strategy to detect and prevent fraud.

CHAPTER 12

Accounting information systems development

Introduction

This chapter examines the importance of accounting information systems development, in particular the need for a cohesive accounting information systems development strategy and the socio-economic problems associated with accounting information systems development. It also considers the political nature of accounting information systems development; explores processes and problems associated with the key stages in the life cycle approach to corporate accounting information systems development, and looks at prototyping.

Learning outcomes

By the end of this chapter, the reader should be able to:

■ Consider and explain the socio-political context of accounting information systems development

■ Describe the major characteristics of the six key stages of a systems development life cycle, and the prototyping approach

■ Illustrate an appreciation of alternative planning, analysis and evaluation techniques

■ Demonstrate a critical understanding of the risks associated with accounting information systems development

Accounting information systems . . . and the need for change

'There is nothing permanent, except change' (Heraclitus of Ephesus[1])

As we have seen in previous chapters, whether they operate as simple paper-based manual systems or as highly complex internet-enabled computer-based systems, accounting information systems are essentially socio-political constructs. They exist as imposed unifying structures, employing both tangible and intangible resources to collect, store, process and transform selected transaction data into business information and provide constructed representations for decision-making purposes to both internal and external stakeholders.

And yet, as semi-open, output-orientated systems, accounting information systems are neither permanent nor stable. They are, like many artificially constructed corporate systems, subject to almost constant change – a process of change conditioned by the chaotic interaction of an increasingly complex array of environmental factors.

All corporate systems operate within a multidimensional environment, an environment comprising many different interrelated layers. It is the interaction of the various macro and micro factors and characteristics that comprise each layer which creates what is often referred to as environmental turbulence. And it is this environmental turbulence that is the source/cause of change within a system, or the trigger for change within a system – whether that system is a company or organisation, or a subsystem within the company: for example an accounting information system. More importantly, it is the unique combining of these macro and micro factors and characteristics within the layers that comprise an environment which determines the nature and scope of any reaction to such environmental turbulence.

Broadly speaking, in a systems context we can classify external environments into three categories – based on the level/scale of turbulence within the environment:

1 A stable environment (also known as a closed change environment)[2] – that is, a steady state environment in which there is little or no change, or an environment in which change is cyclical, repetitive and expected.

2 A predictable environment (also known as a contained change environment)[3] – that is, a dynamic environment in which change is intermittent, and while neither cyclical nor repetitive, is nonetheless predictable and manageable.

3 An unpredictable environment (also known as an open-ended change environment)[4] – that is, a volatile environment in which change is turbulent, fast moving, frequent and unpredictable.

In addition, within an organisational context there exist three varieties of change:

1 Smooth incremental change – that is, change which is slow, systemic, predictable and planned.

2 Rough incremental change – that is, change which occurs periodically and which is concerned more with realignment and readjustment rather than substantial change.

3 Discontinuous change – that is, change which occurs rapidly, sometimes unpredictably, and causes substantial change as a result of for example a new discovery and/or new development.

Within a stable environment, change would generally be smooth incremental with occasional periods of rough incremental change, but with very few periods of discontinuous change. Within a predictable environment, change would generally be smooth incremental with increasing periods of rough incremental change and fragmented periods of discontinuous change. Within an unpredictable environment, change would generally be rough incremental (with limited periods or no periods of smooth incremental change) and extensive periods of discontinuous change.

In essence, as the environment become more unpredictable, systems become increasingly uncertain – an unpredictability/uncertainty that is constantly fuelled by, for example:

- the changing needs and demands of users/stakeholders,
- the changing structure and content of finance-related regulations,
- the continuing impact of information and communication technology, and
- the increasing consequences of an ever more globally competitive business environment.

Indeed, as suggested by Stacy (1996):

- a stable environment (or closed change environment) has a tendency to be close to certainty, with change often being linear and planned, whereas
- an unpredictable environment (or open-ended change environment) has a tendency to be far from certainty, with change often being discontinuous and unplanned.

Types of change

In an accounting information systems context, change can be defined as any amendment, alteration and/or modification to the structure and/or operation of a system or a component subsystem. This would include amendments, alterations and/or modifications to:

- data input procedures,
- data capture and filtering processes,
- data management protocols,
- internal documentation and control procedures,
- data processing procedures,
- information output procedures, and
- feedback/feedforward control procedures,

and can be classified by:

- type (or nature), and/or
- level (or scale).

In terms of *type (or nature)*, change can be divided into two subcategories:

1 Hard change – that is, change emerging from the introduction/integration of new information and communications technologies.

2 Soft change – that is, change resulting from organisations restructuring and/or procedural adaptations.

In terms of *level (or scale)*, change can be divided into two subcategories:

1 Minor change – that is, change which has only a limited impact on a small number of components, procedures, processes and/or subsystems within a system, and is commonly referred to as 'fine tuning' and/or 'incremental adjusting'.

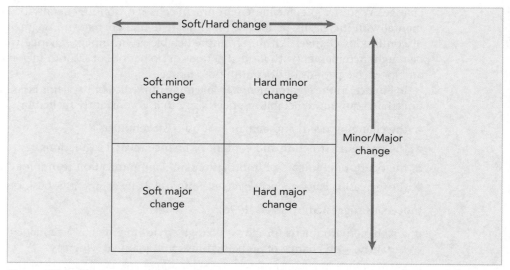

Figure 12.1 Change matrix

2 Major change – that is, change which has a substantial impact on a significant part of a system, and/or number of systems, and is also referred to as 'systems adaptation' and/or 'process transformation'.

Have a look at the 4-quadrant matrix in Figure 12.1. Using this matrix, we can classify change (within an accounting information systems context) into four different categories:

1 Soft minor change.
2 Hard minor change.
3 Soft major change.
4 Hard major change.

Soft minor change

Soft minor change can be defined as component, procedure and/or process change(s) resulting from organisational restructuring/procedural adaptation. It would include, for example:

- the consolidation of data input procedures, or
- the introduction of new documentation, or
- the introduction of minor software amendments/updates.

Hard minor change

Hard minor change can be defined as substantial technological change(s) resulting from organisational restructuring, and would include, for example:

- the introduction/addition of new network facilities, or
- the extending of existing capabilities.

Soft major change

Soft major change can be defined as a substantial modification/reorganisation of systems procedures, process and practices, and would include, for example:

■ the introduction of new wide ranging internal control procedures, or
■ a change in company-wide data processing procedures – from batch to on-line/real-time processing.

Hard major change

Hard major change can be defined as the widespread introduction of new information and communications technologies, and would include, for example:

■ the development of web-based transaction processing facilities, or
■ the introduction of chip and PIN or alternative non-card-based payment systems, or
■ the introduction of new RFID technologies.

Change management

Clearly, whether change to an accounting information system constitutes a minor amendment or a fine tuning adjustment or, indeed, a major structural adaptation, it must be adequately planned, properly implemented, and appropriately monitored and controlled. Why?

For four reasons:

1 The economic reason – to ensure adequate resources are available to fund the change.
2 The social reason – to ensure that the consequences of any associated organisational/ procedural change is clearly understood.
3 The political reason – to ensure that any potential resistance is minimised.
4 The technological reason – to ensure that all regulatory consequences are understood.

Who would be involved in managing and coordinating information systems change?

As we have seen, information systems (including accounting information systems) are – in an organisational context – goal-orientated, political resource structures, designed to process (selected) data and provide (selected) users with information, to:

■ support organisational decision-making processes,
■ facilitate organisational control, and
■ fulfil internal and external organisational obligations.

It is perhaps unsurprising, therefore, given the nature, scope, and possible impact/ consequences of any accounting information systems development, that a range of company staff will often be involved – staff from, for example:

■ the information systems function,
■ the management and/or administration function,
■ the human resource management function,
■ the financial management/business function, and (where necessary)
■ other functions/services and/or external agencies.

Such a coordinating team is often referred to as a systems development team.

Accounting information systems development – alternative approaches

There are many alternative approaches to information systems development – in particular accounting information systems development – the most common approach being the **systems development life cycle approach**. However, a variation of this approach – the **prototyping approach** – is also widely used, especially where a systems development involves either the introduction/development of new operational systems, or the introduction/development of new information and communication technologies, and requires the determination of end-user requirements – that is, an understanding of what end-users want from the system/technology.

The systems development life cycle approach

There can be little doubt that in a modern commercially active company, a well-designed, user-orientated information system(s) can contribute to/assist in:

- increasing operational efficiency,
- reducing operational costs and increasing business-related revenues,
- eliminating non-value-added activities,
- improving the coordination of organisational activities,
- improving customer-related services, and
- improving management decision making.

It is, therefore, perhaps not surprising that information processing systems – in particular accounting information systems – are regarded as one of the most valuable assets a company can possess.

What is the systems development life cycle?

In essence, the systems development life cycle is a practical framework – a sequential multi-stage framework – which provides a broad context for the pre-development stages, development stages and post-development stages of an accounting information system.

In fact, the systems development life cycle (see Figure 12.2) involves six critical stages:

1 Systems planning and the identification of systems and/or subsystems within a (business) information system that requires further development, amendment, improvement, renewal or replacement.

2 Systems analysis and the assessment of existing system or subsystem problems.

3 Systems design and the development/formation of a blueprint/conceptual design or range of alternative blueprints/conceptual designs for a completed system or subsystem.

4 Systems selection and the determination of how the system will be acquired/developed.

5 Systems implementation/conversion and the implementation of the selected design and/or conversion of an existing system.

6 Systems review and the operational maintenance, monitoring and evaluation of the selected system/subsystem performance.

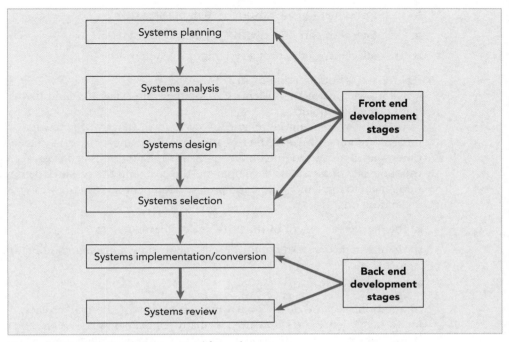

Figure 12.2 Systems development life cycle

The first four stages (systems planning, systems analysis, systems design and systems selection) are often referred to as the *front end development stages* since they are mainly concerned with 'what' the system will do, whereas the latter two stages (systems implementation and systems review) are often referred to as the *back end development stages* since they are mainly concerned with 'how' the system will accomplish its objectives.

Before we look at the systems development life cycle it would perhaps be useful to define what the term **systems development** means.

For our purposes, we will define the term systems development as the development of an accounting information system by a process of investigation, analysis, design, implementation and maintenance, the primary objectives of such systems development being to ensure that:

- all company systems/subsystems function effectively,
- all company systems/subsystems resources are used efficiently,
- all company systems/subsystems objectives are consistent and comparable,
- all company systems/subsystems are adaptable, and
- all possible systems/subsystems duplication is minimised.

What can a systems development project involve?

A systems development project can involve, for example:

- the construction of a new system or subsystem;
- an amendment to an existing system or subsystem (for example, a reduction in, addition to, and/or re-design of a system's internal procedures/processes);

- an improvement to an existing system or subsystem;
- the renewal of part of an existing system or subsystem;
- the replacement of part of a system, or subsystem.

(Or, indeed, a combination of any of the above.)

Before we look at the systems development life cycle, it would perhaps be useful to clarify three key points.

First, the systems development life cycle is an iterative framework, which can, and indeed often does, involve the repeating of a stage and/or stages – possibly a number of times – until an agreed outcome/consensus to that stage is achieved. As a consequence, the timescale of a systems development, the cost, and the resource commitment – from initial plan to implementation and post-development monitoring – can vary enormously, depending on:

- the nature and extent of the systems development,
- the size and complexity of the development team managing/coordinating the development, and
- the urgency of the development.

In addition, because of the increasing complexity of the marketplace, and indeed the increasing variety of pressures faced by many companies, it is possible, and quite probable, that a company may will have a number of systems development projects in progress simultaneously – all at different stages of the development life cycle.

Second, (as suggested earlier) the wide ranging impact of many systems developments often necessitates the creation of a systems development team containing a wide selection of skills and capabilities from both inside and, where appropriate, outside the company. Although the responsibilities of such a systems development team would vary from company to company, invariably, given the eclectic nature of the individuals that comprise the systems development team, and the wide ranging portfolio of responsibilities of such a team, it is not surprising that in many instances the systems development process can become fragmented, disjointed and highly politicised, especially where development team members feel personally and professionally threatened by a proposed development and/or developments.

Third, the complex and interrelated nature of the accounting information systems often mean that changes to one system or subsystem may necessitate changes/amendments to another related system or subsystem – the so-called indirect development consequence. Clearly, it is important for a systems development team to possess a clear understanding both of how systems and subsystems are interrelated/interconnected, and of how changes in a system/subsystem may affect other interrelated/interconnected systems/subsystems.

Systems planning

Systems planning involves the identification and prioritisation of system(s)/subsystem(s) that require/may require further development, amendment, improvement, renewal and/or replacement. The systems planning stage is often divided into two distinct sub-stages.

1 A strategic planning stage.

2 A systems developing planning stage.

Strategic planning stage

The purpose of the strategic planning stage is to provide a framework or context for any planned systems developments – a reference framework which for our purposes we will consider as comprising three interrelated strategies:

1 the strategic mission and objectives of the company,

2 the strategic information plan of the company, and

3 the information and communications technology strategy of the company.

Note: Although strictly speaking the strategic planning stage is not really part of the systems development life cycle – because the life cycle is concerned primarily with the development of specific systems and applications, whereas the strategic planning stage is concerned primarily with the corporate/organisational context of such developments – it nonetheless provides an important 'starting point' for all systems developments, whether such developments are:

■ formal developments – that is, developments which are timetabled and resourced as part of a company's/organisation's cyclical strategic review programme, or

■ informal developments – that is, developments which emerge as a result of an ad hoc request from a departmental manager and/or the identification of errors or problems by a system(s)/subsystem(s) user.

Systems developing planning stage

The purpose of the systems developing planning sub-stage is to ensure that any planned systems developments are appropriately identified, suitably defined, accurately evaluated, and correctly prioritised in accordance with the company's strategic mission. This stage can be regarded as comprising four interrelated phases:

1 an *evaluation phase* in which the rationale for, and feasibility of, a systems development project is assessed;

2 a *development phase* in which a systems development project proposal is prepared;

3 a *prioritisation phase* in which systems development projects are prioritised; and

4 a *design and scheduling phase* in which a preliminary systems design for selected/accepted systems development projects is produced.

Evaluation

The evaluation phase is concerned with appraising the feasibility of a proposed system(s)/subsystem(s) development project, and would consider three key issues:

1 Economic feasibility – for example: What are the estimated potential costs[5] of the systems development, and what estimated tangible[6]/intangible[7] benefits will accrue for the system once it is implemented?

2 Technical viability – for example: What information and communication technologies will be required to realise the systems development, and are such information and communication technologies currently available?

3 Operational/implementation capability – for example: What resources will be required to realise the systems development, and are such resources currently available – in particular, human resources?

In addition to the above, it may also be necessary to assess the legal/regulatory aspects and consequences of a systems development – especially if additional costs may need to be incurred to satisfy legal/regulatory requirements.

Clearly, any evaluation/feasibility study would invariably be quantitative in nature, and may involve the use of a wide selection of financial management/financial planning and analysis techniques, especially investment appraisal/capital budgeting techniques including, for example:

- discounted cash flow – that is, net present value and/or internal rate of return;
- business rate of return – for example, return on investment; and
- payback – including discounted payback.

While most companies will use a discounted cash flow variant/measure, and will consider the longer-term net present value of a systems development, invariably liquidity and the conversion of any net benefits into actual cash flows will be a major concern. It is, therefore, not uncommon for a company to use a return on investment variant and/or a payback variant as primary evaluation measurements.

Development

The development phase is concerned with preparing the systems development project proposal.

Following the completion of the systems development project evaluation, such a project proposal would provide a basis on which the systems development team can decide whether to proceed with, or to abandon, the systems development project, and would in general seek to:

- establish a rationale for the systems development project, and explain the relevance of the systems development project in terms of the current operations of the company;
- illustrate the potential contribution that the systems development project (if accepted and implemented) would make to the overall strategic objectives of the company; and
- summarise the net benefit/net cost of the systems development project.

Prioritisation

The prioritisation phase is concerned with the prioritising of system(s)/subsystem(s) development projects, the key assessment criteria being an assessment of the potential strategic contribution of the proposed system to the company in terms of increased wealth creation, improved resource utilisation, improved information provision and enhanced decision making.

How would such a prioritisation phase/process be undertaken?

While there are a number of alternative approaches that may be used to prioritise systems development projects – many of which would be company unique – it is likely that the majority of such approaches would seek to quantify any strategic contribution, possibly using a predetermined weighted scoring system in which a selected range of factors and issues would be considered.

Design and scheduling

The design and scheduling phase is concerned with confirming a preliminary system(s)/subsystem(s) design for selected/accepted development project(s), and providing a definitive schedule of development – that is, a development schedule for each stage of the systems development life cycle, detailing:

- a capital and revenue expenditure budget for each stage,
- an implementation time plan for each stage,
- a critical analysis of core activities (usually a critical path analysis) for the project,
- an acquisition schedule, and
- a resource schedule for each stage.

Systems analysis

The systems analysis stage seeks to formally assess the functional attributes of current/ existing system(s)/subsystem(s), the aim being to identify any operational problems within the current/existing system(s)/subsystem(s) and determine the precise nature of such operational problems.

Why is such an analysis required?

Put simply: to solve a problem, it is important to understand first what the problem is, and second where the problem is!

The systems analysis stage (see Figure 12.3) involves the following four phases:

1 A survey of the current/existing system.
2 An analysis of system requirements.
3 An identification of user information needs and requirements.
4 The preparation of a systems requirement report.

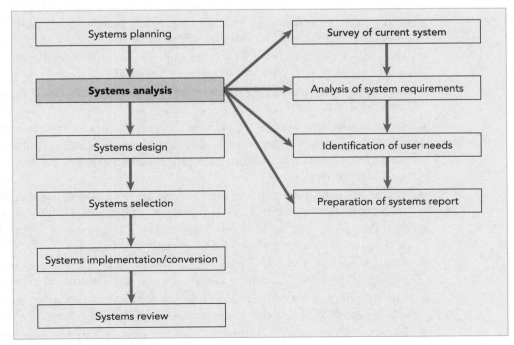

Figure 12.3 Systems analysis

Survey of the present system

This survey is designed to provide a fundamental understanding of the operational aspects of the target system(s), the aim of this survey being not only to identify problem areas within the current existing system(s) (to provide important data for modelling/design purposes), but, more importantly, to establish a working relationship with system(s) or subsystem(s) stakeholders.

Why? Because the success or failure of any system(s)/subsystem(s) development will to a large extent depend on the quality of data collected, the relationship developed between the system(s) development team and system(s) stakeholders, and, of course, the viability of the system(s)/subsystem(s) proposal.

Identify/determine system requirements

Once the systems survey has been completed, this phase of the systems analysis process seeks to identify/determine:

- the input requirements of the current/existing system(s)/subsystem(s),
- the processing procedures within the current/existing system(s)/subsystem(s), and
- the output requirements of the current/existing system(s)/subsystem(s).

For example:

- What are the main sources of data – for example, are the data internally or externally generated?
- What is the nature and structure of the data – for example, are the data narrative-based or numeric-based or a combination?
- What types of data are processed – for example, are the data subject to disclosure requirements and/or processing restrictions (see the Data Protection Act 1998)?
- Who processes the data – for example, is the data processing in-house, or is the data processing outsourced to an external service provider?
- What data input controls exist – for example, what type of application controls are used to ensure the security and integrity of the data?
- How are the data stored – for example, on manual documentation or on computer-based documentation?
- Where are the data stored – for example, are the data stored on-site or off-site?
- How are the data processed – for example, is data processing manual or computer-based and, if computer-based, are data processed in batches or are they processed on-line and/or in real time?
- What are the data flow trends – for example, are data processing transaction levels seasonal, and are any data processing trends linked to any other identifiable activity?
- What data processing controls exist – for example, what type of application controls are used to ensure data are processed accurately and securely?
- What are the data processing transaction levels – for example, is the current/existing system(s)/subsystem(s) operating at capacity, or is spare processing capacity available?
- How efficient is the data processing system – for example, what are the current error levels within current data processing procedures, and are such levels of error acceptable?
- How effective are data processing systems – for example, are there excessive delays in data processing procedures, and are such delays acceptable?

- What are the current resource costs – for example, are costs excessive when compared to other similar systems, and if so are such costs justifiable?

- Do any redundant operations/processes exist – for example, are all systems processes and procedures in use?

- Does any redundant documentation exist – for example, is all system/processing documentation appropriate?

- What data output controls exist – for example, what type of application controls are used to ensure data are output correctly, timely, accurately and securely?

- Who are the system(s)'/subsystem(s)' users – for example, are users internal and/or external?

Such facts can be gathered in many ways, perhaps the most common being:

- by questionnaires,
- by personal interview,
- by observation,
- by participation, and
- by documentation review.

Identify user information needs and requirements

Based on the data/information collected earlier on the physical nature/characteristics of the current/existing system(s)/subsystem(s), and the information requirements of current/existing system(s)/subsystem(s), this phase of the systems analysis process seeks to assess:

- the current nature of user information needs and requirements,
- the current level and complexity of such needs and requirements, and
- the current format of user information needs and requirements.

It also seeks to determine the appropriateness of such user information needs and requirements, and the continued relevance of such user information needs and requirements.

This is predominantly a cost/benefit-based rationalisation process, designed to evaluate the relative importance of user information needs and requirements, eliminate inconsistent and/or conflicting user needs and requirements, and minimise excessive duplication of information.

Preparation of a systems requirement report

Once the analysis of the current/existing system has been completed and all appropriate facts have been collected, collated and assessed, it is important for the systems development team (or its representative) to prepare a formal report for the company management (or a delegated management committee/group).

Such a report should provide:

- a complete appraisal of the results of the initial survey,
- a detailed review of the problems/issues identified,
- a summary analysis of user needs/requirements, in particular information needs and system(s)/subsystem(s) requirements, and (perhaps most importantly)

■ a comprehensive report providing a detailed description of the suggested/recommended requirements of the new system(s)/subsystem(s).

Although the structure of such comprehensive systems requirement reports would vary from company to company, from organisation to organisation, in a broad sense they would all contain some, if not all, of the following detail:

■ A rationale for the study – explaining the background to the systems analysis.

■ The scope of the analysis – detailing the parameters of the systems analysis.

■ A description of overall problem/issues identified – detailing the results of the survey.

■ A summary of system requirements and specification of user requirements – detailing *what* the new system(s)/subsystem(s) should do.

■ A summary of resource implications – net cost/net benefit (and proposed timescale) of the development.

■ Recommendations – for example, on whether the development should continue and, if so, what priority should be assigned to it.

Systems design

The systems design stage (see Figure 12.4) involves two key phases: a **conceptual design phase**, and a **physical design phase**. Both undertaken by perhaps a subgroup of the systems development team, the conceptual design phase is concerned with developing a design (or a range of alternative designs) for the completed system(s)/subsystem(s) – that is, a schematic outline or blueprint for *how the system(s)/subsystem(s) will work*. The

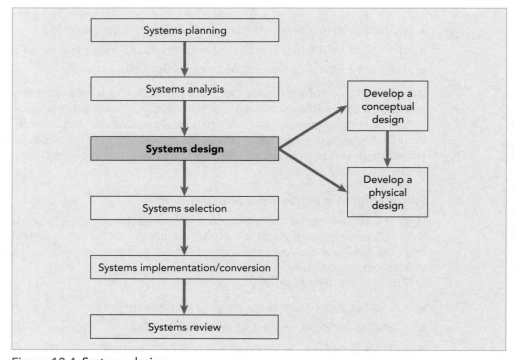

Figure 12.4 Systems design

physical design phase is concerned with establishing the physical design of the completed system(s)/subsystem(s) – that is, *what the system(s)/subsystem(s) will look like.*

Conceptual design phase

In a broad sense, a conceptual design is a theoretical/abstract design that seeks to provide a representation of the structure of a system(s)/subsystem(s). In a systems development life cycle context, it is concerned with the nature of the relationships between process and flows – that is, how such processes and flows are connected, and how such processes and flows interact; the purpose of the conceptual design stage being to develop a general framework within which the needs and requirements of users/stakeholders can be met.

There are many alternative approaches to the conceptual design phase, of which the function-orientated approach (or the top-down approach) and the object-orientated design approach (or the bottom-up approach) are perhaps the most common.

The function-orientated design approach

The function-orientated design approach (or the top-down approach) is also referred to as the structured design approach. It is an approach which commences with an overview of the proposed system/process – that is the *primary* or *context level*, which is then separated/divided into its constituent subsystems/sub-processes – that is, the *transitional level*, which is then separated/divided into constituent subsystems/sub-processes – that is, the *foundation level*, until the basic data components of each of the subsystems/sub-processes within the proposed system/process are identified.

The advantages of the function-orientated approach are that it can minimise fault replication and it promotes flexibility. However, the disadvantages of the approach are that it can be time-consuming, and it can be costly. Despite such disadvantages, the function-orientated design approach is still widely used in information systems design – especially for accounting information systems.

The object-orientated design approach

The object-orientated approach commences with analysis of available standard system/process objects (or more appropriately system/process components and/or modules), and uses such objects as a basis for the conceptual design. Such an approach is widely used in software development projects.

The advantages of the object-orientated approach are that it can significantly reduce design time, and it can reduce overall design costs. In addition, because system/process components/modules are already available, it can improve system/process maintenance, and improve user support. The disadvantages of the object-orientated approach are that it can lead to problem inheritance (problems may be replicated from one system/process to another system/process), and it can limit innovation – using existing components/modules may limit design possibilities, suppress creativity and restrain originality.

What design considerations would the conceptual design phase address?

It would consider, for instance:

- Systems/process communication – for example:
  - what communication configurations will be used,
  - what form of communication channels will be used, and
  - what type of communications network will be used.

- Data input – for example:
  - what forms of data input will be used,
  - what source documents will be required and how they will be structured,
  - what input medium will be adopted/used, and
  - how input data will be validated.
- Data storage – for example:
  - what data storage medium will be used,
  - how data will be stored,
  - what file format will be used,
  - how data files will be organised, and
  - how access to data files will be controlled.
- Data processing – for example:
  - how the data will be processed, and
  - when and where the data will be processed.
- Data output – for example:
  - what format of data output will be used,
  - how frequently data output will be produced,
  - what data output medium will be used,
  - how the data output will be validated, and
  - how data output will be scheduled.

Once a broad palette of design alternatives has been determined and agreed by the sub-group, it would be necessary to prepare a conceptual design specification for the systems development team, detailing the range of possible input, process, storage, and output alternatives considered suitable/appropriate for the new system(s)/subsystem(s), the purpose being to provide the systems development team with a design template/design guide for the physical design phase of the systems development.

Physical design phase

The physical design phase is primarily concerned with determining how the conceptual design can be/will be implemented, and would involve identifying and determining the precise nature of:

- the data input(s),
- the system(s)/subsystem(s) process/procedure,
- the data files,
- the system(s)/subsystem(s) programs,
- the data output(s), and
- the system(s)/subsystem(s) internal controls.

Again such a task would more than likely be delegated to a systems development team subgroup – their role being to consider the 'real world' complexities of making the conceptual design a reality.

Design considerations – data input(s)

Determining the precise nature and variety of data input(s) – for example, the source of data input(s), the format and medium of data input(s), and the type, volume and frequency of data input(s) – is often considered to be the most important design consideration of any physical design. This is especially important where it is likely that a number of alternative data input format/medium may be/will be used in the new system(s)/subsystem(s).

Why? Primarily, to minimise the possibility of data input errors, but also to ensure:

- the cost-effectiveness of each data input format/medium,
- the accuracy and uniformity of all data input(s),
- the appropriateness and relevance of all data input(s),
- the integrity and security[8] of all data input(s), and
- the compatibility of all data input(s).

Clearly, issues of data source, data type, and input volumes and frequencies will have a major influence on determining the medium used to collect/input data – that is, for example, whether data are collected and/or input using:

- a hard document based input (usually a physical paper document), or
- a virtual document based input (usually a computer-based input screen) or
- a combination of both hard document based input, and virtual document based input.

For example, a high frequency, low value and data input (such as customer-based ATM transactions[9]) would, of course, be suited to a virtual document based input procedure. However, a low frequency, high value, high risk data input would of course more likely be suited to a hard document based input procedure.

Design considerations – processing procedures

It is, of course, more than likely that the processing procedure selected will be partly, if not completely, computer-based. There are many alternative types of processing procedures available, for example:

- Periodic (batch) processing (off-line processing).
- Immediate processing:
  - on-line processing,
  - real time processing.
- Distributed processing.

However, the selection of the precise design nature of system(s)/subsystem(s) processing procedure will normally be determined by the so-called 5 Ws:

- For *whom* are the data to be processed – for example, who are the users/stakeholders, and what are their needs and requirements?
- *What* data are to be processed – for example, are the data predominantly quantitative or are predominantly qualitative?
- *When* are the data to be processed – for example, are the data to be processed at a single scheduled time or at number of scheduled times?
- *Where* are the data to be processed – for example, are the data to be processed at a single location or a number of geographically separate locations?
- *Why* are the data to be processed – for example, is the data processing for data collection/data storage purposes, or is the data processing for data analysis purposes (such as for decision making)?

Answers to the above should provide not only an indication of:

- the overall complexity of the data processing procedures,
- the repetitiveness of the data processing procedures,
- the uniformity of the data processing procedures, and
- the frequency of the data processing procedures,

but also an indication of the possible limitations/restrictions that may exist – for example, limitations on current processing abilities and/or communication capabilities and/or even technological resources.

What are the key design criteria?

Put simply, any selected processing procedure (or combination of processing procedures) should be:

- cost-effective,
- compatible with existing processing procedures (if required/necessary),
- accurate,
- appropriate,
- relevant,
- secure, and
- designed to minimise the possibility of data processing errors and/or data loss.

Design considerations – files

In a design context the structure of data files, the content of data files, and the storage of data files will invariably be influenced by a number of issues:

- the source and format of the data input(s),
- the procedure(s) adopted to process the data input(s),
- the destination and frequency of the data output(s), and
- the existence of external requirements (for example, the requirements of the Data Protection Act 1998),

with the aim being to maintain data integrity, maximise data security, and minimise data errors, whilst ensuring availability of and accessibility to data input(s) and data files.

Design considerations – programs

The decision as to whether a program (software system) is either developed in-house or acquired (purchased) from an external supplier/developer should be influenced and determined by user/stakeholder needs and requirements – and not, as is often the case, by cost alone. Remember, a program that does not satisfy the needs/requirements of its users/stakeholders is a waste of money!

We will look at both alternatives in a little more detail later in this chapter (during the systems development life cycle systems selection stage). For the moment, however, let's assume that the program is developed in-house – how would that process be undertaken?

There are, as you would probably expect, a number of alternative program (software system) development processes, some of the more common being:

- the waterfall approach,

- the prototyping approach,

- the synchronise/stabilise approach,

- the spiral approach.

The *waterfall approach* is a sequential development approach which establishes goals and assessment targets for each development phase. The advantage of the waterfall model is that it simplifies the development process because there is no iteration; however, the main disadvantage is that it does not allow for revision to take place.

The *prototyping approach* is an approach in which a prototype (or early approximation of a final program) is constructed, tested, and reworked as necessary until an acceptable workable program is achieved.

The *synchronise and stabilise approach* is an approach in which a program is divided into individual application modules on which separate specialist teams work in parallel. The key to this approach is to ensure that the separate programming teams frequently synchronise their programming activities/coding activities to ensure that a stable final product/program will be produced.

The *spiral approach* is an approach in which the program development combines the features of the prototyping model and the waterfall model. The advantage of the spiral approach is that there is/can be continuous revision/reviewing of development progress to date; the main disadvantages are that such an approach can be costly, resource intensive and time-consuming. Nevertheless, the spiral approach is an approach that is often used in large, complex, company-wide program (software system) developments.

In addition to the above, there are also the following:

- the Rapid Application Development (RAD) approach, in which program developments are undertaken using workshops or focus groups to gather system requirements – the aim being to speed up the program development process, and

- the Joint Application Development (JAD) approach, in which users/stakeholders are directly involved in the program development – usually through the use of collaborative workshops/development sessions.

Assuming that the spiral approach is adopted, for the program (software system) development, what stages would be included in the development process?

The main stages would be:

- Analysis of the feasibility of the program.

- Identification and analysis of the program requirements.

- Preparation of a detailed design specification of the program.

- Coding/programming of the software system.

- Testing the program.

- Maintenance of the program.

The key criteria would be:

- functionality,

- accuracy,

- integrity,

- security,

- compatibility,
- usability,
- appropriateness, and
- relevance.

Design considerations – data output(s)

The primary design consideration of any physical design phase is determining the precise nature and variety of data outputs – for example, the destination of data outputs, the format and medium of data outputs, and the type, volume and frequency of data outputs.

Main categories of data output(s) are:

- supply-led output(s) or (more appropriately) scheduled output(s),
- demand-led output(s),
- special purpose output(s),
- exception reports.

As with data input(s), design consideration is especially important where it is likely that a number of alternative data output formats/mediums may be/will be used in the new system(s)/subsystem(s). Why?

Primarily, to ensure:

- the cost-effectiveness of each data output format/medium,
- the accuracy and clarity of all data output(s),
- the timeliness and relevance of all data input(s), and
- the integrity and security of all data input(s).

Clearly, issues of data destination, data type, data output trigger, and output volumes and frequencies will also have a major influence on determining the medium used to issue/distribute output data – that is, for example, whether data are distributed and/or output using a hard document based output or a virtual document based output, or a combination of both hard document based output and virtual document based output.

Design considerations – internal controls

System(s)/subsystem(s) internal controls should prima facie be designed to ensure the efficient and effective operations of all system(s)/subsystem(s) processes and procedures, and the security of organisation assets and resources; that is, prevent and minimise the occurrence of errors, undesirable events, and adverse threats, detect and identify errors and adverse threats that have occurred, and correct and remedy the causes of adverse threats and/or undesirable events. Such internal controls will invariably be influenced by the source of the data input(s), the procedure(s) adopted to process the data input(s), the destination and frequency of the data output(s), and the existence of external regulatory requirements.

Such internal controls could comprise:

- documentation checks (preventative internal controls),
- authorisation checks (preventative internal controls),
- validity assessments (preventative/detective internal controls),
- accuracy assessments (detective internal controls),
- security checks (detective internal controls),

- integrity checks (detective/corrective internal controls), and
- audit checks (detective/corrective controls).

Systems selection

Once the blueprint/conceptual design specification of the system(s)/subsystem(s) has been completed, approved and adopted, and the underlying physical/operational design has been agreed, the systems selection stage – that is, the process of selecting how the system(s)/subsystem(s) will be put together – can commence.

There are, essentially three possible alternative selection approaches:

1 An acquisition approach in which hardware/software components are purchased from an external supplier/developer – also known as an out-house acquisition.
2 A development approach in which hardware/software components are developed internally – also known as an in-house development.
3 A combined approach in which some hardware/software components are purchased from an external supplier/developer and some hardware/software components are developed internally.

Within each approach there are of course a number of subsidiary issues that would need to be considered, for example:

- If the system(s)/subsystem(s) is to be purchased as a complete system:
    - how will the purchase be financed/arranged, and perhaps more importantly
    - how will the supplier/developer be chosen?
- If the system(s)/subsystem(s) is to be developed in-house:
    - what resources and competencies will be required, and
    - how will the development be managed?
- If the system(s)/subsystem(s) is to be partly developed in-house, and partly purchased from an external supplier/developer:
    - what hardware/software components will be developed internally, and
    - what hardware/software components will be acquired externally?

How would a company decide which approach to use?

In general, the decision would be made by the systems development team (in consultation with other relevant management representatives), and would be based on a combination of internal and external factors, perhaps the most important of these being:

- the net cost/net benefit of purchasing and/or developing the system(s)/subsystem(s);
- the levels of skills, competencies and capabilities available within the company;
- the availability of appropriate suppliers/developers for the hardware/software components; and
- the operational compatibility of any developed and/or acquired hardware/software component(s).

Which approach is most commonly used?

Although it is difficult to say with any degree of certainty which of the above approaches is the most common, it is often the case that the combined approach is used in large developments and/or projects involving company-wide systems/subsystem(s).

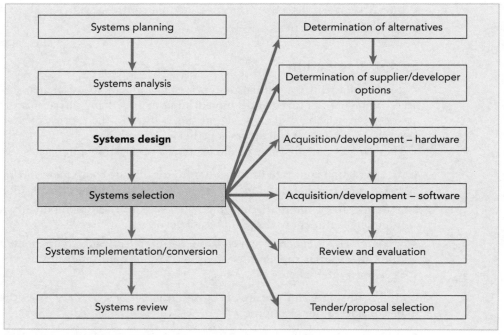

Figure 12.5 **Systems selection**

What are the main phases within the systems selection stage?

The selection stage (see Figure 12.5) would involve the following six phases:

1 Determination of alternative selection options.
2 Determination of supplier/developer options.
3 Acquisition/development of system components – hardware.
4 Acquisition/development of system components – software.
5 Review/evaluation of alternative tenders/proposals.
6 Selection of successful tenders/proposals.

Determination of alternative selection options

If a company chooses to pursue an acquisition approach, or indeed a combined approach, within which some hardware/software components are acquired from an external supplier/developer, what alternative acquisition options are available? While the precise details of any acquisition would depend on the specific features of the systems development, the nature of the components and (as we have already seen) the extant capabilities of the company, in general there are three alternative acquisition options available: *purchase*, *lease*, or *outsource*. In addition, within each of these options, the company could use either a single supplier/developer or multiple suppliers/developers.

Let's look at each of these acquisition options in a little more detail.

Purchase

In a broad sense, a purchase can be defined as an agreed transfer of property and/or property rights from one person to another in exchange for a valuable consideration, and is a method of acquisition that has historically dominated the commercial activities of many companies. While such a method continues to form the commercial foundation of many revenue-based transactions, purchasing has – certainly since the late 1970s/early 1980s – become less popular for specific categories of capital assets, especially those capital assets which are subject to high levels of value depreciation due to rapid technological obsolescence.

Why? Have a look at the following advantages/disadvantages of purchasing.

The advantages of purchasing are: there is an immediate transfer of legal title and ownership; the purchaser can claim immediate tax (capital) allowances – sometimes up to 100 per cent of the cost; and, in the longer term, there is, overall, a smaller cash outlay. However, the disadvantages of purchasing are: there is a large initial capital outlay – the full cost at purchase; there may be an increase in gearing if the purchase has to be financed through borrowing; all the risks related to the purchased asset(s) (for example risk of failure, risk of obsolescence) are borne by the purchaser; and all the repair and maintenance costs related to the purchased asset(s) are borne by the purchaser.

Clearly, purchasing high-value capital assets which may require regular servicing and maintenance, constant upgrading, and frequent replacing – in particular, capital assets (including both hardware, and in some instances related software) related to the provision of information and communication technology facilities/capabilities – could place an excessively heavy strain not only on a company's/organisation's longer-term borrowing (if the acquisition is to be financed by debt) but also, and perhaps more importantly, on a company's/organisation's working capital.

An alternative to the purchasing of such capital assets is, of course, to lease.

Lease

A lease can be defined as a legal contract between the owner of the asset(s) (the lessor) and another party (the lessee), and relates to the transfer of possession and use of an asset(s) for a valuable consideration for a specified period of time. While there are many named variations, in a business/finance context, there are essentially two types of leases:

1 A finance (or capital) lease, which involves a series of payments over the majority of the expected life of the asset(s) and for the majority of the cost of the asset(s), and in which the lessee acquires all the economic benefits and risks of ownership.

2 An operating lease[10] which involves a series of payments over a period (usually 1 to 5 years) that is less than the expected life of the asset(s), and in which the lessor remains responsible for all servicing and maintenance.

Mainly for fiscal reasons, the popularity of leasing grew enormously in the late 1970s/ early 1980s for a wide range of assets. Indeed, during the latter part of the 1990s and the early part of this century leasing has become a much more asset-focused industry, and it is not uncommon for companies to lease a range of assets – for example premises and buildings, plant, machinery and equipment, vehicles, and information and communication technology hardware/software.

What are the advantages and disadvantages of leasing?

The advantages of leasing are:

- there is only a small initial cash outlay – it avoids large capital outlay;
- it can reduce/eliminate risks of ownership, and can lessen the impact of technological obsolescence;

- it can help to conserve working capital and minimise cash outflows;
- it minimises the need for borrowing; and
- lease payments are a tax deductible expense.

The disadvantages of leasing are:

- the ownership of the asset(s) does not transfer from the lessor to the lessee, and
- the lease may involve a long-term commitment for the lessee, and may therefore be very expensive.

Determination of supplier/developer options

Before deciding whether to use a single supplier/developer and/or multiple suppliers/developers, it is of course important to first determine whether the supplier(s)/developer(s) under consideration are appropriate and are the type of supplier(s)/developer(s) with whom the company should deal.

Selecting a supplier/developer

There are many factors/issues that a company should consider when selecting/approving a supplier/developer. These would include, for example:

- Is the supplier/developer well established?
- Is the supplier/developer an experienced information and communications technology supplier/developer?
- Is the supplier/developer industry-recognised/approved?
- Is the supplier/developer reliable?
- Are external third-party references available?
- Does the supplier/developer offer guarantees and/or warranties on the products/services they provide?
- Are the supplier's/developer's products/services up to date?
- Does the supplier/developer provide finance for the purchase/development of hardware/software systems – if not, does the supplier/developer provide alternative acquisition means (for example leasing)?
- Does the supplier/developer provide implementation and installation support/maintenance?
- Does the supplier/developer provide post-implementation and installation training and support?

In some companies this (pre)selecting of a supplier/developer is often referred to as 'pre-qualification', inasmuch as potential suppliers/developers may be asked to demonstrate their financial, commercial and technical capabilities.

Okay, so what are the advantages/disadvantages of using a single supplier/developer, or multiple suppliers/developers?

Single supplier/developer

The advantages of using a single supplier/developer are that: it can simplify the acquisition/supply process; it may ensure compatibility; and it may be a more reliable service. The disadvantages of using a single supplier/developer are that: it may limit product range; and it may increase risk (supplier/developer stops trading etc.).

Multiple suppliers/developers

The advantages of using multiple suppliers/developers are that: it may result in cheaper prices (due to competition); it may result in increased product range; and it can spread risk (supplier/developer stops trading etc.). The disadvantages of using multiple suppliers/developers are that: it can be inconvenient; it can be complex; it may increase administration costs; it may be less reliable; and it may result in possible incompatibilities.

The acquisition/development of system components – hardware

Invariably, information and communications technology hardware will be *bought into* the company – that is, developed, constructed and supplied by an external third party. Because such acquisitions can have a significant cost/benefit implication, as well as representing a substantial long-term commitment, it is essential that an appropriate hardware supplier is selected, and an appropriate hardware *system* is selected.

Selecting a hardware system

The main factors/issues that a company should consider when selecting a hardware system would include, for example:

- Specificity – what are the main features/capabilities of the hardware system?
- Technology – is the hardware system's technology up to date and relevant?
- Comparability – are any external third-party evaluations of the performance of the hardware system available?
- Compatibility – if necessary, can the hardware system be integrated into existing hardware systems?
- Availability – is the hardware system available now, and is it reasonably and competitively priced?
- Maintainability – what guarantees and warranties are available with the hardware system?
- Expandability – can the hardware system be expanded to include external facilities (for example, external data storage)?
- Affordability – is financing available and/or are specific discounts available?

The acquisition/development of system components – software

In a broad sense, software can be either developed or acquired (purchased). There are two alternative approaches to the in-house development of software:

1 the top-down approach (or management specific approach), and/or
2 the bottom-up approach (or end-user development approach).

There are also two alternative approaches to the acquisition of software (where it is not developed in-house):

1 the acquisition of generic software, and/or
2 the acquisition of commissioned software.

In addition, where software is acquired, it is important to ensure that an appropriate software retailer/supplier is selected.

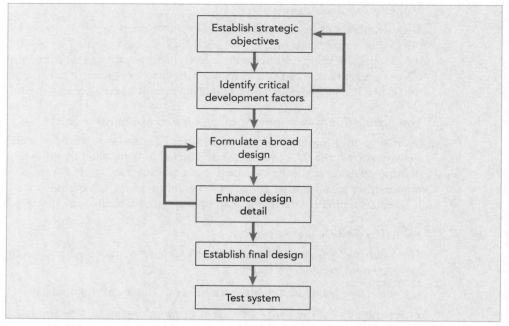

Figure 12.6 In-house development of software – top-down approach

In-house development of software – top-down approach

The top-down development approach (see Figure 12.6) is an iterative process which commences with an overview of the development/design project, in which the strategic objectives of the development are established, the critical development factors of the development are identified, and a broad design structure is formulated, the emphasis being on establishing an understanding of the context of the development project/design.

Once a broad development/design structure has been established, a greater level of detail is introduced. The introduction of this further level of detail – in particular its impact on the development/design structure – is assessed and reviewed and, where necessary, a refined overall development/design structure is produced. Once agreed, a further level of detail is introduced, again its impact on the development/design structure is assessed and reviewed and, where necessary, a newer refined overall development/design structure is produced. Again, once agreed, a further level of detail is introduced, which leads to . . . etc . . . , until a complete and detailed development and design specification is available – and the software design can be fully tested.

Such a process is, of course, not too dissimilar from the function-orientated conceptual design approach discussed earlier.

What are the advantages and disadvantages of the top-down approach?

The advantages to the top-down approach are that the overall strategic context of the development/design minimises the risk of development/design errors, and ensures/promotes compatibility with existing software systems; the iterative reviewing and refining of the overall development/design structure results in better testing, less development waste, and a reduction in bad documentation.

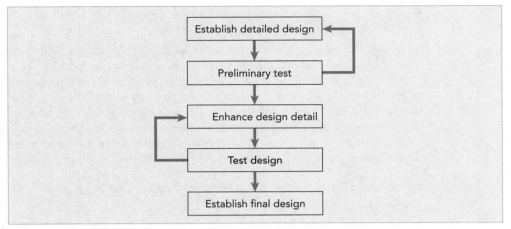

Figure 12.7 In-house development of software – bottom-up approach

The disadvantage of the top-down approach is that the development is often divorced from user needs and requirements – that is, the development process may produce 'what we think you want', as opposed to 'what you really need'. In addition:

■ the process can be very time-consuming and resource intensive;

■ full testing of any development/design cannot be undertaken until a complete and detailed design specification is available; and

■ end-users may resist the imposition of newly developed software because of a lack of involvement in the development/design process.

In-house development of software – bottom-up approach

An alternative to the above approach is a bottom-up approach (sometimes referred to as end-user development). The bottom-up approach (see Figure 12.7) is a design process which focuses on the detailed aspects of individual parts/modules within a development/design, and emphasises early preliminary testing of individual parts/modules within a development/design specification. Once complete and fully tested, the parts/modules are then linked together with other parts/modules to form larger composite modules/structures, which are then linked to other composite modules/structures . . . etc . . . , until a complete and detailed development and design specification is available.

Such a process is, of course, not too dissimilar from the object-orientated conceptual design approach discussed earlier.

The advantages of the bottom-up approach are that the development/design process is controlled by software end-users, ensuring that the development/design meets their needs; and user software implementation and control procedures are managed by software end-users, producing greater flexibility, versatility and adaptability.

The disadvantages of the bottom-up approach are:

■ development errors and logic issues may emerge when parts/modules are linked to other parts/modules;

■ development errors may result in incorrect or inconsistent documentation;

■ poor development/design control may result in parts/modules being inadequately tested;

■ parts/modules may be incompatible; and

■ there could be excessive duplication and waste, resulting in increased costs and the inefficient use of resources.

In reality, the modern approach to software development and design usually combines both the top-down approach and the bottom-up approach. Why?

Put simply, while an understanding of the complete picture in terms of the strategic context of any development/design is considered by some to be a necessary, if not essential, prerequisite for good design – that is, adopting a top-down approach – most software development/design projects often use existing software specifications as a base development platform (usually to aid integration with existing software) rather than start a development/design project from a zero base – that is, adopting a bottom-up approach.

What would be involved in this combined approach?

The main stages would be:

■ Analysis of the feasibility of the program (software system) – that is, a detailed evaluation of the program development project, and a determination as to whether it is feasible.

■ Identification and analysis of the program requirements – that is, once the program feasibility has been confirmed, detailed requirements of the program should be established, in which variables and processes[11] are precisely identified and defined.

■ Preparation of a detailed design specification of the program – that is, once the program requirements have been established a design specification should be developed focusing on three key areas:

   1 High-level design issues – for example, what specific program (software systems) will be required, what will the program inputs and outputs be, and what will be the relationship and/or interaction between the program and existing programs (including for example existing/current operating systems)?

   2 Low-level design issues – for example, how will the program function, and what modular components will be used/required?

   3 Data design – for example, what will the structure of data inputs and outputs be?

■ Coding of the program (software system) – that is, once the design is complete the designs are translated into a functional program (that is, the program code needs to be created).

■ Testing the program (software system) – that is, once the coding/programming is complete, the complete program will require testing to ensure that its functions are as intended/required and on the intended platform(s).

■ Maintenance of the program (software system) – that is, once the program has been tested, authorised as complete, and delivered to the users, it will invariably/inevitably require regular maintenance and/or updating.

Out-house acquisition of software – generic software

The main factors/issues a company should consider when selecting a generic software system would include, for example:

■ *Specificity* – what are the main features/capabilities of the software, and is the software package well documented?

■ *Usability* – is the software user-friendly, and are on-line enquiry facilities available?

■ *Controllability* – does the software contain appropriate and adequate control features?

■ *Comparability* – are any external third-party evaluations of the performance of the software available?

■ *Compatibility* – is the software compatible with existing company software?

■ *Availability* – is the software available now, and is it reasonably and competitively priced?

■ *Maintainability* – what guarantees and warranties are available with the software?

■ *Expandability* – can the software system be expanded/amended/customised to meet specific company requirements?

■ *Affordability* – is financing available and/or are specific discounts available?

Purchased software is often referred to as *canned software*.

Out-house acquisition of software – commissioned software

Commissioned software – also known as bespoke software – can be defined as software which is specifically created for a company to meet pre-agreed conditions and requirements. Such software can be either newly developed software or modified/amended generic software.

Where a bespoke software package is commissioned, it is important for the company commissioning the work to ensure an appropriate software developer(s) is/are appointed. More importantly, it is essential that a detailed development plan is agreed in advance with the software developer(s), a price/detailed costing is agreed in advance with the software developer(s) and, a detailed performance/delivery timetable is agreed in advance with the software developer(s). Where appropriate (especially for a larger development, to be delivered in stages over a number of months), a contract detailing the nature of the development project and the rights and responsibilities of all parties to the contract should be agreed and signed.

Review/evaluation of alternative tenders/proposals

Where a systems development project represents a major undertaking for a company it may be likely that a number of suppliers/developers may be asked to tender or submit a proposal for some, if not all, of the development work.

A tender can be broadly defined as an unconditional offer to enter into a contract which, if accepted, becomes legally binding. There are of course many alternative types of tendering, the most common being:

■ open tendering,

■ restricted tendering, and

■ negotiated tendering.

Open tendering is essentially a single-tier bidding process, in which all interested suppliers/ developers can submit a tender in response to a tender notice issued by the company. Normally, such a tender notice would stipulate the conditions that apply to the tender process, how the tender process will work, where tender documents can be obtained, and the last date by which tenders will be accepted.

Restricted tendering is a multi-tier bidding process in which suppliers/developers are initially requested to submit an 'expression of interest'. These expressions of interest are evaluated, and a shortlist of appropriate suppliers/developers is then created. Those suppliers/developers on the shortlist would then be invited to submit a formal tender, which would then follow the open tendering procedure discussed above. This restricted tendering procedure is most likely to be used where a large number of suppliers/developers are expected to submit tenders.

Negotiated tendering occurs where a company negotiates a tender with one or more approved suppliers/organisations following a pre-qualification process (see earlier). This negotiated tendering procedure is most likely to be used where specialist services and/or components are required, or where compatibility with existing services/components is crucial, or as a means of reducing the numbers of tenders – for example, as part of the restricted tendering process.

Whatever tender process/procedure is used, once all tenders have been submitted and received, they need to be objectively reviewed and evaluated, and, of course, a selection made.

During this review and evaluation process, it is important that the integrity of the tender process as a competitive procedure is maintained, and essential that the evaluation of submitted tenders is undertaken fairly, objectively and impartially.

What would the review procedure look for?

Put simply, the review process would primarily consider how well the submitted tenders comply with all the requested criteria, and would usually be reviewed and evaluated using a predetermined set of criteria, and a pre-agreed scoring and weighting system to evaluate individual aspects/components of the tender – perhaps also incorporating benchmark performance measures and/or test simulation scores and evaluations for specific aspects/components of the tender.

Such predetermined criteria could include for example:

- the price of the tender,
- the financial viability of the tender submission,
- the experience of the supplier/developer,
- the technical merit of the tender submission,
- the suitability and compatibility of the tender submission,
- the expandability and flexibility of the tender submission, and
- the projected completion time period of the development.

Clearly, while the precise nature of the award criteria would differ from tender to tender, from company to company, organisation to organisation, it is very unlikely that any tender would be successful on the basis of price alone. Rather, a tender would be awarded to the supplier/developer based on value for money.

Who would undertake this review/evaluation?

It would probably be undertaken by a specialist subgroup appointed by, and accountable to, the systems development team. It may also include specialist consultant advisers from outside the company where appropriate.

Selection of successful tenders/proposals

Once the objective review and evaluation has been completed by the specialist subgroup, and reported to the systems development team, it would be the systems development team – in consultation with appropriate users/stakeholders – who would be responsible for taking one of three possible courses of action:

1 Where the specialist subgroup had identified a clear successful tender – the systems development team would be responsible for **confirming and awarding** the tender to the successful supplier/developer.

2 Where the specialist subgroup had identified a number of successful tenders – the systems development team would be responsible for **selecting and awarding** the tender to the successful supplier/developer.

3 Where the specialist subgroup had identified no successful tenders – the systems development team would be responsible for **reviewing** the tender process, **assessing** the reasons for a lack of successful tenders, and, where appropriate, **recommencing** the tender process.

Systems implementation/systems conversion

Systems implementation/conversion (see Figure 12.8) involves the implementation of the selected design, and/or the conversion of an existing system(s)/subsystem(s). The *systems implementation* stage would normally contain the following seven phases:

1 Establishment of an implementation timetable.

2 Allocation of system(s)/subsystem(s) responsibility.

3 Establishment of performance criteria.

4 Preparation of location resources, including human resource management – acquisition, training and education.

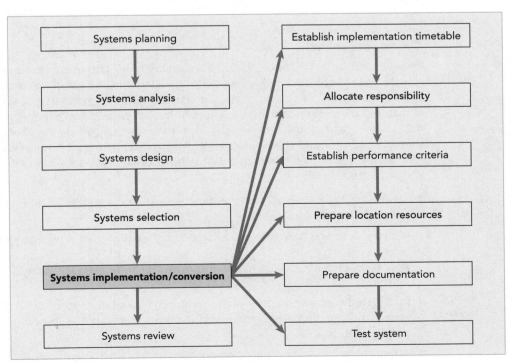

Figure 12.8 Systems implementation/systems conversion

5 Preparation of system(s)/subsystem(s) documentation.

6 Testing of system(s)/subsystem(s).

In addition to the above, where a systems development involves the changing/moving of an existing operational system to a new operational system, consideration should also be given to issues regarding:

- systems conversion – that is, how the conversion will be managed, and

- data conversion – that is, how/what data will be converted.

We will look at systems conversion and data conversion later. For the moment let's look at systems implementation in a little more detail.

Systems implementation

Establishment of an implementation timetable

Clearly, the first phase of any implementation process is the establishment of an implementation schedule – a timetable of activities and events which will ultimately result in the installation of a fully operational system(s)/subsystem(s). Because such an implementation schedule will often contain a vast array of events and activities, it is critical that within the implementation schedule there is a prioritisation of the key implementation/development activities and events, and an identification of the so-called critical path of the implementation schedule – in other words, a recognition of the sequence of activities that limit how quickly an implementation can be completed.

There are, of course, a number of techniques available to establish an implementation timetable/schedule, the most popular – perhaps somewhat unsurprisingly – being critical path analysis.

Critical path analysis

Critical path analysis can be defined as an analysis/planning technique – a form of analysis that can be used to diagrammatically represent the continuous chain of activities and events critical to the successful implementation of a system(s)/subsystem(s) by its scheduled completion date. By focusing on those events and activities which are critical to the implementation schedule – that is, those activities and events to which attention should be devoted and/or resources allocated – critical path analysis provides an effective tool for the planning, monitoring and control of complex implementation schedules, and provides a means of:

- identifying the nature of implementation events and activities – that is whether events and activities are considered:
  - dependent and therefore must/can occur in sequence (that is, one after the other), or
  - non-dependent and therefore must/can occur in parallel (that is, at the same time);

- prioritising events and activities within an implementation schedule – that is, whether events and activities are considered core events and activities or non-core events and activities; and

- determining the minimum duration over which such events and activities can be completed.

In essence, the critical path of an implementation schedule is the longest sequence of dependent activities and events that leads to the eventual completion of the implementation plan – inasmuch as any delay in any event/activity on the critical path will delay the system(s)'/subsystem(s)' implementation, unless the duration of future sequential events and/or activities can be reduced. There are two main ways in which the critical path can be presented, using either:

1 a scheduling chart – for example a Gantt chart, or

2 a PERT (project evaluation and review technique) chart.

Scheduling chart

Scheduling charts are often used in the planning, development and implementation of a system, the most popular and indeed the most widely used scheduling chart being the Gantt chart. The Gantt chart is extremely useful in:

- assessing the maximum period of a development project,
- determining and prioritising resource requirements during a development project,
- establishing an order/timetable for development events/activities within a development project,
- identifying and managing interdependencies between development events/activities, and
- monitoring the progress of a development project.

PERT (project evaluation and review technique) chart

PERT is a variation on critical path analysis that takes a slightly more sceptical view of time estimates made for each event/activity of the development project. For each event/activity time estimate, PERT uses a weighted average of the shortest possible length of time each event/activity will take, the most likely length of time each event/activity will take, and the longest possible length of time each event/activity will take, and calculates the weighted average time for each event/activity using the following:

$$\frac{\text{shortest time} + (4 \times \text{likely time}) + \text{longest time}}{6}$$

Allocation of system(s)/subsystem(s) duties and responsibilities

Within any systems development, however large, however small, it is inevitable that at some point during the implementation stage, discussion regarding the allocation of duties within the system(s)/subsystem(s), and the assignment of responsibilities within the system(s)/subsystem(s), will need to take place.

Why? Because duties and responsibilities associated with for example data capture procedures, data security procedures, data processing procedures, data storage facilities, and system(s)/subsystem(s) management will invariably cut across a range of company departments. It is therefore important that a suitable allocation occurs in order to ensure that sufficient separation of duties and responsibilities will exist post-implementation, and to ensure the existence of adequate internal control and appropriate security within the new system(s)/subsystem(s).

Within a company's accounting information system, it would be important, for example, to ensure (as a minimum) the existence of the following separation of duties and responsibilities:

- User/stakeholder department – duties/responsibilities related to data capture and data preparation;
- IT operations – duties/responsibilities related to data processing, data management and data file library maintenance; and
- IT development – duties/responsibilities related to systems analysis, systems management and systems programming.

That is, within the above:

- Staff members of IT operations **do not** undertake duties/responsibilities related to data capture and data preparation, or duties/responsibilities related to systems analysis, systems management and/or systems programming.
- Staff members of IT development staff **do not** undertake duties/responsibilities related to data capture and/or data preparation, or duties/responsibilities related to data processing, data management and/or data file library maintenance.
- Staff members of user departments **do not** undertake duties/responsibilities related to data processing, data management and/or data file library maintenance, or duties/responsibilities related to systems analysis, systems management and/or systems programming.

In many cases, this process of allocation of duties, of assignment of responsibilities, and of determination of line accountabilities will emerge from, and be established by, reference to the structure and nature of the new system(s)/subsystem(s), and will therefore be a simple, if somewhat formal, routine exercise – an objective and apolitical systems development allocation/assignment exercise. In some cases, however, this process can become very political, very divisive and, indeed, very disruptive, especially where:

- the nature, scope and impact of the new system(s)/subsystem(s) on the company (or a large segment of the company) will be significant;
- the manner in which the new system(s)/subsystem(s) is to be implemented is unclear and/or uncertain; and/or
- the impact and/or effect of the new system(s)/subsystem(s) on employees and/or groups of employees within the company will be substantial.

Clearly, it is in the best interests of the company to minimise any attempt at politicising the development and/or implementation process.

Why? Because such politicisation (whatever its origin/whatever its cause) may provoke unwarranted resistance – resistance to the development and implementation of the new system(s)/subsystem(s) and the adoption/use of related information and communication technologies. Any such resistance, if left unresolved, can become extremely costly in both a financial and a business context.

We will look at the politics of accounting information systems development and the management of resistance a little later in this chapter.

Establishment of performance criteria

An essential part of the post-implementation assessment is a determination of the success or otherwise of the new system(s)/subsystem(s). A part of this post-implementation assessment is, of course, an assessment and measurement of the performance of the new system(s)/subsystem(s), the criteria for which will invariably be established during the systems implementation stage. In establishing performance criteria, it is important to determine:

- what performance criteria will be used – for example, qualitative or quantitative factors;
- how performance will be measured;
- when performance will be measured – for example, every week, every month, or every year;
- who will perform/be responsible for performing the assessment; and (perhaps most importantly)
- who will review the assessment results.

The preparation of location resources

The preparation of location resources (often referred to as site preparation) involves ensuring that:

- adequate and appropriate location facilities are available for the installation of information and communication technology hardware,
- appropriate integrity and security measures will be implemented to control access to the installation facilities,
- sufficient power supply services will be available at the location,
- appropriate communications facilities will be available at the location, and
- appropriate environmental controls (for example, humidity controls/temperature controls) will be implemented to protect the installed information and communication technology hardware.

Clearly, the costs of such preparation can be substantial, especially where such location preparation requires any (or a combination of) the following:

- the construction of new premises,
- the development of newly acquired premises,
- the refurbishment of existing company-owned premises,
- the leasing of additional premises,
- the acquisition/installation of specialist equipment/facilities (other than information and communication technology hardware) – for example:
  - backup power facilities – for example, additional power generators,
  - property security facilities – for example, CCTV systems,
  - environment management systems – for example, air conditioning systems.

Human resource management – acquisition, training and education

Resource preparation (often referred to as employee recruitment/employee orientation) involves ensuring that:

- the appropriate and timely recruitment of qualified and/or experienced staff is undertaken to satisfy any shortfall in employee skills and/or knowledge, and
- the appropriate and relevant levels of training and education are provided for those staff members who will be involved in using and/or managing the new system(s)/subsystem(s).

Regarding training, it is important that:

- any training and education programme should include not only training and education on the system(s)/subsystem(s) hardware and/or software, but also training and education on the processes, procedures, policies, and protocols developed to support the new system(s)/subsystem(s); and

- any training and education programme should cater for the level and status of the audience undertaking the training programme, and:
  - focus on their needs and requirements, and where appropriate,
  - combine both formal and informal activities as part of the training and education programme.

While such resource preparation activities can be very expensive (especially where new employees are required), extremely time-consuming (especially where substantial long-term training and education is required), and, of course, very disruptive, such resource preparation activities are vital to any system(s)/subsystem(s) development.

Why? Put simply, an inadequate availability of skills and/or knowledge once the system(s)/subsystem(s) are operational could result in not only substantial operational problems but, perhaps more importantly, significant additional costs.

The preparation of system(s)/subsystem(s) documentation

As part of the systems implementation process, it is essential that the systems development team ensure appropriate system(s)/subsystem(s)-related documentation is available not only for management and for technical support staff, but – perhaps most importantly – for system(s)/subsystem(s) users and stakeholders.

Such documentation would include, for example, a development narrative, an operational guide and a user/stakeholder manual.

A *development narrative* would normally include:

- a description of the development process;
- a description of the system(s)/subsystem(s) input, process, and output procedures;
- a description of the system(s)/subsystem(s) data management procedures;
- an explanation of the information and communications interfaces;
- a listing of system(s)/subsystem(s) programs and coding structures; and
- a description of system(s)/subsystem(s) security.

It would also include, where appropriate, relevant flowcharts and data flow diagrams and, where necessary, example copies of systems documents. The purpose of such a development narrative is to provide a detailed technical specification of system(s)/subsystem(s).

An *operational guide* would include for example:

- details of system(s)/subsystem(s) operating schedules/timetables;
- details of system(s)/subsystem(s) hardware and software components;
- a description of the system(s)/subsystem(s) files and databases; and
- a description of system(s)/subsystem(s) users.

The purpose of such an operational guide is to provide detailed information on how to operate the system(s)/subsystem(s).

Note: For system(s)/subsystem(s) security purposes, it is important that the operational guide does not contain information such as systems flowcharts and program codes. Why? Because a system(s)/subsystem(s) operator should not under any circumstances have access to data/information that may reveal the system(s)'/subsystem(s)' internal logic.

A *user/stakeholder manual* would include:

- a system(s)/subsystem(s) reference guide;
- an overview of the system(s)/subsystem(s) and its major functions;

- examples of data input procedures and data analysis tools;
- a comprehensive guide to error messages, error codes and error descriptions;
- a tutorial guide;
- a training programme – usually task or topic orientated; and
- a help/problem referral guide.

The purpose of such a user/stakeholder manual is to describe how to use the system(s)/subsystem(s), and it is likely that much of the above would be provided as an on-line facility.

Testing the system(s)/subsystem(s)

A final, and perhaps crucial, phase prior to any systems implementation is the system(s)/subsystem(s) test. It is important that the system(s)/subsystem(s) is correctly tested – to ensure that any faults and defects are appropriately rectified, any weaknesses and imperfections are suitably repaired, and any limitations and inadequacies are correctly resolved prior to implementation. Such testing would include:

- data capture/input tests,
- data processing tests,
- data/information output tests.

Testing would seek to determine:

- the appropriateness of system(s)/subsystem(s) documents;
- the reliability, integrity and security of user input processes and procedures;
- the availability of output information and the timetabling of system(s)/subsystem(s) reports;
- the processing capacity/ability of the system(s)/subsystem(s);
- the appropriateness of system(s)/subsystem(s) data processing procedures;
- the reliability and effectiveness of operating and control procedures;
- the appropriateness of data backup/data storage/data management procedures; and
- the suitability of disaster contingency recovery procedures.

A final testing of the system(s)/subsystem(s), often called an acceptance or transfer test, would involve users providing data (preferably actual data) for the final test phase of the new system(s)/subsystem(s). Such end-user-related testing is designed to confirm to the users the credibility and integrity of the new system(s)/subsystem(s).

Systems conversion

System conversion can be defined as the process of changing/moving from an existing operational system to a new operational system. There are essentially four approaches to systems conversion:

1 Direct (or immediate) conversion.
2 Pilot (or modular) conversion.
3 Phased conversion.
4 Parallel conversion.

Direct (or immediate) conversion

Direct (or immediate) conversion is the most risky of all conversion processes/procedures, and consists of an immediate switch over from the old system(s)/subsystem(s) to the new system(s)/subsystem(s). Such a conversion process (also known as the *cold turkey approach*) is appropriate only where:

- the system(s)/subsystem(s) being replaced is of little or no value;
- the new system(s)/subsystem(s) is very different (operationally and/or technically) from the existing system(s)/subsystem(s);
- the existing system(s)/subsystem(s) and the new system(s)/subsystem(s) are simple; and/or
- the need for conversion from the old system(s)/subsystem(s) to the new system(s)/subsystem(s) is urgent.

The main advantage of the direct (or immediate) conversion is that the conversion process is immediate and inexpensive. The disadvantage of the direct (or immediate) conversion is that the process can be very risky, especially where conversion problems occur. Such problems could result in for example, the incorrect processing, and/or incorrect management of data as a consequence of a loss of system(s)/subsystem(s) integrity and/or a failure of system(s)/subsystem(s) security.

Pilot (or modular) conversion

Pilot (or modular) conversion occurs when a new system(s)/sub/system(s) is tested and introduced at either specifically selected locations or specifically selected functions/services. If tests prove successful, then the new system is gradually introduced throughout. Such a conversion process (also known as the *localised transition approach*) is suitable where both the old system(s)/subsystem(s) and the new replacement system(s)/subsystem(s) are crucial to the ongoing survival of the company.

The main advantage of the pilot (or modular) conversion is that such a conversion process allows for the testing of (and training on) a new system(s)/subsystem(s) in a live functioning environment, resulting in the identification and correction of operational procedure/process errors (sometimes referred to as debugging[12]). The main disadvantage of the pilot (or module) conversion is that such a staged/segmented introduction can extend substantially the time period of the conversion process, and as a consequence can increase the overall cost of conversion.

Phased conversion

Phased conversion occurs when a new system(s)/subsystem(s) is gradually introduced in different phases, per subsystem or module, and the old system(s)/subsystem(s) is gradually removed. Such a conversion process (also known as the *incrementalist approach*) is suitable where the new system(s)/subsystem(s) is very different (operationally and/or technically) from the existing system(s)/subsystem(s), and/or both the old system(s)/subsystem(s) and the new replacement system(s)/subsystem(s) are crucial to the ongoing survival of the company.

The main advantage of a phased conversion is that there is a greatly reduced risk of system(s)/subsystem(s) failure, because the transition to the new system(s)/subsystem(s) is gradual, with resources and capabilities introduced/transferred in a programmed, coordinated and managed approach. The disadvantages of phased conversion are:

- the conversion process may take a considerable time;
- additional costs may be incurred as a result of creating temporary connections/interfaces to facilitate the gradual transfer of procedures and processes;
- incompatibilities may arise between the old system(s)/subsystem(s) and the new system(s)/subsystem(s);
- the timetabling of the conversion process, unless closely managed, may become problematic, especially where large complex transfers are involved.

Parallel conversion

Parallel conversion occurs when both the new and the old system(s)/subsystem(s) are operated simultaneously for a period of time – which could be days, weeks, or months. Obviously, the longer the period, the greater the overall cost. Such a conversion process (also known as the *dual approach*) is suitable where the data processed, and the information produced, by system(s)/subsystem(s) being replaced are of substantial value to the company, and/or both the old system(s)/subsystem(s) and the new replacement system(s)/subsystem(s) are critical to the ongoing survival of the company.

The main advantage of a parallel conversion is the greatly reduced risk of conversion failure, because the transition to the new system(s)/subsystem(s) only takes place once the parallel running has indicated that no procedural/processing problems exist with the new system(s)/subsystem(s). The disadvantages of phased conversion are:

- the conversion process to the new system(s)/subsystem(s) may take considerable time,
- additional costs may be incurred as a result of the parallel running of the old and new systems, and
- operational problems may occur (for example, employee resistance) as a result of the need to maintain two different systems and/or subsystem(s) simultaneously.

Data conversion

Where there is a system(s)/subsystem(s) conversion, there will invariably be a need to convert data from the old system(s)/subsystem(s) data format to the new system(s)/subsystem(s) data format.

Why? For a number of reasons, for example:

- the data structure used within the new system(s)/subsystem(s) may differ substantially from the old system(s)/subsystem(s),
- data file content used within the new system(s)/subsystem(s) may be significantly different from the old system(s)/subsystem(s), and/or
- data storage media used within the new system(s)/subsystem(s) may differ from the old system(s)/subsystem(s).

Such a conversion process can of course be time-consuming, extremely repetitive, very tedious and enormously expensive, especially where a substantial amount of data and a substantial number of data files exist.

It is not uncommon for a company facing a substantial data conversion task for such a task to be outsourced to an external company. There are essentially three stages to the data conversion process:

1 data file selection,
2 data file conversion, and
3 data file validation.

Data file selection

Data file selection involves:

- identifying the data files that require conversion to the new data file format, and
- evaluating the integrity of the data contained in the data files, for example:
  - measuring the accuracy of the data,
  - determining the relevancy of the data, and
  - assessing the consistency of the data.

Data file conversion

Data file conversion involves the adaptation/alteration of the data files – that is, changing the formatting of a data file – and can be defined as the process by which data files created for use in a system/application are modified and/or transformed to a data file format that can be used in another system/application.

Data file validation

Data file validation involves ensuring that all data/data files have been correctly converted, evaluating the accuracy of the content of the converted data files, and ensuring that no data/data files have been lost and/or corrupted during the data conversion process.

Systems review

'. . . there is no better teacher than history' (Anon.)

Systems review involves the monitoring and evaluation of the selected system(s)/subsystem(s) performance, the primary aim of such a review being to determine the success (or otherwise) of the company's systems development process.

The systems review stage (see Figure 12.9) involves the following two phases:

1 A post-implementation assessment.
2 A resource management assessment.

Post-implementation assessment(s)

The post-implementation assessment(s) will normally occur sometime after system(s) implementation – the duration and the frequency of the assessments obviously depending on the importance/criticality of the system(s) developed.

The aim of the post-implementation assessment is to measure/assess the success or otherwise of the system(s) development process, and determine whether the objectives of the system(s) development have been achieved. Often undertaken by the systems development team, such a post-implementation assessment would ask questions such as, for example:

- Are users satisfied with the system(s) operations – if not, why not?
- Are system(s) procedures functioning reliably and effectively?
- Are data input/capture procedures functioning correctly?
- Are data being processed accurately and appropriately?
- Are data output procedures functioning properly and in a timely fashion?
- Are processing errors correctly identified and resolved?

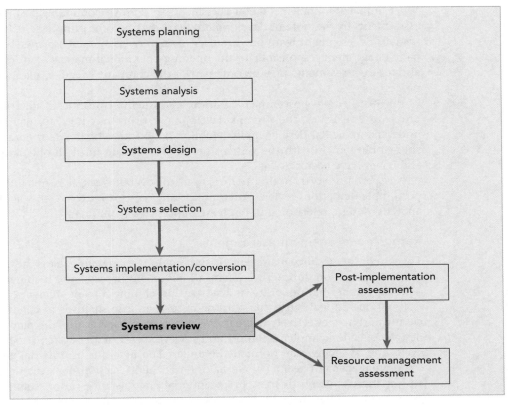

Figure 12.9 Systems review

- Are there any ongoing inter-system(s) compatibility issues?
- Are control and security processes and procedures functioning efficiently?

In addition, the post-implementation review would also assess:

- the appropriateness of conversion/transfer/introduction procedures – for example:
  - Was the process clearly explained to users/stakeholders?
  - Was the conversion/transfer/introduction timetable appropriate?
  - Were any data and/or files lost during the conversion/transfer/introduction process?
- the effectiveness of user training provided as part of the system(s) implementation procedures – for example:
  - Was adequate and timely training available for users/stakeholders?
  - Was the conversion/transfer/introduction training documentation appropriate?
- the effectiveness of organisational/operational changes made as a consequence of the system(s) development – for example:
  - Were the organisational/operation changes appropriately timetabled?
  - Was the rationale for the changes clearly explained to users/stakeholders?
  - Was any consultation process with users/stakeholders undertaken?
- the appropriateness and usefulness of user documentation produced as part of the system(s) implementation procedures.

Where initial post-implementation assessments are positive, continuing post-implementation assessments by the systems development team may become unnecessary. In this case, the systems development team may transfer (or sign over) system(s) ownership to the company department responsible for the ongoing operational management of the system(s) and future assessments may become part of the company's regular, planned monitoring process.

However, where post-implementation assessments continue to identify operational problems and issues, the systems development team may need to/may be required to undertake remedial design/implementation action, in which case the system(s) ownership would remain with the systems development team until all outstanding problems and issues have been resolved.

It is perhaps worth noting that in terms of overall costs, it is not unknown for the post-implementation review costs/monitoring costs to exceed the actual planning, analysis, design, selection and implementation costs combined.

Resource management assessment

The aim of the resource management assessment is to measure/assess the effectiveness of resource utilisation during the systems development process, and is sometimes regarded – perhaps somewhat unfairly – as a systems development team efficiency audit.

In an operational sense, the purpose of such an assessment is to determine how efficiently and how effectively company resources were used during the planning, analysis, design, selection, implementation and review stages of the systems development life cycle, and as such would normally be undertaken by either an internal audit team or a senior management team (where an internal audit section/department did not exist within the company). It may, in exceptional circumstances – for example, where the assessment requires specialist knowledge – be undertaken by external consultants.

Such a resource management assessment would ask questions such as:

- Was the system(s) development process adequately coordinated, and appropriately managed?
- Did any conflicts of interest arise during the system(s) development process, and if so were they adequately/satisfactorily resolved?
- Were original system(s) development cost–benefit estimates accurate?
- Were there any significant departures from the original estimates/budget, and, if so, were such departures assessed, approved, and authorised?
- Were the system(s) development benefits fairly valued?
- Have the system(s) development benefits been realised?
- Was the system(s) development timetable realistic?
- Were there any significant departures from the system(s) development timetable, and, if so, were such departures assessed, approved and authorised?
- Was the system(s) development process adequately communicated by the systems development team?

Clearly, where problems/issues are identified, remedial action by company management would need to be taken, especially where such problems/issues are significant.

The final outcome of the review stage would be a post-implementation review report.

Systems review report

Once the post-implementation review has been completed and all appropriate facts have been collected, collated and assessed, it is important for the systems development team (or its representative) to prepare a formal report for the company management (or a delegated management committee/group).

What would such a post-implementation review report contain?

Although the structure of such reports would vary from company to company, in a broad sense they would all contain some, if not all, of the following detail:

- An overview and background of the systems development – explaining the background to the systems development.
- An evaluation of the systems development – for example, were objectives achieved and were expected net benefits realised?
- An evaluation of user/stakeholder satisfaction/comments.
- An evaluation of the systems development team.
- Recommendations for future systems developments.

The prototyping approach

In an accounting information systems context, prototyping can be defined as the incremental development of new system applications and/or procedures using an interactive and iterative feedback process, the objective of the prototyping approach being to produce a system specification from which a fully functional system and/or systems can be developed (Emery 1987). The basic premise of the prototyping approach is that end-users find it easier to identify *what they do not want*, as opposed to *what they want*.

Note: Although the prototyping approach can be used as an alternative to the systems development life cycle approach, it can be (and often is) used as part of the systems development life cycle approach. For example, it is often incorporated into the initial (or front end) stages of the systems development life cycle approach as a means of identifying and clarifying end-user requirements.

The prototyping approach (see Figure 12.10) involves four stages:

1 Specification of user needs and requirements.
2 Development of an initial prototype.
3 Modification of the prototype.
4 Acceptance or rejection of the prototype.

Let's look at each of these stages in a little more detail.

The specification of user needs and requirements

This specification stage will involve/include:

- identifying the systems and/or subsystems requiring development,
- analysing and assessing the development need,
- specifying end-user needs and requirements, and

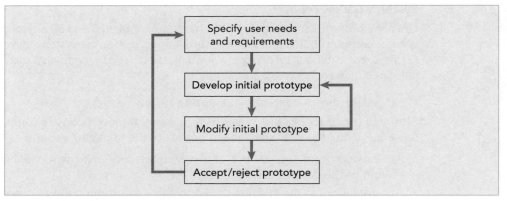

Figure 12.10 Prototyping approach

- formulating a blueprint/conceptual design and/or range of alternative blueprints/ conceptual designs.

The development of an initial prototype

This development stage will involve determining an initial physical/operational design – or prototype – of the blueprint/conceptual design to be adopted.

The modification of the prototype

This modification stage will involve/include:

- presenting the prototype to end-users,
- obtaining end-user feedback on the prototype, and
- changing/amending the prototype based on end-user feedback.

As an iterative process, this modification process may be undertaken a number of times, depending on the feedback offered by end-users.

The acceptance or rejection of the prototype

Where user feedback regarding the prototype system(s) is positive and constructive, and end-user needs and requirements are well defined and agreed, the prototype system(s) may, after a number of modifications, be developed into a fully functional system(s). This type of prototype is often referred to as an *operational prototype*. However, where significant and continuing disagreement exists over the feasibility of the prototype system(s) and/or the definition of end-user needs and requirements, the prototype system may be discarded and the system development pursued using the traditional systems development life cycle approach. This type of prototype is often referred to as a *non-operational prototype*.

When is prototyping used?

In general, prototyping is used for developments that involve management related and/or decision support related systems – that is, systems developments where there is, or may be:

- a high level of ambiguity about the systems development,
- substantial uncertainty regarding the nature and/or structure of the system(s) processes,
- considerable problems and/or difficulties in defining system(s) requirements,
- significant uncertainty about the outcome of the systems development,
- a considerable number of alternative system(s) designs.

Prototyping is also ideal for system(s) developments which involve experimental system(s)/investigational system(s), high risk system(s), infrequently used system(s), and/or continually changing system(s) – for example, developments involving strategic/executive information systems and/or on-line data retrieval/information recovery.

However, prototyping is generally unsuitable for systems developments that involve standard, large and/or complex company-wide systems – especially those that have limited design alternatives, and/or well-defined system(s) requirements, and/or predictable processing procedures – for example, developments involving a company's debtor management system(s) and/or a company's purchasing system(s).

What are the advantages and disadvantages of prototyping?

The main advantages of prototyping are that it can:

- provide for an improved definition of end-user needs and requirements,
- offer an increased opportunity for modification/change,
- facilitate a more efficient and effective development process,
- result in fewer development problems and errors.

The main disadvantages of prototyping are:

- It can involve a significant amount of end-user commitment, and may therefore result in a less efficient use of systems resources.
- The continuous modification of the systems specification and/or end-user requirements may result in excess time delay and/or the development of:
  - an incomplete system, and/or
  - an inadequately tested system, and/or
  - an inadequately documented system.
- The continuous revision of the systems specification and/or end-user requirements may create negative behavioural problems.

Managing resistance

> . . . there is nothing more difficult to carry out, nor more doubtful of success, nor more dangerous to handle than to initiate a new order of things
>
> (Niccolo Machiavelli, *The Prince*, 1532)

In today's ever more chaotic, ever more interconnected, ever more technology-orientated market environment, change is inevitable, especially change involving information and communication technologies. Yet, while such change may be seen as unavoidable – even perhaps inescapable – the consequences of such change can be, and indeed often are, perceived and understood in different ways.

For example, for some, change may be seen as bad, and its consequences destructive and malevolent – the intention being to replace, even destroy, long and well-established practices and procedures. For others, such change may be seen as good, and its consequences as beneficial and constructive – the intention being to break down traditional barriers, remove out-dated and inappropriate practices and procedures, and engage with the new 'brave new world'!

How can such a diverse range of alternative understandings arise?

Put simply, they arise because change (certainly within a corporate context), while motivated by an increasingly vast array of interconnected factors and issues, is invariably political in nature, with its consequences affecting different socio-economic groupings within a company in different ways. For example the introduction of 'chip and PIN' technologies in many high street retail stores during 2003–04 affected lower-level operational employees differently to tactical-level junior/middle managers, who were themselves affected differently to strategic-level senior managers.

For example:

■ lower-level operational employees, such as retail assistants, required an understanding of the operational aspects of the new technologies and the use of the new customer payment procedures;

■ junior/middle managers, such as store managers, required an understanding of the control requirements and reconciliation aspects of the new technologies; and

■ senior managers required an understanding of the longer-term cost–benefit impact of such technologies.

It is the potential impact of change (especially information and communication technology orientated change) on different socio-economic groupings within a company – the social and economic consequences on an individual and/or groups of individuals within the company – that will, if sufficiently negative and/or adverse, stimulate an agenda of defiance, of opposition, and of non-cooperation from an individual and/or groups of individuals.

Sources of resistance

Clearly, how an individual and/or a group of individuals perceive or understand a change/proposed change – whether it involves the adoption of information and communication technologies and/or the introduction of new/revised processes, procedures and/or protocols – will, of course, determine their reaction to such change, in particular the level of opposition/resistance that may arise. But why does such resistance emerge?

What are the sources of such opposition?

Resistance to change – whether in the form of defiant opposition or merely non-cooperation from an individual and/or groups of individuals – will often emerge where:

■ the nature, scope and context of the change/proposed change is ambiguous;

■ the manner in which the change/proposed change is to be introduced and coordinated is unclear;

■ the possible impact/affect of the change/proposed change on individuals/groups of individuals is uncertain; and/or

- the level of support (and reassurance) offered by those coordinating the change, to those affected by the change/proposed change (for example, re-training), is limited and/or vague.

That is, resistance and opposition emerge where there exists considerable bias/ambiguity and significant fear and uncertainty regarding the change/proposed change. Furthermore, the intensity of any resistance and opposition offered can be influenced by:

- the individual/personal characteristics/profile of those affected by the change/proposed change, and
- the level of personal loss that an individual and/or groups of individuals may incur as a result of the change/proposed change.[13]

Types of resistance

Resistance can, of course, take many forms. It can range from hostile aggression, to defiant opposition, to negative projection.

Hostile aggression

Hostile aggression can be defined as an unprovoked violent act or hostile action designed to damage and/or possibly inflict injury. Examples of hostile aggression would be:

- the deliberate impairment of information processing hardware – for example, the wilful destruction of input/output devices;
- the intentional sabotage and/or theft of data storage facilities;
- the theft of data;
- the deliberate introduction of software viruses; and
- the intentional removal of control procedures and protocols.

Defiant opposition

Defiant opposition can be defined as a deliberate act of avoidance and the wilful resisting of procedures and protocols. Examples of defiant opposition would be:

- the deliberate failure to follow appropriate internal control procedures;
- the intentional processing of transactions using incorrect/inappropriate documentation; and
- the purposeful (perhaps even fraudulent) omission of authorisation procedures.

Defiant opposition differs from hostile aggression inasmuch as there is no intention and/or deliberate act to damage, destroy and/or inflict injury or harm.

Negative projection

Negative projection can be defined as the transference and/or allocation of blame or responsibility. It occurs when:

- the introduction of a new system, or subsystem,
- the development of new procedures and processes, and/or
- the integration of new information and communication technologies

is inappropriately blamed for errors and problems. Examples of negative projection would be:

- where new procedures and processes are blamed for excessive error levels in the processing of transactions, and/or

- where new information and communication technologies are accused of increasing time delays in the production of information.

Clearly, no matter how resistance emerges – no matter what its source, or indeed, what form such resistance takes – such resistance needs to be effectively managed. Why? Because continued resistance to change, in particular continued opposition to change from different socio-economic groupings within a company, may create unrest and escalate into internal conflict, which could, if sufficiently significant, be politically and economically damaging for the company.

Managing resistance and resolving conflict

Where resistance and opposition does arise, it is important to identify and define the nature of the resistance/opposition, identify and define the symptoms of and reasons for the resistance/opposition, and develop a strategy to manage/contain it. Indeed, in managing change, it is important that those assigned with planning, developing and implementing any change, succeed in:

- establishing a sense of importance and urgency about the change/change process,

- developing an acceptable rationale for any proposed change,

- creating a sufficiently powerful coalition to support any change/proposed change, and

- resolving any obstacles/hindrances to any proposed change at an earlier stage in the change process.

There are, of course, many strategies which can be adopted to assist in minimising resistance – although perhaps not fully eliminating opposition. It is, for example, important to ensure that:

- open communication and discussion takes place during the planning, development and implementation stage of any change/proposed change;

- adequate support (and reassurance) is offered to those affected by the change/proposed change;

- open and honest feedback is available at all stages during the planning, development and implementation stages of any change/proposed change; and

- user participation is encouraged during the planning, development and implementation stage of any change/proposed change.

Is resistance futile?

Well not really! Indeed, not all resistance is bad. While there can be little doubt that in some instances resistance to change, especially unprovoked and unwarranted hostile and aggressive resistance, can be not only socially harmful but, more importantly, economically damaging to a company, some resistance – although perhaps initially unwelcome and inconvenient – can be politically constructive and economically beneficial. How?

For example, such resistance may help to:

- focus attention on critical issues which may have been overlooked by the systems development team,

- identify operational faults within a proposal which the systems development team may have failed to recognise, and/or

- identify technical issues which may have a detrimental impact on operational control procedures.

As a consequence, resistance may actually result in a more cost-effective and operationally efficient system(s)/subsystem(s).

Concluding comments

Change – especially in the context of information and communications technology and accounting information systems – is, as we have seen, inevitable. Consequently, it is important for a company to control such change, to identify when and where it is needed, what form it should take, and how the introduction of this change – and any consequences arising from it – should be managed. Failure to do so could be disastrous – certainly in the longer term.

Self-review questions

1 Describe the six main stages of the systems development life cycle.

2 Distinguish between the following categories of change:

    (a) smooth incremental change,

    (b) rough incremental change, and

    (c) discontinuous change.

3 Distinguish between the following:

    (a) soft minor change,

    (b) hard minor change,

    (c) soft major change, and

    (d) hard major change.

4 Explain the key phases you would expect to find in the systems analysis stage of the systems development life cycle.

5 Describe the four main stages of the prototyping approach to systems development.

6 Distinguish between the following types of resistance:

    (a) hostile aggression,

    (b) defiant opposition, and

    (c) negative projection.

7 Explain the main factors/issues a company should consider when selecting a hardware system.

8 Distinguish between a top-down approach and a bottom-up approach to the in-house development of software.

References

Emery, J.C. (1987), *Management Information Systems: The Critical Resource*, Oxford University Press, Oxford.

Machiavelli, N. (1532), *The Prince*, trans. Marriot, W.K. (1912), Macmillan, London.

Stacy, R. (1996), *Strategic Management and Organisational Dynamics*, Pitman, London.

Notes

1 Heraclitus of Ephesus (*c.* 535–475 BC) was known as 'The Obscure', and was a pre-Socratic Greek philosopher from Ephesus in Asia Minor.

2 See Stacy, R. (1996), *Strategic Management and Organisational Dynamics*, Pitman, London.

3 Ibid.

4 Ibid.

5 Such costs would include, for example, hardware/software acquisition costs, design costs, programming and testing costs, data conversion costs, training and education costs and hardware/software maintenance costs.

6 Such tangible benefits would potentially include, for example, increased sales incomes, reduced payroll costs, and better working capital management.

7 Such intangible benefits would potentially include, for example, improved decision making, more efficient operations, improved communications and greater stakeholder satisfaction.

8 Such security would also include restricting/confirming user access.

9 Individual ATM withdrawals are normally limited by the account-holding institution/bank. Although the precise nature of the restriction will differ from bank to bank, from institution to institution, it is not uncommon for a restriction/limit of £200–£250 per day to apply to ATM withdrawals from an individual personal current account.

10 Sometimes (somewhat incorrectly) referred to as a service lease, or contract hire.

11 Variables are data which change over time, whereas processes are activities which, in an information and communications technology context, transform data.

12 Debugging can be defined as a process of detecting, locating and removing mistakes, defects and/or imperfections in a system(s)/subsystem(s). Debugging tends to be harder when various subsystems are tightly coupled, as changes in one may cause bugs to emerge in another.

13 For example: a loss of financial rewards, a loss of power base, and/or a loss of utility.

Index